Praise for Rick Bragg's

THE BEST COOK
IN THE WORLD

"Rick Bragg serves up a feast. . . . [A] love song to the woman who raised him and who has been his greatest muse."
—*The New Orleans Advocate*

"The stories, as much as the portrait they paint of [Bragg's] family and their times, are baroque and profane, simultaneously moral and amoral, loving and blunt." —*San Francisco Chronicle*

"One of my favorite writers of all time. . . . Both an incredibly evocative portrait of [Bragg's] mother and a collection of his mother's recipes." —Ed Levine, Serious Eats

"Bragg has a bone-deep empathy for people who endure hard times. . . . [He is] a leisurely, soulful storyteller, a reporter with a poet's eye, and an appreciative diner. Most of all . . . he's a ferociously devoted son." —*The Christian Science Monitor*

"Affectionate, funny, and beautifully written. . . . Heartfelt, often hilarious stories from an Alabama kitchen, a place from which issue wondrous remembrances and wondrous foods alike."
—*Kirkus Reviews* (starred review)

"An engaging read about food that is dear to me."
—Hugh Acheson, *Food & Wine*

"A testament that cooking and food still bind culture together."
—*Publishers Weekly* (starred review)

RICK BRAGG

THE BEST COOK
IN THE WORLD

Rick Bragg is the author of eight books, including the bestselling *Ava's Man* and *All Over but the Shoutin'*. He is also a regular contributor to *Garden & Gun* magazine. He lives in Alabama.

THE BEST COOK
IN THE WORLD

THE BEST COOK IN THE WORLD

Tales from
My Momma's Southern Table

RICK BRAGG

VINTAGE BOOKS

A DIVISION OF PENGUIN RANDOM HOUSE LLC

NEW YORK

The Library of Congress has cataloged the Knopf edition as follows:
Name: Bragg, Rick, author.
Title: The best cook in the world : tales from my momma's table / Rick Bragg.
Description: First edition. | New York : Alfred A. Knopf, 2018.
Identifiers: LCCN 2017024979 (print) | LCCN 2017028840 (ebook)
Subjects: LCSH: Bragg, Rick—Family. | Cooking, American—Southern style. |
GSAFD: Cookbooks.
Classification: LCC TX715.2.S68 (ebook) | LCC TX715.2.S68 B725 2018 (print) |
DDC 641.5975—dc23
LC record available at https://lccn.loc.gov/2017024979

Vintage Books Trade Paperback ISBN: 978-1-4000-3269-3
eBook ISBN: 978-0-525-52028-3

Photograph of author and his mother by Terry Manier
Book design by Maggie Hinders

www.vintagebooks.com

Printed in the United States of America
10   9   8   7   6   5   4   3   2   1

To the cook

CONTENTS

Let your speech be always with grace, seasoned with salt,

that ye may know how ye ought to answer every man.

COLOSSIANS 4:6

Good stuff always has a story.

MARGARET BRAGG

THE BEST COOK
IN THE WORLD

IT TAKES A LOT OF RUST
TO WIPE AWAY A GENERAL ELECTRIC

Three generations of great cooks, from left to right: Great-Aunt Plumer,
Aunt Juanita, Cousin Mary, Cousin Betty, Aunt Edna, my mother at 13,
Cousin Louise, Aunt Jo, Cousin Norma Jean, Grandmother Ava, Aunt Sue,
Aunt Fene, and Cousin Jeanette in diapers

SINCE SHE WAS eleven years old, even if all she had to work with was neck bones, peppergrass, or poke salad, she put good food on a plate. She cooked for dead-broke uncles, hungover brothers, shade-tree mechanics, faith healers, dice shooters, hairdressers, pipe fitters, crop dusters, high-steel walkers, and well diggers. She cooked for ironworkers, Avon ladies, highway patrolmen, sweatshop seamstresses, fortune-tellers, coal haulers, dirt-track daredevils, and dime-store girls. She cooked for lost souls stumbling home from Aunt Hattie's beer joint, and for singing cowboys on the AM radio. She cooked, in her first eighty years, more than seventy thousand meals, as basic as hot buttered biscuits with pear preserves or muscadine jelly, as exotic as tender braised beef tripe in white milk gravy, in kitchens where the only ventilation was the banging of the screen door. She cooked for people she'd just as soon have poisoned, and for the loves of her life.

She cooked for the rich ladies in town, melting beef short ribs into potatoes and Spanish onions, another woman's baby on her hip, and sleepwalked home to feed her own boys home-canned blackberries dusted with sugar as a late-night snack. She pan-fried chicken in Red's Barbecue with a crust so crisp and thin it was mostly in the imagination, and deep-fried fresh bream and crappie and hush puppies redolent with green onion and government cheese. She seasoned pinto beans with ham bone and baked cracklin' cornbread for old women who had tugged a pick sack, and stewed fat spareribs in creamy butter beans that truck drivers would brag on three thousand miles from home. She spiked collard greens with cane sugar and hot pepper for old men who had fought the Hun on the Hindenburg Line, and simmered chicken and dumplings for mill workers with cotton lint still stuck in their hair. She fried thin apple pies in white butter and cinnamon for pretty young women with bus tickets out of this one-horse town, and baked sweet-potato cobbler for the grimy pipe fitters and dusty bricklayers they left behind. She cooked for big-haired waitresses at the Fuzzy Duck Lounge, shiny-eyed pilgrims at the Congregational Holiness summer campground, and crew-cut teenage boys who read comic books beside her banana pudding, then embarked for Vietnam.

She cooked, most of all, to make it taste good, to make every chipped melamine plate a poor man's banquet, because how do you serve dull food to people such as this? She became famous for it, became the best cook in the world, if the world ends just this side of Cedartown. But she never used a cookbook, not in her whole life. She never cooked from a written recipe of any kind, and never wrote down one of her own. She cooked with ghosts at her sure right hand, and you can believe that or not. The people who taught her the secrets of Southern, blue-collar cooking are all gone now, and they did not cook from a book, either; most of them did not even know how to read and write. Every time the old woman stepped from her workshop of steel spoons, iron skillets, and blackened pots, all she knew about the food left with her, in the way, when a bird flies off a wire, it leaves only a black line on the sky.

"It's all I've ever been real good at, and people always bragged on my cooking . . . you know, 'cept the ones who don't know what's good," she told me when I asked her about her craft. "When I was little, the old women used to sit in their kitchens at them old Formica tables and drink coffee and tell their fortunes and talk and talk and talk, about their sorry old men and their good food and the good Lord, and they would cook, *my God,* they could cook. . . . And I just paid attention, and I done what they done. . . ."

Most chefs, when asked for a blueprint of their food, would only have to reach for a dog-eared notebook or a faded handwritten index card for ingredients, measures, cooking times, and the rest.

"I am not a chef," she said.

Yet she can tell if her flour is getting stale by rubbing it in her fingers.

"I am a cook."

I remember one night, when she was yearning for something sweet, she patted out tiny biscuits and plopped them down in a pool of milk flavored with sugar, cinnamon, vanilla, and cubes of cold butter. She baked this until the liquid, half whole milk, half thick, sweetened condensed milk, steamed into the biscuits, infusing them with the flavors underneath. It created not a dense slab, like a traditional, New Orleans–style bread pudding, but little islands of perfect sweet, buttery dumplings; the spacing, not the ingredients or cooking time, was the secret here. "Momma taught it to me, and Grandpa Bundrum taught it to her, and his momma taught it to him, and . . . well, I guess I don't really know no further than that."

In the roadside cafés, cooks in hairnets with *Semper Fi* on their forearms taught her to build the perfect burger from layers of charred, thin patties, melting cheese, rings of sweet Vidalia onion, and wheels of fresh tomato. They taught her crisp, fork-tender chicken-fried steak, and how to dress steamed foot-long hot dogs with homemade hot chili, just the right trickle of yellow mustard, and lots of finely diced onion, to make the pulpwooders weep. She learned to slow-cook pork barbecue from old men who lived in the smoke itself. "The workin' people wouldn't pay good money for food that wasn't fit to eat. I didn't make no money in a café . . . fourteen or fifteen dollars a week was the most I made. But at Red's café we got all the puddin' we could eat. Your uncle Ed's momma, Granny Fair, waitressed at Red's when I was there. You remember her? She was kind of a big woman? Well, she'd bust through the double doors to that kitchen, snatch up one of them little chocolate puddin's, and eat it in three bites on a dead run—and not miss a *step*."

Her big sister, Edna, taught her to fillet catfish, crappie, and tiny bream with a knife as thin as aluminum foil. A brother-in-law, a navy man, taught her how to pat out a fine cathead biscuit, but could only bake them a battleship at a time. Her mother-in-law showed her how to craft wild-plum pies, peach, apple, and cherry cobblers, and cool banana puddings, all in pans as big as she was. Her daddy shared the secrets of fresh ham and perfect redeye gravy, and tender country-fried steak. And her momma taught her to do it all, even with a worried mind. Then, finally, it was her time, and it has been for a long, long time.

"I have to talk to myself now to cook," she said. "I have to tell myself what to do, have to tell myself to handle the knife by the right end. I have to call myself a name, so I'll know to listen to myself."

"By what name," I asked, beginning to be concerned, "do you call yourself?"

"Why, I use my name, hon. I ain't so far gone I don't know my name. I'll say, 'Margaret, don't burn yourself,' and 'Margaret, close the cabinet so you won't bump your head.' It's when I do call myself by somebody else's name that y'all got to worry about me. Till then, hon, I'm *alllll right.*"

She had hoped for a daughter to pass her skills and stories to— that or a thoughtful son, someone worthy of the history, secrets, and lore; instead, she got three nitwit boys who would eat a bug on a bet and still cannot do much more than burn a weenie on a sharp stick, and could not bake a passable biscuit even if you handed us one of those whop-'em cans from the Piggly Wiggly and prayed for bread. We ate her delicious food without much insight into how it came to be, which was not all our fault. She banned us from her kitchen outright, much of our lives, because we tracked in red mud, coal dust, or some more terrible contaminant, or tried to show her a new species of tadpole as she made biscuit. We are still barely tolerated there, though I have not stomped in a mud hole or hidden a toad in my overalls for a long time. So she would be the end of it, then, the end of the story of her table, unless we could find another way.

I made up my mind to do this book not on a day when my mother was in her kitchen, making miracles, but on a day she was not. Most days, unless she is deep in Ecclesiastes, or Randolph Scott is riding a tall horse across the TV screen, she will be at her stove, singing about a church in the wildwood, or faded love, or trains. In the mornings, the clean scent of just-sliced cantaloupe will drift through the house, mingling with eggs scrambled with crumbled sausage, and coffee so strong and dark that black is its true color, not just the way you take it. At noon, the air will be thick with the aroma of stewed cabbage, sweet corn, cornbread muffins, and creamed onions going tender in an iron skillet forged before the First Great War. Some nights, you can smell fried chicken livers as far as the pasture fence, or barbecued pork chops, pan-roasted pig's feet, potatoes and pole beans, or blackberry cobbler in a buttered biscuit crust. But as I walked into the house in the winter of 2016, to find some clothes to take to her hospital room, the kitchen smelled only of lemon-scented dishwashing detergent, and a faint aroma of old, cold, burnt iron.

.   .   .

In her life, she saw weeds creep over the Model T, and church steeples vanish beneath the man-made lakes of the TVA. She saw great blast furnaces go up, and go dark, and ancestral mountains clear-cut down to bald nobs. She saw circus trains, and funeral trains, and the first gleaming diesel engine roar through these hills. She saw a Russian monkey in a spaceman suit, and figured, well, now she had seen it all. "It made me sad, when they shot him into outer space. They showed him on the TV again when he come back down, but I ain't sure it was the *right* monkey, you know, the *same* one." The point is, I had convinced myself she was somehow immune to passing time, that she lived outside and above the events of the twentieth century, and the twenty-first. She could no more wear out than the whetstone she used to sharpen her ancient butcher knives, even if she had seasoned most of the vegetables she ate with pork fat.

"Gettin' old ain't easy," she told me, as she passed seventy-nine, "but it's best not to try and fight it too much. You know how

I live with bein' old? I just don't look in the mirror, 'cept when I part my hair."

She passed eighty in April of 2017 with a baseball bat beside her bed, for assassins. In the past five years, she survived heart failure, serious cancer, dangerous surgeries, and harsh follow-up treatments that left her thinner and weaker over time. Still, I rarely saw her stumble, or waver in her resolve to live as she always has, to walk her garden, gripe about the weather, and rattle her pots and pans. She survived *everything,* but in the late winter of 2016, the hospital entrance had become a revolving door, and she was admitted and readmitted for regimens of strong medicine and rest. Again, the young doctors said she would recover, if she would eat the dull, bland food and drink the foul-tasting medicine that was made, she believed, from the manure in her donkey pasture. She could go home again, the doctors told us, if she would behave herself, and if, after so many hard, hot, long days, she still had the will. She was not an ideal patient.

"That stent they put in my heart a year or two ago, well, they didn't really have to do that," she grumbled from her bed. "That was just the style then. Ever'body was gettin' one. I didn't *need* it. I was fine."

She spent most of the spring on an IV. While she slept, my big brother and I talked quietly beside her bed about being boys, running buck wild through her kitchen, about big fish, and ugly dogs, and a pearl-white '67 Camaro he never let me drive. The past is where we go when we are helpless; the past, no matter what the psychiatrists say, can't really hurt you much more than it already has, not like the future, which comes at you like a train around a blind curve. But our conversation always circled back to the thing that mattered most. I am not a particularly optimistic man, and feared for her. Sam told me I was being foolish. She would get better this time, too; it was just a matter of time before she got tired of this place and walked out, grumbling. He said he knew her better than I did; he was living his life within three miles of her, while I went gallivanting God knows where. He said the same thing over and over, like a prayer. "That old woman picked cotton . . . did stuff the regular people can't do. They don't know who she is."

"Do you remember the junk stoves? Remember that grave-yard?" he asked me one evening, and I shook my head. He seemed deeply disappointed in me, as if I had somehow failed my heritage by not remembering every anthill, blown-over willow tree, vicious blackberry bush, and rotted-down rope swing on the Roy Webb Road. "How," he asked me, "do you not remember that many burnt-out stoves?"

And then I did remember them, a ragged row of scorched, rusted relics banished to the deep backyard, worn out, shorted out, and dragged out of the little frame house to a place past the rusty bicycle junkyard and the doghouse, to the edge of the cotton field. The years bring down everything here, in the heat, damp, and rot, but it takes a lot of rust to wipe away a General Electric. The number varied, but at one time there were thirteen derelict stoves abandoned there, bound to the earth by honeysuckle, briars, and creeping vines: Westinghouse, Kenmore, Hotpoint, GE, and more, in white, brown, and avocado. She used them till there was a near electrocution, or an electrical fire, till there was not a spark left.

"Momma wore 'em all slap-out, one after another," he said. "She cooked every meal we ate, seven days a week . . . except when she got us all a foot-long from Pee Wee Johnson's café, every payday, every Friday night. To be honest, I guess most of them ol' stoves was second- and third-hand to start with, but it's still a lot of stoves, ain't it? Just think . . . think what it took to wear out that many stoves."

"I had a big forty-two-inch stove in my kitchen one time, when we lived with Momma," the old woman said from the hospital bed, her eyes still closed. She pretended to be asleep sometimes, so she could hear what was being said about her. "But it wadn't no-'count, to start with. I melted the buttons off of it."

There, in Room 411, she even dreamed of food, or maybe just

remembered it. She saw herself waist-deep in rows of fat, ripe tomatoes hanging heavy on vines that ran green for as far as she could see. She reached into a vine and pulled one free, rubbed it clean on her shirt, and took a saltshaker from a pocket of her clothes. She ate it, standing in the blowing red grit, salting every delicious bite, until it was all gone, the way she'd done when she was young. She told me about it later, amid the alarms of the IV machines, the barking intercom, and call buttons that never went quiet, even at 3:00 a.m. "And it just seemed so real I could taste it," she said, and I told her she must be on some fine dope if she could taste a dream.

She lay there day after day, and planned what she would cook once she got home, what she would grow in her garden and pepper pots, or gather in the woods and fields for jellies, preserves, and pickles.

"I lost the spring," she told me one morning, after a particularly bad few days, and for some reason that simple declaration haunted me more than anything else. "I lost one whole spring."

I would like to say that something profound happened after that, something poetic. The truth is, as my big brother predicted, she just got mad. It bothered her that she could not tell if she was dreaming or remembering, there in her narrow bed, and she told the nurses, "I don't want no more of that strong dope." She had eaten very little in the hospital; the cooks did not know how to use a saltshaker, she said. It irked her that her vegetable garden was still deep in weeds with hot weather coming on, and that she had to dream a ripe tomato to get a good one. One night, she just opened her eyes, demanded some Hi Ho crackers, an ice-cold Fanta orange soda, and her shoes. "And tell the nurses," she said, "tomorrow I'm goin' home."

I told her the doctors would have to decide.

"Well," she said, "doctors don't know everything, do they?"

I told her a little more rest, just a few more days of care, fluids, and observation in her hospital bed, under the kind and careful watch of the fine nurses and doctors, could not do her any harm.

"You don't know about Irene," she said.

I told her I did not remember any Irenes.

"She was my cousin, I guess, and she was trouble, son, trouble all her life. She argued three days over what color dress to bury my aunt Riller in, and Aunt Riller was still *alive,* still a-layin' in that hospital bed, *listenin'* to her. Don't tell me there ain't no harm can come to you in a hospital room. . . .

"If I can just get home, I'll cook me some poke salad, and I'll cure myself. . . . And I'll tell you something else. Salt is good. It says so in the Bible."

You learn, if you live long enough down here, not to push too much against what these old, hardheaded people believe. If an old woman tells you there is magic in an iron pot, you ought not smile at that. "The iron gets in you, through the food," she believes. "It gets in your blood, and strengthens you." I have heard French chefs say the same, but the old people who raised her believe the iron left something much more powerful than a mere trace of mineral; it left something from the blast furnace itself, a kind of ferocity. But how do you explain that to heathens? She has cooked in iron all her life, and she is cooking in it now.

But since that day in her cold kitchen, I knew I had to convince her to let me write it all down, to capture not just the legend but the soul of her cooking for the generations to come, and translate into the twenty-first century the recipes that exist only in her mind, before we all just blow away like the dust in that red field.

. . .

I am a roving gambler
I've gambled all around
And wherever I see a deck of cards
I lay my money down, lay my money down
I lay my money down

She came home to her small, cluttered kitchen and the aroma of one-hundred- and two-hundred-year-old recipes and the words to even older songs again drifted through her cedar cabin, which rises, like it grew there, from the ancient rocks, oaks, and scaly-bark trees in the lee of Bean Flat Mountain, in the hilly north of Calhoun County. It always made me smile, how she would not sing a note unless she was alone in her kitchen, at work. All my life, I've listened to my mother sing, faintly, through walls, and through the kitchen door.

I've gambled down in Washington
I've gambled over in Spain
I'm goin' down to Georgia
To gamble my last game
Gamble my last game

"The Scripture says we are not supposed to glory in the things we make with our own hands," she told me, not long after she came home from the hospital, in the late spring. "But when I got out of that place, that last time, I stood in my house and it just dawned on me, 'I'm home. I'm back in my own house. I'm back in my own kitchen.' And God forgive me, but I gloried in that."

The day after she got home, she went to her flour barrel, sniffed it, made a face, and cooked a big pan of biscuits and a massive iron skillet of water gravy, for the dogs. Then she scattered the remainder of the abomination into the front yard, for her birds; I sniffed it and it just smelled like flour, but she could not rest, knowing stale flour was in her house. She sent me to the grocery with a list written on an old water bill in No. 2 pencil, and it occurred to me that those lists, saved in desk drawers and sock drawers and between the pages of books, are the only record of her food I had. I will keep them the rest of my life.

"It was a hard life," she told me once, "but we ate like we were somebody a good bit of the time." They worked hard for it and prayed over it, even when, sometimes, our ancestors had to steal it. If I could capture just some of that, somehow, it would be a book worth doing, not a broad or deep treatise on the history of Southern cooking—of plantations, cotillions, and divinity candy—but of one old woman's story of working-class mountain food, or, as she calls it, "plain food, well seasoned."

I could claim a more cosmic reason for doing it. In a South that no longer seems to remember its heart, our food may be the best part left. It is the opposite of the bloody past, the doomed ideals, and our still-divisive, modern-day culture; it is a thing that binds us more than it shoves us apart, from each other and the rest of the world. It is the one place in our culture where living in the past makes a lovely sense, not an antidote for all the rest of it, but a balm. There is a reason why many black Southerners—and some white ones, like my mother—still call this kind of cooking soul food, because it transcends the pain and struggle of the everyday, a richness for a people without riches. We are not so arrogant as to believe that the genre of Southern country cooking hangs by a thread as thin as ours; it will live on, of course, carried from the kitchens of other old women and men like her . . . but not *just* like her.

Mostly, I just wanted to hear her talk about her food.

My mother is not a student of haute cuisine and would not care about it even if she was altogether certain what that was. She has heard that old people are supposed to keep learning and trying new things, so as to remain relevant. She would rather remember and preserve, rather remain a master of simple ingredients we grow ourselves, or forage from the Winn-Dixie, or find in an ever-shrinking wild, like the highland cress she wilts in an iron skillet with a little bacon grease and slivered green onion. "I ain't doin' no yoga at my age," she said, and made a face. She pronounces it "yogurt," and she is not doing any of that sour mess, either. But she will have a cold glass of buttermilk, thank you, and a slow walk to the mailbox.

She laughed out loud when she first heard the term "farm-to-table." They had it in her day, too; they called it a flatbed truck. She knows her food is not the healthiest, yet her people live long, long lives, those not killed by gunfire, moonshine, or machines. She has never tasted ceviche or pâté, but can do more with field-dressed quail, fresh-caught perch, or a humble pullet than any-one I know. With a morsel of pork no bigger than a matchbox, salt, a pod of pepper, and a sprinkle of cane sugar, she can turn col-lards, turnips, cabbage, green beans, and more into something finer than the mere ingredients should allow. With bacon grease and two tablespoons of mayonnaise, she turns simple cornmeal into something more like cake. I watched two magazine photog-raphers eat it standing up in her kitchen, with slabs of butter. I do not believe they were merely being polite. "They even eat the crumbs," she said. "They were nice boys."

Her food is not the world-class cuisine of Charleston, Savan-nah, or New Orleans, not reliant on the Gulf, or the Atlantic, or estuaries of the coast and the Low Country. It is the food of the high places, of the foothills, pine barrens, and slow brown rivers. It is not something done by the great chefs in Atlanta or Birming-ham for people who spend more on a table for four than a work-ing family spends on groceries for a month. It was never intended for everyone, but for people who once set a trotline, or slung a wrench, or rose from a seat in the city auditorium to testify during an all-night gospel singing.

Her brothers would pitch legendary drunks when they were younger men, and would inevitably wind up on our couch to sleep it off. My brothers and I, little boys then, used to stand and stare at them, thinking perhaps they might be dead. But my mother cooked for them as if they were sultans or senators, cooked to bring them back to life. Sometimes, if they had the terrible shakes, she had to help them to the table for plates of baby limas, backbone, corn muffins, stewed cabbage, and tea as black as her coffee, but not so sweet as to be silly. My uncle Jimbo is not a gourmet, or an unbiased and veracious critic; he once ate a bolo-gna sandwich sitting on a dead mule, to win a bet, and can out-lie any man I have ever known. But he would tell her, hot tears rolling down his cheeks, that he had not eaten stewed cabbage that fine since his momma was alive. My mother never needed much vali-dation beyond that, no grander praise.

It truly never occurred to her to open that lore to a wider world and share her skill with cooks she never even met, to translate into the twenty-first century recipes from a time when marching off to war meant foraging for shell corn in the Cumberland, and people still believed that if you chopped a snake in two with a hoe the pieces would rejoin in a circle and roll off like a hula hoop. It would be like singing a song to people in a language they do not understand, or one they knew long ago, as children, but can no longer recall.

"A person can't cook from a book," she told me.

Her mother, Ava, baked tea cakes and put them in a clean white flour sack to keep them soft and warm, because even a Philistine knows they taste better, somehow, lifted from that warm cloth. My mother would feel foolish, she said, trying to explain why such things should be honored in a modern world.

"A person," she said, "can't cook from numbers."

She believes a person learns to cook by stinging her hands red with okra, singeing her knuckles on a hot lid, and nicking her fingers on an ancient knife as she cuts up a chicken, because a whole chicken tastes better than one dissected in a plant and trucked in from Bogalusa. You learn by tasting and feeling and smelling and listening and remembering, and burning things now and then, and singing the right songs. Jimmie Rodgers, who sang of trains, chain gangs, and the shooting of untrue women, lived in our kitchen. "We had a whole big ol' box of his records that we played on the Victrola," before the awful summer of '47, when they warped and melted in the heat. The great Hank Williams lived there, and the Dixie Echoes, Patsy Cline, the Carter Family, and anyone from the *Heavenly Highway Holiness Hymnal.* "I guess you *can* learn to cook from a book," she relented, "if it was a real, real *old* book.

"It takes an old person to cook, or . . ." She struggled to find her meaning, but the closest she could come was a young person with old ways, with an old soul. The recipes inside her head come from across an ocean, from the French countryside, where my mother's people once lived, and from the Irish, English, Scots, Germans, even the Nordic people. Others came from those already here, from the Creek, Choctaw, and Cherokee, as the blood of them all mingled over the passing years. There is a recipe for coconut cake that, we are pretty sure, tumbled straight from God. "Young people *can* cook some stuff, I suppose," she said, grudgingly, "but, you know, they'd have to go to school."

I told her we could preserve it all, dish by dish, not by doing merely a litany of recipes, as in a traditional cookbook, but by telling the stories that framed her cooking life and education, from childhood to old age. The stories behind the food would not be difficult to gather; they well up here, from a dark, bottomless pool. The harder part would be the recipes themselves, the translation from the old ways, and her own peculiarities in the kitchen.

"Does that mean I am peculiar?" she asked, when I read her this.

"Well," I said, "yes."

She does not own a measuring cup. She does not own a measuring spoon. She cooks in dabs, and smidgens, and tads, and a measurement she mysteriously refers to as "you know, hon, just *some.*" In her lexicon, there is "part of a handful" and "a handful" and "a real good handful," which I have come to understand is roughly a handful, part of another handful, and "some." It would be romantic to believe she can tell, to the tiniest degree, the difference in the weight of a few grains of salt or pepper in one cupped hand, but it would be just as foolish to say she guesses at the amounts, or cooking times, or ingredients. She just remembers it, all of it, even if she cannot always remember when or where she learned, and you can believe that or not, too. She can tell if her cornbread is done, and all the rest, by their aromas alone—that, or the angels mumble it straight into her ear. It's not the clock that tells you when it's done; the food does.

She does not own a mixer or a blender. There is a forty-year-old lopsided sifter for her flour, and a hand-cranked can opener. She mixes with a bent fork and a big spoon, smelted, I believe, during the Spanish-American War. We got her a microwave once, which lasted one week before the first nuclear accident and resulting blaze; I am pretty sure she did it on purpose. Her stainless refrigerator, which she does not approve of and secretly wishes would die, is shiny, new, complicated, and as hard to operate, she complains, as a rocket ship. "And it's too quiet," she says. "You don't know when it's working." She preferred her old Frigidaire, purchased during the Johnson administration, even though she had to chip out her Popsicles with a butcher knife. It ran like an International Harvester, shook the floor every time it throbbed to life, and caused lights to flicker as far away as Knighten's Crossroad.

"I don't like new stuff," she likes to say, usually as she stirs a pot so battered and dimpled it will not sit flat on the stove and spins on the red-hot eye like it has been possessed. Her knives, most of them, are as old as she is, the wood handles worn to splinters, the blades razor-sharp and black with age. She had to dig her nine-inch iron skillet, her prized possession, from the ashes of her burnt-down house, in 1993. Well-meaning relatives offered to get her a new iron skillet, but she said she would have to season a new one to get it to cook right, and that could take the rest of her life. She would just keep the old one, thank you very much. How do you hurt a skillet, anyway, in a fire?

Other well-meaning people send her gadgets and diamond-coated pans and garlic presses, and even cookbooks on Southern country food; she sells them at yard sales, next to her pickles and preserves, for ten cents apiece, and she worries that she is asking too much for something of so little practical use.

That said, she recognizes progress when she sees it, or tastes it. Self-rising flour and cornmeal were perhaps the finest inventions since the polio vaccine, and even canned biscuits and store-bought pie shells have their limited use. Electricity was, she concedes, also a fine idea. But she would like to meet the man who invented the telephone, she says, and smack him a good one.

Progress is fine, in all. But with food, she says, you should not be able to taste it.

You should taste the past.

"What would you even call it?" she asked me, of a cookbook on her food.

"*The Best Cook in the World,*" I said.

"I wasn't even the best cook that lived on our road," she said. "Your aunt Edna was a fine cook. Our momma was a fine cook."

I told her we couldn't call it *The Third-Best Cook on the Roy Webb Road,* because that just didn't sing.

She thought about that a bit, about its veracity, and her reputation. Her momma was an excellent Depression-era cook, but was widowed young and never had the variety of ingredients to flex her muscles in the kitchen the way her daughters would, in somewhat gentler, fatter times. Edna Sanders, my mother's oldest sister, was a true master of Southern country food, in every way, who could grow it from the dirt, fish for it, run it down and kill it, skin it, and make gravy from it, on dry land or floating on a houseboat or bateau. "I guess me and Edna did run a pretty good race," my mother said, her humility slipping a little bit.

I told her I believed she was the best cook in the world, and I got to say.

"Well," she said, "I did wear out eighteen stoves."

I told her there were only thirteen stoves, off and on, there in the weeds.

"I wore out some since then," she said.

I could tell, after a while, that I was beginning to wear her down. She is otherwise humble, a woman who buys her clothes at the City of Hope thrift store on Highway 431, and has been to the beauty shop twice in forty years. My cousin Jackie cuts her hair in the living room, the same style for sixty years. But she can be a hardheaded old grouch when it comes to cooking. Though her face has been on the cover of a great many books, her food is her identity closer to home. And it saddens her that her iron skillet might one day become a relic, a curiosity, like a butter churn or a flea-market lazy Susan, or that her home-canned vegetables, peppers, jellies, and jams would be something vaguely remembered, like the name of that third cousin who moved to Detroit in the fifties to work on the auto assembly lines, or like a long-gone dog.

We already live in a culture where people line up at buffets of canned turnip greens cooked to green ooze, macaroni and cheese that glows like a hunter's vest, and vacuum-sealed coleslaw that went bad on the back of a truck somewhere on Interstate 59. She has seen home-cooking recipes dwindle even from the kitchens of her kin, slowly fading, generation by generation. She has watched the cafés, truck stops, and barbecue joints of her youth—places that took pride in their simple, savory food—go out of business forever, to be replaced by themed restaurants, and kitchens that produce what could be called food only in the most generous sense. Southern is more a fashion, a marketing tool. She knows there are world-class restaurants out there that produce fine, fine Southern food, but she will never sit down in one, most likely, nor will most of the people she has ever known, most of the people she has cooked for in her lifetime.

She wondered, aloud, if people outside the family even see value in food like hers anymore.

"What if people don't like it?" she asked.

I told her some people don't like Patsy Cline.

The culture around her has changed, of course; country means something different now. The entire region walks around in camouflage, to belong, and the last of the Roosevelt Democrats have long vanished in the mist, with the last panther, and the last local dairy, and most of the good butchers. The fish in the Coosa River, fish that fed generations, are unfit to eat, and the wild things in the forest taste different now, she believes; the venison tasted better when our men walked in the woods without a GPS, and deer did not hurl themselves into every third Subaru on a six-lane thoroughfare. Wild turkey roam subdivisions now, and can be shot from the bathroom window by a data processor in his Scooby-Doo drawers. Thank God, she says, she can still see the fresh-turned red earth of gardens in the springtime, mostly in the yards of old people like her, who will cling to their traditions, and their hoe handles, till the bitter end.

But mostly, outside the living museum of her kitchen, she has seen a great silliness envelop Southern cooking, something she sees when we drag her, griping, to eat catfish or barbecue, or to the last few meats-and-threes; she sees no reason to drive a half-hour to a strange place, to sit on a hard bench built from two-by-fours so as to appear rustic, just to be sad. She believes that most outsiders, including Southerners who have never stood in a field and salted a tomato, have forgotten what Southern country food used to be, or ought to be. "I mean, it ain't s'posed to be *easy*."

She believes this food cannot be purchased, only bestowed, or cooked with your own hands. Do not order it in a restaurant, at least in most of them, and assume you will be getting anything akin to genuine Southern mountain food. Think of restaurant grits, which are likely to be an inedible, watery, unseasoned abomination. Restaurant beans, of all kinds, are likely to be mass-prepared, chalky, bland, and bad, almost without exception. Try to find a piece of ham in them and you will go blind; none will have the concentration of lean ham, fat, skin, and that little something extra the ham bone brings as it disintegrates into the dish over hours of slow cooking. By the same standard, if you have ever had good sausage gravy over hot biscuits, or good greens, stewed squash and onions, fried green tomatoes, or slow-cooked cabbage, *then* order them in most restaurants; you will put down your fork in dismay.

"I can eat it, if I'm starvin'," she said, after searching for something nice to say. "I'd just hate for people to think that's what country food is. . . . I don't want the people to think it's what real food is. . . ."

It is soul food without soul, but mostly without a story.

"Good stuff always has a story," she said.

The great chefs might snort at her, but she believes good Southern cooking is not all about excess or overindulgence; pork is more often served as a seasoning than a whole hog on a spinning spit, as a way to add a richness to fresh vegetables, dried beans, collards, and more. Her fried foods, like chicken, fish, or pork, or fried vegetables, like green tomatoes, squash, and okra, are dusted lightly with dry flour or cornmeal, salt, black pepper, and sometimes cayenne, not drowned in a thick dredge of gunky egg batter and deep-fried, obscuring or even erasing the flavors underneath, like a fried mushroom in a sports bar. My mother believes you can tell if a thing was cooked right by listening as people eat it. Any sound a fried food makes should be crisp, maybe even delicate. A group of people eating fried chicken should not sound like someone smashing a glass-topped coffee table with a ball-peen hammer.

She has watched the signature dishes of Southern food become parody. Hot, spicy food has become sideshow. She loves heat, and her pickled pepper would be dangerous in the hands of children, but it is not hot for the sake of heat alone. The point is to taste the food, not to take a bite, squeal, blister hideously, and flee to the closest emergency room. Her soups, relish, sauces, and chili are spicy, rich in tomato, onions, peppers, and sometimes garlic, which you savor even as it bites you a little bit. I told her about a trip to Nashville where I had hot chicken seasoned with what appeared to be some kind of nuclear runoff. It almost sent me to a hospital, to have my eyes flushed, lips salved, and stomach pumped. I literally blinded myself, temporarily, just by wiping my face with a red-peppered napkin. "Seems like you'd want to taste the chicken," my mother reasoned. "You ain't supposed to burn your own fool self up. You ain't supposed to eat nothin' and sit and suffer. That's just ignorant, ain't it?" I told her ignorance is in.

It is the same with sweets. She loves sugar, as most Southern cooks do, but there was once an art to it, a layering of flavors such as cinnamon, vanilla, and fruit or nuts. Now it all seems designed by a thirteen-year-old boy high on Little Debbie, as if a treacly, gritty icing will hide the fact that the cake layers are as dry as a Lutheran prayer meetin'. Her muscadine jelly is faintly sweet, a flavor that makes you think of flowers. Her cobblers taste of butter, plums, apples, and cherries. Crabapples, she said, do take a lot of sugar to cook with, and are also good for throwing at itinerant tomcats.

Not long ago, I went searching in a Piggly Wiggly for a Coca-Cola bottled in Mexico, because they still use cane sugar instead of inferior beet sugar, a thing I only recently learned. She had known it all along. They haven't tasted right on this side of the border since Lawrence Welk was wishing her champagne dreams.

She knew that affordable, simple Southern food had turned the corner to banality when she saw that a chain restaurant had introduced a barbecue sauce purportedly flavored with moonshine. Moonshine, as any Southerner not born at a cotillion knows, tastes like kerosene. Men did not drink moonshine for its bouquet, but because they wanted to dance in the dirt, howl at the moon, and marry their relations. When they took a slash and said, hoarsely, "Man, that's smooooooth," they meant smooth for paint thinner. Her daddy made smooth liquor and peddled it in old kerosene cans; sometimes it ate through.

On TV, Southern cooks are often portrayed mixing a julep, or staggering under a Kentucky Derby hat the size of a Fiat, or planning a wedding with antebellum gowns and at least one cannon. That, or they are trust-fund bohemians in actual berets, and more pierced nostrils than a rooting hog. She has seen very hip chefs prepare things that were, in her mind, not something serious people would do, like pork-belly ice cream, or sweet meats in caramel sauce, or collard purée squeezed onto a tofu hoecake. She has nothing against fusion cooking, whatever that is, or something called, honest to God, "shrimp foam," or "bright rice," or recipes involving algae, or three-year-old duck eggs, or yellow catfish pounded into a fermented paste. "People is used to different things now," she says, "but don't you bring it into *my* kitchen."

She did not expect to find good, affordable food among the effete, but neither does she have much in common with modern-day blue-collar cooks who are regularly portrayed in popular culture as camouflaged, shirtless, excessively hirsute, and hollering *sooooo-ieeee*. They are often filmed cleaning a poor groundhog, or boiling a raccoon skull, or studiously sautéing squirrel brains. And the sad thing is, it all looks so put on, like the beards would come off if you pulled on them, like a bad strip-mall Santa.

She does not cook raccoon, which is rich but strong and a little rank-tasting, like the small member of the bear family it is, and she sees no reason to sacrifice an animal as intelligent as a raccoon as long as there is a sparerib or chicken thigh lying around. Even possum has all but faded from the family diet, although my aunt Juanita, a possum-eating fiend, is the bon vivant of roasted marsupial. Tradition requires that we include a recipe for it, though my mother does not believe she is preserving her heritage by skinning and eating something that, when confronted with its mortality, keels over and plays dead, "and a whole lot of trouble for some oily meat." Squirrel brains taste like you have licked the inside of an old, smutty beer can. Still, she knew how to cook it all, when it was all there was. "You mix your squirrel brains with scrambled eggs, to cut down on that metal taste. . . . Anything you got to hide real good, ain't good."

She does not cook chitlin's, because she knows what God made them to do. That said, she has eaten many of them, when it was all there was. We have eaten many succulent pig's feet, split, roasted, and pickled. We have eaten poke salad and more than a few varieties of bitterweed, but we have never in our lives deep-fried a peanut-butter-and-banana sandwich, or a Snickers bar, or served a cheeseburger on a Krispy Kreme doughnut; there is a reason why such food is found in carnivals, next to a goat that reads minds. We demur on frog legs; they may sound rustic, but they taste like an unholy union of a chicken and a Gila monster. But we ate a bunch of them, too, when it was all there was.

The closest she will come to such exotica in her own repertoire is quail, which is delicious, and dove, which she can clean and dress using only her thumbs; she does not like to cook doves anymore, because they sound so lovely in the morning. Nor will she cook any rabbit, because she thinks they are adorable. She used to roast a little venison, which is lean, mildly gamy, and prone to toughness and stringiness, and has to be soaked in buttermilk and expertly prepared (grind a little pork into venison for a tasty burger or meat loaf) to be all that good. But fawns run across her driveway now, so she will not do it again.

Snapping turtle remains in the diet, but that, too, is complicated. She will, if you bring her one already cleaned and quartered, dust it lightly with flour, salt, pepper, and a little hot sauce, and fry it up like pork chops or chicken, but she says it is best prepared in a strong, spicy tomato broth, to mask the strong essence of lizard. "Turtle makes a good soup," she said, "long as you don't think too much about it."

She would rather cook you something for the simple pleasure of eating than in some attempt to be picturesque. If you have time, she will show you how to make a catfish stew with okra, tomatoes, onions, and garlic, the way old drunks cooked it on a riverbank in '47, between long swallows of white liquor, marathon lies, and the occasional fistfight; the French called it catfish *court bouillon*, but that language faded from her people a long time ago. Could the flavors, the memory, be that far behind?

She will show you how to make delicious pickled onions, and jelly from hot pepper, honeysuckle blossoms, or kudzu blooms. She can show you how to bake a juicy meat loaf from ground beef, day-old bread, bell pepper, and sweet onion, all worked together by hand, because it is the bread, absorbing the liquid from the meat, spices, and vegetables, that gives the dish such rich flavor and smooth, almost creamy texture . . . if it's cooked right. Drown it in tomato sauce and it's prison food. Cook it too long and it resembles a tar-paper shingle; cook it too little and it looks like something the French would do and call a terrine. "Use a iron skillet, 'stead of a bakin' dish or pan," she said. "It'll make the outside more crispy. You want the onion and green pepper inside to be so tender it almost ain't there."

She will show you the secret to perfect mashed potatoes,

whipped together with only butter, milk, and one special ingredient, with no lumps or skins; lumps are for Philistines, and came into vogue only as an underhanded way for insecure cooks to prove they actually started with a real potato in the first place. You don't whip 'em, "you just mash 'em till they're just right," and she grew a little testy that such a thing needed to be explained. She will not even discuss skins, though they are good for you. "They can be good for the hogs, then," she said, which puzzled me a little, because we have not had a hog for seven years.

She can show you how to prepare sweet peas or green beans so that they will not taste as if you got them on a tray in junior high school, and how to put up a jar of creamed corn so naturally sweet in its own sugar you will want to save it for dessert. She will show you how to make a coleslaw that will be the antidote to every miserable, gone-bad, chemically masked slaw you ever endured, how to spice pickled pepper and pickled onions and concoct a vegetable soup with a short-rib base that takes two full days to get right. She will show you how to make creamy porridge with rich broth, and twice-cooked watercress, a dish that was here long before the Spaniards came clanking in their rusty iron armor through these hills.

She could show you all of it, if she only had someone she trusted to pass it on. In the end, the greatest obstacle to this book was finding a qualified person to write it, because this, apparently, was not me. She has eaten my cooking with regret and pity and not some small amount of genuine fear that I might actually poison her with undercooked pork or poultry, poorly washed vegetables, or alien spice. She did allow I once made some savory baked beans topped with thick-cut bacon in the summer of '84, and served up a barely scorched ham in Atlanta in the spring of '96; that she remembered it all, and the dates, insulted me more. She also recalls I once set a small kitchen fire with a grilled cheese sandwich, beat a smoke alarm to death with a broom handle, and—cooking on high heat, against her advice—caused a permanent molecular bond between her favorite biscuit pan and a box of freezer-burnt Pizza Rolls.

I told her I am no more a gourmet than my uncle Jimbo, but I know what tastes good. I have eaten good roasted lamb on a rooftop in Peshawar, and excellent curry just outside London's Kensington Gate. I celebrated high tea in a mountain outpost in Kashmir, had antelope steak in the Masai Mara, shepherd's pie in Addis Ababa, and chateaubriand in bone-marrow sauce in Port-au-Prince, in the shadow of a coup d' état. I had succulent Korean barbecue in Los Angeles, fine *tres leches* in South Florida, and spicy grilled shrimp, slivered onions, and garlic aioli on hot, sweet cornbread in New Orleans. I had buttery clam chowder in Boston *and* Portland, tasty dim sum on a slow Sunday in San Francisco, and a sizzling, world-class steak in Oklahoma City. The best salad I ever had was diced heart of palm, avocado, and fresh tomato in a mildly sweet, garlicky oil and vinegar, in Santo Domingo. I cannot cook; I love to eat.

None of that made her feel any better about me; it just made her more suspicious, as if I had been caught spearing snails with little-bitty forks in the perfect bistro, or gone shopping for a three-hundred-dollar pair of pointy shoes. It all sounded like fancy, worldly, exotic food to her, to this woman who has been out of Alabama only three or four times in her adult life, if you don't count Chattanooga, Pensacola, and Ringgold.

The truth is, no matter where I went or how hungry I was, it has always been working-class food that made me happiest, made me feel close to home, like the black beans and rice, fried sweet plantains, and ham croquettes on Calle Ocho in Little Havana, deep-fried fish and chips in a thick white fog in Edinburgh, red beans and rice and boudin on the Bayou Teche, glorious fried chicken in Memphis, murky seafood gumbo on the Mississippi Gulf, ham shank and white beans on Canal Street, roast pork in San Juan, stewed turkey wings and cornbread dressing in Harlem, raw oysters on saltines with cocktail sauce and an extra daub of horseradish on a causeway on Mobile Bay, corn pudding on a buffet line in Fairhope, Alabama, and fine tortillas cooked atop a blazing oil drum in Everglades City.

This, I told her, *was* her food, just working-class food with a different accent, often cooked with the cheapest ingredients to hand, by old women and men in their own ancient pots, stirred with their own steel spoons, with their own drunken uncles and freeloading kinfolks to feed. If I could write about all that, with respect, then maybe I had sense enough to write about hers, too. I wanted to do this book, I told her, not just because her food will live on forever in some kind of dusty archive. The truth is, I like the notion that my mother's recipes might one day be attempted by cooks who live far, far away from here.

I like the idea that her delicacies might be crafted on designer countertops with ergonomic knives and simmered on ten-thousand-dollar stoves. I like that her daddy's fine redeye gravy might one day be prepared with coffee from a French press and organic tomatoes from a market on the Upper East Side. I like that cooks accustomed to extra-virgin olive oil might go slumming with lard, and maybe even stare down a pig's foot, not to be picturesque, but because it just tastes good. I like the idea that an amateur chef who has never been anywhere close to the Coosa backwater, who has never swung a hammer or slung a wrench, might one day call up the words to my grandpa's train songs on a touch screen embedded in his or her refrigerator door, while discussing how to craft the perfect hush puppy without access to any government cheese.

But mostly I like the idea that her food might one day be prepared in a mobile home or a little wood-frame house right down the road from her, by young people who vaguely remember that their great-grandmother used to make it just this way. And, after a while, my mother came to like that notion, too.

The stories and recipes in this book are of long memory. Many come, skillet by skillet, from my mother's teachers and the teachers before, and others come from the foot of my grandma's bed, where I slept as a little boy, listening night after night to endless stories of her life and her kitchen when she was a child bride, in the early twentieth century. Later, when my grandma's mind began to slide a little sideways, she carried on long conversations with her mentor, my great-grandfather, as if he were sitting with us in the dark, and so many others I had never known. It would be years and years before those conversations made sense to me, as I listened to my own mother talk about cooking and what it meant to us, and what it used to be. Though, in my defense, I had covered up my head with a quilt during some of my grandmother's one-way conversations. The stories and recipes in this book come from great cooks who have passed on, and from aunts, uncles, and other living kin who did not write down their favorite recipes, either, but had the great good sense to pay attention, as my mother did, when the old people had something to say.

These recipes and stories come, one by one, from the beautiful, haunted landscape itself, from inside the lunchboxes of men who worked deep in the earth and out in the searing sun, from homemade houseboats in the middle channels of slow rivers, or in the dark, high places as we chased the beautiful sound of our dogs through the hills and pines. They come from feasts and damn near famine, from funerals and other celebrations, and a thousand tales that meandered to no place in particular, and some I will never forget for as long as I live. I tried to write them as they were lived, tried to write them richly, because we believe that a dull people will rarely cook rich food, and sure will not appreciate it when it is laid before them.

As my mother said, it is not for everyone; it is heavy, probably a little too greasy, and perhaps deadly. You would not cook and eat it every day, even if she does.

I guess you would call it a food memoir, but it is really just a cookbook, told the way we tell everything, with a certain amount of meandering. Even the recipes themselves will meander, a little bit, because a recipe is a story like anything else.

We have learned that you can never tell what people would remember about food, or the people they cooked it for, like those young soldiers she fed in Red's café back in '65, across the four-lane from Fort McClellan. We remember it was banana pudding they had before they left for war, and know it for sure. We remember because she would bring their discarded comic books home to me—*Sgt. Fury and His Howling Commandos, Tales to Astonish, Amazing Adventures, Wonder Woman, Mandrake the Magician,* and more—and as I flipped through the pages crumbs of vanilla wafer would fall into my bed.

. . .

I had to be away for a while not long after she got home. I came in from the airport to find the house quiet but the stove hot to the touch. Dusk is feeding time here, for her mule, donkeys, goat, two dogs, untold cats, the wild things she has tamed, even the crows in the trees, and any kin who might wander in, hungry or just pretending to be. I have learned not to fret when I do not find her right away; she cannot move that fast and won't be far off. She has forty acres, but the mule is eight feet tall and not right in the head, so she does not go into the pasture anymore, for fear of being stomped to death. I asked her, many times, if she wanted me to give it away, or shoot it, and she told me she loved the mule and had paid a hundred dollars for it besides, so her eventual decision was to surrender the entire property to it, every fenced acre, till it died of ripe old age. It is in excellent health and will outlive all of us. If that makes no kind of sense to you, then you do not understand the terrifying logic of the Southern woman.

I circled the house and found her in the side yard, listening to the clouds. The weather prophets on Channels 6, 13, and 42 said we would have storms that evening, and thunder growled in the distance from clouds we could not yet see. The heavens can be seen only in slashes and slivers here, blacked out by the ridges and the trees; the horizon ends before you get to the mailbox. I can hit the horizon with a rock.

Sometimes, dissatisfied with their prophecy, she flipped from one weather prophet to another, looking for a forecast that suited her; today they all agreed she should go sit in the basement with a good flashlight and a weather radio, and maybe a fistful of Fig Newtons.

"The Lord's crying," she said.

"At what?" I asked.

"At the wickedness in the world," she said.

I started to ask her if it might just be weather and not the End of Days, but I so badly wanted to eat.

"My house is in order," she said. "I am not afraid."

"Well," I said, "that's easy for you to say."

I walked beside her to the house, but not too close. Someone is with her almost all the time now, but she does not like us to hover, as if we are waiting on her to fall. Inside, I stood in the room just off the kitchen, and we talked as she finished cooking supper, and I noticed how she has to work harder now to do what used to seem so easy. She cannot see well anymore, and sometimes she salts things two and three times. She forgets. "I ain't the cook no more that I used to be," she said, but that is not necessarily true.

At Thanksgiving last year, she roasted a juicy turkey, golden brown and swimming in a lake of melted butter, maybe not as pretty as a *Southern Living* holiday photo shoot, but tender and delicious, and perfect in its way. She had surrounded the great turkey with cornbread dressing, green beans cooked with pork, buttery mashed potatoes, hot biscuits, sweet potatoes, creamed onions, a pan of hot cathead biscuits, and more. It might have been the greatest meal of her life, or at least the greatest in recent memory.

Then, just a month later, she petrified a Christmas ham. She cooked it like she was mad at it, cooked it and cooked it till it looked like an old, scorched baseball glove laid atop a desiccated bone; cutting into it was more archaeology than anything else. "I guess I just lost track of the time, hon," she said, genuinely stricken. I told her it was good ham anyway, if a little chewy and, well, smoky, because it is my prerogative to lie to my mother in times like these. Everyone else lied to her, too, right along beside me; we lined up to lie to her. We should all be loved like that old woman is.

We came in so she could finish supper, and I left her in the kitchen; she prefers to be alone when she cooks, or at least as alone as she can be. But even from the next room I could tell there was something remarkable there on the stovetop of number 22, or 23; we have lost count. I could hear her for a long time, still talking.

"You know, I always wisht I could whistle," I heard her say to no one in particular, as she put the finishing touches on supper. I wonder whom I will talk to, when the day comes, and if they will answer? The institutions here could not hold all the people with our blood who walk around talking earnestly to Bear Bryant, Teddy Roosevelt, or the air. "Momma could whistle, whistle like a bird singin'. . . .

"It's done," she said after a while, softly, but, like dogs listening for thunder, we seem to be able to hear those words for miles. She handed me a heavy ceramic plate minted two generations before I was born, the same one I ate from before I left to catch the yellow school bus across from my grandma's house. The plate has a faded cluster of red roses at its center and a thumbnail-sized chip in the rim. I cannot recall how the chip got there, so it must have happened before I was born, and maybe even before she was.

I raised the lid of the old pot bubbling on the stove and gazed into a molten, aromatic pool: pinto beans and ham bone, with hunks of lean ham, disintegrating fat, and luscious skin floating in the liquid that melted from the ingredients to form a lovely, translucent elixir on the surface. A pot of deep-green collards, the liquor steamed away, waited on the back of the stove, next to a skillet of pale-gold creamed onions, and a tray of crisp cornbread muffins baked with melted butter *and* bacon grease.

"Well, now you're just showing off," I said.

The recipes, like so many of her recipes, precede the Civil War, though some are relatively modern and stretch back only about a century or so, to a time when the Doughboys rode home on trains festooned with American flags after the First Great War. She was not yet born when the best of those recipes traveled to Alabama from the mountains of North Georgia on muleback, inside the mind of a mean ol' man. I suppose, in the long history of my mother's food, it is as good a place as any to begin. It is not, of course, *the* beginning, only as far back as we can reach. The true beginnings of some of these recipes are so old there is no beginning anymore—only, if we are not careful, an end.

She handed me a steel fork.

"I hope it's good," she said.

1

"THEM SHADOWS GET TO DANCIN'"

Butter Rolls

Jimmy Jim Bundrum, his first wife, Mattie,
and their boy, Charlie, my grandfather

IT BEGINS not with a recipe at all, but with a ghost story.

The Buick was a '50, maybe a '51, long and slick and gleaming black, and sparkled with more chrome accessories than a Shriner's hat. It rolled up to their porch on the Littlejohn Road, and my mother thought for a minute it must be the governor, drunk again, or a judge, or some other rich man lost on the dirt roads. But it was only her second cousin Buck Bundrum, who had stolen his daddy's car, again.

His daddy, Richard, ran a bulldozer for the county, and there was good money in it—maybe not Cadillac money, but Buick money. "Let's go for a ride," Buck shouted, but when my mother and her older sister Juanita looked in the car, they saw his daddy snoring softly in the backseat, well and truly drunk, passed out cold. "Buck's daddy never would let him drive that car. I think Buck saw the keys in it and just took off, and he didn't see his daddy back there till it was too late, till he'd gone on down the road a ways. Buck wasn't old enough to drive that car no-how. . . . I was just fifteen then, and I know he wasn't no older'n me. . . ." But his daddy seemed deep in dreams, even smiling the faintest little bit, so Buck just kept motoring, and with any luck he could take his favorite cousins for a spin before his daddy even came to. It was in the late summer of 1952, and, "Well," my mother said, "we didn't have nothin' better to do."

Night was falling when they rumbled out of the driveway, three abreast on the front seat, with Richard, oblivious but breathing regularly, still curled up in the back. Buck spun the radio to WHMA.

I'm walkin' the floor over you
I can't sleep a wink, that is true

"We had us a nice car for a little while, by gosh," said my mother, the rebel. They drove to the Mill Branch, a clear, lovely stream in northern Calhoun County, where my people went in the daylight to picnic, or sneak a warm sip of Pabst Blue Ribbon, or wade in water so cold it burned their feet red. The branch was only a few inches deep here, rippling over clean, smooth pebbles, the streambed bordered by thick carpets of watercress. With Ernest Tubb warbling from the speaker, they slid out of the car to look at the moon and count the lightning bugs. Unsure how long Richard's slumber might last, they were walking back to the car to head for home when the calm around them was rent by a terrible scream from the backseat.

Richard was awake.

"Oh God!" he screamed. "Not here!"

He had awakened befuddled, unsure where he was or how he got there, and looked out the car window to see the moon reflecting on the rippling surface of the Mill Branch. And in that moonlight he saw . . . something. He thrashed, and wailed, not in foolishness but in genuine terror.

"The Haint! The Haint!" he sobbed, and begged his boy to drive them away from this damned and haunted place. Then he curled up into a ball on the backseat, arms wrapped around his knees, and began to rock and moan. His fear spread to the young people, who jumped back inside the car and locked all the doors. If Richard, a big, solid block of man, was so frightened, it had to be real. "Please, please," he begged, "he's comin' for us. Get us *away from here.*"

Buck left rubber on the blacktop. My mother turned to peer through the back glass, to see what was coming after them. All they could get from Richard was that he had seen "the Haint," an indistinct, manlike shape astride what seemed to be a great red-eyed mule, coming at them through the glimmering stream.

This was the night she learned that the Bundrums saw things at the Mill Branch other people did not see. If there was wrong done here, it was our wrong, and if there are ghosts, well, we put them here.

And it was the night she first heard the story of where so much of the good food she had eaten as a child, and had already learned to cook herself, truly came from.

The story behind it varies, depending on whom you ask, but this much we know: In 1919, James J. Bundrum, her grandfather, fought a bloody battle with another man on the banks of the Mill Branch. They were both dog-drunk at the time, and fought with knives. The other man, a drifter, was maimed and believed killed—was likely killed, for James J., who was called Jimmy Jim, was a furious man, and rarely fought to wound (he was also known to be a biter). While the blood was still bright on the leaves, he leapt on a tall black mule and fled across the state line and deep into the North Georgia mountains, leaving his family behind. His failing wife, Mattie, and a sickly boy, Shulie, would die as he hid deep in the trees. He would later say, "I couldn't have helped them none in prison no-how." And when people spoke of him, even years after, they said good riddance, because all the mean old man had wrought in the world was bloodshed, violence, and pain. His saving grace—and it was no small thing, this—was his skill in a kitchen, where he was known to make fine cornbread, delicious ham and beans, and lovely greens.

Since that awful fight at the Mill Branch, my people have seen moonlight and shadow differently here. Some believe it is the restless soul of the unnamed drifter who rides forever here after dark. Others say it is old Jimmy Jim Bundrum himself, or perhaps both of them, who linger here under a bright moon.

My uncle James, who is ninety-three and has created more mythology with his own stories than can be easily recalled, will not even joke about this tale. His customary foolishness sloughs away when he tells how the shadows of two ghostly figures come together when the moon hits the water just the right way, and how "them shadows get to dancin', but t'ain't dancin', a-tall. . . . It's fightin', turrible fightin', and they fight till you get clos't up on 'em, and then . . . and then they ain't there no more, son. . . ."

And still others say that is foolishness, of course, just country people scaring themselves bug-eyed in the dark, usually after sipping on some liquid imagination. My big brother has seen it, and some cousins, serious people and chuckleheads alike. "It's just the moon in that water, trickin' you," says Sam, my level-headed brother, but my mother warns that it is not wise to discount such things out of hand.

"I just know I never went back there after dark," she said. " 'Cause if you believe in the Lord, if you believe in His goodness and His mercy and His miracles, then you got to believe in them ol' demons, too, don't you?"

Still, she doubts if it is the old man himself, my great-grandfather, who haunts the branch. Old Jimmy Jim's spirit rests in her kitchen with all the rest of them, most likely inside the saltshaker.

I guess we should not be surprised that a ghost story and the story of our food are entwined. One of the first lessons my mother learned, which was one of the first her mother learned, was that the greatest sin a cook can commit is to serve bland food carelessly prepared, devoid of salt, seasoning, and crisping fat. Our people, our cooks, learned that long ago, from the mean ol' man himself. It was old Jim who taught them the difference between savory and nothing special. They just had to go fetch him first, from exile.

· · ·

1924

The boy had always been thin, but now his bones threatened to cut right through his clothes. He had been just a child when the old man left them, steps ahead of the law. Now he sat astride a gray mule that was better fed than he was, as it picked its way up and down a narrow trail through the Georgia mountains, up toward the Tennessee line. He had left the tiny towns and family enclaves of the Piedmont far behind, riding through small fields of cotton and corn and along zigzag lines of split-rail fence, till the forest closed in around him altogether. He rode for hours with no sign of humankind except a rare, thin tendril of smoke rising through the trees. He always sang out as he rode near one of these, and was careful not to come too close. It was not smart to ride up on a man as he cooked his liquor, and some of these old bootleggers had not seen a strange face, one that was not their kin, in years. The boy, just seventeen years old, then, had never been so far back in the still mountains before; he had been born in the high places.

He was not afraid, but there were noises in the night up here that made him wish he had stayed home: the owls screeched, like a woman's awful, anguished cry, and the wind hissed at him from the trees. One morning, when he was half asleep in the saddle, his mule shied wildly as a great, feral hog, as big as a washing machine, rushed, snorting and squealing, down the trail, right at them. The mule bucked wildly, crazed, and the boy lost his seat and landed hard on the rocky ground. But when he scrambled to his feet, expecting to be cut to pieces by those long yellow tusks, the monster was gone, like it had all happened in his mind. He was not sorry; his rifle was a rusty single-shot .22, and it would make only a bee sting, like thumping it with a cherry pit, to go at a hog so big with such a puny firearm. He remounted, cussed his quest as a damn poor idea in the first place, cussed the mule for its foolishness, and pushed on.

He had stopped at a shack here and there at the beginning of his search, asking where he might find the old man, and some people turned their backs to him and some told him just to go home, son, if he knew what was good for him, but he was on a quest and would not be scared away. Sometimes the trail vanished completely in the creeping vines and dark trees, and the briars all but clawed him from the saddle. Finally, after three days, he came to a small clearing in the green, and a one-room tumbledown shack.

A bleak old man in ragged overalls sat against a tree at a small, cold campfire, sliding a rough whetstone in a slow arc around the cutting edge of a small limbing ax; it was what he did to ease his mind. He had the sharpest steel in the foothills, people said of him, and was nowhere close to easy in his mind yet.

The old man did not acknowledge the boy at all as he rode in, did not even look at him, that he could tell, and when the boy drew closer he saw a double-barrel Belgium 12-gauge, which was the only thing of value not taken from him, leaning against a tree close to the old hermit's hand. The old man hid his eyes beneath a slouch straw hat, and concealed much of the lower half of his face under a massive bushy red mustache. The bones of his face stood out around eyes that most people could not hold for long, even if they wanted to. He was in his sixties then, but he was old only in the way that iron, or good hickory, gets old.

"You look starved, boy," said the old man, who was mostly rags and bone himself.

"I am," the boy said.

The old man scraped the stone against the blade.

"I have little here," he said.

The young man noticed that the black mule was missing, and thought the worst.

But he just shook his head; that was not why he was here.

"I've come to fetch you, Daddy," he said. "I need you."

The old man said nothing. His children had turned away from him after he fled. He had been a wrathful father, quick to use his strap, and worked his boy children like beasts, snaking logs down the mountainside with teams of mules. When he rode away, blood on his hands, he doubted he would see any of them again. While he was in hiding, his wife, Mattie, passed away, and then his youngest boy, Shulie, died from sickness. He had owned some land before the incident—not valuable land, but pretty mountain land—and he lost that, too, when he fled the state. He lived as a fugitive for three years or more, trapping, setting trotlines, hunting deer, turkey, pigs, squirrel, rabbit, possum, and raccoon, and gathering poke salad, muscadines, and persimmons on the mountain. He was as close to invisible as a man could be and still walk the firmament. His kin seemed content with that. They dug a deep, dark hole for him, and filled it in.

He had not asked his son to get down from the mule.

"What do you want of me, boy?" he said.

"You have to come with me," the young man said, "'cause I've married a pretty and hardheaded woman who can't cook a lick, and I do believe that I am a-starvin' to death."

His beloved was barely sixteen when he stole her away from her family in Tidmore Bend, not more than two or three months before, but he was bamboozled, hoodwinked, sold a blind mare. He was lured by her wit and her raven hair and lithe form, and was not thinking right. She had sealed the deal at a barn dance with a box supper he paid a dear dollar for, only to learn that the delicious fried chicken, potato salad, and slab of pie had been prepared by her older sisters, to get her married off and out of the house. They were tired of her, for she could be a little peculiar, and was often ill-tempered.

In the ensuing days, she cooked him greens that tasted like grass, and beans with the consistency and flavor of river rock. Her meat was scorched and smutty, or so rare it was damn near still matriculating, and her cornbread did not rise much higher than a Mexican tortilla; when he questioned this, she quoted the Bible, about unleavened bread and the body of Christ and such. He could not live like this, could not live hungry, not when there was steady work to be had and money for food, and a good garden growing chest-high just a few steps from the back door. His daddy just said no, he reckoned not, and went back to sharpening. The old man was not loquacious; he considered most conversation to be a form of weakness.

"I need you to teach her how to cook, and I don't know where else to go." The boy's new wife was contrary and would not listen to anyone, least of all her new husband.

"I need to fight fire with fire," the boy said.

He pronounced it "far with far."

"I can't come back," the old man said. "They'll ketch me if I do. They'll send me off for certain."

The boy told him no, there were no posters out on him, no warrants, "no paper on him, a-tall." The drifter, nameless to begin with, had just vanished from the earth as if he'd never been, and must have stumbled off to die elsewhere. He had not been missed, apparently, wherever he was from. The old man did not speak of it, then or ever, not with pity, regret, or relief. He nodded, but did not say he would go.

He told the boy it was too dark to go back through the mountains, and the path was dangerous in the dark; there were deadfalls steep enough to kill man and mule. He told him he was welcome to share his supper, such as it was. He had knocked down a single quail with the Belgium, in a clearing down below.

The boy sat quietly as the sun went down and watched the old man, working with just his hands and a wickedly sharp pocketknife, clean and pluck the bird. He rubbed the skin and the inside of the body cavity with salt from a tobacco pouch, which appeared to be his only seasoning, then ran a wire through the flesh and hung the bird from a thin, dangling limb over the fire. He had built the fire tight against the tree, so the branches would filter the smoke, spreading it into nothing but a vague gray that blew away on the wind. In a while, the quail began to smell good, and he would nudge it with a green twig now and again, to make it sway over that fire, back and forth, back and forth, to cook both sides. His daddy was good at stuff like that, the boy believed. The old man broke the quail in two with his hands, just ignoring the heat, and gave half to the boy.

He had not spoken as he cooked. He was out of practice, the boy supposed.

The bird was excellent, with just the right char. There is not much meat on quail, usually hunted for here, my people maintain, as a good excuse for biscuits and gravy.

The boy ate it in a grubby hideout, cooked by a fugitive whose kitchen was a tree limb and a bag of salt, and it was still the best thing he had eaten since he said "I do."

The old man rolled up in a wool blanket and was asleep immediately; whatever demons he lived with were afraid to follow him into sleep, or so it seemed. What he had lived, in one bitter lifetime, could not easily be described. He had been born in the ashes of the Civil War South. He had almost starved in a failed Reconstruction, and as a boy he swung an ax for both the hateful carpetbaggers and what was left of the hateful failed aristocracy, educated only in the law of the jungle, in brutal logging camps, and by bitter, beaten Confederates and the hidden-out Union sympathizers, each growing old inside their doomed ideals. He learned how to hunt and fish and fight and cut and curse with such color there was almost a beauty to it. He should have perished in the century before, in a time that at least made some sense, because he did not seem to belong in a time of mills, federal marshals, and great machines.

The next morning, without announcing his intentions, the old man stuffed his few belongs into a burlap sack and stood waiting as the boy saddled the mule. He climbed up behind his son, and my grandfather and great-grandfather headed down the mountain together. And, in this way, we were saved.

"Does this girl have a name?" the old man asked.

"Trouble," the boy said.

.   .   .

The boy had tried everything else. He and his bride had even moved in, soon after their marriage, with his uncle Tobe and aunt Riller, who was said to be an excellent cook. But Riller was also somewhat of a harpy, and she and the girl clashed, it seemed, every day. The older woman could not believe the sixteen-year-old girl could not cook so much as a cathead biscuit or a pan of grits. She derided her, mocked her helplessness, and the girl had the ill manners to talk back to her. When Riller caught the newlyweds dancing to the radio in the middle of the day, in front of God and everybody, she forgot her Scripture and called the girl some bad names. The boy took up for his bride, at which point his uncle Tobe, who at more than six feet and three hundred pounds would have made two and a half of the skinny boy, balled up one big fist and knocked him ass over teakettle across the room. He was lumbering toward the boy to do even more harm when his visiting brother-in-law, Henry Wilder, broke a cane-back chair across Tobe's oxlike shoulders, then went against his head with a chair leg, just to make sure. "Go, children," said Uncle Henry, "afore this great fool gets up an' I have to smite him agin."

"I always loved my uncle Henry," my mother said as she told it to me.

The young couple moved out of Tobe and Riller's house and into their own little rented place in East Gadsden, which the boy paid for by hammering down shingles, swinging a pick, digging wells, working as a hired hand for cotton and cattle farmers, and packing illegal whiskey out of the mountains on muleback; there was always a dollar in moving whiskey for a man unwilling to risk prison in Atlanta to peddle it himself. As he worked, other would-be tutors—great-aunts, aunts, second and third cousins, others—came and went over the next few weeks, trying to teach the girl something, anything, about cooking, with no positive results. They left defeated, and angry. The child was willful, they said.

The boy could cook a little himself; he had learned a bit from his father, which only made the bad food he had been choking down, for the sake of his marriage, even more awful, because he knew the difference. He told her he could teach her, and she told him to go to hell. Then he told her not to worry, that he could cook for them himself, when he was not working late or on second shift or chasing work on the freight trains or leading a mule down the mountain loaded with liquor. This caused her to weep piteously, her sobs building to a crescendo of awful shrieking. The boy had to choose between starvation, it appeared, or hysteria. He had decided a man could live a long time hungry before he fell to clattering bones, but his head would explode in a day, listening to shrieking like that. He would have ridden around the whole world, oceans and all, and drowned a hundred mules doing it, to find a solution to this terrible state.

His daddy was his last hope, the boy truly believed, or they would soon find his remains propped in a cane-back chair at the kitchen table, his teeth empty, a knife and fork in his skeletal hands, poised over a plate of food that even the hounds would only stare at, in dejection and dismay. And a hound will eat rocks and pine bark and pig iron if you rub some grease on it.

His bride was waiting on the porch as they rode into the yard. She was spooky that way. She just knew. The boy slid off the mule and introduced his daddy as the man who would, finally, teach her to cook.

"Daddy's a fine cook, and he can learn you easy," the boy said, not unkindly. They had married for love, against all common sense, but the girl still scared him a good bit.

She did not pitch a fit—you never knew what the girl might do—she just stood there and looked the old man up and down. He seemed in sorry shape, for a legend.

Ava Hamilton Bundrum was already prone to fits of anger and the occasional descent into deep melancholy, another thing her kinfolks had neglected to tell the boy. She was a great reader of Holiness Scripture, newspapers, and literature, and might have made a fine teacher, perhaps even a woman preacher. She had her own mind, and had since she was a child. And this ragamuffin would teach *her*?

"I don't see how," she said, finally. The grimy, dusty old man looked like he had walked, flapping and rustling, from a cornfield, where he had been propped and wired on a stake to scare off the blackbirds.

She cared not one whit about the craft of cooking, anyway; she had only half listened to her own momma's tutelage, and ignored her recipes altogether. Why would she listen to this old felon?

The old man stood without a word, too, but took off his wide-brimmed floppy hat, out of courtesy. She could see his face now, for the first time. She met his steel-gray eyes and held them, waiting, but the old man just walked right past her and stepped inside, uninvited, to peruse the kitchen. He needed to see if there was coffee in the can, for morning. If there was coffee in the house, there was hope for the future. There was a little.

"I'll make us a pot," he announced, without turning around.

The girl stood on her porch, frozen.

Whatever theatrics she had planned were taken from her.

How do you stomp mad *into* your own house to have a cup of coffee?

He moved in that day to the small house just outside the industrial heart of Gadsden, still in the country, but close enough so that they could see the blast furnaces of the steel plants glow beyond the trees. Her cooking lessons began almost immediately, but it would be a fat lie to claim that her tutelage began with anything remotely akin to enthusiasm on her part. And it would be that way for quite some time.

She had married a poor boy, enthusiastically, but might not have thought it through. Her people had been what the boy's people called the better-offs—not wealthy, but gentle, civilized, and churchgoing, with their own legacy of fine Southern cooking, of Mississippi mud cake, ambrosia, and sausage balls. Most of the fine cooks she had known in East Gadsden lived with flour on their clothes and their plump cheeks, and smelled warmly of baking bread and peach cobbler and pecan shortbread, the acidic tang of home-canned tomatoes, and the scent of frying bacon and pot roasts. They waved big rolling pins in the air as they talked, which was mostly of Jesus and money and the socialist Democrats or the money-grubbing Republicans, an affiliation that seemed to change from breakfast to dinner and, by supper, back again.

This old man smelled of wood smoke, Brown's Mule chewing tobacco, the barnyard, and, sometimes, corn liquor or hard cider, and had no use for a rolling pin whatsoever, though he had told her, in as few words as was possible, he once had to knock a bull to its knees with a mattock handle when it tried to run him down. He had no use at all for preachy Democrats and would have fed a fat Republican to his dogs, had no use for their religion, either, not the gentle, watered-down kind, which he called "Escapalians," nor the real God-botherers, the shoutin' and tongue-talkin' people of the mountain Pentecostals. He was a straight-up sinner and blessedly free of hypocrisy, because that would have required him to give a damn what people thought of *him*. He was stubborn, and he was mean, but when he took on a job, a contract, he would by God see it through.

Still, he had knocked the tops off mountains that were easier, it seemed, than this. He would discover that his son had not exaggerated. She could not cook any of it, her people's food or his, and did not even eat, or so it appeared. She ate like a baby bird. The foolish boy should have noticed that right off.

"Next time," he told the boy, "go get yourself a big woman. You ever see a big woman can't cook?"

That first evening, he let the girl cook supper without comment. She made a pan of cornbread devoid of all flavor—even, he would later swear, corn, which was by God a trick. As the cornbread sat on the counter, growing colder and sadder, she cooked a woeful half-gallon of vegetable soup by emptying cans of beans, tomatoes, and corn into a pot. In the years before refrigerators, cooking from a can was no sin, but there was no seasoning in it, either, no stock, no base, nothing to give it taste. She did shake in a dash of black pepper—that much, at least, she remembered from her mother—and then, making sure the old man was watching, she shook a saltshaker over it. She did not, however, check to see if any actually came out. The old man took a brave spoonful; it would do if a man was starving, but he had tasted better simmered in a work-camp cookhouse by murderers, arsonists, and dope fiends, dragging shackles across the floor.

The old man forced down a spoon or two more, trying not to make a face like an urchin staring down a dose of castor oil, then choked back a couple bites of the flat, tasteless cornbread. Before she could ask him if he wanted more, which might have been more than even he could bear, he got up and washed the bowls. There was a good quart or so of the awful stuff left in the pot, since no one wanted seconds.

"We can have it tomorrow," the girl said.

The boy had more iron in him than the old man had figured, to endure such a hell as this.

He lit his pipe, and in the quiet of the little kitchen heard his own stomach growl.

"I'll rustle us up some dessert, children," the old man said, rising, and did not wait for the girl's assent.

First he checked to make sure they had in their larder the few things he needed. They did—it was a simple dish. He quickly pulled together a biscuit dough, mixing flour, salt, soda, lard, and buttermilk, not in a bowl, not on a counter, but in the flour can itself, hunched over the bin in a straight-back chair, which the girl believed to be barbaric. Inside the bin, which he held steady between his bony knees, he shaped a depression—what amounted to a bowl made from the flour itself—and in the bottom placed his lard and his wet ingredients, drawing the dry flour down into the wet till he had his dough just right. He worked silently, almost grimly, but that was his natural state. He was actually almost happy, cooking, though his angry, desolate face and his happy, content face were eerily the same. "We'll need biscuits for this," was his only comment, but when the girl went to fetch the open-ended can she used to cut them out, he waved her away. He shaped them in his two hands, like a big, grim child making mud pies.

When the girl peeked over his shoulder, she almost laughed. He had patted out what seemed to be biscuits for a dollhouse or a child's tea party, a third the size of a real biscuit; it appeared such an odd thing, to see the rough old man's hands, which looked like they had been jerked at the last minute from a fire and nicked with a million knives, crafting such a dainty thing. Then, in a deep pan, he made a lake of sweetened, buttery spiced milk for them to swim in, and dropped them in with a plop, making sure they were coated. It was ready for baking in less than twenty minutes, and ready to eat in thirty more, a pan of buttery dumplings steeped in a liquid thickened to something like a pale-yellow caramel, but cleaner-tasting, milder, somehow. The boy was so happy he almost floated off the chair; the girl was mystified that it came out of *him,* but would not admit this for another half-century or so.

He learned it, he would say later, cooking for the men who skinned logs out of the woods, who fought each other with ax handles for sport, and worked for timber barons who considered them of lesser value than mules. He worked from the ingredients at hand, inside a kitchen tent with a dirt floor and flapping canvas walls. But, in a way, it was the best job a cook could have, because when he set this dish down on a rough table amid workingmen, he knew, and they knew, there was not a rich man in the fanciest house on the highest hill who was eating any better than they were, right then.

Butter Rolls

She has two methods for this, one a little harder, more traditional, and at least 150 years old. The other, much easier, is only sixty years old. "It's new," she said.

She prepares her biscuit dough just as Jim did, in the way he taught her mother to do it. Because she bakes every day, she keeps her flour in a ten-gallon can, and every time she bakes a pan of biscuits or needs other dough, she shapes a bowl of dry flour inside the flour can itself, pours her wet ingredients and fat into the depression, and uses the ends of her fingers to push the dry dough down and pull the moisture up the sides until she has just the right consistency. But this is not something you want to try right away: you run the risk of contaminating your flour. Better, for the first twenty to forty years or so, to use a clean, flat surface, such as an un-nicked cutting board or a large, separate bowl. Some use the clean countertop itself. "The flour is your bowl, and don't say 'depression'; just say 'make a hole in it.' "

"If you already know how to make biscuit dough, you won't need me," she said, "not for the first part. But I guess it wouldn't hurt to tell it."

The Traditional

WHAT YOU WILL NEED

for the biscuit dough

 3 to 4 cups self-rising flour
 4 tablespoons lard or Crisco
 ¾ cup buttermilk
 ¼ cup water

for the sweetened, spiced milk

 1 teaspoon ground cinnamon
 1 can (12 ounces) sweetened
  condensed milk
 ½ cup whole milk
 1 cup sugar
 1 teaspoon vanilla extract
 1 stick unsalted butter, kept cold

HOW TO COOK IT

First lay out a sheet of wax paper, and another sheet, both large enough to hold or cover a dozen or more small biscuits. You will not need a traditional baking sheet for this recipe; you just want something to lay the biscuits on as you make them, "before you take 'em swimming," she said.

Sift the flour, all of it, into a large bowl or whatever work surface you choose for mixing your dough. Some of our people keep a large wooden cutting board just for this, or use a clean countertop. Sifting is mandatory, even for self-rising flour. The sifting will catch any impurities in the flour, and mass-milled flour will have some mysterious specks here and there.

"I sift *all* my flour," she said. "Some people don't, and I eat their bread, but I don't really want to. You know, I just do it to be polite." But, she concedes, she usually points it out.

In the mound of sifted flour, use your fingers to create another bowl. Leave about an inch or two of flour at the bottom of the flour bowl. The idea is that the wet ingredients never actually touch the bottom of the bowl, or board.

"Reach and get a handful of lard or Crisco," she instructed. "My hands are not real big. I guessed at the four tablespoons." Work, break, or squeeze the Crisco into pieces, into the bottom of the depression. " 'Hole,' " she said.

Carefully pour most of the buttermilk and water into the depression, or hole, saving just 2 tablespoons or so, in case your mixture goes a tad dry and you need to moisten it. Gradually work the flour into the liquid and fat, pushing the flour down with your fingertips from the sides into the wet ingredients.

"Pull it from the sides, and work it into the liquid and lard in the bottom till it begins to get more firm. You don't want sticky, and you don't want dry, neither, but right in the middle."

The lovely thing about this is, if you have pulled the dry flour into the liquid gradually, it is hard to miss the consistency you are aiming for. You want to be able to roll the finished dough into rough balls, no bigger around than half-dollars, then flatten them slightly between your hands, so you have biscuits no bigger around than silver dollars.

Do not worry about waste. You can sift the leftover flour, and reuse the flour that is still perfectly dry.

Pat out about a dozen small biscuits, or a few more if you have some dough left over, and lay them on the wax paper. Sprinkle about half the cinnamon, but no sugar, lightly over the top of the biscuits—they will be sweet enough—and cover with the other sheet of wax paper.

Now it is time to make the bath. Into a clean bowl, pour the sweetened condensed milk; then fill the empty can with whole milk and add that to the bowl. You could ask why she does it this way, instead of measuring it into a cup, but she would only tell you because she just does. Add the sugar, the vanilla, and the rest of the cinnamon to the pool. Do not try to mix the cinnamon thoroughly, meticulously. "It will just make you mad," she said. "Cinnamon likes to trail and clump and swirl."

Cube the whole stick of butter, and let it go swimming in the milk mixture.

"That's why we call 'em butter rolls," she said.

Preheat your oven to 350 or 400 degrees, "depending on whether your oven runs hot or not," she said.

Pour the liquid into a 1-quart baking dish or pan, about 8 by 8 inches—though the shape does not matter—and gently drop the biscuits one by one into the liquid. Take your fingers and press each one down in the liquid, then let it bob back up.

"You want them wet, but do it just before you put 'em in the preheated oven, at the last second, so they won't get too mushy or soggy."

Do not crowd them as you place them in the dish. Leave space between them, about an inch or so. This does not have to be exact, but if you squeeze them in, "they will gum together, and just not do right," my mother said. "This is the most important thing in this, I believe. It won't hurt nothin' if one or two of 'em sticks together; you just don't want 'em covering the whole pan as they cook."

When I asked her to be specific about the oven temperature, she snorted at me.

"How in the world do I know how their oven cooks? I ain't never been in their house, and I don't even know who they are."

Bake about 15 to 20 minutes, depending on the mysteries of your oven. Then—and this is a little tricky—take a large spoon and turn each little dumpling over. It should be coated in the thickening liquid, and so should remain moist for the remainder of the cooking time. Cook another 10 to 15 minutes, until the liquid has formed a thick soup, not evaporated completely or cooked to a true caramel, but till the milk has cooked up into the biscuits and they have begun to brown just a little on top.

"You want 'em done, not somethin' soggy, but golden brown and still kind of creamy and buttery. The soup needs to be still thin enough to spoon out and drizzle some on the butter rolls."

They should be moist throughout, more like a buttery dump-ling than a flaky biscuit. Sometimes she sprinkles a little more cinnamon on them at the end, but sometimes she does not. If they seem a little gooey, she says, "then they're prob'ly just about right."

"How long, in minutes, altogether?" I asked her, pressing.

"How would I know?" she said. "Just till they're right."

Her wild guess was about 30 to 40 minutes or so, in all, "but you have to check, and smell. You'll know they're ready by the smell." When I asked what that smell is, she just said, impatiently: "Good."

Serve them while they're hot, or throw them out. They should be sweet, but not sickening, treacly; the first thing you should taste is the butter.

"But be careful, 'cause they can burn you."

I told her we could just leave that to common sense.

Some people, she explained, "don't have none."

She looked at me a little longer than was necessary.

The Cheatin', Whoppin' Version

"Came up with this 'un on my own," she said.

This recipe is quicker and easier, and still tastes very good; even I can make these. She fought against it for a while, she and her conscience, to see so much family history compressed into a cardboard tube. But she knows that many younger people, whippersnappers of sixty or seventy or so, may be intimidated by having to make real biscuits, or just believe they have something better to do, and may never attempt it otherwise.

First follow the directions for the milk mixture, as given in the traditional recipe, and set it aside.

Now, in shame, walk to refrigerator, retrieve a tube of canned biscuits, and—following directions on the label—peel off the outer label and whop the tube smartly on the edge of the counter; try not to drop the biscuits on the floor when they open in that alien, unnatural way.

I have never had a gallbladder go bad, or appendicitis, but I think it is probably something like this. "I don't care if I open a million of 'em. It just don't look right," my mother said.

My mother has the usual biscuit chef's snobbery about canned biscuits. She believes they are all but useless for breakfast, and especially for breakfast sandwiches, like a sausage biscuit. They don't even look like biscuit, any more than a bowl of plastic fruit looks like a curb market. But with a little sleight of hand, to hide the processed, uniform, somewhat mechanical nature of the average whop 'em biscuit, they can be useful in a limited way. "And this might be the best use of a canned biscuit I can think of," she said.

You will divide these biscuits into quarters, so a tube of small canned biscuits, a ten-count or so, will more than do. Do not try to doll them up, pat them out, or shape them in any way. You will just have a tacky mess.

"And don't worry about how they look. Sprinkle 'em with some cinnamon if you want to, and drop 'em in the milk. They won't be pretty at first, not like them pretty little real biscuits. They'll look fine when it's done."

You may have more so-called biscuits, or dumplings, and smaller ones than in the traditional recipe using whole, real biscuit, but this is fine, too. But, again, be careful not to crowd the biscuit pieces, or they will gum together and create a single slab, just like the real biscuits.

Bake roughly the same way, remembering to press them down into the milk at the beginning, and to turn them after 15 minutes or so. Again, it will depend on the stove, and also on the brand of biscuit, so keep watch as they brown.

Hide the biscuit tube in the trash, and "put the butter rolls on the counter on top of a pot holder, or on the stove eye, and let 'em cool a bit. Won't nobody know no different . . . but, you know, the cook." Pray about it, she said.

The somewhat ragged texture of the torn-up canned biscuit pieces will brown in such a way that, she says, "it'll look like you meant it to be that way."

Like the preformed pie shell, it is a small sin, and one of those rare, rare shortcuts that actually lead somewhere good, instead of to a bleak dead end, like vacuum-sealed macaroni salad, or fast-food fried chicken, or a microwaved anything.

"The only reason I even mention it is, I know a lot of people wouldn't never cook this if I didn't, and these butter rolls is a whole lot better than no butter rolls a-tall," she said.

. . .

Ninety-two years before, with the glow from the iron stove warm on their backs, the mean old man and his boy ate their butter rolls in thick ceramic soup bowls, with spoons rescued from an old army mess hall. They made sure to scoop out some of the thickened, sweetened, buttery milk from the bottom of the pan, and spoon it over the dumplings. It was the only way to eat them right, "to just kind of drizzle it on there," the old man said. Old people like to do that to young people in my family, like to tell them how to eat their food; they figure that, since they had the good sense to cook it, they should surely know how it should be eaten, too. They will lecture, in the middle of a delicious mouthful, "You just ain't eatin' that right."

Ava, after being told to use a spoon and a bowl, ate hers in a saucer with a fork, and would for seventy years, just to get even in some small and pointless way, till she could plot a better one. You had to know her.

It was just the beginning, of course. Some people give up on a good grudge after a while, maybe because the weight gets to be so heavy over time, or else the accumulated years make it a little slippery in the mind. And then there are people like my maternal grandmother, who could carry a grudge the size of a pachyderm around till Kingdom Come. It does not matter if their feelings about a thing, or a person, decline or improve in time; it's how they felt in that moment, in that misbegotten sliver of time, that endures, and they will bring it up at least once a week forever, till their minds just collapse around it. How *dare* that old rascal show her up like that, in front of her half-starved husband, by cooking something so good?

But there was no denying it, she would admit to us one day, many, many days from then: it was a fine and delicious thing the old cuss laid upon their table, maybe even the best dessert she had ever tasted, and her people were wizards with German chocolate cake and pineapple upside-down cake and chocolate and lemon pies. Even people who don't really like food like a little dessert—ask them, and see if they don't. Even very skinny people, supermodels and swimmers and the like, enjoy a good, rich, sweet butter dumpling, for the same reason that a sick dog with no appetite will always eat a can of sardines.

She knew, as she left the old man and boy that night, sitting quietly by that warm stove, that she probably needed to say something kind, maybe even make some slight gesture of friendship or at least civility toward the mean old man, maybe even go so far as some halfhearted stab at gratitude. But the beautiful thing about her, all her long life, was, she truly did not give a damn what she was supposed to do.

"That baking pan," she said to them, as she went to bed, "is gonna be hell to clean."

2

"SALT IS GOOD"

*Cream Sausage Gravy, Buttered Grits with a Touch
of Cheese, Sliced Tomato, the Perfect Fried Egg*

My grandfather, Charlie Bundrum, and his baby brother, Shulie

THE NEIGHBOR saw the girl wandering in the overgrown pasture near her house, and asked her if he could be of assistance. She did not seem to be in distress, merely searching for something.

"Sir," she said, "I hear there used to be an old well hereabouts."

"Yes, young miss," he replied.

Then the neighbor, a bashful farmer, just stood there.

"Well?" she asked.

Ava did not suffer fools, either, and she was quick to decide if someone might be one.

"Miss?" he replied.

"Well, where is it?"

"It used to be right yonder," he pointed, to the remains of an abandoned, broken-down house that had almost been reclaimed by the pine saplings, tall weeds, and gathering vines.

"Well," the girl said, "did it get up and move?"

"Did what move, miss?"

"The well."

"No, miss," he replied, beginning to think he should have minded his own business and kept walking. "It was filled in, not too many years ago. It was dangerous. A couple people fell in, I heard."

"Pity," Ava said, though it was unclear if she meant it was a pity that two or so people fell into the well, or that it had been filled in and was no longer suitable for what she had in mind.

"Oh, they fished 'em out," he said, earnestly, "afore they filled it in."

Then he did not so much walk away as hastily retreat.

It is doubtful, to those of us who knew her, that she would have pushed her father-in-law down an abandoned well. But we do know she went looking for one, just to sit by it for a while and think about it.

Some Southern damsels, those of a different class, might have gone searching for a well to hurl *themselves* into, but my grandmother was not built that way. She was not forlorn; she was mad.

Her plan was to tell him there was a hog down it, or a calf, and when he bent over to peek, well . . . But people should not see her as cold-blooded. If she had pushed him in, she always said, she would have called down to him now and again, to see if he was still alive, and might even have sung him a song from the rim, so as to prevent him from becoming lonely. Eventually, she might even have thrown down a rope, or at the very least gone to find her young husband, to make a full confession of it:

"Papa Bundrum," she would say, with sorrow, "fell down the well."

I was too small to tell, the first time she told it, if she was kidding or not. I do know I walked around, till about third grade, afraid to make my grandma mad. There was an old well near our house, too.

. . .

Just that morning, the morning of the second day, she and the boy awakened to a lovely smell. Running around it, through it, was the scent of strong black coffee; you could almost smell the color of it. Then came the rest, that glorious blend of frying pork and baking bread. Like a spell, a good breakfast can draw you from the bed no matter how dog-tired and drowsy you are, and make going back to sleep unthinkable, because a hot breakfast only lasts for a fine minute or two, whereas a cold breakfast can disappoint you all day, over and over again. Try to walk past a good hot real breakfast without regret. Try.

The boy thought he might be dreaming. He had been a child the last time he smelled a morning like this. His momma and baby brother were alive the last time he had awakened this way.

The girl had awakened and sniffed the air, and was mad all over again.

She, truly, had never understood the power of food.

· · ·

The old man had awakened long before dawn to begin, being of the opinion that no decent breakfast in the history of the world had ever begun after the sun had slipped free of the horizon. The girl might not have known how to cook a blessed thing, but she and the boy had laid in some sensible staples every payday, and he found all he needed here. There were grits, muscadine and crabapple jelly, pear and blackberry preserves, hard black-rind cheddar, and even a little leftover smoked sausage, not enough to fry up in links for all of them, but plenty for what he had in mind. He would need some more milk, but that was handy: the couple's one great wealth was a fine milk cow, and the girl, by some miracle, had learned to churn butter. There were chickens raising hell in the yard, so he suspected there were eggs; a man could cook a fine breakfast, a breakfast anyone would envy, with no more provision than this. He set to.

He stoked the fire in the woodstove, fed it some more wood, and quietly gathered his skillet, pots, and pans. He liked the quiet in the morning, when the world was still mostly in dark and most of the chuckleheads and nitwits were still held safely captive in dreams. He would not destroy it himself by rattling iron. He had heard that the Texas bandit John Wesley Harden had once killed a man in the early morning, just for snoring; he had understood, perfectly.

After his inventory, he milked the cow, then went behind the house, hopeful, to peruse the small vegetable garden. Good. There were still some late-season tomatoes left. He could have given a whole lecture, sung a sonnet, on the importance of the tomato in the Southern breakfast, if it had not involved actually talking to people and, even worse, having them talk back to him.

He went to work on the biscuits first, using roughly the same recipe as the night before, the one countless thousands of workingmen and -women had already approved, a basic, simple recipe with a little extra twist, a recipe that would endure for generations. This was before the miracle of self-rising flour, so he had to mix his soda and salt, measuring it in his cupped hands. He did not roll them out and cut them this time, either, as many people did, but patted out each one in his hands, as he had the night before, in domes on the baking pan, not discs, but bigger than the dumpling biscuit, just big enough to rest in his palm.

He worked not so much fast as smoothly, to bring everything to doneness at roughly the same time, a skill that some cooks still have trouble with even after a lifetime, forgetting that temperature can completely change the taste—and enjoyment—of food. First he prepared his ingredients for the sausage gravy. He diced the smoked sausage with his sheath knife, since the girl's knives were as dull as spoons. He wanted no more than a good handful. Then he went through their bin of potatoes and onions for a tiny white onion. What he needed was something not much bigger than a pearl onion, than his thumb, just enough for a teaspoonful minced fine; he wanted just a taste of it, a sprinkling that would cook to nothing but would be the thing that set his sausage gravy apart. Anything else, anything more than a taste, would make it a true onion gravy, and working people did not overpower their breakfast gravy with such exotica as that.

He set it all aside and went to work on the grits, a simple two-to-one ratio of water to grits, seasoning them with a little salt and pepper. As they began to thicken, he added a dollop of fresh milk, for taste and to thin them a bit; grits will run a little thick sometimes, but it's better to start thick, and thin a little, he believed, than to start with a watery mess that could not be rescued in any way.

He had seen grown men brawl over a sorry breakfast, over a watery plate of grits. He did not blame the men; any fool should be able to thicken a pot of grits, even a drunken or inept fool.

The gravy, the main course, was simple, too. Into a little slick of bacon grease, melted and just beginning to spit and pop in an iron skillet, he tossed the diced smoked sausage and smidgen of onion. The smoked sausage was too lean and slow to render, so the bacon grease was essential, to help it along. We know this because he never cooked a thing, a single thing, without adding a touch more bacon fat, and cursing the sausage maker or the butcher or grocer for being too damn dumb to know that good sausage needed plenty of fat, not just for taste but for the cooking itself. The world, it seemed, was full of dull-witted butchers and inferior pork sausage, but he was too old to educate the whole dad-gum planet earth.

When the inferior fat in the inferior sausage had begun to render, he tossed in a single pat of butter, then quickly stirred in a few tablespoons of flour, working from sight and smell more than time, than arithmetic. He let it brown only a little before he added the milk, but enough to erase that raw, chalky taste, then tossed in a little salt, and a more impressive dose of black pepper. He wanted a black-speckled white milk gravy, not a brown gravy, and as it thickened he stirred it with the big spoon till it was just about right.

The grits—good, coarse-ground yellow grits that had not had the taste and the texture and the color milled and bleached out of them—were about right, and as they finished he added a big chunk of real butter, and wished he had just a little cayenne, not for the heat so much as for that nice taste. Some pepper was all heat and whang, but cayenne had flavor. He took just a few crumbles of the hard, sharp cheddar and tossed them in as the grits began to thicken. Plain grits were fine for children, but grown people needed grits with some damn taste. He despised a plate of dull grits almost as much as he did thin ones. And if you tried to put sugar in them, he would slap the spoon out of your hand. No one—no one—put sugar in grits.

If anyone had bothered to look closely, they would have seen he stirred with both hands, in separate pots.

He pushed both the pan of grits and the skillet of gravy to the back of the stove to keep warm, and, still working quickly, went to work on the eggs. He would have preferred some good lard, but the bacon grease, which the girl had the good sense to hoard, was handy. He selected the smallest skillet she had and cracked and fried two at a time, carefully angling the pan to run the hot fat over the surface of the eggs, till he had six perfect medium-cooked eggs in about six minutes. Hard-cooked eggs had no flavor, he believed. People only insisted on a yellow cooked as hard as a dirt clod because they despised a runny white, but if you ran that hot grease over the sunny side before you flipped it, you could erase that probability and serve an egg that had a molten yellow but a done white and "still actually had some goddamn taste."

He had not timed the biscuits, and there was no glass window on the old iron stove to peek through to see how they were rising. He knew from the smell when they were done. The secret to a good biscuit, he believed, was a soft, domed top but a thin, crispy bottom. You got this with a little extra lard on the biscuit pan's bottom—not a whole lot, just a little more—so that the flour on the bottom crisped as the rest of the biscuit baked. Some people did not like it and preferred a soft, fluffy biscuit through and through, which concerned him not at all. Those people could make their own damn biscuit, if they did not see the glory in his.

He broke a biscuit for each plate, ladled on the sausage gravy, spooned some buttered grits to the side, added two eggs, and—as a last touch—sliced one of the late-season tomatoes. He laid two thick slices beside the gravy biscuit, dusting them with just a little salt and pepper. Breakfast gravy needed a tomato, or, better yet, a slice or two of cantaloupe, the sweeter the better, for a cool balance. People here have been eating biscuit and gravy and fresh tomatoes, or cantaloupe, side by side for going on two centuries.

Finally, working fast, he buttered the leftover biscuits, spooned in some muscadine jelly that the young couple had received as a wedding present, and set them back on the stove, to keep warm and to let the jelly liquefy into the melted butter and hot biscuit, for dessert.

The whole breakfast took less than forty-five minutes to prepare, and it was cheap to make; only the pork sausage and the biscuit flour were dear in 1924. The eggs were gathered from the few scraggly hens in the yard, and the tomatoes from the red clay, and the grits ground from hominy that the boy prepared himself, mixing ash into shell corn. It was cheap food, and good food, if you only knew the way of it.

The coffee was smelling like it might be ready, too. He made it strong—too strong, the girl would complain—but not foolishly so. He knew men who liked it like mud, the same men who ate hot peppers from the jar, standing up, to prove they were somebody tough.

Philistines.

"Hit's ready," he hollered, in case the boy and girl were so slothful as to sleep through a breakfast such as this.

. . .

From that first night, and certainly after the glorious breakfast that followed, the old man would be the beneficiary of her crackling, sizzling moods, which the boy might have considered all along. The old man made a fine lightning rod. The boy had some mild concerns, he later said, that his beloved and his daddy might actually kill each other, if the old man's reserve cracked and his infamous temper was unleashed, or if she could catch him from behind with a poker or a small stick of firewood. He had not even considered the abandoned well till his betrothed mentioned it, casually, sweetly, one day. But his daddy's stoicism usually only washed away in liquor, so as long as he kept an eye on the old man's moonshine and hard cider, he believed his bride would be secure.

The old man would quickly discover that the girl, who could not have weighed ninety pounds with her apron pockets full of lead sinkers, responded to criticism with rants, fits, fist shaking, and foot stomping. He responded to this, for a while, by simply ignoring her and—in mid-rant—just strolling onto the porch, or into the woods, or down the road, to have a peaceful smoke or chew of tobacco while she calmed down or, sometimes, just wound down from exhaustion.

People still wonder why he bothered, since the old man had never shown any outward affection for even his blood kin, and little patience, even tolerance, with anyone. My mother thinks perhaps it was because her daddy went to find Jimmy Jim when no one else wanted him, when the rest of the world seemed content to let the hot-tempered old booger rot in the trees, and pretend that he had never existed at all. It may be, though less likely, that he was lonely. And, also unlikely, it might be he was penitent for what he had wrought; either way, he was by God going to teach the brat to cook. It seemed to be what he had left.

It was not like he was trying to teach her how to be a fancy chef, but, in a way, there was more at stake; there was even more of a burden on a working-class cook. The country people, the working people, subsisted mostly on beans, greens, potatoes, sweet potatoes, onions, pork, and sometimes chicken, when one could be spared or perhaps stolen; beef was a rich man's food, mostly, and the old man could count on the fingers of both hands the times he'd had real beefsteak in his life, not just tripe and soup bones. In warm weather, his people ate richly from the green beans, green and ripe tomatoes, okra, squash, sweet corn, and more from their small gardens, which they canned to help get them through the cold, bare weather, when the diet would be plainer, poorer. They hunted then, for deer, rabbits, squirrels, raccoon, and possum, and wild turkey, quail, and doves. They gathered water and highland cress, and poke salad. They fished in warm weather, in the rivers, creeks, and backwater, for crappie, bream, catfish, jack salmon, and turtle. But you could not count on it, on almost anything in the wild, because it was a natural fact that if you did the fish would not bite for a fortnight, and the last deer would vanish in the mist.

It was plain food they ate, for the most part, cooked with simple tools.

"This is what you need, to cook," he said, and smacked an iron

skillet against a biscuit pan, to make sure he had the girl's attention. It rang so loud she held her ears.

"And a big spoon, and one deep pot," he said.

It was the most words she had heard him say. These backwoods
people seemed to live on rocks and sticks; maybe it should have
been no surprise that her new husband had brought in a mulish
ditchdigger to teach her how to prepare food.

"Where did you learn?" she said.

"Got hongry," the old man said.

"Not *why*. When? How?" she asked.

"I've always knowed," he said, which was not far from true, a
thing I have heard my people say over and over again, rather than
try to tell a thing that they themselves did not fully understand. In
the same way that some people could hear a song and play it right
then, the old man was almost a savant with simple food, which
was the only food in the world he had ever tasted or cared about;
everything else was mystery and theory. His mother died when
he was a boy, but not before he learned biscuit, cornbread, and
the essentials, and he practiced that craft in the woods, cooking
for the logging crews, and on riverbanks with other rough men,
cooking wild game, fish, turtle, and birds. His wife, Mattie, had
been crippled after being kicked by a mule, so he cooked for his
children for years; it was the only kindness from him that they
could recall. Some people, the sort who hold grudges, said of
course the old man knew his way around a fire, since he had apparently been born in flames and would return to them d'rectly, by
and by.

The boy would never explain how the old man, who had taken
such great care in feeding his children when they were small,
could then leave without a backward glance when he heard the law
coming for him. We always just supposed there were some men
who did not give one whit about death, who even grinned in its
teeth, but whose blood was iced by the idea of shackles and leg
irons and confinement.

The kinfolk just watched from afar, to see who might kill

whom. As it turned out, the old man was at first respectful of the volatile girl, and, for him, patient. He was insistent that she at least pay attention, but it seemed to be coming to naught. For days, he taught, and taught, but she did not seem to be learning, or even trying all that hard. One day, after another fit, he stood quietly beside her on the porch and told her the way it would be.

It was either pay attention and learn to cook, he told her, or crawl up on the same mule she rode in on and go home to her people in Tidmore Bend. The boy had never said that, of course, and would have chased after her, running his mount to death, his heart broken, but the old man knew mulish when he saw it, and hated to waste his breath for months on end when one good made-up threat would do.

The girl was so shocked her mouth closed for the first and perhaps last time in her life, but she did not cry. She just bored a smoking hole in him with her own spooky blue eyes. The old man would later say he admired that; he would say the hardheaded girl had spine *and* guts. She just didn't know which end of a spoon to hold, was all, or how to tell the difference between raw, burned, and a nice in-between.

"I ain't got no mule," she said, hotly.

He pointed to her feet, and walked away.

The main problem, other than attitude, was an almost total disregard for seasoning. Like a lot of people who are not eaters, or who eat mostly just to stay alive, she did not understand the importance of it; it was seasoning, the old man believed, that made the difference between living life and merely enduring it. It was not a profound notion . . . well, maybe a little, coming from a man in hobnailed boots. He told the girl, in as few words as possible, that she had to think about what suppertime, and all meals, really meant to working people. It did not just mean food was on the table; it meant the backbreaking labor was done, at least for a while. These meals, dinnertime and especially suppertime, were as close as most of them would come to a worldly reward. They ate supper early, because they went to bed early, to be up at four the next morning, to do it all over again; the time a workingman or -woman spent hunched over a bland, dull plate was wasted, empty, disappointing time. The cure to that malaise was salt, black pepper, ground cayenne, pork, onion, garlic, cinnamon, vanilla, and more, and a few Yankee greenbacks to buy it all with.

"A man has to eat to swing a ax or a hammer, and a woman's got to eat to work the field, and to bring the children into the world . . ." which might have sounded a little backward, but hardly so for 1924. "But you shouldn't just *have* to eat," the old man would tell her, and he would say it over and over, across the months and years. "You ort to *want* to eat. Poor folk ain't got much more'n that, not these days."

Some people have Commandments or Golden Rules. He had this. He went about his cooking with the same single-minded purpose that he went about drinking and fighting with, and if the food had no taste, if the biscuit was burned or the meat was tough, he had failed, failed at what he saw as a fundamentally simple task.

"Salt is good," the old man told her. "It says it in the Bible."

She rolled her eyes. If the old man had opened the Good Book, she believed, it would have turned to ashes in his hands.

"How do you know?" she asked, smug.

" 'Can that which is unsavoury be eaten without salt? Or is there any taste in the white of an egg?' " quoted the old man.

She stood amazed.

"I believe that's Job," the old man said.

"I know that," she said, even more amazed that this old sinner had taken the fight to her on her own high ground.

He would tell her, one day, that such things tended to stay with you when they were beaten into you, and that was as close to an explanation of his nature as he offered anyone, that we know. But it stuck with her forever; in a harsh time, when "spare the rod, spoil the child" was not just cliché but the law of the land, she would never be that type. Her children would not walk through this life grim and hard, but would laugh out loud, and tell tall tales and stories. But although the old man seemed to take little joy in anything else, there was an odd, grim satisfaction in him in the preparation of good food, and even, in time, in the teaching of it. It might not have been joy that he found, exactly, only something like it.

Cream Sausage Gravy

The smoked sausage that Jim used, which was the only sausage he had to work with then, in the twenties, is probably easier to prepare than the fresh sausage recommended in this dish. It is already cooked and only has to be chopped and rendered a bit to bring out the flavor and provide the fat needed to cook the flour, but may require, as Jim's dish did, a little extra pork fat to form the roux.

But my mother insists that, since the invention of the refrigerator, only fresh pork sausage will do for this dish. Fresh sausage was a true delicacy then, available only in hog-killing season. I like them both, but since this is her story, and her modern-day recipe, we will hold to her ingredients. Smoked sausage is also much more likely to contain sugars, which will affect the flavor.

WHAT YOU WILL NEED

¼ to ½ pound fresh mild pork sausage, or equal
amount smoked sausage

1 teaspoon minced raw onion (no more)

¼ cup flour (no more)

Bacon grease (optional)

2 cups whole milk

½ teaspoon salt

½ teaspoon black pepper

1 dash cayenne pepper

HOW TO COOK IT

Turn your stove eye to medium. My mother cooks damn near everything over medium. In a 9-inch cast-iron skillet, scramble the sausage, and brown it till the pink has begun to fade, then toss in the minced onion. Continue to fry over medium heat until some of the scrambled sausage begins to crisp the slightest bit, and the onion has gone clear. The bits of crisped sausage, the nice brown bits, will add nice, nice flavor.

The rest of the process happens quickly.

Leave the sausage in the skillet, and sprinkle in the flour, still over medium heat, stirring as you go, till all the flour has been incorporated. "Just say 'mixed up good,'" my mother said.

There should be plenty of fat from the rendered sausage to do the job, and you should stir until you have a smooth consistency in the cooked flour. If there is not enough fat and the flour is still dry and crumbly, quickly add a little bacon grease to thin it a bit, or the gravy will clump. Do not just add cooking oil, such as vegetable oil: "It will have a taste to it, a whang, if you do, no matter what kind of oil," my mother believes. Mixing pork fat and butter is always a good idea; mixing pork and other fats, like vegetable oil, is not.

The flour will cook quickly. She does not particularly like white gravy, which she believes can have a raw, chalky taste, so the cook has to be aware of nuances here, she believes. As soon as the fat and flour are well mixed and smooth in texture, and the flour has begun to take on a little color, to darken just a bit, you are ready to add the milk.

This will not be the rich yellow of chicken gravy, more a nice tan. Continue to stir as you slowly pour in the milk. Some people use a whisk. She does not; she thinks cooking with anything but a big spoon is just putting on airs (and, besides, the damn thing is hard to clean). The flour-and-milk mixture will begin to thicken immediately. Reduce the heat, add the salt and peppers, and continue to stir. If it does not thicken, you can turn the heat up a little to finish it off. This is no great sin, and will not hurt the taste at all. If you fear you have browned the flour a little too much before adding milk, do not panic; the milk will lighten the color, and, in a way, the taste. You'll see what she means, in time. Gravy is a more subtle dish than most cooks concede, but it can also be forgiving.

Thickness is a matter of preference. We like it not too thick, not too thin, but right in the middle. If the gravy is too watery, it will make the biscuits soggy. I know that sounds perhaps a little persnickety, but the first time you slop watery gravy on a good biscuit you will know what we mean. The gravy should not lie thick, like a paste, either. It should just kind of linger there, running down the sides to pool on the plate.

"That sounds about right," my mother says.

It is incomplete, as Jimmy Jim told Ava, without a slice of cantaloupe, or a slice or two of ripe tomato, on the side. This balances the richness of the dish, and if you try hard enough, you can almost convince yourself it makes the dish a little healthier.

"Sausage gravy," she said, "ain't that hard to do, to tell the truth. But really good sausage gravy may take a time or two, to get just right. The thing about cooking is to not get mad at yourself too much. In the old days, if you messed up, you might not have nothin' to do with for a while. But there ain't no need to get mad at yourself too much now."

This gravy is so rich, so satisfying, that sometimes we cook it for supper.

"The good thing about bad gravy is, it don't never go to waste, even if you do mess it up," she said. "The dogs love it. The grease is good for their coats. Makes 'em shiny."

Buttered Grits with a Touch of Cheese

WHAT YOU WILL NEED

2½ cups (more or less) water

1½ cups yellow grits

½ teaspoon salt

¼ cup whole milk

¼ teaspoon black pepper

¼ teaspoon cayenne pepper

¼ cup salted butter

¼ cup American cheese shredded or torn into small
pieces

HOW TO COOK IT

Bring the water to a boil, add the grits and salt, and stir. Reduce the heat and let it simmer, being sure to continue to stir, for about 15 minutes. Grits will stick, she warns, "if you don't pay attention. They'll go gluey." As they begin to thicken, add the milk. If the grits seem to thicken too much or too quickly, add a little more milk, for a little more creaminess. Add the black pepper, cayenne, butter, and cheese, and cook over low heat, continuing to stir, until the cheese is mixed in good and melted thoroughly.

Grits are not hard to cook if you pay attention, but like to spit at you as they thicken, my mother says. Expect it. The first time you get burned, you'll know what she means. This is a sign that the heat may be too high.

Thick grits are good, even if they seem a little too thick, she said, parroting her own mother, who was parroting Jim. Watery, thin grits are always an abomination, a thing not even food. Some chefs try to mask this by serving grits in a bowl, as if they meant them to be a watery mess. Grits should not be served in a bowl, like, ugh, cream of wheat, but should be thick enough to hold up in a pool or puddle on the plate. They should not need butter, salt, or pepper after the fact, but some people like saltier grits and more buttery ones. Some people go crazy and put diced ham or bacon in them. These people are Philistines. The cayenne will give them a little heat, but not so much as to be silly.

The switch from Jim's cheddar to American cheese is her only other real alteration, besides the sausage. The hard cheddar adds a nice bite, but it melts poorly and gives the grits an irritating stringiness, whereas the American cheese adds a nice creaminess to balance the little kick of cayenne. Grits, as Jim declared, should have taste. This is how you know you are not at the breakfast buffet at the Marriott, or the Hilton, or any other place that boils grits in unsalted water and serves them to human people that wretched way, unbuttered, unsalted, without care or conscience or consequence, because they know that by the time you have worked up a real good mad you will be on a crowded airplane or in a rental car on your way out of the time zone. It is no wonder that Northerners, after tasting grits for the first time in Southern restaurants, either make a face like they just ate a stinkbug, or make a U-turn and flee for Grand Rapids.

The only real thing you need to know about grits is that they are not a thing unto themselves, any more than a blank, white canvas is a work of art.

"Grits is to carry the other flavors of stuff," my mother believes. "Grits ain't nothin' just left by their self."

The Perfect Fried Egg

WHAT YOU WILL NEED

Lard

Eggs

Luck

Salt and pepper (to taste)

Obviously, you get to fry your eggs to taste, and if you like over-easy, sunny-side-up, or more hard-cooked fried eggs that have the rough texture of automobile upholstery, this recipe is simply unnecessary. But all eggs in her kitchen, all my life, have been medium, neither hard nor runny, with perfectly done whites (because nothing is so awful as a runny egg white), a firm but not well-done yellow on the bottom, and molten yellow on the flip side. This is how she does it, which was how her momma and the old man did it, which is the ultimate answer just about every time I ever asked, "Why?"

The greatest mistake in the long history of egg frying is trying to cook too many eggs at one time, my mother believes. Cook two or at most four at a time, unless you are cooking for Napoleon's army; when they are done, just ladle them onto a warm ceramic plate at the back of the stove to keep them from turning cool.

"Use brown eggs when you can get 'em," she said. "They're more like real eggs."

You will need a cast-iron skillet. She refuses to recognize any material that has come into vogue since the Iron Age, and Teflon might actually have been invented by space aliens. Place about 3 tablespoons of lard in it. You want about ¼ inch of lard to work with, at least. You will have more fat than you are probably accustomed to using for the average, more healthy egg. Turn the heat to medium, and heat till the fat begins to roil and spit just a little.

Make sure it is lard, or—if you must—Crisco.

"Bacon grease is *not* perfect for eggs," she believes, "and ham grease is worse. The eggs will stick in bacon grease, and really stick in ham and sausage grease, and really, really stick in smoked-sausage grease, 'cause it's all got sugar in it. The best thing for eggs is good lard." When I asked why, she answered: " 'Cause it is." When I asked her what she would recommend for people who did not want to go through that much trouble for a fried egg, or just had a natural disinclination toward lard, she suggested this:

"Scramble."

Do not, no matter how health-conscious you are, lubricate your skillet with cooking spray, and shame on you for thinking about it. She would no more spray a skillet than she would braid the hair of her dog, and thinks PAM is an airline Elvis used to ride on to make a picture in Miami.

Assuming you have adequate good-quality, properly heated, lightly spitting grease, lower the heat to medium-low, crack two eggs into the fat, and then, as the undersides of the eggs cook, use a large spoon to ladle the hot fat over the top of the egg white, which will cook the surface slightly as the bottom cooks quickly, in seconds. If you like your eggs sunny-side-up, this method will lightly, lightly cook the sunny-side whites, avoiding awful still-raw whites. Do not try just to manipulate the skillet, as Jimmy Jim did, because your chance of slopping hot grease into the stove is too great, and no egg is worth a paramedic.

As Jim believed, this method of spooning the fat onto the sunny side lightly cooks the whites and firms up the top of the eggs so that when you flip them they will hold together much better, and will not require so much direct heat to finish the process. Or she may just like to do it that way because her people did it that way. "There ain't nothing wrong with that, is there?" she asked, but it did not sound like a question.

Then, carefully, flip each egg, being mindful not to spill the fat into the stove eye and burn the house down. A few seconds more, and your eggs should be ready. My mother does all this by sight, not time, and using only the spoon, as Jim did, but most people in the twenty-first century like a spatula.

Depending on skill—or, in my case, luck—you should have eggs that are neither hard nor runny, the whites done but not rubbery, one side of the yolks more firm, the other more molten—or, as she calls it, "just right." Salt and pepper them to taste, or try a dash of cayenne pepper.

She has, successfully, educated me on breakfast. I can make fine grits and even a good sausage gravy. The perfect egg still mostly evades me. I cannot do it more than once or twice in a row before I create an abomination. She can do it a few dozen times, maybe a hundred, without fail. I would like to meet the fool who originated the phrase "can't fry an egg" as a minimum standard for cooking, and punch him in the snoot.

"You ain't got the patience for good eggs," she told me. "You got to have patience, not to ruin a egg, or to make a good biscuit, or to cook anything, hon."

"Could you teach me to make a biscuit?" I asked.

"No," she said.

.   .   .

After the old man laid down his ultimatum to the girl, after the shock of it had worn away and the subsequent plotting of his murder had gone unrealized, the girl seemed to pay a little more attention, though the old man was probably lucky that he was a light sleeper. She looked at him sometimes with hellfire in her eyes, too, but he had been right to fetch him, the boy believed.

"Far with far," he had said.

Here the phrase is more than a cliché. Fire on the mountains is as much of the lore here as the black panther, or the rolling snakes, or the Mill Branch ghost. When the mountains caught fire, and they always did, there were only two ways to keep the flames from the little wood-frame houses built in the lee of the hills. You could build a break, frantically scratching the mountain itself down to the dirt with picks and shovels, till there was nothing to burn. But the fire often jumped a break, traveling on a leaf on the wind. The other way, which was tricky, was to try to set a backfire to control or alter the burn, so that when the fire raced forward it was met not with more fuel but with more fire, and behind that a landscape, for at least some distance, with nothing left to consume. Sometimes that worked, and sometimes both fires raged out of control in whatever direction they pleased, and scorched the whole damn mountain down to black trunks and gray ash and woe. This, the boy knew, was a possibility in his home, but at least they would eat.

After the first week, the little house was still standing, though the girl had burned a few simple meals to cinder, just to show the mean old man she could. Still, he endeavored to persevere, and believed it was time to show the girl something more complicated, something that was perhaps as close to a feast as most poor men might ever see. He began her education, in earnest, with the nature of beans.

3

A MAN WHO KNEW BEANS

Pinto Beans and Ham Bone,
Creamed Onions, Buttered Boiled Potatoes,
Carrot and Red Cabbage Slaw, Cornbread

James B. Bundrum, my great-great-grandfather, who taught his son,
Jimmy Jim, that a bland bean was a poor bean, and unfit for men or hogs

1924

FIRST he had to make the world straight, just a little bit.

Soon after he arrived, he had taken inventory of the small, ragged smokehouse that leaned, a little drunkenly, in the far back of the yard. In the cool gloom inside, he saw only naked hooks and empty rafters; the boy had told him he was making a living, but not enough, apparently, to fill the smokehouse with even the barest essentials, and the young couple did not yet have a hog of their own to fatten and kill. The girl would never be a good cook until they had their own pork, but it could take a year to fatten a hog and slaughter it, and that was just too long. One day, the old man just rose from his chair, cursed the air around him, and left, his one great possession, the Belgium shotgun, swinging in the crook of his left arm, and a sharp, long scabbard knife riding at his side.

The girl believed that, beaten and dejected, he had simply given up on her and walked away, and she rejoiced. She felt like doing a buck-and-wing, or maybe even a little do-si-do, but was afraid her fellow Pentecostals might catch her dancing as they passed by; a good Christian, as that harpy Aunt Riller had lectured, only danced when no one was looking. She had always loved dancing *and* church, but you had to be careful when you walked that fine line in the community of East Gadsden, in Etowah County, Alabama—you couldn't swing a dead cat in East Gadsden and not hit a Congregational Holiness—so she just sat gleefully in her rocker on the high front porch, free as a bird, and rocked with wild abandon.

As it turned out, as sin goes, dancing was the least of it.

The old man returned after midnight, his hands bloody. Ava's usual belligerence evaporated in fear, and the boy stood, worried, waiting for an explanation. The old man just washed his hands and went to bed. The next morning, instead of discovering a dead body or a pack of bloodhounds on the doorstep, they spotted smoke rising from the smokehouse. Inside, they found small hams, shoulder, and sides of bacon. Slabs of fatback were packed in salt, to cure. At least it had not been murder.

"Where did you get it?" she asked, drumming up her courage.

"From people who won't miss it," he said, as she tried, and failed, to stare him down.

The truth was, the old man believed he was entitled. He took it not from a pen, but from the land itself, roaming loose, as some people allowed their pigs to live. This one roamed the land he had once owned, before the law ran him to Georgia and the tax barons and lawyers took it from him in absentia. The old man knew only a little about the law, and what he did not know he could ignore, but there were some things a man was owed, and if you did not believe that, you should pen your hogs.

Besides, it was just a shoat. It wasn't like it was a prize hog.

"Sin little, sin big," Ava said.

The old man told her to tell that to a judge and see what happened; by her reasoning, if you picked a penny off the street, you might as well knock off a bank on the way home, or rob a train.

Besides, it didn't make much difference to the pig.

"If I coulda come across a fat 'un," he confessed, "I'd of kilt a fat 'un."

In as few words as possible, to get the child to shut up, he tried to explain the law according to the common man. He had decided, the day before, to teach her how to cook a fine pot of beans, "and you natcherly can't have beans without pork," he said, as if this made it all right somehow. In his mind, maybe it did, since the old man had never known a world in which the people, his people, could live without good beans.

. . .

Dried beans, just a few cents a pound, were life itself for the people of the hills, he told the girl after she had calmed down and it seemed they were not all going to prison after all. Butter beans,

Great Northerns, baby limas, black-eyed peas, and others, sim-mered on the woodstoves of sharecroppers and landowners alike, because they were not only filling, cheap, and nutritious; if they were properly seasoned, usually with just salt, pepper, onion, pork, some sugar, and sometimes a little stray red pepper or garlic, they were delicious. But for the poor, in hard times and pretty much every time, they were the very foundation of the diet. Families lived almost completely on beans and cornbread in cold weather and early spring, with the largesse of a skillet of fried potatoes.

The rest of the world could demean the bean, say that some-thing "ain't worth beans," or say that someone "didn't know beans." In the foothills of the Appalachians, a man who knew beans was worth something, by God.

And at the very top of this pyramid of a billion beans, shelled over a few hundred years, was the pinto, the bean you cooked for company, or in celebration of all important things. Pinto beans were less chalky and starchy and more flavorful than other beans, he claimed, with a nutty, rich flavor. Besides, the old man liked them best, so of course that was where he would begin. But, as fine as it was, the pinto was, on its own, incomplete. Pinto beans could not be prepared without pork, even if it was just a piece of skin, or a scrap, to enrich the natural flavor. But a ham bone— now, a ham bone was *fine*.

"You can't make brick without straw," the old man said, and it made her so mad she almost levitated. Who was he, to quote to her the tribulations of the children of Israel?

"I ain't stealin' no pigs," she told him, and then, to cover all possibilities: "Nor no chicken, neither."

"No," he said, "they'd ketch you, short and bowlegged as you are."

She stomped to the door, but wheeled around at what had seemed to be, of all things, a shard, a fragment, of a chuckle.

"Hee," went the old man, who had the rare ability to laugh without mirth or joy.

It took a long time for her to wind down this time; self-righteousness is without a true bottom. But before he could teach the child actually to cook something truly fine, he had to teach her to build and maintain a fire. Electricity had not arced so far as the little rented house. He split wood for the stove, and tried to show her how to do it herself. The boy would lay wood by, of course, but she needed to know how. "I know how to chop wood. I ain't helpless," she said. She took a mighty swing and almost lost a toe, and the second time she brought the heavy ax head down, the block of wood flew into her shin, knocking her, bloody, onto her backside. She sat there alternately praying and cursing, with tears in her eyes, as the old man finished his smoke. He had the thing in his mouth, lit and unlit, from dawn till bedtime.

He would admit, much later, that it was amusing to watch the girl try to split wood. She was a true Pentecostal, despite her hubris and dancing and occasional cussing, and however far she might have backslid from time to time, which seemed daily. But she was true to her doctrine. She wore her hair to below her waist then, and her skirts to her shoe tops. Around a cookfire, the girl was a human torch. At the woodpile, she was little more than a backstop.

"It's be easier on your shins if you was to put on some pants," he said. "Be easier to get out the way, when that wood comes flyin' at you. Hard to chop much wood, anyway, in a damn bedsheet."

She told him that, like thievery, drinking, fighting, and smarting off to ladies, to wear pants would be a sin.

"Hell is a wide place for y'all, ain't it?" the old man said.

While she composed herself, he chopped the wood, gathered it, and showed her how to sort the beans.

What made Jim remarkable, like all good Southern blue-collar cooks, was the distance he could bring the simple ingredients, the transformation he could achieve in a simple bean, or a bitterweed, or the pieces of meat that would be discarded, in a more affluent culture and easier time, as scrap. This does not, however, make him unique. It was true in the slave quarters of the Old

South, and in the mill villages of the early twentieth century, and the coal fields. The villain of taste was expediency, impatience, and before a cook got near a fire, he had to make sure that the food he was preparing was fit.

He told her to find a quiet place with good light and pick through the dry beans, swirling them round and round in a pan, like she was panning for gold. He told her to discard any black ones or shriveled ones, and to feel for grit, or tiny pieces of trash.

"Can't I just rinse the trash off of 'em? Won't the trash and the grit come off in the wash?" she asked.

"No. Hit might just stick to the wet beans. They'll get tacky after you wash 'em."

It seems such a little thing, till you think about what a speck of grit tastes like, feels like, in your teeth. It is hard to enjoy your meal once you taste grit in your teeth, he said, and she allowed that was probably true, her being a fastidious housekeeper herself. But, again, such a notion did not fit the man, who brushed his teeth with a sweet-gum twig, and ate slices of his apples off the wicked blackened blade of the same pocketknife he used to whittle stick and shave off his tobacco.

He rinsed the beans with clear, cool water, once, twice, then put them in a pan to soak for an hour or so. "They'll cook better, and cook a little bit quicker, if you soak 'em," he said. "You don't have to, but hit's better to."

He tested the edge on the butcher knife and found it to be useless, and spent ten minutes putting an edge on it. She would learn this was what the old man did to relax. Then he went to work on a small fresh ham, one from the mysterious pig. He sliced off some meat to set aside for breakfast, till he had the ham bone he was looking for—not a bone at all but just a skinnier ham, with some nice meat still on it.

A pound of pinto beans cooked with a ham bone would feed a family of six, maybe more, he said. He stoked up the fire, aiming for a slow boil, and put the beans on. He tossed in a tiny peeled whole yellow onion, with a tablespoon of salt and a teaspoon of sugar. "If we had some garlic," he said, "we'd add a little some-thin' extry." He had learned garlic from a man on the Gulf Coast; they put garlic in everything there.

He laid the ham bone in the boiling water with the beans and seasonings, then gathered up the trimmings of fat and skin from the chop block and dropped them into the pot. He told his daughter-in-law that even a small piece or two of pork—salted, smoked, or fresh—would help the flavor, but a ham bone was the foundation of a feast, and the trimmings of fat were an extra blessing. "Cook it all slow, so it all gits together," he said. The fat would literally melt into the beans and the cooking liquid, and become that fine elixir.

Bland beans, he lectured, would keep a man from starving, but there was no goodness in them whatsoever.

It occurred to Ava that, for someone who did not particularly like to talk, whose answer to most questions outside the kitchen was a baleful stare, the old man grew more and more talkative as long as he was talking about food. He was never exactly gabby, but at least he did not speak in hisses, curses, and nods. He seemed almost fascinated with the nature of beans.

When the girl lost interest, the old man did not rant or yell.

He just stabbed his temple again with one scarred, bony fnger.

"Cook *thinkin'*," he hissed. He pronounced it "thankin'."

And remember.

Then he showed her how to make the dish that complemented it all. He showed her how to thin-slice the white onions and a few green onions and put them on to cook in just a daub of bacon grease and a little butter, bring them to a quick sizzle to get the fla-vors working, but cook slowly from then over low heat. "You don't want fried onions," he said. He showed her how to make them go soft in their own sugars by slowly adding spoonfuls of water and covering them with a lid, so that they did not fry or steam so much as just kind of melt in the butter and pork fat.

"This little thing," the old man said, "is what folks will remem-ber."

"Onions?" she said, aghast.

"You'll l'arn," he said.

She was prone to wandering off in the middle of a thing, even a sizzling skillet, causing him great distress that she might actually burn the house down, but this dish, he lectured, could not be prepared at all unless the cook was willing to stare into the skillet and monitor its cooking at least every few minutes. You had to cook it covered but routinely stir—gently, so the onions did not break into mush. Now and then, you had to be sure to add a spoon or so of water when the liquid was about to cook away. If the onions turned brown, they were cooking too fast; you wanted a gold color, he told her.

She did not concede it then, but she was amazed at how careful, how almost delicate, the rough old man was in the kitchen. Over the months ahead, she would see him take a discreet swallow of liquor now and then as he cooked, but, as much as she disapproved of such as that, she learned that cooking, much like banjo picking and sometimes preaching, was one of those things a body could do when about half drunk, as long as he did not get his testaments mixed up or fall into the fire.

As the beans and then the onions cooked, the old man put a few potatoes on to boil whole. There were only two kinds of potatoes, in the vernacular of his people: there were sweet potatoes, and white, or Irish, potatoes, which, in his accent, was pronounced "Ar'sh." These were "Ar'sh," peeled and boiled whole.

Then he showed the girl how to bake a decent skillet of cornbread, how to measure out the salt, soda, and meal, stir in just enough cool water. "Now I'll show you the secret," he said. They had no ice box, but had a quart jar of mayonnaise—even then, there was mayonnaise—cooling in a springhouse. He showed her how to mix a double spoonful into the cornmeal, for richness, and how to line an iron skillet with lard so the cornbread would come out crispy on the edges but soft and crumbly inside. He melted some butter and drizzled it across the top of the meal before putting it on to bake, for a little something extra.

Last, he coarse-chopped a simple cabbage slaw, or at least she thought it would be simple. But the old man had a lecture for everything. Save as many of the dark-colored leaves as you can when you begin to strip it down, he said. "Hit'll taste better if you do." He mixed in only enough mayonnaise to give it taste. He stirred in a liberal dose of black pepper, but no salt at all: "Hit'll wilt that cabbage down," and defeat the very purpose of a good slaw, which is to cool, or somehow level, a heavier, saltier meal.

And, again, the girl wondered how such an idea ever even took root in the smutty old man. But slaw was not an invention of the twentieth century. It was a staple in the mountain South, and the old man, like a lot of people here, had eaten it all his life. He made his own mayonnaise sometimes, by the half-gallon, and cabbage was about the cheapest thing in the dirt. Carrots, which he considered another essential ingredient, did not grow well in the clay, and often had to be store-bought, or bought from peddlers who brought them in from sandier soil. But they were worth it, because of that sweet taste they gave a slaw.

That said, he would not allow sugar to be added for taste.

"You don't want sugar-sweet, but carrot-sweet," he explained. "Good fer yer eyes, too, carrots," he told her.

She already had to wear glasses to read, and was sensitive about it.

"Ain't nothin' wrong with my eyes," she said.

"Wadn't speakin' of yourn. Talkin' 'bout ever'body's eyes in the natural world," he clarified.

It was a small kindness by the old man to say that, she would later decide.

At the time, she told him to kiss her foot, anyway.

.   .   .

The boy had been away, doing pick-and-shovel work. He came back on a Friday evening, about done in. He was digging wells that day, ten hours at the bottom of a deep hole, praying for mud.

Some men would not pay till you struck the damp, till you felt the red clay begin to slide a little under your boots. He was smeared with it from his boots to the crown of his head as he walked in, and it had dried in patches; he looked like a golem. He washed it off on the back porch, or at least he washed off some of it, and sat down at a tiny homemade pine table, almost too tired to sit upright.

The plate the old man placed before him was a thing of beauty, another memory of his simpler past, with its puddle of beans rich in ham fat, with tender hunks of the reddish lean in the broth; to the side, mingling with the broth from the beans, the old man had spooned a big dollop of the creamed onions, so tender they slipped through the tines of the fork. Ava watched, a little mystified, as the old man took his own fork and pressed down on a single red potato till it broke apart, steaming, spooned a little melted butter on it from the pot, then peppered it liberally, as if his teenage boy were still a child, helpless. It was almost too much, the addition of that single potato, but the old man said a working-woman or -man needed a little tater in almost every meal, if they were going to swing a hammer or a pick, or drag a hundred pound of cotton, or herd a passel of young'uns all day, and not misplace any.

The slaw he placed at the edge of the plate, so it would stay cool; it was such a tiny notion, but it stuck in her mind. Finally, the old man unscrewed the lid on a home-canned jar of hot chowchow— he had swapped a few pounds of mysterious swine for some pickles and hot relish—and dished it out onto the heavy ceramic plates with a dainty teaspoon, like a fancy waiter spooning caviar in a New Orleans hotel.

The boy leaned over his plate, breathing it in, and sighed.

"Good Lord," he said.

Ava told him to wait a damn minute, and said a long and torturous grace, which would also become a tradition in our family on days when we could least stand the wait. The boy set upon the food like he had been living on maypops, boiled okra, and artichokes, as the girl sat across the table from the old man and glared. But even she had to admit that she had never seen the boy so happy, even hunched over the butter rolls and the fine breakfast, and it *did* taste very good, though she usually did not give a flying flip about such hearty food. The boy scraped the serving bowls clean, all of them, and then, bone-tired, went to sleep in his hard, straight-back chair. He often would, when he was exhausted, or a little bit drunk, or if his mind was easy. He was down so deep it was as if body and soul had already quietly departed, like a cat leaving a room.

Ava looked at the ham bone on the boy's plate. It was so pristine, so clean, it looked like it had been polished. She had seen bones in the dog pen that had been worried less than that. The boy dozed on, listing; he fell out of his chair altogether some nights. The old man smoked his pipe, and drank his black coffee. The only light in the pitch dark was from a single kerosene lantern in the middle of the table. The cool days seemed even shorter here in the foothills, when the sun slipped behind the mountain like it had dropped down a shaft, and you had a feeling it was still daylight somewhere, just a hill or two away.

"I will pray for you," she told him, "for your thievery."

The old man rose and headed for the door, to drink his coffee in the night in peace.

"The one who cooks," he said, "don't do no dishes."

It was not a victory, for either of them, not yet even a peace.

But it was a truce.

> *For every one shall be salted with fire, and every sacrifice shall be salted with salt. Salt is good. . . . Have salt in yourselves, and have peace one with another.*
>
> MARK 9:48–50

.   .   .

Pinto Beans and Ham Bone

WHAT YOU WILL NEED

1 pound dried pinto beans

1 ham bone, with about 1 pound or so of meat still on it

1 pound or so trimmings of fat, skin, and lean,
   from the outside of the ham

1 small clove garlic, whole

1 small onion, whole

1 tablespoon salt (cut by half, or exclude completely,
   if the ham is salty)

½ tablespoon sugar

HOW TO COOK IT

First understand that this pot of ham and beans is not intended as a side, but as a rich, decadent main course. If you are preparing pinto beans as a side, you will use a scant fraction of the pork suggested here.

To get started: In a quiet, well-lit place, devoid of children and cell phones and worrisome or trifling spouses, place the beans in a large, glazed ceramic bowl and, with the bowl on your lap, carefully pick through the beans to remove any discolored or shriveled ones, or grit, or trash, just as Jimmy Jim showed my grandmother. Swirl them round and round, with your fingertips on the bottom of the bowl. You will feel the bad ones, and feel the grit and trash, before you see them. "It's something you can't do distracted," my mother says. It may be that it is more tradition now than anything else, more ritual, since the milling process has changed over the years, and the beans seem cleaner now. But is there any true harm in sitting quietly for a minute or two and just thinking about your food, or just thinking?

The truth is, as her vision has declined, this is the only way she can be sure she catches all the impurities in milled beans.

Cover the beans with water by about two inches, and let them soak for at least 2 hours. Some people still insist on letting them soak overnight, but my mother thinks that may break down the beans too much and leave them a little mushy in cooking.

As they soak, prepare the ham. The ham can be fresh or smoked—the smoked ham will add a nice flavor—but never use sugar-cured ham, not only because of the sugary taste but because of the thoroughly unnatural chemicals in the modern-day curing process. The ham should not be presliced; the thin slices will not provide the ragged texture you want for the ham in this dish; it just won't look right presliced. The ham needs to come apart in cooking, not begin that way. When I asked my mother what difference it makes, she told me, " 'Cause it just does."

With a sharp knife, trim away the fat and skin from the outside of the ham, and do not worry if some lean comes off in the process; you are not taking this off to discard, but to eat, to have it slowly, slowly melt into the dish, bolstering the flavors of the ham bone. The trimmings of fat probably will not have to be cut up any more, because they will render a good bit, but the skin may have to be cut into smaller pieces so as not to frighten more delicate people; some good country cooks dice it before adding it to the pot. Even a small ham will render about a pound or so of fat and skin. Set these pieces aside. You should now have a perfectly lean, whole ham, and it is time to trim it down to the ham bone. (If you go to the market searching for a lean ham to start with, you probably need to close this book right now.)

Do not try to be a master butcher as you whittle; just cut frying slices from it, as Jimmy Jim did, to cook for breakfast, for ham and eggs, ham and biscuits, or sandwiches. Bigger pieces can be set aside to bake for another supper, or to be diced for an excellent navy-bean soup. Leave about a pound or so of meat on the bone. It may be a cliché, but the meat closest to the bone, even if a little fatty or held together with chewy gristle, is incredibly flavorful, "the most flavor there is on the whole pig, except maybe in the feet, or in a cracklin'."

If you truly do have grave concerns about using both the ham bone and the trimmings from the ham to season a single pot of beans, you can use just the ham bone, or just the outer trimmings. Such sensible, reasonable thinking is not recommended here, but reducing the concentration of fat in the beans will make the dish less rich, and of course more healthy; you can adjust the combinations over time, to get just the right concentrations of flavor to suit. Some people like a less savory pot of beans.

"Who?" my mother asked.

"People not like us," I said.

Once you have prepared the ham, and the beans have soaked, you are ready to cook. In a large pot, combine the beans, the ham bone, and the trimmed fat. Cover with about 2 inches of water, though it is fine if parts of the ham bone are not covered completely. Bring to a boil, then reduce the heat to medium, or medium-low. All stoves vary. What you want, at first, is a slow boil.

Peel the small garlic clove and the small onion, but leave them whole; add them to the pot with the salt and sugar. Cover with a lid, but check it every 15 minutes or so, to stir gently and turn the ham bone in the pot. This is not a dish where you want the beans to disintegrate, or cream, like some recipes for white beans or even butter beans.

After about 1 hour, reduce the heat to low, to simmer another hour or so, but stir two or three times, for luck.

"You'll likely have to add water, just a little at a time, as it cooks out, just to keep the beans from stickin', but you don't want to drown it in water to start with and just walk away from it," my mother said. "You'll have mush. You want about an inch or two of soup, of that liquid, on top of the beans as it simmers, but not more than that."

Cook until the beans are tender and the meat begins to fall off the bone, about 2 hours, depending on the stove. Her stove takes about 2½ hours. If you have done it right, a translucent nectar from the beans and fat will have formed on the surface of the beans, not quite murky, not quite clear, but a kind of golden broth.

Taste a little of the liquid as you cook. If the beans need salt, add a little, taste, and keep on till it satisfies. The greatest mistake people make with beans is salt—usually too little, but too much and they are inedible.

To be sure they are done, and to look like a real chef, take a few beans from the pot and press gently with a fork. If the bean is slightly firm but mashes easily, they are good and done. If the bean splits into two pieces, lengthwise, and remains more or less intact, they are not done. This is not a tragedy. Just cook them some more, to be sure. If you are still not sure, eat a few. No one will know.

Before serving, remove the onion and the garlic clove. I like to eat them both; you decide.

You can use tongs or a fork to tear some of the meat from the ham bone if needed, though much of the fat will have melted into the elixir of the beans, and even the lean should be coming apart. The skin is an acquired taste; even some country people do not eat it, but they still believe it adds that little something extra in flavor to the dish. My mother loves to eat it, and I do, too.

Some important things to know, about the nature of beans

1. Do not be surprised if the beans cook differently from pot to pot. Bean producers have a greedy nature, my mother says, and will ship old beans from time to time, especially in summer or early fall. "You'll get beans shipped not from this season, but held over from the last year's beans, from the summer before, so they can be more than a year old. And they *do* get old. They're harder to cook when they're old, and don't make a good soup, and you can taste the difference in it." Spring is the worst season for old beans, she believes: producers clear out their warehouses to make room for the new crop. I had no idea that beans were such a cutthroat commodity, but if she says there is a difference, there is a difference.

2. Pinto beans are not supposed to be spicy, but savory. Hot sauces, or pepper sauces with a vinegary base, will stand out sharply in the flavor and ruin it. Many outsiders believe the first thing you do with a Southern meal is to douse it with pepper sauce. That said, a side of hot pepper, or of chowchow, hot raw onion, green onion, and the like, is a fine garnish, but only on the side. Some people, like Texans, like to add about a quart of chili powder to pinto beans. Bad beans and big hats is how you know they are Texans.

3. Some older people, like my big brother, crumble their cornbread and cover it with beans; it is tradition. To me, this ruins the consistency of the dish, and you don't really get to savor either the taste of the crunchy cornbread or the texture of the beans. It makes the beans taste mealy. Still, a lot of ancients swear by it; it made a pot of beans go further in hard times.

4. Do not cook more than you will need for one meal and perhaps one more serving of leftovers. Unlike gumbo, or some soups, stews, and chili, beans are not better the second day, and the soup will grow murkier, thicker, the more they are reheated. They will still be pretty good that next day or next meal, but never so good as that first day, that first supper. Many Southern agrarian families cooked them as a noon meal, left them on the stove, covered, and reheated them for supper. But the mill culture, the industrial South, changed this, and made supper the big meal of the day, often prepared by the older children or grandparents while the mother and father worked.

5. Some people like to mix pinto beans and white beans, or other beans, in all sorts of unnatural alliances. Even my mother does this when she has about ½ pound of each left over. She is trying to be frugal, and I have to remind her that the Great Depression has eased and Herbert Hoover walks the earth no more. And since pinto beans still cost only a dollar a pound or so in 2017, we can afford some new ones. Do not mix your beans. This is not succotash, another conglomerate. It is not that they taste bad; they just don't taste like anything.

6. You will be tempted to add heavy doses of black pepper to the cooking beans, to enhance the flavor, but don't. Black pepper can be added on the plate. The beans should have a rich, nutty flavor, and will, of course, absorb the flavor of the pork and salt; black pepper can leave the beans with a slight whang amid the other, more delicate flavors. You can sneer at this. We do not care.

7. It is considered ill-mannered, even after everyone has been served and most of the lean meat has been pulled from the bone, to plunk the whole ham bone down on your plate. So do it only when no one is looking, or if you are among family or good friends. If I tried to do it as a child, I'd have had to fistfight my brothers for it. But a busted lip was a small price to pay for such a delicacy as this. The thing is, my mother believes, someone has to do it, sooner or later. "It's just too good a thing," she said, "to throw to the dogs."

8. Beans and cornbread are almost one word down here, so pair them, unless you are a Philistine. Instead of plain cornbread, for a change serve the beans and ham with cornbread muffins, which have more crunch. Mexican cornbread, augmented with sharp cheddar cheese, white onion, green onion, and sweet corn kernels, is especially good with beans and ham. Sweet cornbread, though my mother rejects it as not being "real" cornbread, is also a good complement to pinto beans. But you will need cornbread of some kind; when I asked my mother if hot rolls or the like would do, she looked at me, again, as if I had been abandoned on her doorstep. Some of my kinfolks, hungover, would sometimes eat their pintos with biscuits, or even sliced bread. She regards this as unholy.

Creamed Onions

There is no actual cream or milk in this dish, as in the creamed Bermuda onions of old. The sugars in the onions will create a lovely creaminess if the onions are cooked right. Young, sweet onions are best, but this does not require Vidalia onions in particular; the dish can be prepared with Texas sweets, and even white and yellow onions. "Just try to get new onions, not ones held over for several months," she said.

WHAT YOU WILL NEED

4 large sweet onions, such as Vidalia

2 green onions, blades and all

1 teaspoon bacon grease

¼ teaspoon salt

1 cup water

¼ teaspoon finely ground black pepper

HOW TO COOK IT

Slice the sweet onions into wheels about ¼ inch thick, then cut across the wheel so you will have not circles but crescents. Cut the green onions into slivers. Any green onions, or even fat leeks, will do fine in this dish. Leeks have a sweet, mild flavor and are a nice substitute for green onions, but the smaller, more pungent green onions add a more distinctive flavor.

In a cast-iron skillet, melt the bacon grease, and add the onions and salt. Cook over medium heat only until the white onions begin to go slightly, slightly clear and the green onion blades begin to wilt "and get to smelling good," she says. Slowly add about ¼ cup of the water, being careful of the steam, then cover, and cook over low heat, gradually adding water as needed.

The idea is to let the onions steam in the fat and water, not fry to crispiness. Add the black pepper as the onions begin to go soft, and continue to cook slowly until they begin to go creamy. If you use coarsely ground black pepper—rich folks cannot resist using this, because they consider boxed pepper to be pedestrian—you may find it a little gritty in such a delicate dish. Plain ol' boxed black pepper works better with this. No one will know.

Following Jimmy Jim, try not to break them up as you stir, so stir gently once the onions begin to soften. Do not be dismayed if the onions seem to cook down to almost nothing. They are so rich, a spoonful or two is usually enough per serving. If you really like this, "next time use more onions," my mother said.

The cooking time will vary, too, but the onions should be done in about 20 minutes.

This dish will appear a little oily, but in that oil, as in good garlic oil, is a wonderful flavor. It would probably complement a sheet of drywall. My people will not discard the leftover oil in the skillet. Old women in the family used to save the onion-infused oil to season everything from fresh garden vegetables to beans and greens, or to add its essence to cornmeal porridge.

This dish is harder than it seems; do not be disappointed if it takes a time or two to get right. Even if it is wrong, it will still be very good. I have been trying it for only forty-seven years, but with clean living I may have time to get it just right before my people sing me into the sky.

Buttered Boiled Potatoes

Even I can boil potatoes, but there is a trick or two. For this, red potatoes are best. They are the only kind of potatoes my mother will even consider leaving the peel on. Do what makes you happy.

WHAT YOU WILL NEED

6 to 8 red potatoes, depending on size

1 tablespoon salt

1 teaspoon black pepper

¼ teaspoon garlic powder or dried garlic

1 stick butter

HOW TO COOK IT

If you are using large potatoes, quarter them, but smaller ones can just be halved. If you have small new potatoes, cut them in half anyway, so they can better absorb the seasonings.

Cover the potatoes in cold water and bring to a boil until they break easily with a fork.

Drain the water, and to the still-hot pot add the salt, black pepper, garlic powder, and stick of butter, cut into sections so it will melt easier. Stir the potatoes, butter, and seasonings so that the potatoes are coated.

Serve immediately.

"There's a line in a song that says, 'Take a old, cold tater an' wait,'" my mother said. "There ain't nothin' worse than a cold tater."

Carrot and Red Cabbage Slaw

WHAT YOU WILL NEED

½ head red cabbage

1 large carrot

½ cup mayonnaise

1 teaspoon black pepper

½ teaspoon garlic salt

HOW TO PREPARE IT

Coarse-chop the cabbage and carrot. You want crunch in every bite. Use a knife, not a peeler, on the carrot.

Here's how: Just hold the carrot near the top and whittle it down with the knife, as if it were a piece of wood. If you use the peeler, you will have long, limp, flat strings of carrot in the crunchy cabbage.

This is bad.

Mix the mayonnaise, black pepper, and garlic salt for the dressing; then, in a large bowl, work the dressing into the carrot and cabbage.

Do not salt.

"If you ain't got slaw, well, it ain't Christmas," she said, which would make more sense if she did not also say it in April, and July.

Cornbread

You will notice the title is just "Cornbread." "Gettin' fancy with cornbread will mess it up, usually." This is a Depression-era cornbread recipe that some find a little crumbly, even dry, if they are accustomed to box recipes. Some people insist on adding sugar to the recipe, to make a sweeter cornbread, or milk and eggs, for a more cakelike cornbread. "Don't never, ever put sugar in cornbread. It will ruin it, and you will have to throw it out."

WHAT YOU WILL NEED

1½ cups self-rising yellow cornmeal

1½ cups self-rising white cornmeal

1½ to 2 cups cold water

¼ stick butter, softened, or lard, bacon grease, or
  shortening

(No salt. It's already in the self-rising meal)

1 heaping tablespoon mayonnaise

HOW TO COOK IT

Preheat the oven to 450 degrees.

Mix the cornmeals in a dry bowl. Slowly add the cold water until the meal has a nice, smooth consistency, like pudding. Different meals will take more or less water, at different times of the year. Take a spoonful and tilt it. If the mixture drips, it is too watery and the cornbread will be an abomination. Some people like to add bacon grease or lard to the mixture of plain cornbread, but it is not necessary. There is already enough fat, and flavor, in the dish.

Using your fingers, grease a 9-inch cast-iron skillet with butter or lard. It's your choice, and it will taste good either way. The butter will add another little level of flavor. If you do not own a cast-iron skillet, shame on you; go get one. If you have no lard, you can use bacon grease or any good shortening. The shortening, though, will not have the delicious pork flavor that the lard will, though it would be healthier. So, of course, would eating a salad.

Pour the cornmeal mixture into the skillet, and bake until the top is golden brown, usually around 20 minutes. If the top turns dark brown, the cornbread will be mealy, dusty, and dry.

"Cook it right the first time, and pay attention to the smell. You will smell it when it's done, that kind of nutty smell. For the rest of your life, you can time it with your nose."

There is an art to serving it. My people never gave much of a damn about presentation. We do not build towers of green tomatoes, picked crab, and goat cheese, or fan out our quail so it appears to take wing off the rutabagas. But we are neither heathens nor Philistines, and there is something to be said for the beauty of food on a plate, no matter who cooks it or how humble it might be. Photographers love to shoot Southern food, because it is one of those rare genres in which you can almost see the flavor, almost smell it coming off the print or the page.

Do it as Jim did it, on a plate instead of in a bowl, with that puddle of beans and ham and dollop of creamed onion and that single red potato to the side, and a generous dab or two of the cabbage-and-carrot slaw. I know this seems a little bit much, all in all. I know delicate people, those who eat a celery stick and half a rice cake and have to go lie down, will fret and perhaps tremble. I think this meal, even unadorned, might actually kill them—not over a lifetime, but instantly, like a bullet, or a subway train.

. . .

I asked my mother to translate these recipes because they were Ava's first real feast, a lesson she passed down to my mother, and because they constitute what might be my favorite meal. As much as anything in her repertoire, it is timeless, as much a part of the landscape as the pines, and the legend of the mean old man himself. It would become the meal my grandmother—and my mother, after her—cooked to celebrate birth, and to ease the pain of death, and to celebrate the arrival of the Pilgrims, the Baby Jesus, the leprechauns, and the Easter Bunny. Not even the invention of electricity has significantly altered the way it is prepared; only thin-crusted fried chicken, hot biscuits, and good chicken gravy, with fresh green beans and new potatoes, rival it in our history, and appetite.

It does take hours to prepare, which is a lot of time for a plate of beans in the twenty-first century, and requires an antiquated

attention to detail, to try to find that place between nothing special and just too much. Even veteran cooks concede that such
a place cannot always be found, though the old man seemed to
know, inherently, and so could lead others to it. My mother, the
beneficiary of three generations of experience, knows there is
no magic in it, knows that cooks who tend their pots with care,
who do not rush, and do not settle, will find it every time, though
things might get a little tedious for those who get anxious waiting
for a Pop-Tart.

As my South becomes less familiar to me, I think more and
more about what the old man said about his food, about how he
believed supper should be the finest time of day, a reward for
climbing out of that well, or laying down one more hundred-
pound sack, or stepping away from the blast furnace and into the
cool of the evening, one more time. Though he, of course, used
fewer words.

4

SWEETER, AFTER THE FROST

Collard Greens, Baked Hog Jowl,

Baked Sweet Potatoes

Ava

1924

IT WAS BAD ENOUGH she had to stand at that woodstove and listen to the old man preach on food as if he was the John the Baptist of beans and grits and pigs and such. At least he kept his sermons short, plain, and to the point. The hateful truth was, it was beginning to sink in; she was beginning to appreciate the difference between food and good food. She did not appreciate her lessons enough to stop griping and stomping, but this was her natural state, in the way that grimness was his, and did not always mean a lot. But then, on top of everything else, he made her follow him into the weeds and sad remnants of the fall garden, where he preached on, curtly, about the changing season, and the position of the moon, and early frost. She walked behind him like a petulant child, and even kicked at the dirt every few steps.

The old man turned and saw her standing in the middle of a rising cloud, her socks—she wore big, thick men's woolen socks with her high-ankled, old-fashioned shoes—red with kicked-up dust. He just shook his head and pointed to the tumbledown shed that passed for their barn, and the mule stabled within.

Working people, he warned her, could not afford to remain ignorant of the sky, the rain, and the chemistry of the turned earth underneath. They could not ignore the frost and pests and blight, or fail to see the potential in a seed the size of a speck of dust that could save your life if your luck was running high.

The boy had learned how to grow a fine garden from his momma before she passed away, and before that from the old man himself, before he vanished into exile. Most of the good things were gone, of course, the tomatoes, the squash, the sweet corn, the okra. A fall garden could still feed you a good while, though, and as he talked, he gathered a good mess of collards—the best green there is on earth, he believed. While he was there, he searched for and found the last of the hot pepper, a twisty little pod of turning cayenne.

The collards were taller than his knees, and she had been gathering them a few at a time since they first started to come in. But the old man had ignored them till now. The first frost had settled cold and silver on the garden just a day or so before.

"They ready now," he said.

Just because a row of collards were tall, even as high as your hip bones, did not mean they were ready to eat, he believed.

"You can pick collards as soon as they start to come in," in late summer and in early fall, as the weather begins to go cool, "if they're all you have," he said. But though young, small collards were tender, they were a little bland. If you could wait a bit, he said, wait to pick them after the first light frost has touched them; "the frost does somethin' to collards that just makes 'em a little bit better. . . . I think they're sweeter," he said.

He tapped his temple again, for emphasis. *Remember.*

"Just this, and a pan of good cornbread, is pretty fine," he said.

"Is this all we're having?" she asked.

"Not by a damn sight," he said.

. . .

He had a nice piece of hog jowl, a pound or so, slowly curing in the smokehouse. It had not cured much, but some smoke was better than none. He rubbed it all over with a little bacon grease and a heavy, logging-camp dose of coarsely ground black pepper, and set it aside.

He needed an iron rack to slip inside the pot, to raise the hog jowl an inch or so, as the fat rendered. The girl did not have one, so he went searching. He came back with three railroad spikes—the black iron clean, not rusty. The boy picked them up in the rail yards, and when he walked the tracks; he used them as weights, in fish and turtle traps, and more. The old man rubbed them clean, then rubbed them again with some bacon grease, and lined three of them across the pot, to rest the pork on. He covered it with a heavy lid, and slid it into the baking box on the iron stove. Ava stood beside him, aghast, making a face.

Who cooked with stuff that shook out of a cross tie when the trains roared by?

Hog jowl is not as exotic as some people think. Granny, in *The Beverly Hillbillies,* introduced it to much of America in the 1960s. It is, though, exactly what the name implies: the fatty meat at the hog's jowl. The flavor, to many, is like a cross between fatback and pork belly. It is an excellent seasoning in boiled beans, but it bakes to something close to heaven.

The piece the old man used was mostly fat, but had a thin streak of lean. Salted, the lean could be a little strong, in this as in most side meat, though it was excellent for seasoning; smoked, or fresh, it was milder. There were people in the hills who believed all other parts of the hog were inferior to the jowl, and he was one of them. He had cooked them every way you could, even sizzling, dripping, skewered on a stick over a campfire. He had scored it with a knife and slow-cooked it in an iron pot outdoors, surrounded by bubbling beans. But the best way, he told the girl, was to bake it slow in its own running fat, maybe surrounded by some sweet potatoes, till all that was left was the crisp, crumbly ghost of what you'd started with.

No one seems to recall the brand, but the woodstove in his daughter-in-law's kitchen was a good one, a solid one, the child's only dowry. The old man had done most of his cooking in the fireplace itself, or in outdoor kitchens, but he liked this invention, tremendously. Still, he would not give it his final seal of approval until he had tested it on some good hog jowl.

"That's all we do to that jowl," he told the girl, "till we throw in the sweet taters. Now let's get to the greens."

He showed her how to wash them thoroughly, and chop them so that they would cook down to pieces about the size of a playing card. Then he put them on to cook with salt, sugar, a single pod of hot pepper, and a small piece of fat. "White meat [what he called fatback] is better for collards, or a nice little chunk of streak o' lean, but anything will do, whar it's smoked or fresh, or salted," he said. But there was a science to it.

"You don't want no real whole lot of meat in your greens. You want your greens to be seasoned, but you don't want no big ol' hunks of seasoning meat . . . don't want your greens to get greasy, and they'll get that way if you use too much meat." He had heard of a Frenchman who seasoned greens with a piece of duck fat, and though that seemed a little fancy-pants to Ava, the old man surprised her. "I ain't had much duck, but that don't seem like no bad idea, a-tall. We shoot some ducks this winter, we'll see about it."

Collards, like any green, had to be smartly seasoned; if you used salt meat of any kind for your seasoning, you should reduce the salt you added, he lectured, or they would be inedible. Greens should taste mildly sweet and hot at the same time; the sugar, working in concert with the seasoning meat and salt, would reduce their natural bitterness.

"Why can't you just add more sugar to your young greens, 'stead of waitin' for the frost?" the girl asked him. It was the first logical question she had asked since her lessons began.

"T'ain't the same kinda sweet," the old man answered.

As with the beans, the amount of water, and its gradual addition to the pot, was important. He showed her how to begin with just a few cups of water, just enough to cover, and slowly add more as it cooked away; his own momma had taught him that, "to keep from washing the taste right out of good stuff."

If the pinto was the bean of kings, then the collard was their green. Even people who didn't like greens liked collards, because the leaves were naturally dense, not mushy or weedy. But he said the truth about cooking collard greens was that sometimes, no matter how good a cook a person was, the greens would still taste a little strong, or the texture might be a little tough, even after two hours or more of cooking. There was some luck involved, the old man told her; there was luck involved in cooking just about anything on a woodstove, in a time when a spice rack often consisted of little more than a pepper pot and a box of salt.

Everyone knows about potlikker; even the girl knew about it, but he told her anyway. "Save the juice in the pot's bottom, to mix with your cornbread the next day. Hit's better than soup, 'specially if you've got a few scraps of collards left." It was a poor folks' version of the Italian wedding soup, and a fine meal in lean times. The old man called it broth. He called every savory liquid that, whether it was from greens, beans, squash, or chicken.

But if beans were the foundation of a poor man's diet, greens were his apothecary. The broth from the greens, fortified with pork, was also an excellent meal for the sick, rich in iron, to get them out of the bed and back in the mill or the field, back down the ladder to the bottom of a well. No one, no one with cash money, the old man told his daughter-in-law, "has got no use for a helpless poor man. Greens is medicine. All greens is medicine. Beans will steady a body, but greens will cure one . . . but t'ain't no reason it can't taste good, too."

He finished the meal by peeling four sweet potatoes and, without seasoning them at all, raising the lid of the iron pot and easing them in, to cook as the hog jowl finished.

Then, leaving the girl to watch the greens, he went to have a smoke.

She wandered out to the porch two or three times, but was ordered inside to supervise.

The greens were done in two hours, roughly dense and leafy, but tender. They were sweet, and hot, and savory, as the old man had predicted.

The hog jowl crumbled to the touch. The sweet potatoes had soaked up some of the flavor, and in turn had added just a little sweetness to the pork as their flavors swirled inside the pot.

The boy was getting used to being glad it was suppertime.

"He started," the girl told him, "but I had to do most of it."

Collard Greens

WHAT YOU WILL NEED

About 2 or 3 large bunches of collard greens
1 small piece fatback or hog jowl, or about
    2 slices bacon
1 small whole pod hot pepper, such as cayenne
1 small clove garlic
1 tablespoon salt
1 tablespoon sugar

HOW TO COOK THEM

Wash the collards at least three times; grit clings to collards, in the wrinkles at the edges of the leaves and between the stalks. Chop the small stalks and leaves into pieces about the size of your hand, and wash them once more. Do not be alarmed if you have a monstrous pile of collards; they will cook down. How much of the stalk you use—the thick, main stalk closest to the cut—is a matter of taste. My mother uses almost no stalk, though some cooks say it will add a little flavor, and a little texture, to the finished dish. She thinks such people just don't know collards.

You do not have to cover the collards with water. Just use 2 or 3 cups, and bring them to boil in a large covered pot. Add the fatback or bacon (if you use bacon slices, cut them into thirds), and the whole pepper, the whole clove of garlic, and the seasonings. If you must, substitute for the pepper pod three good dashes of hot, clear pepper sauce, but no more than a good teaspoon.

Reduce the heat to low, cover, and cook for about 2 hours, adding water, if necessary, as it cooks out, still being careful not to drown the leaves with too much water. Stir every 15 minutes, at least. Some cooks like to use a set a tongs instead of a large spoon to move the collards around. "There should be very, very little liquid left in the bottom of that pot when your collards are done," my mother said.

Time is of secondary importance, she stresses, as a measurement in the cooking of collards. Texture is paramount. Cook them until the leaves are tender, but not till they disintegrate. So pay attention as they cook, and take a leaf or two from the pot and test it, after about 1½ hours. You should be able to cut easily through the collards with the edge of a fork when they are done. Collards should be leafy, and should seem, well, substantial, almost dense, and not be in shreds or ropes after they cook, as other greens can be.

Do not confuse collards with turnip greens, spinach, or mustard greens, and never mix them. Though it is acceptable for turnip greens and mustard greens to go mushy, mushy collards are terrible. "If you want real mushy collards, open a can," my mother believes.

And be sure to taste when you test them for texture. If they are too bland, add a little salt to the pot.

You do not want overpowering heat in this dish, so be careful when choosing the fresh pepper. She likes cayenne, but some people like a jalapeño, or even a serrano. A good rule is to avoid anything bigger than your little finger. And try not to break it as you stir the collards. This is a fine point, but an important one. Never, ever slice or dice the pepper—or the garlic, for that matter—as it will make those flavors overpowering.

Dried pepper will suffice in this dish, but, again, use a whole pod. But you can find hot pepper year round now in grocery stores, about the only great improvement my mother seems to admit to in the last 30 years. My mother grows her own, in cut-down milk jugs, shaded by a rock wall.

Many people, like me, like sweeter collard greens. You can adjust the sweetness, to taste.

Again, try to season your collards as they cook, instead of just smothering them with extra pepper sauce on the table or in the serving bowl. It will greatly alter the flavor—not the pepper so much as the strong pickling vinegar the peppers are preserved with—sometimes to such a degree that you cannot even taste the savory greens. Stick to a clear hot-pepper sauce; if you want to slop a lot of red-pepper sauce on your greens, she believes, you should never be offered any good greens to start with.

"I don't know why people feel like they got to mess stuff up," she said.

Unlike beans, which can be cooked to a more or less reliable formula unless they are old, collard greens can be a little more complicated, as Jimmy Jim warned. "Some collards will be tough when you pick them late in the season, but they'll have more flavor," my mother said. "Sometimes collards can be bitter. I think it's because of the dirt they come from. Nowadays, you can get collard greens out of season in the grocery store, but I don't know them collards. I don't know where they're from, or who grew 'em, or nothin'. I like to eat my collards in season, took from our own dirt. But even odd collards is better than no collards, I suppose."

The old ways are hard to discard. The secret to good collards is the old admonition to pick them, or buy what you believe to be fresh-picked greens, after that first frost, which might sound like folklore but may have some scientific basis.

"It ain't no myth. It's nature."

You cannot trick nature by just chucking them in the freezer for a minute or two, she believes. Frost falls from heaven, my mother says, as dew. Dew does not exist in a Frigidaire.

Baked Hog Jowl

WHAT YOU WILL NEED

1 tablespoon salt

1 tablespoon black pepper

1 teaspoon cayenne pepper

1 pound or so fresh or smoked hog jowl

1 tablespoon cooking oil

HOW TO COOK IT

This is not a pork roast. The cooking is more a rendering, and the finished product should be flaky, crumbly pork fat, similar to a giant cracklin'.

Preheat your oven to 350 degrees.

Mix your salt, black pepper, and red pepper in a small bowl, or shaker.

The cooking time, and seasoning, will depend on whether you use fresh or smoked meat, of course. If you are ambitious, select a piece of fresh jowl of between 1 and 1½ pounds. Rub it all over with a little oil, then sprinkle it with your spices and rub it in.

There is no need to add oil or water to the pot, as long as you have a raised rack inside it.

In a baking dish, bake the jowl, covered, at 350 degrees for about 1 hour to 1½ hours, or until the flesh has rendered to the point where it is golden brown and almost comes apart at the touch.

Save the fat in the bottom of the pot; it is excellent, seasoned lard, and can be used in other dishes, for cooking eggs, or just to add a little flavor to beans or greens; it's excellent on green beans.

When you are ready to serve it, carefully remove the jowl onto a platter or cutting board, and slice with a sharp knife. It is so rich that a little bit goes a long way, so do not cram a big piece of it in your mouth and expect to be pleasantly surprised, any more than you would take a huge bite of expensive chocolate, or knock back a tin of caviar.

"This is maybe the easiest way to do it, to just bake fresh hog jowl start to finish, but sometimes I like to boil mine for about an hour, on medium heat, till it's done through, and then bake a little, to render it. I think it makes it a little better, but that's just me." That is her way of saying, "But what do I know? I've just been cooking for a hundred years."

The smoked jowl is a little quicker and easier. If you use smoked jowl, it has already been slow-cooked in the smoking process and already contains salt, so lower or even eliminate your salt, rub with black and red pepper, and bake for 1 hour or less, again checking to make sure the color and texture are correct.

"I don't know about that smoked flavor," she said, "not done in no factory."

Then she made a face.

I told her it might just be that they smoke it in bigger batches than her grandfather did, with his mysterious pig. But, as with most things in her cooking, she trusts no smokehouse she cannot see leaning on a hill. She has not had a decent slice of bacon in a half-century or so.

Baked Sweet Potatoes

WHAT YOU WILL NEED

4 sweet potatoes (or 1 for each person,
    with 2 extras)
½ stick butter
1 tablespoon cooking oil

HOW TO COOK THEM

She does not like to cook the sweet potatoes in the baking dish with the hog jowl, as Jimmy Jim did, because if you add them at the time you begin baking the pork they will likely overcook and shrivel to wretched lumps, and if you try to add them during the cooking you may guess wrong and get both burned pork and raw potato, or fricassee yourself with the hot pig fat. It happens.

Plus, the hog jowl is so rich that you may want a cleaner taste in your sweet potatoes, for balance, though there is no denying that a good sweet potato perfumed with the rendered fat is perhaps one of the most decadent tastes—and smells—in our repertoire.

"What I do is, I get me some aluminum foil, and I rub them

sweet potatoes, with the skin still on, all over with the cooking oil, and then I wrap 'em in that aluminum foil. Bake 45 minutes to an hour and they'll be done. And that oil, it'll make that skin on that sweet potato a little crispy, and if you want to peel it, it'll peel right off."

Just in case she might be confused with someone attempting to cook healthy, she said the sweet potatoes are best served "mashed open a little bit, with a nice pat of butter, and nothing else."

I told her that some people like to add brown sugar.

"Why?" she asked.

"To make it sweeter."

"It's a sweet potato," she said.

"I know," I said.

"It's already sweet," she said.

I told her it was the same thing, the same idea, as a sweet-potato casserole, which is sweetened and seasoned with all manner of things, even marshmallows. Sweet potatoes are just not sweet enough for some people.

"I never have liked marshmallows," she said.

"Some people are just different from us," I said.

"Then they prob'ly won't like the hog jowl," she said.

Serve the greens in a generous mound in the middle of the plate, with a slice or two of the hog jowl on the side. Unwrap the foil from the sweet potato before you slice it, lengthwise, down the middle, mash it carefully from the sides to get it to open up, and then butter it. Be sure to take the foil off before you prepare the potato, and certainly before you eat it, she warns. "Aluminum ain't like iron. It ain't good for you." When I told her the discount steakhouses, like Western Sizzlin', left the foil on, she did what she has done all my life. She told me I was not Western Sizzlin', was I? Besides, there is just something unnatural about eating something from a blanket of tinfoil, something that reminds her of powdered orange drinks, and lunar modules, and that wayward monkey from outer space. They wrapped him in tinfoil, too, or so it seemed, and look what happened to him.

. . .

The old man told Ava that she was already on her way to knowing much of what really mattered in mountain cooking: beans, greens, potatoes, and that essential Southern vegetable, cream gravy.

She knew a few simple ways to cook pork, and was beginning her mastery of the more complicated staples of cornbread and biscuit.

But there was still much, much to learn, and he was very, very old.

Which was, she thought, a shame.

It was about then that she had ceased wishing that he was dead.

5

"A CHICKEN . . . AIN'T LIKELY TO KETCH ON"

Chicken Roasted in Cider with Carrots, Turnips, and Onion,
Chicken Gravy, Mashed Potatoes

My uncle James, left, and Grandpa, Charlie Bundrum,
in a borrowed soldier hat

1925

SOMETIMES, in the dying light of evening, the old man liked to sit on the porch and watch the chickens peck. He got cold more easily now, and wrapped himself in a half-mile of woolen shawl and a long gray army-surplus campaign coat from the First Great War, as if he were building a shed around his aging bones to keep out that yammering girl. Uninvited, she often sat there beside him anyway, and tried to engage him in conversation, since even a mean, mute, glinty-eyed ol' blasphemer and swine thief was better than sharing her thoughts with the lone cow, or hopping crows, or creaking pines. Sometimes the old man would even nod the slightest little bit, his face and glowing pipe hidden deep inside his shawl and upturned coat collar, blue smoke rising from inside his failed, imperfect solitude.

This day, he tried to ignore her altogether.

"Hush," he hissed.

"Why?" she said. "You ain't doin' nothin'."

"I was," he said.

"What?" she asked, and was further ignored. The old man just clenched his corncob pipe in his teeth and, like a divining rod, swept it slowly across the yard, back and forth, back and forth. Now and then, it would hold still for a deliberate second, before beginning to track again, back and . . .

Finally, the trajectory of the pipe ceased, and he held it ominously still on a belligerent young rooster that was worrying an uninterested hen.

"I don't see why I can't talk? It's my damn porch," the girl said, and the old man, finally losing his temper, rose to his feet with such force and with such a bellow that the chickens in the front yard burst, shrieking, into the air around him. Chickens do everything like it is the end of the world.

The girl backed up, but only a step or two. She had figured

out, early, that the old man would never put a hand on her; he only looked at her as if he would like to murder her in her sleep. He sank back wearily into his chair, and gathered his greatcoat around him against the chill of the gathering dusk.

"I am trying," he said softly, "to *choose.*"

The old man eased back down to his chair, the storm passed, and, as patiently as possible for a man like him, he tried to explain to her the ritual of the sacrifice.

. . .

"Got my mouth set," the old man said, "on some chicken gravy."

City people like to think my people just grabbed a chicken up off the yard or out of the coop at random, just snatched up whichever unlucky bird wandered within our grasp. This is untrue. There was a process to it, almost a kind of science. But it was a personal thing, too, a kind of blood reasoning.

The actual capture, up to a point, was not difficult, the old man told her.

"A chicken is not a intelligent critter," the old man said, and so "ain't likely to ketch on" when there is murder in the air. The problem is, they are just as apt to run from a flower blowing on the breeze as from a hydrophobic fox. A chicken cannot reason, he said. It might think, and react, but it cannot reason. A fox can reason, and a cat, and a bear. A chicken would react, like a tick on a hot rock.

A chicken lived every situation, every moment, like it was brand-new, and so lived in a constant state of wonder and surprise. "It's hard to get clos't to a chicken goin' at him head-on," the old man said, because, though chickens had tiny brains, most of these brains seemed devoted to suspicion. But chickens, he told her, are easily bamboozled. "And once you're clos't . . ." and the old man made a twisting, wrenching motion with his two big hands; that might have made some girls wince, but it made this one smile.

First, he said, you sit in judgment.

"It's best to go with a young rooster," he said, and her second great lesson had begun. She had hoed in her momma's vegetable garden and understood something, at least a little, about planting, tending, and harvesting growing things, but she had never before spilled blood for the sake of the table. She listened, for a change, with great interest. A lot of religious people are like that, as to bloodletting; read the New Testament, let alone the Old one, and measure the wars and sacrifice and endless smiting therein.

"Roosters is good for only two things: for eatin', and for gettin' with hens," he said, and a smart manager of the chicken yard had to play God routinely, to cull the weaker or apparently brain-dead roosters regularly from the flock, or a chicken apocalypse would befall. Too many roosters in one barnyard, and they would kill each other off to establish dominance, but till then they would also worry the hens to death, like a ship-full of sailors on leave in New Orleans, the old man explained, as much of the story of the birds and bees as he was willing to impart to a Pentecostal.

He hated to kill a truly good fightin' rooster, he said, a real neck-cutter and eye-pecker. He felt a kinship with them. Game roosters fight from a hatred of their rivals that most men will never understand, but a game rooster that dies in battle is useless for the pot, unless you discover the loser quickly, and roosters did not always have the good manners to perish on the doorstep.

But, as a practical measure, you only need a rooster or two to get the job done in a barnyard, he explained, and the best fighter was usually the best breeder, and the one most likely to produce the best and hardiest line of biddies. "Spare that one," he said. "You prob'ly won't get clos't to that 'un no-how."

Of those younger, inferior roosters, you went first for the peckers, the ones whose violence was not channeled, directed, with purpose. Some game roosters could be picked up and handled, like pets; some old men handled them as if they were parakeets. Those birds reserved their violence for each other. But other roosters were mindless peckers, who thought they had to assert their dominance on everything that moved, including squatting babies, small dogs, or the bare legs of just-married young women who were naturally inclined to hold a grudge.

Ava's legs were already streaked with tiny scars, from flying blocks of wood at the chop block, briars, Johnsongrass, and mean-spirited roosters. She was, as we have said, of long memory, and already had an inventory of pecking roosters she intended some-day to erase violently from this earth.

Next, the old man said, you went for the soft brains, the roost-ers who were not malevolent so much as just a half-bubble off plumb. Chickens are not intelligent to begin with, with brains the size of black-eyed peas. But some chickens are even dumber than average; these are the ones who suddenly begin running in end-less circles for no apparent reason, then keel over from sunstroke in the middle of an Alabama summer, or go halfway across a road and forget why they were crossing in the first place. It comes to them, usually, about the time the first tractor-trailer comes rum-bling down the centerline. A run-over chicken, Jim said, can be salvaged if you actually witness its destruction. These soft-brain chickens are not long for the world anyway, he said, and should be eliminated before they take their own lives, or somehow do man-age to spread their affliction to offspring.

He mentioned the names of several families who lived nearby who had not been judicious in this, as to their own, human off-spring, and the girl nodded that she completely understood.

"Heard about chickens in Mexico can play checkers," the old man said.

"Uh-unh," said the girl, but the old man swore that it was so.

"You ain't got none of them," he said.

He had perused the yard and decided that the smartest chicken there would drown just looking up at the rain.

If you are going to eat a hen, he told her, select a hen that is not a good mother. A hen that watches over her biddies is a valuable thing, season after season, and is a builder of wealth; a hen that ignores her biddies is just a layer, and of less value than a steadier hen that would tend her young and therefore increase the population. Ava did not like the idea, new to her, that a hen would not tend her biddies, as if she were running off to Florida in a convertible with a rooster in a plaid suit and a rakish hat.

Young chickens, pullets, were to be spared. A pullet might be more tender than an older bird, and in fat times there was nothing more delicious than a young chicken, but a mature chicken has more meat. Spare the young when you can, and let them grow into fat hens or good roosters. It might be as tough as a two-by-twelve, but would be good for broth, or dumplings, or stew.

And if you have to eat a chicken your kids have named, wait till they are visiting relatives, and blame the foxes.

Ava stood in the yard a minute or two, beside the old man, with all this running through her mind.

"I'll pick," the old man said, "if you got no stomach fer it. . . ."

Her eyes settled on a young but very hefty game rooster, a known pecker, with no emotional entanglements.

"That 'un," she told him.

. . .

They sat there on the porch, huddled against the cold, and plotted. Some people, the old man said, used a fishing pole, not with a hook and line, which would have been unconscionable even for such as him, but as a striking instrument. It is not hard to run a chicken down, he explained, if you still have your wind and are still fairly nimble and at least partly sober; but it can be tricky, that last step or two, as you stoop to snatch it up, and nobody runs all that good bent over. Chickens change direction much better than most humans can, leaving a whole lot of hungry people empty-handed and red-faced and cursing.

With a cane pole, a long one, you don't have to get close to the chicken, or break stride. You just have to get within six or seven feet, and whip the end of the fishing pole with a wicked snap at the chicken's fragile neck, and send it to its reward. His momma did it like that; she was hell on chickens, he said.

"That's blasphemy. Beasts don't go to glory," she said.

The old man saw little reason to argue this; they were merely discussing technique. Some people used a broken broom handle, he said, but the cane pole gave you another couple of feet to work with.

"That's cheatin'," Ava said, as if it were a footrace at a July Fourth picnic.

"Well, it ain't s'posed to be sportin'," he said. "It's gettin' groceries."

"Do you use a cane pole?" she said.

He sniffed, offended. "O' course not."

"Tell me how you do it," she said, so he did.

He rose to get to it, when his narrative was done.

"No," she said. "I can do it."

· · ·

It was diabolical.

First she caught the chicken's eye, which can be a trick in itself, when you think about it. Try it sometime. Chickens are not known for their attention span. They are physically incapable of a long stare.

She sidled to within a few feet of her victim, just close enough to get it to watch her but not so close as to spook it; this took several tries to get right. Once she got within about ten feet or so, she dropped a few pieces of crushed corn to the ground at her feet. The chicken did not trot over immediately. The advantage to being afraid of everything is that it cannot help being afraid of the right things sooner or later.

As soon as it appeared to notice the corn, she moved a few steps away, and the chicken trotted over to the kernels. She waited as it pecked up the corn, then dropped another few kernels at her feet and moved again. The secret was to time the drop so that it fell just as the chicken was finishing the previous one, and move not toward the chicken but away from it, so the chicken would feel secure.

Sooner or later, the old man had assured her, the chicken would just go stupid.

Ava dropped another few kernels at her feet, but this time just froze, and as the chicken trotted over and began to peck, she snatched it up by the neck, as quick as a mongoose. Before even half a squawk, she covered the bird's eyes with a grip around its head, and, with a violent, twisting motion, killed it quick.

The old man just nodded from under his halo of blue smoke.

The girl was a quick study, by God.

She asked him later if she was supposed to grab its head and cover its eyes out of mercy. He told her the head just offered the best grip, and she nodded. It did indeed make a sure handle.

This would be a skill she passed to her own children and grandchildren. Sometimes, near the end of her life, she forgot and dispatched a few that her grandchildren had named, but she did not mean to.

"She was quick, even when she got old," my mother said. "My God, she was quick."

It was not always a perfect plan. Sometimes more than one chicken, more than the doomed one, would be attracted by the bait, making the whole process impossible. "Keep a rock or hickory nut in your apron pocket," he told her, to scatter the other birds, but she was such a poor marksman that she was just as apt to break a window or hit the old man himself, which was probably an accident, though we cannot say for sure. But she was usually good at stalking chickens, and she stalked them across decades, never asking for help, even in her old age. I watched her do it myself as a child, fascinated, bloodthirsty, because it meant there would be something delicious on the stove as soon as the bloodletting was done.

Once the chicken was dispatched, she and the old man went to work immediately with the plucking and cleaning, which had to be accomplished with dispatch in a world without refrigeration. We are not often a finicky people, but have a suspicion of poultry, so much that it is hard to believe we have any European blood in us at all. The idea that our ancestors used to hang game like pheasants and duck so they would "go high," to improve the flavor somehow, causes only tremors now. We took no chances, and it was not uncommon for a chicken to go from blissfully pecking in the yard to Sunday dinner in an hour and a half. The Deep South does not lend itself to aging much of anything, not even liquor; to use smoke or salt to cure ham, bacon, or sausage is a true art form. But with chickens, it was right then or nothing, even in cool weather.

Ava fetched down the big skillet, but the old man said no, they would fry a chicken another day. This bird, which had a nice little bit of fat on him despite his battles in the dust, was going in the oven. First, though, the old man told her, he needed to get it good and drunk.

"Seems like that would have been easier before you cut its head off," Ava said.

. . .

The old man loved his cider, and always had a few jugs cooling somewhere—in the barn, or springhouse, or just under the bed. The law did not bother a man much for making cider—not like for corn liquor, for sure—but the old man had learned that the law bothered a man sometimes for no good reason at all, so he made some halfhearted effort to be sneaky about it. The old man did not even consider cider-drunk to be a true drunk, like from moonshine. Cider-drunk was play drunk, half drunk, pretend drunk. He could drink a jug of cider, he said, maybe even a jug and a half, and walk a bridge rail, or recite the Exodus. She would remember it as the first true foolishness to pass the old man's lips in a long and serious time. "But we only need a cup or so," the old man said, "to get this chicken drunk enough."

First he rounded up his vegetables. Roast or baked chicken was a plain thing, he said, if you didn't flavor it, same as anything else. He needed carrots, which were not grown easily in the soil here and had to be store-bought, sweet onions, and some turnips, which would cook into the chicken and absorb the chicken fat in turn. There was little on the earth, the old man said, better than turnips cooked in the renderings of a nice fat bird.

The closest thing to a baking dish the boy and girl had was a Dutch oven, and that would do. He prepared the chicken by rubbing it all over, both on the skin and inside the body cavity, with good homemade butter, and put a good half-pound, it seemed, inside the bird. Then he rubbed the whole thing again, first with coarse salt, and then with black pepper. They had a little red pepper—her momma had given her some spices as a wedding gift—and he dusted the chicken all over with that, too, but only lightly, and laid it in the iron pot. He did not chop the vegetables, only peeled them, and put them in whole. Then he mixed about a cup of hard cider with a cup of water and poured it around the chicken, so it could steam up into the bird as it cooked slowly in the woodstove.

Do not cook the liver and gizzards in the bird, but let them cook outside, with the vegetables, he told her. She would need them later, he said.

"Some people put apples inside the chicken," he told her, but the apple cider had a spice the apples didn't have. The hard cider had a different taste from the sweeter soft cider, a kick, and the cooking would steam the liquor out of it, he said, and just leave the rest.

He said a young bird would cook, covered, in two hours on a woodstove, but that halfway through he liked to take off the lid and, using a big spoon, ladle some of the cider liquid and rendered chicken fat over the bird. This kept the breast from drying out quite so much.

"But the truth is, I don't think the smartest cook in this whole world has figgered a way to really keep the breast meat from drying out, at least a little, in a chicken cooked thisaway, nor a fried chicken, neither."

When it was about three-quarters done, he said, it was time

to put on the mashed potatoes. The mashed potatoes, he said, were the easiest thing to mess up completely in the long history of cooking food; you could cook the flavor right out of them.

Cook them, he told her, with just enough salted water to cover—gold, white, red, it didn't matter—till the corners on the quartered potatoes began to melt and round off. Cook them until there is almost no liquid left, at which point you slowly, slowly stirred in the butter and the milk, began to mash, then stirred in more milk and maybe more butter if needed, and mashed some more, till they went fluffy (he did not actually say "fluffy"; it was not in his lexicon), and only then added the secret ingredient, the thing that made them sing.

The chicken should be golden brown but tender, from the steam, and the liquid should have cooked to a thicker, buttery, delicious residue. Then you took a little of the liver and gizzards and diced them fine—careful, because the liver would try to go to mush, he said—and combined that with two tablespoons, at least, of the golden fat from the pan, in a skillet.

"Use that with your flour," the old man said, "to start your gravy."

She would say, a half-century later, that this was the meal that taught her not merely to cook food but to love eating it, more even than beans and ham.

The chicken was tender and moist, even the troublesome breast, but it was the turnips, carrots, and whole onions that made it work. The bite of the cider, as with all alcohol, had steamed away, like the spirit it was, leaving just a little something, something she did not have the words to explain.

"Why, t'ain't drunk a-tall," she said.

The old man told her that a cook who could prepare a juicy roast chicken was already halfway home.

A cook who could prepare a good pot of mashed potatoes, he said, was even closer.

But a fine turnip, salted and peppered and cooked in chicken fat and butter, was "rare fine."

Rare fine.
They talked as pretty as they cooked.

Chicken Roasted in Cider
with Carrots, Turnips, and Onion

Buying poultry in modern times is a conundrum. A fat hen is the best modern-day alternative to the scrawny, battle-hardened game rooster. This is one of those times when tradition must yield to common sense. Still, except for the tenderness, and the greater fat content, the chickens of old probably did have a superior, much cleaner flavor, before the age of fish meal, before the time of the mutant, hopped-up, chemically and genetically sculpted poultry you see in the supermarket. Free-range chickens, as much as I hate to admit it, are more than a pretension; they taste more like the chickens I remember from my childhood.

WHAT YOU WILL NEED

2 carrots

1 large turnip, or 2 medium-sized ones

2 medium sweet onions (can substitute 2 large leeks)

1½ sticks salted butter

1 fat baking hen

1 tablespoon coarse salt

1 tablespoon coarsely ground black pepper

1½ cups cider, hard or soft

1½ cups water

Cayenne pepper (to taste)

HOW TO COOK IT

First prepare the vegetables, and set them aside. They are meant to be eaten, not just as seasoning. Chop the carrots into pieces about 2 to 3 inches long, and peel and chop the turnips into pieces about 2 inches square. You want chunks, not small, diced, bite-sized cubes. Peel and quarter the onions, or if you prefer, cut chunks of leeks, which work very, very well in this dish.

Preheat your oven to 350 degrees.

Let the butter soften to room temperature. Take the half stick and cover the skin of the chicken all over with it, and, as Jimmy Jim did, butter the inside of the body cavity. Then, with a devil-may-care look on your face, toss the other, whole stick of butter inside the bird. It will feel good to do it.

"Some people put lemons and oranges and other stuff, but I think you just don't need it," said my mother, echoing her grandfather.

Salt and pepper the outside of the bird, then let it sit about 5 or 10 minutes. My people believe the flesh will absorb the salt better this way. Pour the cider and water into the roasting pan, being careful not to wash your handiwork from the bird.

Dust the chicken lightly with the cayenne. You are not going for heat here, just a little dash of flavor.

Place the chicken in the oven and cook, covered, between 2 and 2½ hours. You do not need to uncover the bird. "It'll go golden brown. Watch your drumsticks. If they're going dark brown, it's about past done, you know?"

Do not be dismayed if the white meat is not as juicy. "White meat is trouble," my mother says. "It's a shame, with all the messin' around with nature them mad scientists has done, that they haven't made a chicken with all dark meat."

I told her we should try duck, and she believed she would stick to chicken. "It's a little too late to be tryin' crazy stuff now."

You can let the chicken rest a few minutes before carving, if you can wait that long.

Chicken Gravy

WHAT YOU WILL NEED

½ cup whole milk

1 cup water

2 tablespoons drippings from the roasting pan

1 tablespoon butter

2 tablespoons flour

½ teaspoon black pepper

½ teaspoon salt

HOW TO COOK IT

Combine the milk and water, and set aside. My mother sometimes does this dish with water alone, but the milk adds a slight creaminess.

In a 9-inch skillet, combine the drippings from the roasting pan with the butter, and bring it to a nice sizzle over medium heat. Stir in the flour. This is not milk gravy, in the traditional sense, so you want it to cook a little longer, still stirring, till you get a nice medium-brown color.

Slowly, add the milk-and-water mixture, continuing to stir as it thickens, and sprinkle in the pepper and about half the salt. Turn off the heat. It should thicken fine.

Thickness is a matter of preference. We like not a thick, pasty gravy but a fairly thin one—though not watery—which goes well on your potatoes. For biscuits, you may want to let it thicken a little more. Taste it. If it needs salt, add more until it makes you happy. If you think to yourself, "I could just about eat this with a spoon," you have done well.

Mashed Potatoes

WHAT YOU WILL NEED

2 to 2½ pounds white potatoes, gold- or red-skinned

1 teaspoon salt

1 cup whole milk

½ stick butter, softened

1 teaspoon mayonnaise

HOW TO COOK IT

Peel and quarter the potatoes; larger potatoes, cut into eighths, or near abouts. Do not dice them. They will "turn watery," she believes, if they are cut too small.

Salt the water and potatoes as you begin cooking, not the cooked potatoes after they are done. Boil, as Jimmy Jim mandated, till they are done but the corners have not begun to melt, to blunt. If you are unsure, just take a piece of potato out and gently press down on it. If it mashes easily, it's done.

My mother mashes with a large fork, gradually adding the milk and butter. You may not need all the milk, but you will damn sure need all the butter. At the end, stir in the mayonnaise, being sure not to use too much, and to incorporate it thoroughly.

You want fluffy potatoes, not chunky ones. You do not want to whip them. You want just enough texture so that they will hold together in a perfect but ragged mound, with little peaks and valleys. I do not care how froufrou this sounds. We take our potatoes seriously.

.   .   .

The use of mayonnaise in such dishes dates back to harsh times when butter and milk were scarce. I guess it is a little funny, but the world never seemed to run short of mayonnaise. The secret ingredient remained in the recipe long after the hard times eased, just one more little thing about which, when you ask my mother why it is, she tells you that it is because it has always been. You can add all the butter and all the milk from all the cows who have ever been, and if you leave the secret ingredient out she will taste its absence, and I will, too, after all this time. I guess it does not speak to any great sophistication in our cuisine, but "it tastes good, I believe," my mother says, "and ain't that what we're going for?" Besides, how do you erase something that was never written down in the first place?

. . . ,

In that long-ago kitchen, Ava watched, over his shoulder, as he stirred it in.

"That don't seem like much of a secret ingredient," she said.

She had expected something odd or rare, or whispered by the fairies.

He told her to get a fork and take a taste.

"Well," she said, "yeah, that's pretty good."

Then she tasted the golden chicken gravy.

"Well, yeah, that's pretty good, too."

The chicken itself, though, was perfect, maybe even the best chicken she ever had.

It could be it really was just that good. It could be, knowing her, and knowing the chicken, she still held a grudge.

"It tastes better," she liked to say, "if you was mad at it to start with."

. . .

I asked my mother if she needed to have a bad feeling about a chicken, in the old days, before she prepared it for the pot. She said she knew the fates of chickens at the hands of other cooks, and knew that sometimes there was malice there, but her heart was too soft for her actually to do in a chicken with her own hands. She has gone a lifetime without killing anything except mosquitoes, flies, spiders, and a snake or two, which makes her a bad Buddhist but does not count off if you are a Congregational Holiness. She hired her killing done, bribing her children with the promise of baked, fried, stewed, and barbecued chicken, and we rushed into the yard with blood in our eyes. Ava would watch from the porch, rock, and nod. Now and then, she would just point, and, even in her frailty, play god of the barnyard.

Even though the chicken may not be as good now as it was then, it is easier on the conscience, my mother believes. She is pretty sure that, staring into the cooler at the IGA, she had nothing against any of them.

6

THE FOURTH BEAR

Cornmeal Porridge with Chicken and Watercress,
Stewed Cabbage, Fried Apples

The oldest boy, James, with a wagonload of babies

1926

IT WAS a damn dicey time to be a chicken with an attitude.

"We'll need one, a fat 'un if we can ketch one," the old man said.

The girl came back in about twenty minutes with another rooster.

She'd had her eye on him.

"Now," he told her, "I'll l'arn you to make porridge."

"Like in the story about them bears?" she asked.

"No," he said, not altogether sure what bears had to do with anything; he had eaten bear as a boy, and it was loathsome, strong and oily with an essence of what seemed to be axle grease. Literature, and especially fairy tales, did not figure in the old man's experiences. The last books in the Bundrum family had been left behind long ago, in Virginia, as the family drifted south during the previous century; even the name changed, as that literacy slid away, from the original Bondurant to Bundrum, as if it had been blurred or muddied somehow on a page soaked with corn whiskey.

But porridge had been in the family history forever, it seemed, on both sides of a wide, deep ocean; our people called it merely "broth," because of the chicken stock that is its twentieth-century foundation. But its origins envelop just about everything. My European ancestors—French, English, Irish, German, Viking— lived on it, but flavored with pork fat or poached game. The Creek and Cherokee, who are just as much a part of our lineage as the Europeans, ate it flavored with squirrel and rabbit. My mother and her sisters made it, often, with quail, and even doves. But the best it ever was, my people believe, was with a good fat chicken— or, barring that, a tough and stringy one—and maybe a few aromatics to season it with.

It required no sides, just a bowl and a spoon. The old man, though, liked to eat it with a savory side or two, like stewed cabbage, which was mildly sweet and a fine complement to this simple porridge, and apples fried in butter and cinnamon, which, he said, was like having dessert but not having to wait on it.

To Ava, the porridge sounded like a terrible notion, like the meals the evil kings fed to their prisoners in the dungeon. They called it gruel.

"It ain't like chain-gang food, is it, like mush? 'Cause we had some kin on the chain gang, and they said all they had to eat was mush and white beans and beets and such."

He told her to hush, and, no, it wasn't; she should wait and see—but, mostly, hush.

"It's cheap food, shorely, but you need to learn to cook cheap food. Times will always get hard, harder than reg'lar," he said, as if he could feel the coming Depression in his bones. "But cook it rich," he said, "and you won't need as much meat, and you won't need as much of nothin' else." The meaning of that would become especially clear to her, in the worst of times.

The meal could be made with either cornmeal or flour, but the cornmeal version, he believed, was more savory, more satisfying. The flour recipe was similar in consistency to the broth with dumplings.

"Never have liked dumplin's," he said. "Pasty-tastin' bastards."

Since they had only the liver and gizzard from the one bird, there was not enough to fry, so the old man set them aside to use as bait on his trotlines. They would not do in the stockpot, he said, because they would muddy up the clean taste of the chicken broth, especially the heavy, murky taste in the liver.

He liked his coffee like tar, and smoked cheap, strong tobacco that would all but knock birds from the sky, and could out-curse any other man she had ever known, but he was not ham-handed as to food. It may be, all in all, he really was just an excellent fish camp cook, akin to all those fine short-order chefs who worked the truck stops. But the old man had a light touch for such an unapologetic ruffian; he even understood the value in a little fresh-picked watercress.

It seemed, to Ava, to be a puzzling ingredient, not just for a porridge, but for almost anything. The peppery taste seemed to go with nothing. He had gone to the creek to pick it himself, from the cold water, but came back with a bunch so small he could hold it in one hand, more like a bouquet than something a grown man would put in a pot. He boiled it first, then fried it, quickly, in bacon grease. He diced it with a sharp knife, ending up with a handful or less of what looked more like wilted parsley, and set it aside.

He showed her how to season the water and boil the chicken with a little onion and a dear, store-bought carrot, and how to bone and break the chicken into pieces without burning herself. Then he returned the chicken to the stock, and sprinkled the watercress into the broth. The only real trick was in combining the chicken stock with a mixture of seasoned cornmeal stirred into cool water. It had to be done slowly and carefully, because in this dish the consistency mattered just as much as the seasoning. He cooked it down to a smooth, creamy consistency.

The key ingredient, he told her, was a quarter-pound of the pure cow's butter that they had churned themselves, which magnified and complemented the richness of the broth. As the porridge slowly bubbled, pushed to the side of the stove, he washed, chopped, and stewed a head of white cabbage in a daub of bacon grease, frying it a little to get it going, add some flavor, and improve the sweetness a bit, but finishing it more with hot steam than with grease. "It's a plain food, cabbage is, but not plain-tastin'," he said. "I've cooked it all my life, but I ain't never seen none th'owed out."

The apples were easy, a forgiving dish, and good for the late fall and early winter, especially after the garden had already given up all but a few winter vegetables. He worked fast, cutting and coring, but left the skins on, then fried them in butter, bacon grease, and sugar.

"Whar's the damn cinnamon?" he shouted, as he stirred.

Ava just shrugged, insulted. She knew cinnamon, and had

used it in her previous life; cakes and pies were the only dishes she had paid much attention to when she was a child. But it was so odd, too, the old pine-knot asking for a pinch of cinnamon, and she laughed out loud.

"Whar's the damn cinnamon!" she shouted back, and the old man wondered, not for the first time, if the girl might be truly mad. It was hard to tell, under such a great, great mustache, if he smiled, but he did not murder her, so he might have been amused.

The finished porridge was the consistency of warm pudding, with tender chicken in every bite; the old man said it was good to thicken it enough so they could use a fork, so as to make it easy to eat beside the cabbage and apples. As they spooned it up, she told the old man and the boy the story of the bears and the blond-haired little girl and the porridge that was too hot, too cold, and just right. We do not know if he enjoyed the story, but he did question it. Why, he wanted to know, did the bears not just eat the little girl, since they had her already hemmed in good?

When I was a little boy and she told the story to us, she always strayed from the plot and talked of my great-grandfather and his porridge, like he was just another character, like a fourth bear.

· · ·

Cornmeal Porridge with Chicken and Watercress

My mother has altered the recipe only in the sense that she has substituted all dark meat for a scrawny, worrisome yard bird. But the soul is the same.

WHAT YOU WILL NEED

1 small bunch watercress, finely chopped,
    or 1 teaspoon finely chopped fresh parsley
1 tablespoon bacon grease
7 chicken thighs or big drumsticks
½ small onion, or no more than ¼ cup
    finely diced
1 carrot, finely chopped
½ stalk celery, finely diced
1 tablespoon salt
1 teaspoon black pepper
2 cups cornmeal
1 stick best-quality butter

HOW TO COOK IT

First prepare the watercress. Boil it till tender in unseasoned water, or about 30 minutes over medium heat. Drain, then fry in bacon grease for another few minutes. Remove from the skillet, let cool, and dice it fine, like parsley. When I asked my mother why it had to be cooked twice, she just shrugged. "Because we've always done it that way." This explanation will arise again and again.

In a large pot—at least 3 quarts—cover the chicken thighs or drumsticks, with the skin on, with water, and add the onion, carrot, and celery, and the dry seasonings. Bring to a roiling boil, then reduce heat to medium. Continue to cook for about 1 hour, or until done.

Working carefully, lower the heat, then remove the chicken pieces from the water, and set aside to cool, or place in cold water to speed the process. Remove and discard the bones, but keep the skin. Tear the chicken into spoon-sized pieces, being sure to do the same with the skin. Also, do not strain the broth. Leave the vegetable bits in.

"We've done rendered the flavor in the bones and in the skin into the broth, so we've saved that already, but those little pieces of skin will be delicious," my mother said.

In a bowl, make a mixture of the cornmeal and cool water that is about the consistency of grits, oatmeal, or cream of wheat. It should be thin enough, just barely, to pour. Set aside.

Return the pulled-apart chicken to the broth, bring to a boil, then reduce heat to medium. Then, carefully, slowly, spoon the cornmeal mixture into the broth. Add the butter at this point, and a pinch of watercress.

"Cook it till it thickens, which should only take a few minutes," my mother said.

When I asked for a more mathematical timetable, she got a little mad at me. "It ain't like I've ever had to time it, hon," she said, for the thousandth time in my life.

Sprinkle the top with a little more of the watercress. Some of the old cooks, like the old man, liked to cook the watercress into the dish, but the peppery nature of watercress is more of an acquired taste, so it may be best to start small and increase it as desired.

"In the old days, when we had no meat, we'd just have the porridge, cooked with the watercress, with a little salt pork for seasoning," she said. "It was good. Chicken is better."

Stewed Cabbage

WHAT YOU WILL NEED

1 medium or large head white cabbage

3 slices thick-cut bacon

¼ stick best-quality butter

1 tablespoon salt

1 teaspoon sugar

1 cup water

HOW TO COOK IT

Only white cabbage will do. Red cabbage, what we call purple cabbage because that's what it is, will not result in the same sweetness. "Use your purple cabbage for slaw, to eat raw, but don't cook with it, not for somethin' like this."

Wash the whole cabbage carefully, twice. Like the collards, the leaves of a cabbage will harbor grit. Remove any discolored or suspicious outer leaves, but try to save as many of the darker-green outer leaves as you can. There is flavor there, and they will make it look prettier on a plate.

Quarter it, core it, and cut off the stem. Chop the cabbage into pieces not less than about 2 inches square. This part of the recipe is not meant to be exact. If your cut-up cabbage looks ragged, it will still taste good. Do not shred—this is not the texture you are looking for. Set aside.

Cut the bacon slices into pieces about 2 inches long. Fry in a large, high-walled skillet until the fat goes clear, but do not cook until crisp.

While the grease is still hot, add the butter to the bacon and bacon fat, then the chopped-up cabbage, salt, and sugar. Cook over medium heat, stirring, for just a minute or two. It will enhance the flavor if the cabbage fries and there is just a touch of brown on the leaves, no more, before you add any more liquid to the skillet.

Carefully pour in the water, and—stirring occasionally—continue to cook over medium heat until the cabbage is tender and begins to smell very, very good, about 20 minutes or so. The cabbage should be fork-tender, but do not cook to mush. Some older Southerners like it that way, but it is better if you stop cooking before it goes too soft. If it is still crunchy, it has not cooked quite enough.

This dish, like creamed onions, may seem a little oily if you are unaccustomed to Southern food. You can reduce the strips of bacon to one, reduce the amount of butter, and substitute a lighter cooking oil. It makes us sad even to put this down on paper.

Fried Apples

Fried apples are a staple in the Appalachians, served with everything from roast pig to breakfasts, such as fried sausage and eggs and biscuits, and they go particularly well with porridge and other dishes prepared with cornmeal.

Some old, old recipes call for cabbage and apples to be fried together, and others add broken pieces of pecans and even walnuts to the fried apples, but as a side to porridge, the dish is best left plain.

In hard times, when butter, sugar, and cinnamon were scarce, some cooks would simply fry the apple sections in bacon grease, for a less sweet, more savory dish. You can also cube and fry a sweet potato in butter and bacon grease, combine with the apple mixture, and cook for 10 minutes or so, just long enough to let the flavors mix. The old man loved sweet potatoes, and tried to eat one, usually baked, three or four times a week.

These dishes, too, have changed very, very little over time, and would have been on the table in Birmingham, England, in the row houses outside the BSA motorworks, and in the German factory towns and farms after World War I. He learned the porridge and the cabbage from his momma, and the fried apples in the timber camps, as men and mules set about clear-cutting everything beneath the clouds.

WHAT YOU WILL NEED

4 or 5 large apples, any kind
¾ cup sugar
1 teaspoon ground cinnamon
2 tablespoons bacon grease
¼ stick butter
¼ cup water

HOW TO COOK IT

Wash, peel, and core the apples, and cut into sections. The size of the section is not that important, but thin sections of apple will go limp as they cook. Red Delicious and Granny Smith apples are both fine for this, as are smaller Gala apples. The truth is, just about any apple will do.

Mix the sugar and cinnamon in a bowl, and then add the apples and mix them in, coating the sections.

In a large skillet, melt the bacon grease and butter; the stove should be set no hotter than medium heat. Then stir in the apples, sugar, and cinnamon, and sprinkle over them any left-over sugar or cinnamon. Let the apples fry for just a minute or two, then slowly pour in the water and cook, covered, for about 5 minutes. Uncover, stir, and reduce the heat to low. Cook over low another 5 minutes, or until most of the liquid has cooked to syrup and the apples are fork-tender but still have just the tiniest amount of snap to them. What you want, ideally, is a faintly crisp inside, and buttery-soft outside.

. . .

"Your little one will like this," the old man told her. "You may have to beat 'em some to get 'em to eat the cabbage. But they'll like them apples. You heat them apples up at breakfast, and put on a butter biscuit, they'll eat a pan of biscuit."

The girl was so flabbergasted by this soliloquy, by this long-winded recitation, she almost didn't hear the most important part.

"Your little one . . ."

The old man had known almost before she did.

The first boy came in '26. Ava named him James, and they called him Jim, for short.

The second, William, came a year later, in '27.

The first girl, Edna, followed in '29, and another, Emma Mae, a year later.

As she became more proficient, and as the hard times he had warned about seemed to be upon them, the old man went to work in the trees again, cutting timber, sawing lumber. But in the evenings, he always helped with the supper, and rose early the next morning to begin the biscuits and coffee. It seemed that, as he grew older, he grew gentler in their house, in their company. He began to call her "daughter," and though he would never be loquacious, he did admit to a fondness for her, in time.

. . .

He emptied the contents of his own memory into his teaching, showing her not just how to get by, to keep his boy and the children from going hungry, but the foundation of life itself in this bare-knuckle place. The preachers could worry about their souls, he said. There was no point in rushing into it.

They would need, in the years ahead, every inch of the landscape around them. He taught her how to find food deep in the woods, in the creeping vines and wild fruit trees and even in the weeds. He showed her what was good to eat, and what would at least keep them alive when there was nothing else, and what would kill them if she made a mistake. It became part of her.

"My momma loved that old man. I know that. She said it, many times," my mother said. "I don't truly know if she ever told him that. You know, they was a lot alike, them two," like they were blood kin themselves. It was that invisible, unwritten book of recipes that bound them, at least as tight as blood, which had rarely seemed to mean that much to the old man anyway. But even that had seemed to change, pot by pot.

He taught her biscuits, and stewed okra, and catfish, fried and in a spicy stew, and fried green tomatoes, squash, and baked backbone and black-eyed peas. He sacrificed many, many a mysterious chicken, and the boy would walk in the door, day after day after day, to glorious smells.

A romantic would say it was how the old man made amends for leaving his family, but, then, we do like to grind the rough edges off the dead down here, if you give us time. Still, some of his kin say he never left his people a thing except a few welts and bruises, and a legacy of violence. But they never said that in front of her, at least not more than once.

No amount of polishing would make him a saint, or even less a sinner, in some things. As the hard times did descend, and worsen, no one wanted a good roofer, or carpenter, or well digger, and the demand for timber bottomed out. Then, because this is just the way luck will do you, disease ran through their small flock of chickens, and they died one by one. They lived off their garden, and watched their one hog closely, with trepidation. Ava had never been poor, and it was raw and ugly to her.

One day, the old man told Ava and his son he believed he would saunter down to the neighbors and have a little chat if he was to catch 'em outside. They found this especially odd, since the old man did not chat, and would rather eat dirt than make small talk; it all tasted the same in his mouth. He rarely even returned a wave with little more than an almost imperceptible nod, fearing it would be seen as an invitation of some kind, to continue the worrisome interaction.

Later, they saw him coming up the road at a distance, but at an odd gait, and as he got closer it became clear that he was carrying something. It was a chicken-wire cage, crammed with sad, scraggly chickens.

Once in the yard, the old man laid down his burden, turned the chickens loose to spread through the handful that had followed behind him, then turned out one pocket to sprinkle the last handful of crushed corn across the yard. Being chickens, they probably thought they had merely traveled in a circle and were home again. Ava feared the worst, but the old man told her he had swapped for them, fair and honest. She spent most of the next day waiting for someone to come into the yard to reclaim their property, but day passed into night, and no one came. Only then did she notice the old man was not wearing his great wool coat, and her heart broke the slightest bit.

But, just in case, she sat beside him on the porch, to watch the chickens peck, and began to choose.

7

THE FALLING COW

Beef Short Ribs, Potatoes, and Onions

Aunt Edna, who my mother says "run a good race"

1929

THE CATTLEMAN was not accusing, it seemed, only curious.

"I 'uz wonderin'," he asked the old man, "if you seen a cow?"

The old man motioned with the end of his pipe toward Charlie and Ava's milk cow, whose name was Dobbin.

"That 'un ain't mine," the cattleman said.

The old man nodded, as if to say, *Of course not,* and smoked a bit, leaving the cattleman unengaged. He did not like landowners and rich men, and especially did not like them when they came riding up to him on high horses with good leather, asking him foolish or pejorative questions.

The cattleman was not a bad man. He had lived beside the people of the foothills all his life, wading through the muck and pulling the cotton and corn and shoving against the dumb beasts right beside them, except he had papers on the dirt they walked and the beasts they dragged from the bogs, and that, that right there, was the story of the world. They all made the dirt pay, with their sweat; it was the matter of shares that set them apart. Most of the renters and hired hands he lived beside knew their place in this feudal society; then there was this kind here, propped up in his straight-backed chair like he was king of something, the old glinty-eyed son of a bitch.

The old man smoked some more, and the cattleman sat on his horse. Ava, watching from the door, asked him if he would like to get down, but the cattleman said he did not have the time. Rich men's time was always more pressing than poor men's time. Poor men could not even argue the fact. They could dig a ditch to California or a well to Australia, for two dollars. A rich man made a hundred lacing up his boots.

"I could use some he'p," he said to the old man, "findin' her, and ketchin' her up."

The old man removed his pipe, as if he might say something.

It took a full minute to become clear that he would not.

"I've heard you can track a bit," the cattleman said.

"Might," the old man said.

The old man had been born in the last century, in the bleak aftermath of the Civil War, and he could trail deer, and wild pigs, and the last predators to haunt these hills. But the woods and wild things had never seen such stress as this, as now. The wild game had become wary, what with every starving peckerwood in the Deep South trying to run every living thing to ground, to sell or butcher to feed his babies.

"But don't see as how you need me," he said, and left the rest of it unsaid.

A blind fool could find a damn cow, could just fall over it, if nothing else. A cow weighed a ton, and did not exactly move dainty across the earth. But if it had gotten mired in a slough or mud bank, or tumbled off a ridge and crippled itself, or just wedged itself in the thick brush and could not push free, it could expire quickly. The country was wilder in those days; the houses and farms were far apart.

This one seemed to have sprouted wings and flown away.

"I'll pay," the cattleman said, "you find her alive."

The old man looked the question at him.

"One dollar," the cattleman said, "most I can pay."

That was damn near a fortune in '29.

"If it's killed and she's not yet turned, I'll split the meat. Give you a quarter-share. You do the butcherin', though, on your part."

The old man continued to stare, waiting for the rest of it.

"If it's stole . . ."

The old man just shook his head once, to cut him off.

He would not turn in a poor man, not give a name.

"If it's stole," the cattleman said, "just bring back as much of it as you can. You still get a whole quarter. . . . I don't need no name. I just want my property."

No one in this house had tasted beef in a long, long time. The old man got up, a little creakily, and asked just one thing:

"Whar you seen it last?"

It had last been spotted, the cattleman said, outside a rusting, broken-down pasture fence, about five miles from an abandoned community called Tredegar, a true ghost town north of Jacksonville, where a tumbledown train depot and abandoned derelict hotel were being slowly covered up by the weeds and creeping vines.

"I'll send a man with you, to help," the cattleman said. "You might need somebody to send word, or help gettin' her out of the woods. . . ." But what the old man heard in his head was, *to make sure you don't kill and butcher it in the trees.*

But if he was greatly insulted, it did not show. He and Ava watched the cattleman ride off on his horse.

The old man appeared to be smiling, though it was, of course, hard to tell.

· · ·

They needed a break, this family did.

This would do.

It had been a dry and wicked summer, dying into a dusty, uncertain fall. The heat and drought had baked the dirt to iron chunks, bleached the color from the grass, and stunted the corn and cotton in the fields, and all the world—or at least as much of it as they could see—was dull, hot, and thirsty. Some of the wells had gone dry or been reduced to mud and sludge, and the stooped old men who remembered how to witch for water shuffled through the hardpack and dust and brittle weeds, holding to both ends of a green forked stick like the handlebars on a bicycle. They fixed their eyes on the quivering tip; if it dipped, it meant there was good water there, deep underground, but sometimes it was just hope that tugged it down. They had heard that, west of here, whole counties had just blown away, untold tons of red dirt and black dirt billowing across the land. The people of Texas and Oklahoma were blown off with it, and kept drifting west, searching. But that could never happen here, the old people said. The hills could not be swept away. It was all rocks and roots here, rocks and roots, and Johnsongrass, and pines.

Here diseases with old names took people and livestock alike, and the rich men in the statehouses in Montgomery and Atlanta and Nashville just turned away. What did it have to do with them? Did these white trash even vote? Just a year before, Charlie had found wages in the ironworks, pouring steel at the blast furnaces in the city of Gadsden, but when the fires went cold in '29, the steel barons laid him off without a blink or a fare-thee-well, took their company house, and put his family on the street.

They would lose the baby Emma Mae to the deprivations of the time, to poor diet and disease, and the first crack appeared in Ava's mind. She sat for days on the edge of her bed, as she always would when her heart was broken, and did not speak. The boy, a man now, did not know what to do. The old man let her grieve, then went into her room and led her outside, to sit on the porch. It would be grand if he had shown her some wisdom, but they just sat there, neither one talking, for a long time. They would never, none of them, live in town again.

In the trees, you did not rely on anybody in a necktie. The old man was a wizard in making something from nothing. He and the boy set trotlines in the slow creeks, bank to bank, using tossed-out bread from the few cafés and stores that were still open then, and guts from the wild game they took. They ate catfish stew, even if the catfish were the size of goldfish or the big, rank mudcats that were the size of a bateau; you threw nothing back in those days. They made dumplings from squirrel and rabbit he trapped, and he even trapped birds, with intricate, delicate snares. He combed the woods for edible plants, and guarded the garden at night, sometimes all night, with the Belgium shotgun and a handful of rocks; what he used depended on whether the thief had four legs or two. Other nights, he waded the low places with a gig taped to an old hoe handle, and laid low whole legions of frogs. He would not, though, kill snakes for the pot; maybe someday it might come to that, but not yet; the devil owned the serpents, and he would not take them into his body.

On the good days, they had hot cornbread and buttermilk with a blade of green onion as a luxury, or just cornbread and beans, with a smidgen of pork no bigger than a thumbnail, or game, for seasoning. They grew potatoes and onions in the garden, which was their salvation, and tomatoes, squash, and okra. But there was never enough, never enough seed, enough rain, enough luck.

Meanwhile, the boy chased work on the rails, braving the railroad bulls, crisscrossing the state lines of Alabama, Georgia, and Tennessee inside empty freight cars, standing in lines for day labor, while, back home, the old man scrounged and looked after his family. The two boys, his grandsons, followed the old man around like unruly puppies, and Ava told the old man not to teach them any bad habits, like chewin', smokin', cussin', and fightin', or pretty much anything else that ended in an apostrophe. The old man told her the times did not call for gentle folk, but not to worry; the boys were buck-wild, barely house-trained, and mean as scorpions, and he did not believe it was them she should worry about. They followed him into the woods and stumbled out in the evenings with their arms loaded with whatever the old man could find or chase down or hit with a rock, including blackbirds, peppergrass, and groundhogs.

As meager as their fare was, the table remained an oasis, because the old man seemed to know how to coax the most taste from the smallest, meanest amount, and it was the only place where they still laughed out loud, and joked, and sang. Then they pushed back their chairs and realized that everything outside that kitchen door was still unchanged, still bleached to hues of gray, and filmed in dusty red.

But, in a way, the old man was born for this, for a time when the world seemed at its end, and the law seemed mostly absent, or uninterested, and a man took what he could to survive.

· · ·

As he mounted the gray mule to begin his search for the wandering cow, the two little boys came tumbling out in their nightshirts and no pants; it would be years before his grandsons saw much value in pants. The three-year-old, James, with the toddler, William, trailing behind, followed as the old man rode out of the yard, as they were wont to do. The old man did not waste his breath telling them to go back; they were as hardheaded and willful as their momma, as wild as weasels, and did just as they damned well pleased, too. He dismounted, scooped up some small rocks, and threw them at the boys till they ran for the porch.

It took most of the hour, muleback, to get to Tredegar. With the cattleman's man riding beside him, talking about church politics and world politics and other things he did not care about, he found the break in the pasture fence and the tracks of the animal; cows were as easy to track through the hills as a tornado or a freight train or an African elephant. Cows were not climbers; they stuck to the easy places, the trails. Some old-timers let their hogs wander and even go feral, but no one let a thing as valuable as a cow off a rope or out of a fence or lot on purpose. What was odd was that it would wander much out of sight to begin with; cows were social, and very, very rarely ever wandered much beyond the herd, unless they went mad or were led away. He had dealt with mad cows before, usually with a brickbat.

Using a pair of pliers and a roofing hatchet, Jim and the cattleman's man patched the barbed wire, which was rusted almost through along its entirety. The cattleman's man was not much help, lacerating himself twice, cursing, getting in the way. He was not a tracker, either, and seemed to be about as sharp as a mush melon, a big, soft, easy, friendly man whose primary concern was that they might get lost in the woods and somehow miss supper. His wife would feed his supper to the dogs if he was late, a thing he told the old man at least a dozen times. By the heft of the man, it was clear he was religious about being on time.

The old man did not need much help. He followed the sign along an overgrown farm road until the cow, oddly, decided to abandon the soft roadbed for the gravel of the railroad track, where the tracks disappeared. This made no sense.

The old man slid off his mule and followed the track in the direction the cow seemed to be going, to the old Tredegar trestle. It was not exactly a great gorge, but it was the deepest one hereabouts, and little boys, for generations, had proved their courage by walking the tracks from one side to the other. Down below, the shallow water pooled around great slabs of rock.

There he found the cow, deader'n Abraham Lincoln.

The cattleman's man rode off, kicking at his mule's sides, to fetch the cattleman and some men to help hoist the carcass out of the gorge and onto higher ground, so it could be hauled off— that, or to butcher it in the gorge and pack it out. Jimmy Jim stayed behind, to guard the remains. You were talking good money here; a lot of reprobates, hungry ones, would not be above hacking off a decent portion and disappearing into the trees. In flush times, no one would have bothered with it, but in these days, you did not leave beef down a gorge for the turkey vultures and the possums and the other, two-legged opportunists.

Some while later, the cattleman and men with ropes appeared. The cattleman stood with Jim on the trestle and tried to deduce how this tragedy came to be. It seemed to him the cow had tried to cross the trestle, and had been swept off the tracks by an east- or westbound train. Such collisions happened all the time; a cow wandering onto a railroad track, especially on a blind curve, was not even much of a story anymore. It was not the collision but the location that had him flummoxed.

The cattleman had been around cows a long time, and had never known one to have such an adventurous nature that it was willing to cross the narrow trestle for no apparent reason at all.

The old man just shook his head.

"God's will," he said.

The cattleman looked surprised. He had never seen the old man in church.

It took the rest of the day to retrieve the cow from the ravine, the cattleman cursing with every heave, because he had planned to sell this cow, and a few others, any day now. Just damn bad luck, to have it take a header off a railroad trestle, and cost him a quarter of his profit, not to mention what he had to pay to drag it out of the ravine.

"God's will," the old man said again.

The cattleman supposed there were not many atheists left, with Hoover in the White House.

It had been a coarse butchering, there beside the trestle, done by amateurs; the cattleman had always hired his butchering done. His men made a mess of it, with little regard to steaks, chops, or roast, and mostly just stripped the bones. In this, the old man saw an opportunity. He accepted his meat from the cattleman, then asked him if he could also have the ribs, which were still covered with some good meat and rich fat.

The old man packed the beef home behind him on the gray mule. When he turned into the yard with it, it was like he had ridden up with a sack of silver. Beef was rich man's food. Ava cried—Ava always cried at good fortune. The old man hung the big leg of beef in the smokehouse—he would deal with it later—and went into the house with the ribs. He told his daughter-in-law to rest; her health had been poor, for months and months. He would cook their supper that night, by his lonesome.

. . .

When they walked into the little house that night for supper, the smell alone was the richest thing they had known in some time. Some of the babes had never tasted beef, even smelled it.

The old man had braised and then stewed the short ribs in salted water, slowly, in a heavy iron pot, for two hours or more, till the meat all but slipped from the bones. Then he added quartered white potatoes and halved onions, the hot, yellow kind that went sweet as they cooked, and tossed in a generous dose of black pepper. He cooked it over low heat and with little water, until the only moisture left in the bottom of the pot was the liquefied fat from the beef, and the potatoes had puffed up and come apart, and the onions had begun to caramelize in the bottom of the pot. The aroma was so sweet, so intense, it almost had a shape to it, like a fog, and it had tortured the family for those two hours or more. I would ask you to imagine it, with a truly empty belly, but most of us have never been so desperate for such food before.

He had prepared some home-canned sweet green peas with just a little salt and sugar and a pat—well, a block—of homemade butter, baked a small, crisp skillet of cornbread, and prepared a massive bowl of slaw with white cabbage and carrot. He did not drown the cabbage with the dressing, putting just enough in to taste, and dusted it with black pepper, too, but no salt. Fresh food, of any kind, was a blessing; only a fool would cover such a thing in salt, and he was a man who damn near prayed to salt. Besides, he said, a meal this fine, built around meat this rich, a cook did not have to tart it up much to make it taste like something grand. Potatoes, onions, cabbage, peas, even mayonnaise, were cheap, available. But beef, now . . . It was the best meal the people around the table had had in years.

They rose from the table, all of them, as if slightly drunk, wobbled, somehow, by the richness of the food, like there was a drug in it. A whole land hurtin', and the old man fed them short ribs.

"How . . . ?" the boy asked him.

"Fell out the sky," the old man said, which was at least partly true.

. . .

Some years would go by before the damnedest story began to circulate in this part of the world, but it never had much traction, and became swallowed up inside all the other lies and hogwash spread by all the chuckleheads here about the bad ol' days, and what the people had to do to survive them. It was about a bone-thin old man in a slouch hat who was spotted leading a cow across the railroad trestle near Tredegar, when every fool in the county knew the westbound to Birmingham was due on that trestle, just about any time.

. . .

Beef Short Ribs, Potatoes, and Onions

If you have selected good meat, this dish needs no beef stock, no wine, no thickeners for flavor. Just about every culture has some version of it, but this is the simplest, yet richest, I know.

WHAT YOU WILL NEED

7 or 8 beef short ribs, as meaty as possible
1 smidgen bacon grease, or 1 tablespoon cooking oil
1 tablespoon salt
8 medium-sized white or golden potatoes, quartered
4 medium yellow onions (or 2 large ones), quartered
½ teaspoon sugar (no more)
1 teaspoon black pepper

HOW TO COOK IT

Select short ribs that have a good amount of fat and lean. Lean ribs will not provide the flavor, and some short ribs are carved so close to the bone that there is really nothing left but soup bones. Shorter ribs are easier to work with, so have the butcher cut them if need be. The more fat the short ribs have, of course, the better, and more succulent, this will be.

In a large pot—my mother says you will need a thick, sturdy one for this—melt just a tad of bacon grease or about a tablespoon of cooking oil in the bottom of the pot, then lightly brown the ribs on both sides, just enough to give them a slight color and a little sizzle. Cover the ribs with water, and bring it to a slow boil over no more than medium heat. Add the tablespoon of salt at this point. You can add salt later, to taste, if needed, but be careful. This dish is so rich you do not want to make it salty, too.

It seems a universal point in my mother's recipes, but, again, the secret, the whole ambition, is to cook this dish with no more water than is necessary, or you will wind up with a watery, bland stew. Pay close attention to the cooking, and as you add water, add as little as possible to keep the ingredients from sticking and burning. This is the key to the castle in Southern mountain cooking, in so many dishes.

Over medium heat—or less, depending on your stove—cook for about 1½ hours. Add the potatoes, onions, sugar, and black pepper, and cook another 20 to 30 minutes, or until the potatoes have just begun to come apart, the onions have begun to slightly, slightly caramelize in the beef fat, and—and this is most important—there is little or no liquid left in the pot. All the good stuff from the rich beef ribs should have evaporated into the potatoes and onions, and a lovely, clear tallow should have formed in the bottom of the pot.

Some people like a hint of garlic in this, and some of my people toss in ¼ teaspoon minced garlic, or a good couple of shakes of granulated garlic, but absolutely no more. Believe it or not, in a dish so rich, the garlic can mask some of the finer flavors.

You can, at the end, slightly raise the heat, and finish it, stirring to keep it from burning, to cook out the last of the liquid, and to get that lovely, just-right texture to the potatoes and the color in the onions.

The potatoes should be flaky, almost puffy. The onion should be all but melted away, though any whole pieces left will be delicious. The beef will be fork-tender, and rich.

"The beef will be good and done, and some of the fat should have melted off the ribs, and you can slip the bones right out of 'em, easy, if you want to. But you don't want no water, no real liquid at all, except what has melted off the beef ribs. But this is also where you have to be real, real careful not to let it burn."

Just as Jimmy Jim did with the original dish, serve this with cornbread, carrot-and-cabbage slaw, and a side of sweet peas or green beans, fresh if possible, or home-canned. Be sure to season both with a little salt and some butter.

I asked her if there was a secret she was not telling me, since my version of the dish is always a little lacking.

"I have put a little pat of butter in the pot of beef and taters, right at the very end. You know, just a little, little-bitty pat."

"So you cheat?" I said.

·   ·   ·

We call it just that, beef and taters, a vernacular that reaches back to a time in our family history when it really was the only beef my people had, when butchers would save the rib bones for poor men and women who came for scraps, in the worst of times. The ribs in the dish have gotten some good bit fatter and richer since then. Now, when I eat this at my mother's table, even if I eat sparingly, I rise from my chair with that strange, drunken feeling I had been told about, as if I had savored a glass of brown whiskey, as if there really is some kind of spirit in it, in the taste itself. But that is foolish, of course.

·   ·   ·

The old man left them, not long after that.

He told the girl, a young woman now, to try to remember as much of it as she could. After a few years, she would not have to try. She would just know it all, like the words to a prayer, or a song.

He was not a warm and hopeful man, but he wished them well, and just walked away.

He would say, now and then, that if he had known how hard

times would get, he might have stayed. But no one guessed how hard, or how long.

"I can't really remember him that much, because I was so small, but Momma talked about him so much sometimes I forget and I think I did," my mother said. He left her father and mother's house before she was born. "I heard my momma and daddy talk about him when they cooked, and Momma would say things, sometimes, about cooking with him, and I'd ask her how she knew this thing, or that thing, and she'd say, 'Oh, because your grandpa said so,' and so it was kind of like he was with us, you know? It was like he was still there in the kitchen with us. I know what he looked like, from that one picture we had, and I know the things he said, and how he cooked, because it's how Momma cooked, and so it's how I cook, too. Of all the stuff I cook, it's that old stuff, the oldest stuff, it seems like people remember the most." She still thinks of him, and his pupil, when she reaches for the saltshaker, and the pepper, and the bacon grease . . . even sometimes when she touches a hot pan, or the hot handle of those old steel spoons, which he touched in another time. So I guess some of our kin were right about that, when they damned him all to hell. The old man returned to the fire after all.

.   .   .

He had one chapter left to write in his life, or at least have written for him, after he walked out the door of the house that last time. He met and married a lovely young woman, which was the custom there for old widowers like him, and it is said that he treated the woman well, and that he might have been happy for a while. But he lost her, and a baby girl, soon after their marriage, in childbirth. The life just went out of him then, my people remember, as so much of the meanness had before.

He would, in his last days, remarry yet again, and even father another child before he died. He is buried across the state line in Summerville, Georgia, where there are still no warrants out on him, I suppose.

. . .

I heard all about him there at the foot of the bed, and in my grandma's kitchen, which always smelled of tea cakes and frying chicken and sometimes Bruton snuff. But her mind always seemed to loosen somehow at night, and she lay awake with three or four quilts pulled to her chin and a daub of Juicy Fruit stuck on the bedpost, with me curled up on the foot of the bed like some small dog. We listened to her AM radio, the one with the missing dial that you had to tune with a pair of needle-nosed pliers or by slipping a dime into the notch in the grooved post. We mostly just left it alone, and listened to the *Grand Ole Opry*, and wrestling from Boutwell Auditorium, and preachers who convinced me that I was pretty well predestined to burn in hell. As it played, she talked, and talked, and talked. She did not mention the mean ol' man every night, but it was odd how often he would become entangled in the fairy tales and tall tales and memories she told to me, so often that I was greatly surprised, when I was older, to find that he was flesh and blood, that he was, at least mostly, real.

She loved my grandfather, and of this we have no doubt, though, if you believe *his* stories, she had once tried to starve him to death. But I came to realize, when I was a little older, that it was the old man who had become what they called a kindred spirit, and so became, in time, her one great, true friend.

By second or third grade, I was too old to sleep there at the foot of the bed like a baby and moved across the hall, to a bed of my own. But I could still hear her when her mind wandered, hear her pad through the tiny house, into the kitchen, and sometimes call his name.

8

"HARD TIMES, COME AROUND NO MORE"

Sweet Potato Pie, Sweet Potato Cobbler

My uncle Jimbo, keeping the world safe for democracy

CHARLIE BUNDRUM waded through a wide field of yellow broom sage with the seat of his overalls eaten out by hard times and asbestos shingles, but the double-barreled 12-gauge in his hands gleamed with good oil and loving attention, and the stock shone like new money. Through it all, the Belgium gun had never failed, never been dropped, never misfired, not since the time of the Yankee war. Jim left it to him when he disappeared into the mountains one last time, riding off in his funeral black, and this time he would not return. He did not make any ritual of it, and made no speeches. He did not even hand it to his boy. He just left it propped behind the door when he left, as if he had forgotten it there somehow. Still, it was a fine gun.

The gangly boy had not yet fully disappeared inside this lean, hawk-faced man, but the times had ground him down a bit. He cradled the Belgium in his left arm, the barrel resting across his forearm, so that he could slide his right hand into the curved grip, slip his finger into the trigger guard, and snug the stock into his shoulder with one smooth, clean motion. He had loaded the gun with bird shot, for the pasture and tall broom sage and other, clearer places where they might scare up a bird, but had a few loose shells loaded with buckshot and big lead punkin balls in the pockets of his canvas work shirt, for something bigger. He was not hunting for anything special, just anything at all for the cook-pot; he would have run down a groundhog if he had seen one. The Depression still had its teeth in them now, good and deep, and in the fall of 1933, a poor man with a family to feed did not get to be particular.

But even in such grim times, he hated to be without his blood. It must have appeared an unusual hunting party that autumn day. My grandfather walked a few steps ahead of his raggedy gun-bearers, the Belgium pointed safely away, so as not to shoot his progeny. He was flanked by raggedy miniatures of himself, almost identical little boys in almost identical worn-through overalls, one boy lugging a rusty, ancient .22 rifle with a cracked stock wrapped in black electrician's tape, the other stumbling, whispering curses as he dragged a crusty, bloodstained burlap game bag. Jim had left the family with more than recipes and one good gun; the boys could curse with words they did not even yet understand, and were prone, now and then, to thievery. But they were Charlie's, and he liked to have them at his side.

They were begrimed, scabbed over, and skinny, kicking up dust for the joy of it, yammering underneath woolen peaked caps so moth-eaten and decrepit they seemed about to disintegrate upon their burr heads. Their pockets bulged with hickory nuts, for throwing at mailboxes, squirrels, their little sister, and each other. The fact they had made it this far with two eyes apiece Ava could only lay at the throne of God. If they had lived in a city, people would have called them delinquents, urchins; in the hills, there was no adequate name for them. Just that month, they had crawled under a neighbor's house and used a brace and bit to drill through the floorboards and into the bottom of a five-gallon whiskey barrel, then lay on their backs to gulp the dripping liquor and giggle till they were both as tight as Dick's hatband and unable to walk home. Charlie had to carry them back, one on each shoulder. The county might have taken them, but the county wanted no part of it. James, the oldest boy, was seven years old, and William was six.

"Hush," he told them, for the hundredth time.

This time he put some edge to it, and glared that glare, which, I guess, he also inherited.

The ragamuffins went sullenly silent.

There were four children now. Juanita, the baby, had come just that year. Right then, Charlie Bundrum would have swapped any two of them for a good bird dog. He never had a good one, at least one that his children remember. Bird hunting, in his time, was a rich man's thing. So he made do with a coonhound, a redbone that had never pointed at anything in his life except a gravy-and-biscuit. But the big, sloppy dog flushed game by pure accident. He blundered, crashing, through the dry, brittle sage, not altogether sure what he was looking for, and quail and doves would explode into the air with that rustling, whirring noise, and Charlie would snug the shining wood of the stock into his shoulder and pull twice—left barrel, right barrel—and the birds would fold their wings in onto their bodies and fall from the sky. The boys would drop their burdens into the dirt and bolt after the birds, because if the hound got there first he would snatch one up and run off to eat it at his leisure, growling if the boys tried to take it from him, usually on the front porch. Still, together, they all got the job done, somehow.

Sometimes, mostly by accident, the clumsy dog would flush rabbits from the sage, and Charlie would track them with the blue steel of the barrel, though there was little meat there, just a good start for dumplings, or porridge, or a good soup for the children. It seemed, these days, even the wild things were skin and bone. Now and then, the dog would tree a squirrel, and Charlie would reach for the busted-up single-shot .22. It was cheaper; there was no profit in swapping a shotgun shell for a plate of damn bony squirrel.

Sometimes the big dog would run a deer back toward them, not on purpose, just by providence, and if Charlie's aim was good, he would knock it down. But in hard times, the deer had thinned, too, thinned to the point where he could go weeks without seeing one, or even finding sign of them. Most days, what he brought home was just enough, just a few mouthfuls, spread around his growing family. But Ava and her husband could do wonders with next to nothing, as she built on the recipes, the foundation, that the old man had left. On the fat days, they treed a possum or a coon, and Charlie would not waste a shell at all. He would send the little boys up the tree with a hatchet or a stick and a sack, and Ava would cook it with sweet potatoes. She had not been wild about possum, but came to tolerate it over time.

In the evenings, by firelight, her husband cooked, too. He cooked in the trees, coaxing a clear potion from a snake of copper line, drop by drop, from corn he grew himself, and fed the fermented leavings to his hog. The old man had shown him that, too. He worked all day, nailing down shingles in the hundred-degree heat, when there was work, or dug ditches, or did anything he could find, and in the cool of the evening he went up the mountain in the dark and worked until dawn, tending his mash, running off his liquor. He would go days without sleep, then sleep a day straight through. He never made much, but made enough for a few groceries, with some left over to drink, to ease his own worried mind. (There is no recipe in this book for corn liquor. I have tasted prison food, and do not want to do three-to-seven eating lunch meat and beets and working in the prison library for Baby Ruth money.) Ava cursed him for taking such a risk with all their lives, but he told her it was that or go hungry. He said it would be fine. He believed it would.

In the sage, the clumsy dog thumped and blundered and scared up what seemed a whole covey of quail, at their feet. Charlie swiveled and fired almost without thinking. Two birds, what the rich men called "a double," tumbled down, and the boys whooped and took off after them, in a dead heat with the hound.

"Our luck might be changin'," he said, as they headed home.

He was right about that.

. . .

At the house, Ava dressed the birds, fried them, and made biscuits and milk gravy. Even the children were quiet as they ate, except for the smacking. "We got to have more than a few mouthfuls of bird, now and agin," he told her. They had put up as much of their garden as they could spare, but that, too, would dwindle in cold weather.

On the days there was no work, not even a line to stand in, he walked or rode his mule deeper and deeper into the mountains to hunt. On long trips, hoping for deer, he left the boys and clumsy dog at home—no telling how much game he had lost with their help. He still-hunted, moving quietly in the trees, and sometimes, when he found a trail and some positive sign, he hoisted himself into the trees and waited, and waited, sometimes falling asleep, the sling on the Belgium wrapped once around his wrist to keep it from slipping from his grasp and falling to the ground. It had never been on the ground, except to lean on a tree or a fence post.

He had taken to carrying a short board, like the seat on a child's swing, with him when he hunted deer, and would fix it across two limbs with cord to sit and shoot from, or sometimes just to nap in, above all the misery below. The problem was that every other raggedy, hungry man in the foothills of the Appalachians had much the same idea, and he saw more men, even in these high, isolated places, than he saw deer or any other game, except maybe the gray squirrels. Now and then, he would ride or stride past the broken-down slats of another hog pen, and he would think of his daddy, and wonder if he might see another feral hog blunder past, or, in desperate times, a hog of any kind. But Charlie had inherited at least some of his sweet mother's conscience, and none of the old man's sense of humor about property, about "borrowing" things that could not be returned, or letting them follow him home just in time for supper.

But such a hog as the one he had seen crashing through the deep brush that day, years ago, would be a godsend. Such a beast would have begotten others, which would have begotten others, in the intervening years. With all this begetting, in such a wild and distant place, there should be a lot of pork huffing and rooting around up in those deep mountains, good pork that did not belong to anybody, as far as he could figure.

He had heard stories of them, of feral hogs the size of milk cows, living in those mountains, getting fat on hickory nuts and persimmons and whatever they could root—not common, but real.

One night, after fried cornbread patties and a little buttermilk, he lingered long once the dishes had been put away, telling her his plans. As he talked, he packed some cold biscuit, a wool army-surplus blanket, and all his shells, even the bird shot. If he could get close, he would beat it to death with his bare hands if there was a pork chop in it.

"I may scare up a deer, too," he told Ava.

"You may fall off that mountain and make me a widder," she said.

He tried to pat her, but she would not allow it. Ava was against it, no matter what he said. Ava's strategy in life was to be against everything, or almost everything, proposed by the men and boys in her life. Though she was a wonderfully tough woman, she was not necessarily a brave one when it came to some things, and the hard times had touched her soul and broken her a bit inside. She was a little like one of those chickens: if you were afraid of everything, then you just couldn't help being afraid of the right things sooner or later.

"It won't keep," she said, of the pork—or any game, really—he might kill. It would take two days, longer to ride into the mountains, and two days back, if he ever came back.

"You could snag a rich man whilst I'm gone," he told her.

"No one will have me with them hellions," she said of her boy children.

She said they would have to join the circus. The boys could bite heads off things. They would do it now if supper was running late, and if they could run something down.

Her husband said he would only be gone a few days. As soon as he scared something up, he said, he would dress it in the woods, even smoke it there if he had to, and hurry home.

"You'll get et," she said.

"The bears is gone," he said, "and just about all the panthers, too."

"Not the hogs," she said. "The hogs is still there. You done told me." She had a fear of hogs, for it was a known fact that a big feral hog, or a pen of domestic ones if they were hungry enough, would devour a man right down to his boot heels.

The deep mountains scared her, naturally. City people think all the people here were the same, but they never understood the distinction. There were country people, and then there were mountain people. Ava believed the worst. There had also been stories that some of the people in the high-up were not particular as to their diet, either. The deep hills, like the bottom of the sea, pulled at the imagination, and the truth was, she was more afraid of the people he would encounter than the beasts he might find. The hard times had made the mean people meaner, more desperate, and the people in the deep-back made the country people here seem like the Junior League. The people there believed they owned everything under the moon and stars, with or without deeds and fences, and some of them had been there since the first criminals rattled ashore to found the thirteenth colony. They lived by the feud and married only within their clan, and recognized no government; they had ignored the British, the colonials, the Confederacy, the New Testament, and the state legislature.

They had left Jimmy Jim alone, she and Charlie believed, because he was more like them than he was like the people below, and because he kept so completely to himself. He had not fled there despite these people; he had fled there because of them, because they just seemed to know when a stranger's footfall sounded, however softly, in the leaves and weeds and uncut forest, and did not tolerate visitors.

In the morning, before daybreak, she stood on the porch, wringing her hands inside her apron. She would do this, the same way, for all her life. She never took her apron off, except for church. Charlie waved as he rode off, but he did not expect a wave in return. She would be mad forever about this one specific thing, this day, and never forgot it. You could not pile up enough good memories around a thing, enough fine times, so that she could not find it now and then, and prick her finger on the splinter hidden there.

Again he guided the mule into the high places, and again he avoided the smoke and the glow of the whiskey fires. This time, he did not sing out; better to move without attracting any attention, better to hope to slip by, than confront a man before he had taken so much as a ground squirrel. He rode quietly, humming low to the mule. The gray mule liked a little music, till it tried to fling you into the hereafter, or kick your brains out. Faulkner would be right about mules; they really would wait patiently for a lifetime for the opportunity to kick you once—to death, they hoped. The gray was a saddle mule in the sense that it could be ridden, if it felt like it, but only with great care, and never, ever trusted.

The old man had shown him how to track, how to read signs, though he was not exactly the last of the Mohicans. He could find deer, and wild hogs made a clear trail, rooting and trampling. Many of them started tame, escaped, and went wild, and their very physiology changed, like a bad dream. They got leaner and meaner, and their tusks grew and curved. One day, they would trample the landscape underfoot; they were still part meat and part myth at that time, and it was hard to tell if a hog up here was feral or just loose.

But, though he saw the world's densest concentration of squirrel, and heard the crash of deer antlers in the distance, he did not encounter any large game, neither deer nor hog. When he finally did, it was not so much that he found it as that it just materialized, like some kind of magic, at the worst possible time.

As he told it, it was a comedy of errors from start to finish, so bad there was no way to color it to make himself look any more than a witless victim in a string of events in which he was almost killed, first by an invisible snake, then by the mule, then by an illegal hog, and, finally, by the mountain itself. "The only thing I didn't do," he conceded, "was shoot myself."

He remembered how the mule had reacted to the big hog when he came here to fetch his daddy, so in the dense brush, where the trees and weeds closed in on the trail itself, he dismounted and led the animal, wrapping the leather reins around his fist. That was probably unwise, but he had the feeling that, if they were to part company, the mule would run all the way home to Alabama and he would die of old age before he hiked out of these hills. Or, if he were to let his imagination run loose, he feared he would find the mule turning on a spit in someone's yard as he trudged, hungry, back down the mountain in his shoe leather.

He and the mule had stopped at a natural rock spring and were drinking from the cold, clear water when he smelled the musk of a snake; what kind he did not know, because he never saw it, but it was a warm day for early fall, and he feared the serpents might still be out. The mule, suddenly wild-eyed, must have smelled it, too, and spun a perfect 360 degrees, bucking, with the young man's hand still wrapped in the reins, dragging him across the rocky ground. He dropped the Belgium in the water and mud, and banged his hip and head against the rocks before he could get the damn thing settled down. He would have beaten the mule, but that seemed like a damn-fool thing to do to an animal on the edge of a mountainside and a nervous breakdown. He got the beast calmed enough so it would stand and quiver, so he could at least tie it to a sapling, and tried, with murder in his heart, to locate the snake that had caused all this grief. It had apparently slithered off elsewhere, to soak up the sun on one of the last warm days of the year.

He surveyed his wounds. He had a cut on his head and a bruise the size of a mush melon on the point of his bony hip. But, worse, the lovely Belgium was befouled with mud. His daddy had never dropped it, or even laid it flat on the ground, at least not that he could recall.

The mule, except for its nerves, was unhurt. Charlie would wonder, after that, if there even was a snake, but Ava, who knew everything, would tell him that, though a man's mind, imagination, and even his hearing might play tricks on him, his sense of smell was usually dead-on. So, if he smelled a snake, it was a snake. Besides, a mule is not capable of imagining *anything*. Mules are as dumb as doornails but smart like that.

He sat on a big rock to clean the gun, and it was while he was running a rag through the barrels with a green stick that he heard it—heard not a squeal or a snort but a soft, deep, huffing noise, somewhere in the leaves close by.

The great hog, which should have run to Chattanooga after the mêlée involving the mule, stood unconcerned some fifty feet away—it was hard to tell in the thick brush—rooting in the just-fallen leaves and mud. It was hard to tell its size, too, so far away, but it was a true hog, rusty red in color, thicker in the shoulders and leaner in the hips and belly than the domestic hogs, or so it seemed to the boy. One day, to make it sound more exotic, people would call them wild boars; it was still just a souped-up hog, just bacon, ham, and sausage, and a whole lot of it, from what he could tell.

He quietly and quickly clicked the two pieces of the shotgun back together, pleading with the mule, under his breath, to keep quiet just once, then, after slipping a lead slug and a buckshot shell into his shotgun, he began to ease closer. Jim had taught him a trick to hunting anything in the deep woods with a shotgun, which was only worth a damn if you could get close enough. Figure your path as quick as you can, Jim had said, figure the tripping vines, stumps, dead branches, anything in your way, then snug the gun to your shoulder and take some rough aim on your beast; now close in, trying to remember your path. Raise your feet high, instead of shuffling them in the dry leaves. Your sights would wobble, of course, as you moved, but you would still be faster, and more on point than some fool who tried to watch his feet, glance up to relocate his game, throw the gun to his shoulder, and squeeze. You might stumble, might trip, even kill a tree or two by accident, but a man with a shotgun had to get close to do any good. A 12-gauge was not much count, the old man had warned, beyond the length of a bad intention.

He did get close, close enough to see it was about two hundred pounds or more of good meat, and it was like the thing wanted to die, it ignored him so. Then, like something from a bad dream, it snorted a warning, fixed him with its beady eyes, and ran, not away, but straight at him. His legs atremble, he knocked it down with the punkin ball, which is a little like shooting your game with an express train, and finished it, he believed, with a blast from the double-ought buck. It was too close to miss, he would later say.

He was pretty full of himself, standing there with his empty gun over this big, fierce creature. Then it shook and snorted and heaved, and he almost killed himself getting away. He caught his pants leg on a broken, dying trash tree, fell hard for the second time that day, and damn near drove a stob through his palm, but held his gun above his head. He trained his empty gun on the hog, futile, and *then* it elected to die.

One leg of his overalls was ripped half away—where the hog had tried to cut him, he wanted to believe, but, shamefully, he had to admit he had only been attacked by a tree. By some small miracle, he was only scratched up a little bit, and he just had to sit and shake awhile before going to work on his prize. It took him two solid hours, maybe three, to do the rough work of it all. He was trying to decide whether to take the head home with him— not from vanity but because there was good meat in it—when he noticed the ear.

Someone had notched it, neatly, with a sharp knife, probably when it was just a piglet or shoat. The V-shaped notch was how some of the old-timers identified their livestock, like a brand, usually after cutting them to make the meat better. Then they just turned them loose, and let the grubs, roots, and acorns feed them until it was time to harvest the meat. He had heard of it from Jim, and had believed the practice had faded. Whatever had happened, this hog had not been cut; he was somebody's boar, or at least he had been.

He had shot some man's property; there was no way around it, he was a thief. He could have let it rot in the woods and fled down the mountain, but decided that would be twice a crime. He decided he would pack it out on the mule, and if anyone confronted him, he would tell them what had happened, and tell the truth, and try to make it right if he could. Larceny, of any kind, was not in him; somehow, that tendency passed him by.

He would have felt better about it if it had happened down below. But these people lived up here for a reason. He had about a hundred pounds of fresh pork behind his saddle, their pork; if he made it down the mountain, it would be a miracle, and he had never been a praying man.

Still, he almost made it. He was half a day from the state line, maybe a little more, when he rode through a bottleneck cut and saw two singular men lounging in the path, as if they had been waiting for him, and maybe they had. They were not what Hollywood would have cast as hillbillies. They were not passing a ceramic jug around, or scratching themselves; not shirtless and barefoot, or garbed in rags with one gallus dangling. They were lean, hard-looking men, clean-shaven, in fresh-washed overalls, their shirts buttoned to the neck. One had a lever-action rifle swinging easily in one hand. They were hatless and beardless, or he might have guessed Mennonites. Whoever they were, this was their mountain.

The old man had raised him to be a fighter, but, as bad as things were in his house, he hated to kill, or die, for a hog. He raised the Belgium just a bit, but as the men approached him, he saw the man with the rifle step away from the other, to put some space between the two, as the other man, calm as you please, conjured a short-barreled shotgun, a rabbit gun, from behind what seemed thin air. They did not threaten him in any way, unless you count looking hard.

"Fellers," young Charlie said, "I reckon this is your hog."

The men had the look of his daddy about them, unsmiling, curt.

"Thangs be bad down yonder?" one of them asked.

He just nodded.

They left him some of the pork, which was more than he expected, a shank and one small piece of side meat, all the feet, and—he reckoned as a joke—the notched ear. They told him not to come back and shoot no more wandering livestock, and it might be best if he never came back at all. He tipped his hat and rode off with cold sweat running down his back, rode all the rest of the way home slouched in the saddle, miserable, beaten, weary, and sore, but not mad, for, as he would later admit, he was in the wrong. He lacked the outright cussedness his daddy had to be wrong and righteous at the same time.

As he rode into the yard, Ava was sitting on the porch, her face bleak. Some days, bad luck is all there is.

She did not wait to hear his story; such foolishness could wait. She told him the sheriff had been by the day before to take him to jail. He had papers on him, not for making liquor, but for packing it out of the woods for another man, for wages. The sheriff told her to tell him to come into town, d'rectly, and turn himself in. He said it would only be four months or so, maybe six months on the outside, if the judge was not a hard-hearted son of a bitch. But it would be more, much more, if they had to chase him down.

It looked like civilization had decided to include them, after all.

"We'll starve," Ava had told the sheriff, and the man did not meet her gaze. And for some reason, that scared her to death, maybe because his offering no argument meant that it might actually be true.

She took the bloody burlap bag from him, and said nothing about its being so light.

"You should eat," she said, "afore you go."

He had no stomach for it, and just stepped inside to change. He had two pairs of overalls and two ragged shirts to his name. He put on the worst of them—he might be living in it for months if they kept him in the county prison, and there was no point in wasting good clothes. If they kept him in county, he would be shoveling sand or gravel across hot tar, or cutting brush, or loaned out as contract labor to a rich man.

He had not unsaddled the tired mule. He climbed up, and pulled the oldest boy up behind him. It was too far to walk to the county seat, and James could ride the mule home when they locked him away. There was no money for a fine, even if that had been an option, and no need for a lawyer. He was twice guilty: of hauling liquor, and of being too poor to get out of it. He would have to do whatever time the judge handed down.

As they rode to town, he told James he and William could take the Belgium out every day to hunt, but he shouldn't shoot unless he was sure, sure of a deer, a possum, or a coon. There were only a few shells left, and Charlie warned him not to waste them on birds, except maybe a turkey—not enough return on the price of the shell, he told the boy, for a mere bird. Best to use the .22, he said, when he could. He had a tobacco tin full of .22s at the house.

They would have to hire themselves out, him and his brother William, to any farmer who would have them. They might get fed, at least, but he told James to take any wages they might earn home to their momma, and not be tempted to buy hard candy or bubble gum or cigarettes; he knew his boys. They would have to see to the garden. With Edna, who could outwork either one of them, they would need to plant, hoe, and harvest—potatoes and corn especially, but also tomatoes, squash, onions, okra, and water-melons, to sell if they could. Feed any scrap to the hog. And walk the neighbors' fields, after their harvest, for any corn or anything else they had missed, like some late-season melons. "They won't care," he said.

"Do what you can, and don't worry about school," he said, as if either of the boys had worried about it much to start with.

Then, almost as an afterthought:

"Try not to steal nothin', if you can."

Ava did not tell him, as he rode away with the boy gripping him around the middle, that the few handfuls of flour she had scraped together for biscuit dough were the last in the house, the last of pretty much everything. She had a little lard, a little sugar, some spices, and some milk and butter—thank God for the cow. She did not tell him that there was no money, none, in the house.

She did not even tell him I told you so.

William, Edna, and Juanita, who was still toddling, stood with her on the porch. When her man and boy passed from sight, she picked up the small, bloody bundle of meat and threw it as far into the yard as she could, then, after a second or two, sent the little boy, William, to fetch it back to her. They would put it in salt, or hang it to smoke, tomorrow.

. . .

The next year, '34, seemed more like legend than anything else, from a safe distance. My brother Sam, who is older but whose memory is better than mine, remembers sitting with my uncles and aunts and other kin who were just little children in that time, listening to them tell what it was like to be hungry, not just late for supper, but hungry. What he remembers most was the old fear in their voices, and how raw it seemed, even after so much time. Whole careers had passed, mortgages had been paid, children raised, and even a little money saved in the bank, but, even though they were sitting in a warm house, far and safe away, at a table that sagged with food, it seemed just outside the door. "They said they'd walk through a cornfield and pick through the stalks on the ground," he said. "They'd gather the cotton that didn't open, and prize it out and throw the husk in the fire, and sell just that least little bit of cotton back to people, or try to do it."

"I was born after this," my mother said, "and I was glad of it. In my whole life, myself, I never remember being really, really hungry. I mean not truly hungry, where it gnawed on you. But I missed the worst of it, what Momma and James and William and Edna, and I guess Juanita, all went through, though I guess Juanita was too little then to tell much about what was happenin'. That was when Daddy was gone the longest, when they sent him off."

The relatives who had a little extra helped when they could; they gave a limp sack of flour or meal, or some end pieces of bacon, and a few potatoes, or a sack of okra. Ava became farm labor in a time when people were being told not to grow cotton in the first place; there was no market, no need. She became a house servant for people who could barely pay their own bills and paid her in pocket change. She took in sewing, and made quilts to sell till there were no scraps or rags left to piece them together from. In the summer, she hired out to chop cotton for the few farmers who put it in the ground; in September, she hired out again, to pick it. But it was never enough. The boys tried to be the fishermen and hunters that their daddy was, and failed. They were just too small, all of them, to be much help then, but they dragged sacks beside their mother when the season came. It was hard times for everyone, of course, but harder with a man in jail, which was like being a widow till the parole came through. The old people sang about deliverance across the rows, but Ava did not have much hope left anymore. Things had been so bad for so long, it seemed not an aberration, a thing to survive, but just the way it was and would be.

The songs Ava sang that had always been an escape, a way to lift her spirits, were now a prayer.

Let us pause in life's pleasure and count its many tears
While we all sup sorrow with the poor
There's a song that will linger forever in our ears
Oh, hard times, come again no more

The garden did not do well without Charlie's expertise. They ate what they called "poor'do" five days a week. Ava baked a pan of cornbread for one meal, then saved any leftover bread for the evening meal, mixing it with anything and everything to give it taste—the juice from poke salad, greens, boiled back meat, lard, sorghum, whatever they had. She mixed it with water, and baked or boiled it. They were down to two laying hens, and guarded them like gold; there was no broth anymore, so there was none of the golden porridge the old man had made. Children around them grew sick from scurvy and dysentery, but by some small miracle all Ava's surviving children were spared. She would grieve every single day for the rest of her life, but found a terrible joy in the fact it was just the one, just the one.

The two boys, James and William, took on work with their uncle Newt, who seemed immune to the Crash of '29 and the awful decade that followed. He owned his own land and made a good living farming, with a big field of corn, a pasture full of cattle, a pen full of hogs, and a smokehouse full of meat. They peeked inside it when old Newt went inside the house, and day after day they thought the old man might give them a little of his largesse to take home to their momma, but he did not.

He paid them, a quarter or so now and then, enough for their mother to buy beans, enough to keep them alive. At night, they told stories of the smokehouse, of the slabs of white meat in salt and the big hams slowly, slowly melting, dripping, curing in the smoke, and it seemed like something from a fairy tale. They feasted on it in their dreams, night by night. They feasted on it, and suffered.

The one thing they always seemed to have was sweet potatoes. It was a grand year for sweet potatoes, which flourished in the ground of their garden and in the gardens of their neighbors. At the little country stores, sweet potatoes spilled out of the bins, thousands and thousands of them. Ava roasted hundreds of them, as Jim had shown her, both in the baking box and nudged up against the hot coals in the fireplace. The children did not whine. The older ones were too wise as to what was happening around them, and the littler ones were too hungry.

One day, Ava found herself staring into the small spice rack in her kitchen, at the simple things the mean old man had taught her about seasoning. They were covered in dust now, the vanilla flavoring with its lid glued almost shut by age, the cinnamon, an ancient little tin of nutmeg. Her man had been gone less than a year, but it seemed like she was beginning to forget much of what the old man had taught her about the joy of food, the pleasure in eating. She was ashamed of herself.

The worst of it was, the children's ignorance of their situation was being scrubbed away, day by day, meal by meal.

She had only a little flour left, enough for about one pan of biscuit, or . . . She had butter, and milk, and a little sugar and molasses, which the children ate sometimes with their biscuit. And she had a fifty-pound sack of excellent sweet potatoes.

"What we gon' have for supper, Momma?" the boys asked her, not knowing how such a simple question could cut in those days.

It occurred to her, breaking her heart, that the children, even as young as they were, had learned not to trust that she could put good food on the table anymore.

"Well," she said, "I figure we'll have pie."

"Just pie?

"Just pie."

And the rejoicing began.

She decided to make not one but two, since she had sweet potatoes till the end of the world. She baked her sweet potatoes, about three pounds or so, not in the baking box but in the fireplace itself, right alongside the coals, and you could actually see the sugar in them blister out, from the heat. This, she believed, was how you could tell you had good sweet potatoes. Ava let them cool, then set the children to peeling them as she saw to her ingredients.

There was no canned milk in the house—sweetened, condensed, evaporated milk was essential for pies—so she tried a little experiment. She melted her butter, a hunk as big as her fist for the two pies, into fresh milk, with a little molasses, smidgens of nutmeg and cinnamon, and a big dollop of vanilla flavoring. She mashed the sweet potatoes, whipped in the sweetened, flavored milk, and put them on to bake inside a biscuit dough shell. She did not bake the pies till they were done so much as she baked them as long as she could, before the children, who were hopping and whining in anticipation, burst into flame.

The boys eschewed forks and even plates, and each ate a quarter-pie in about three bites.

"Lord, you didn't even taste it," she said.

"I'll taste that other'n," William said.

If it had come down to one single last piece, there would have been blood.

But supper comes every day, and the next night came the inevitable question. This time she just ignored them, and went out to the porch to sit in a straight-back chair as if she simply had not heard.

"Momma?" Edna said.

"Yes, child?" she said.

"What we gonna eat?"

"Well," she said, "how about some cobbler?"

"Just cobbler?"

"Just cobbler."

And the rejoicing commenced again.

She had been meaning to try something new. If blackberries, cherries, and apples could make a fine cobbler, why not sweet potatoes? She baked, again, about three pounds of them, but this time took them away from the fire after only a half-hour or so. She peeled them and cut them into big chunks, the sweet potatoes firmer this time, then poured the chunks into a deep pan, and added about a half-pound of cold butter, also in chunks. Then she sprinkled on a little cinnamon.

Finally, she made a batter of flour, the last of her sugar, a little molasses to stretch it out, and vanilla flavoring, and poured it onto the top of the semi-cooked sweet potatoes instead of crafting a dough for a crust. She baked it until the crust was golden and the potatoes had steamed in their own natural sugar and soaked in the generous portion of butter.

She served it while it was still hot, in big mounds. At least, this time, the children had to use plates. They pronounced it delicious, and pronounced that their momma, if perhaps a little moody, was the greatest momma who ever was. What other momma would feed her children dessert for supper two days in a row, with leftover pie and cobbler for breakfast, and sometimes dinner? This, surely, was the greatest momma, the greatest cook, in the world.

Sweet Potato Pie

WHAT YOU WILL NEED

1 to 1¼ pounds fresh sweet potatoes
  (not canned)
1 can (12 ounces) sweetened condensed milk
¾ cup granulated sugar
¼ cup brown sugar
½ stick butter
2 teaspoons vanilla extract
¼ teaspoon molasses, in Ava's memory
  (no more)
2 eggs
½ teaspoon ground cinnamon
1 good dash grated nutmeg
One 9-inch pie crust, homemade or store-bought

HOW TO COOK IT

Preheat your oven to about 300 or 350 degrees and bake your sweet potatoes—skin on, of course—for about 45 or 50 minutes, until soft. Let cool in cold water, and peel.

Mash them with a potato masher or a large spoon, as my mother does. She does not own a blender and will not have one in her house, and if you gave her one, along with a microwave, she would put the blender in the microwave and turn it on.

"When I get too feeble to mash somethin', I'll quit," she said.

She likes her sweet-potato mixture still to have a little texture to it, "so you'll know you're eatin' sweet potatoes." Add the milk, sugar, eggs, butter, spices, and flavorings, and stir them in thoroughly.

Pour it into a pie crust, and bake for an hour. Let it sit at least a half-hour before serving, if you can beat the children away. Again, if there are a few chunks left, this is a good thing.

Some people down here believe that, in pumpkin pie, canned pumpkin can be even better than fresh. This is not true of sweet potatoes.

"The thing about sweet potato pie is, it's good for you," my mother believes.

"What about the sugar?" I asked.

"The good stuff makes up for it," she said.

Sweet Potato Cobbler

WHAT YOU WILL NEED

3 pounds sweet potatoes

1 stick butter

1½ teaspoons ground cinnamon

2 cups flour

2 cups sugar

2 cups whole milk

HOW TO COOK IT

Preheat your oven to 350 degrees.

Bake your sweet potatoes, skin on, for about ½ hour. Cool, peel, and cut into big chunks. If they're medium-sized potatoes, you can split them lengthwise, and then cut across about three or four times. You do not want bite-sized pieces, but something bigger.

The size of your baking dish will determine your texture. If you want a crispier crust, use a bigger, shallower pan. If you want a fluffier, softer crust, use a smaller, deeper one.

My mother uses a pan that she would use for a large pound cake.

"You don't need no liquid in this. The sweet taters will make a little."

Pour in the sweet potatoes. Cut one stick butter into about six sections, and spread it out among the sweet potatoes. Sprinkle a little cinnamon, no more than a teaspoon, over the potatoes.

"The sweet is in the batter," she said.

Combine the flour and sugar, and stir in the milk, until you get a batter about the consistency of pancake batter or a little thicker. Pour about half of it over the sweet potatoes. Set the bowl down, pick up the baking dish, give it a gentle shake or two, then bang down, smartly but not hard enough to send batter flying or crack your baking dish, on the counter.

"Gets it shook down in there real good," she said.

Then pour the rest of the batter in, and sprinkle with your remaining cinnamon.

Bake for about 30 minutes or so, until the crust is golden brown.

This cobbler can be served as dessert, of course, but it can also be served as a side dish, particularly delicious with roast pork, even if you have to imagine the pork.

· · ·

"There we was, in terrible shape, and the kids was dancin' around, pie on their face," my grandma said. It was one of the lovely things about children, that they were so easy to fool. But they would be fine till the sweet potatoes ran out.

They needed to hope for something, so they sat in the house with the past-due rent and the almost empty larder and talked late into the night about the possibilities of food, like how good that cobbler would have tasted with some thick pork chops, or a roast, or maybe some fat spareribs, or even a platter of her fried chicken. They dreamed it all, meal by meal, and their daddy was always at the table in their imagination. It was not torture to imagine a pork roast when the only meat in the larder was the pig's feet the mountain men had allowed her husband in lieu of murdering him, now cured in the smokehouse. It seemed like so long ago, the night he came home with them.

It was not just make-believe, to imagine a table laid with good food.

Better times would come.
It became a mantra.
When times get better . . .
"I'll cook y'all this."
"I'll cook y'all that."
"I'll cook . . ."

9

"A HAM HOCK DON'T CALL FOR HELP"

Pan-Roasted Pig's Feet (with Homemade Barbecue Sauce),

Chunky Potato Salad

Cousin James Jenkins, left, and my uncle William Bundrum

ONE NIGHT, when there was no moon to speak of, the hellions crawled from their beds, stealthily slipped on their overalls and their brogans, and eased out the door. Or they would have if they had not let the screen door bang like a pistol shot, waking up every soul in the house. But, then, they were still small, the boys, and had much to learn about a jailbreak.

In her bed, Ava, wide awake, did not do a thing.

She had hoped the larceny in her family had ended with the descent of the cow from the Tredegar trestle, and the occasional arrival of an unfamiliar chicken. But, then, she had hoped for a lot of things.

"Some people just don't have no luck," she always said.

If you can't have luck, you might as well have gall.

You might as well have a moonless night.

She knew, being a good Pentecostal, there was no night deep enough to hide within. But she knew, being Jim's protégée, it might be good for a head start.

. . .

The hellions cut through the pines and pastures, and came to the darkened house. Newt was not a man to be fooled with; he might shoot if he heard a marauder, so the boys got down on their bellies and crawled like what they believed wild Indians would do. He had a fair belly on him and was bow-legged himself, and they knew they could outrun him in a straight-up race, but he was not above putting dogs on them, or saddling his horse and trying to ride them down.

But they had chicken thievery—and swine theft—in their genes.

They had plotted this through.

The dogs had been the first problem. Newt did not have biscuit catchers, but good dogs, hunting dogs, chained, and hounds raised hell when there was something to bark at and when there was not; they barked at imagined possums and real raccoons alike, or at a rumor on the wind.

For months, however, the boys had been petting and loving on the dogs, and hoped the dogs would no more bark at them than they would at Newt or anyone in his house.

Besides, they knew Newt, who routinely questioned the intelligence of his dogs. A barking dog, Newt had said, was no reason to light a lantern and freeze your fundament off in the yard.

If Newt were, by some chance, to investigate, to get his horse or mule saddled by lantern light and give chase, they would take to the brush and the thick trees, and slip away. No sane man rode through the thick trees in the dark, even if his dogs had the scent.

"What if he chases us back to the house?" William said.

"We won't go home," James said.

"Ever?" William said.

They discussed this for some time, but could not come up with an acceptable amount of time to hide out. James said he reckoned a year. William said he believed that just till Sunday would be all right, depending on what they stole.

The worst of it was choosing. They had to make a decision between the chickens on the roost or the succulent pork hanging in the smokehouse. They lost their nerve in the end, and settled on a late-season watermelon that Newt had intended to feed to his hogs.

They broke it on a rock, and ate it in the dark with their hands.

The next day, Ava could only puzzle at how her two boys could stay out all night and return with watermelon juice dried in their eyebrows and hair, and a seed stuck here and there on their faces and necks.

.   .   .

A few nights later, they were back. They lay on their bellies in the weeds, looking out on Newt's barnyard, again trying to decide. The allure of sweet potatoes had begun to recede in Ava's kitchen.

"Chicken'd be good," James said.

"Bacon'd be good. Be quieter," Willliam said. He had been involved in a little larceny of his own before this caper, and had not once heard a ham hock squawk for help from the dark.

James was silent, thinking hard. As the big brother, and the larger fistfighter, he made the final decisions.

"Chicken," he said.

"Make a lot of noise," William said.

"Naw, it won't," James said, grimly. He loved to play folly, even then, but when he was serious, he was scary.

Even as a boy, he had hands the size of baseball mitts. He walked up easy, like a ghost, took the first slumbering chicken off the roost like he was pulling a fig, and snapped its neck. They ran a mile, more, before they slowed down. It was not fear that drove them, or conscience, but excitement. They were too excited to sleep, so they made a terrible mess of cleaning and plucking the chicken in the dark, and hanging it on a wire on the front porch, so the dogs could not get at it before morning. They forgot and left the head on—or maybe they did it to give her a scare—so the sad, denuded thing was looking down at their momma when she opened the door just after dawn.

"Where'd the chicken come from?" she asked, though she was pretty sure.

"Got runt over," James said.

William nodded, solemnly.

"Fount it in the ditch," he said.

Ava was a good person, an almost glowing person, deep inside all that personality. But the hardship had taken a lot out of her, too, and made her old too soon. She wanted to punish them, but she just told them that, the next time they found a dead chicken in the ditch, they should bring it home and give it to her, so she could clean it properly. She did not ask how the roads could be littered with run-over poultry in a time and place where whole days went by without sighting a Model A, or even a slow-moving mule and wagon.

. . .

Newt's farm was not the only one they went shopping at, but since they were mad at Newt, they probably visited his place more. A few days after the initial chicken theft, they were back. This time, there was no debate. That morning, early, Newt had killed a hog, and had not asked the boys to help, probably because he wanted to avoid any awkwardness that might arise from not offering them a scrap.

Well, they would spare him that.

"We get caught, Newt'll send us off," William said.

"Newt can't send us off. He's kin," James said.

"Kin can send you off," William said.

"No, they can't," James said. "Daddy done tol' me. It's in the statue."

What his daddy had told him was that a lawfully wedded wife could not be compelled to testify against her husband in court, which was just one of those fine points of the law a poor man needed to know in the 1930s in the Deep South; somehow, in James's interpretation, that shifted a little bit to include everyone, even uncles and second cousins you were stealing from. But there in the dark, when they were plotting the theft of a whole ham or at least some side meat, it was the most reasonable thing that had been uttered in quite a while.

The problem was one of proximity. The smokehouse was just a few feet from the farmhouse, and if Newt came out the door with a shotgun, they would be goners, or at least William would be. To James, it was the same concept as being chased by a bear: only the slower of the two really had anything to worry about, and he could outrun William toting a piano.

They slid like lizards across the dirt of the yard and crept into the smokehouse. The door creaked so loud they almost died right there in the cold, still air, but no lamp was lit inside the house. They worked by feel, and by the light from a single match. The smokehouse had no windows and was well made—Newt took pride in things such as that.

They would have liked just to sling a pair of hams over their shoulders and run for home, but even the two hellions were sure such a large theft would lead to an investigation, and prosecution. They settled, instead, on some pig's feet. Newt had not known if he planned to pickle them or smoke them; it had been a big hog, and the feet were big and fleshy. Surely, the state would not send a boy off for taking feet.

James took just two.

"Get 'em all. I like pig's feet," William said.

"Hush," James said. "We take too much, he'll miss it."

It never occurred to them, as they ran, to consider that such things, feet of any kind, usually came in sets. They crept out with their swag, and as soon as they were out of sight they started to giggle.

Again, Ava asked them where the pig's feet came from.

"Got runt over," William said.

"Fount it in the ditch," James said.

Instead, the next day, she prepared to dispose of the evidence. The stolen pig's feet were not enough to feed her family, but a start. She went to the bare smokehouse and took the last of the scant meat her husband had brought home from his failed trip into the Georgia mountains. There was nothing left but the pig's feet the men had given him. With the two from Newt's smoke-house, and a pan of cornbread, there would be enough for all of them.

For those who think a pig's foot looks like you just lopped it straight off the running hog, it might ease your mind to know that the hoof, what my mother calls "the nail part," had been blessedly removed, and what you had, really, was the last joint, which is why some people called them pig knuckles. It was mostly fat, skin, and luscious cartilage, and utterly delicious when pan-roasted. In better times, my people would dress them with a spicy barbecue sauce.

She rubbed these with a little bacon grease, salt, and black pepper, and then tried something new. She had come into some powdered red pepper—cayenne, she believed—from her kin. She dusted each one of the pigs' feet; the fat she had rubbed on them made it stick nicely. Now, though, she was faced with a quandary. The four cured ones and two fresh ones from Newt's smokehouse would cook differently, so she would have to watch them carefully as they roasted.

She had a few white potatoes left. Odd how there had been a time when she never counted her potatoes. Lately, she knew exactly how many she had, and how many onions, the way a desperate man knows exactly how much change he has in his pocket.

She had eggs, the last of some sweet pickles, and some mayonnaise. She had everything she needed for a good, simple potato salad. They would have a feast, and shove their thumbs in the eye of their bad luck, for at least a little while longer. If it got worse, in the daylight, if the law came and took her boys away, she would beg and pray and, if she had to, go a little crazy. People felt a bit sorry, she had discovered, for a woman who was only a little crazy.

She roasted the fresh pig's feet slowly, for two hours, till they were charred just a bit, and so tender they were almost liquid, and the smoked ones a little less. She was just lifting them from the oven when there was a thumping on her door.

The children peeked out the window.

"Oh, hell," William said.

"Oh, hell," James said.

Ava rushed to see.

"Oh, hell," she said.

Edna jerked open the door, delighted.

They almost never had company, and never at night.

"Hello, Uncle Newt," she said.

Ava could have slid the pan back into the oven, but must have given up a little right then, and just told the children to let him in.

"Ava," he said. "Children."

He sniffed the delectable air.

"I ketch y'all at supper?"

"Not yet," Ava said. "Set."

"I can't stay," he said, "but it smells real, real good."

Ava twisted her hands in her apron.

"What y'all havin'?" he asked.

Ava hung her head, and motioned toward the pan.

It was as if the last of her respectability was drifting up the chimney on that iron stove.

"My," Newt said, and breathed in.

He lingered over the pan of slow-roasted pig's feet an agonizing second or so.

"Well," he said, "I got to be gettin' on. If you'll round up them sorry boys to he'p me, I've got some pork out here in the wagon for y'all."

But the boys were nowhere around.

They had evaporated.

Newt carried in a ham, and some salt meat, and more.

"It must have been a fine hog," Ava said.

"It was a good hog," he said.

He tipped his hat.

"Thing is," he said, "my hogs just come with four feet."

Ava was silent.

"I see yourn is half agin good as mine."

He rode off, laughing.

Ava walked outside, trembling, calling for her sons.

Newt would return with more help, more food, now and then. The Morrisons were all like that, always hard to figure. The midnight raids on Newt's farm ceased after that, and it would be nice to believe they stopped altogether, but times *were* hard. There was, however, a conscience in it, though maybe not a good one. They never took a scrap from a poor man, or a widow woman, or someone whose daddy was in the county prison; they both swore to it, though, well, we know what that's worth.

. . .

Pan-Roasted Pig's Feet
(with Homemade Barbecue Sauce)

There is probably no gentle way to say this, but some people, even those who love pork, will never be comfortable with a pig's foot, or even be comfortable being in the same room with one.

We understand this.

"People's diff'rent," she said. "I mean, you don't have to like *nothin'*."

"Yeah," I said.

"Some people don't know what's good."

WHAT YOU WILL NEED

for the pig's feet
- 4 to 6 pig's feet, split or whole, or about 1 to 2 per person, depending on size (the pig, not the person)
- 1 tablespoon bacon grease or cooking oil
- 1 tablespoon salt
- 1 tablespoon black pepper
- Cayenne pepper (to taste)

for the sauce
- 1 cup ketchup
- 1 cup apple cider
- ¼ cup yellow mustard
- ¼ cup finely diced white or yellow onion
- 1 tablespoon brown sugar

1 tablespoon chili powder

1 teaspoon minced garlic

1 tablespoon Tabasco sauce

HOW TO COOK IT

Pig's feet do not require much seasoning. As much as anything on the hog, they are delicious with next to nothing, and pan-roasted pig's feet are damn near immaculate. But they also lend themselves to a tomato-based sauce, as almost any pork will. My mother likes them plain, or pickled. I like them with sauce, pan-barbecued, or slow-cooked on a grill. The flesh is so succulent, so different from what most people are used to, it does not need the flavor of the smoke, and it's one of those rare meats that might actually be improved by slow-cooking in an oven. I know this is blasphemy.

Rub the pig's feet with bacon grease or cooking oil, as Jim did, and lightly coat them with salt, black pepper, and ground cayenne.

"This one is pretty easy," she said. "You want a baking pan big enough so you can line your pig's feet up so they don't touch, so the heat can get to 'em, and then pour in just a little bit of water around 'em. Cover your pan with some foil, and put it in the oven—get your oven hot first—on about 350 degrees, and cook it for about thirty minutes. That water will steam up into them pig's feet, and get 'em to cooking good."

As they cook, mix all the ingredients of the barbecue sauce. Some people like a bowl for this. We like to put it all in a quart Mason jar, screw the lid on tight, and shake the hell out of it.

Also, if you have some left, it's already in the jar.

After 30 minutes, peel back the foil and coat the pig's feet with sauce, letting any leftover sauce pool in the bottom of the pan. The fat from the pig's feet will mix with the sauce that has dripped down, and create ambrosia. Cover, cook at 350 degrees for another 30 minutes, and ladle or baste the sauce that has mixed with the fat on the feet. Then remove the foil, and cook another 20 minutes or so, till there is just the slightest, slightest crisping of the skin. You want to be able to suck the meat right off the bone.

"Sometimes I like to boil mine for about thirty minutes, then put 'em in the oven to roast, without no sauce nor nothin'. Now, that's good, too."

Chunky Potato Salad

WHAT YOU WILL NEED
(SMALL BATCH)

6 medium or 4 large potatoes

2 eggs

½ cup mayonnaise (at least)

1 teaspoon yellow mustard (no more)

½ teaspoon garlic salt

1 teaspoon black pepper

2 tablespoons sweet pickle relish

1 teaspoon cayenne pepper

HOW TO COOK IT

Peel the potatoes and cut them into chunks. If they're small, quartering them may be enough.

Boil the potatoes till done, but not mushy. Taste to be sure they're done. Pour the water off, and let them cool. Do not pour cold water over them, but you can cover them and put them in the refrigerator.

Hard-boil the eggs, then cool, peel, and coarsely chop them. We like circles. You decide.

In a large bowl, mix the mayonnaise, mustard, garlic salt, black pepper, pickle relish, and ½ teaspoon of the cayenne. When this is mixed thoroughly, add the potatoes and eggs, and mix them in gently till the potato chunks are lightly coated.

This recipe calls for only a little mustard, because mustard will be all you taste if you get carried away. Again, 1 teaspoon, not a tablespoon.

Dust the top with a little more cayenne. Some people like smoked paprika, but we're a little addicted to the cayenne, which gives it a nice, slight kick. Do not overuse, however, or that, too, is all you'll taste.

This is not soupy potato salad, or an exotic one. She has a half-dozen other potato salads, but this is the one that goes best with pig's feet, which is a phrase that I never believed would take shape in my writing life, but that often, when I am dreaming of food myself, takes shape in my head.

Serve it all with cornbread muffins, slightly, slightly sweetened.

. . .

Charlie came home, after a mean six months more. He tried to make it up to her somehow. He worked the garden, and chased jobs across two states and nine counties, and brought home fresh fish from his trotlines and wild game from the mountains, always moving, earning, scrounging. He never really quit making liquor, and she never forgave him for getting caught that first time. He worked himself to rags, inside that disapproval. Ava continued to hire out, picking and chopping cotton every season, sewing clothes and quilts to sell at night. And, together, they beat the hard times from their door. The Depression lingered, through '34, '35, and beyond, but, oddly, after Charlie came home from jail, some local farmers noted that larceny of their smokehouses, fields, and henhouses had shown a marked decline. In late 1936, in the dark heart of it all, Ava told her husband she was to have another child.

10

CAKES OF GOLD

Meat Loaf, Scalloped Potatoes,

Pineapple Upside-Down Cake

My mother, my aunt Edna (holding my aunt Sue), and my aunts Jo and Juanita

THE BIG WOMAN came all the way from Rome. She stomped through the door without knocking, her strong arms full of groceries, of onions, potatoes, store-bought bell peppers, freshly ground beef wrapped in clean white butcher paper, more.

"Whar's the babe?" she said, but the children were too stunned to speak.

The children pointed, in concert, to the small bedroom off the kitchen.

Ava slept, exhausted, the doctor at her side. It had not been an easy birth.

"Has she et?" the big woman asked Edna, who cradled the sleeping baby in her arms.

"Just some broth," she said.

The big woman cursed so loud it woke everyone—not just in the house but in the holler, and perhaps in the mountains beyond. It was that kind of voice, a voice almost biblical, except that every third phrase seemed to be "son of a bitch." Her name was Maudie Morrison, but everyone called her Sis. She was Charlie's cousin, on his mother's side.

The doctor, a respected old man named Gray, was so taken aback he pronounced Ava out of danger and fled the house, pausing only to collect his fee.

"What fool tol' her she couldn't have nothin' but broth?" Sis bellowed, but the doctor was already beyond the porch, bag in his hand, and, impressive for a man his age, had vaulted into his car.

The big woman stomped into the kitchen. Stomping was apparently the only form of locomotion of which she was capable or aware. Her legs were as solid as the posts on a pole barn.

But it was a strange thing: the second those wide feet thumped down in the small kitchen, she moved as light as a dancer, sliding from cupboard to stove, her big hands ripping open the burlap and cloth sacks of the groceries as if they were tissue paper. She did not rattle the pots and pans; they were like something from a dollhouse in her hands. Her knife was almost a blur as she peeled potatoes and diced onions, cranked open cans of sweet peas, and mixed together a big pan of cornbread with her hands. With what seemed a third hand, she fed and stoked the fire until it glowed.

"Need wood," she grunted, and James and William, who had looked on with great curiosity, fled to the woodpile and came staggering back with enough wood to light the lower Appalachians.

"Now get out from underfoot, you little sons of bitches," she said without turning around, "afore I stomp a mudhole in the both of you." The boys stood in disbelief till she took a swing at them with one wide orthopedic shoe. They fled again, this time to the edge of the wood. They were utterly unafraid of their momma, and not afraid enough, perhaps, of their daddy, but they knew peril when they saw it stomp in.

Their daddy had seemed only mightily amused, and had said, "How do," and "Thank you for comin'," and moved to the front porch, pre-emptively, to have some snuff and wonder what he did in life to be blessed with one more girl. Juanita toddled off to hide—under one of the beds, they think.

Inside, the fire roaring, the big woman thin-sliced potatoes and layered them in a deep dish with chunks of butter and cheese, poured on fresh milk, and put it in to bake. Then she went to work on the meat.

She tore up pieces of white bread, what she called "light bread," and kneaded the soft bread into the ground beef, seasoning as she went with the finely diced onion, green pepper, a little salt, just a little canned tomato paste, and a heavy dose of black pepper, using a recipe that had become popular during the Depression because it stretched a single pound of beef to more than two pounds, yet only enriched the flavor of it.

Edna, having lost interest in just one more newborn baby, had handed the child off to her momma and watched every move the big woman made. She was only eight years old, but could already cook a complete meal all by herself, and she knew greatness in a kitchen when she saw it up close.

"It's the bread that makes it," the big woman said, talking without taking her eyes off the food. "It makes it smooth, and creamy. Meat loaf ain't supposed to have big hunks of meat in it, 'cause it gets rubbery, but work the bread in till it's all the same amount of smooth, and the bread soaks up all that good stuff."

She formed a round loaf and eased it into Ava's biggest iron skillet, spread a thin, barely there layer of tomato sauce over the crown, so it would crust a little bit, and put it on to bake. She added a dash of salt and pepper and a third of a stick of butter to the sweet peas, and put them on to simmer, slowly, on the back of the stove. People thought because a thing came from a can it needed little or no seasoning; people, she believed, were for the large part leaping dumbasses.

"Got to have somethin' green with meat loaf, and fresh peas and green beans ain't in season," she said. The gardens were plowed, and some things were planted, but this was the bleak season for fresh vegetables. It might as well be the middle of winter, with ice hanging on the trees, for all they could pick now.

The big woman talked and talked, and Edna stood rooted to the floor.

Her momma talked about food, too, about all she had learned from the mean ol' man who once lived in their house, but not with a passion like this. This was the big woman's religion.

This was the woman she had heard about, the kin from Georgia that her own people had lost touch with, as they moved from house to house over on the Alabama side while Charlie chased work and fled landlords. This was *the* cook, the woman all the other good blue-collar cooks spoke of without spite or jealousy, because she brought her gifts to them in the worst and best times, in times of need and celebration, reaching into her own pocket to buy the ingredients. It was said that she could bake a coconut cake on a hot flat rock, and her fried chicken was so light and crisp it could lift off the plate and fly. Edna, who was practical, half believed the cake story, but not that fried chickens could take wing.

In an hour it was done; meat loaf, scalloped potatoes, sweet peas, and hot cornbread muffins. The big woman called the family in to eat, and took a plate to Ava, and fed her like she was a child.

She herself did not eat, not yet. She returned to the kitchen and, in an iron skillet, layered brown sugar, butter, canned sliced pineapple, and a yellow cake batter she made from scratch, in record time. When it was done, she took a heavy ceramic plate, clapped it over the top of the skillet, flipped it over in one easy motion, and set it on the table with a clatter. The golden pineapple and brown-sugar glaze seemed to glow. A good pineapple upside-down cake will do that, like it has a light in it. Look when you do a good one, and see if it doesn't.

"Serve it while it's warm," she rumbled, and left the rest of it in Edna's hands. The big woman also knew a good cook when she saw one.

She returned to the bedroom and took the baby from Ava's arms.

"Has anybody toted her around the house?" she asked. It is custom here, with a newborn, that when a baby is toted around the house for the first time the child will inherit some of the character and spirit and strength from the kin who carry them around the house.

Ava said yes, the child's father had, but it didn't count if it was the daddy. They would be pleased if the big woman would honor them by doing so.

They believed in this. For a lifetime, as long as anyone was left who remembered, this custom would be an explanation, an excuse, for the child's behavior. If someone was stingy, or mean, or kind, or just knew how to grow a good garden, the old people would say, Well, of course the child was that way, 'cause ol' so-and-so carried her around the house, and you know how *they* were. In a family of loggers, you wanted the best man with an ax or a file. In a family of carpenters, you wanted someone with a good eye on a level. In a family of cooks, you wanted her.

The woman carried the child in one big arm like a kitten, and, as is custom, spoke to her while they made their journey.

"Do you know what she said to you?" I asked my mother, thinking she might have mentioned it when she was older.

She shook her head.

But she would not be surprised, she said, if the big woman had looked down at her and growled, *"Well, look at you, you little SB."*

. . .

Meat Loaf

(small portion, for 4 to 6)

WHAT YOU WILL NEED

6 to 8 slices white bread

1½ pounds ground beef, the cheaper and fattier the
   better

1 large white onion

1 green bell pepper

1 teaspoon salt

1 teaspoon black pepper

¼ teaspoon minced garlic or garlic powder

1 pinch chili powder (no more)

2 tablespoons tomato paste

1 tablespoon lard or bacon grease

HOW TO COOK IT

Preheat your oven to 350 degrees.

First tear the white bread into pieces, each slice into about four pieces, to make it easier to work into the ground beef. In a large bowl, use your hands to work the pieces of soft bread thoroughly into the ground beef, until it is hard to tell them apart.

Then add the onion, pepper, dry spices, and 1 tablespoon of the tomato paste, and work them in thoroughly. Form a round loaf, and place in an uncovered cast-iron skillet that has been greased with lard, bacon grease, or a little cooking oil. Spread the remaining tablespoon of the tomato paste over the top.

Bake for at least 1 hour. The top should be crispy.

Scalloped Potatoes

WHAT YOU WILL NEED

2 medium-sized sweet onions

1 small, tender green onion, with blade

1 tablespoon bacon grease, or more if needed

½ to 1 stick butter

5 medium white or red potatoes

1 cup mild American cheese

¼ cup sharp cheddar cheese

2 to 3 tablespoons flour

¾ cup whole milk, or more if needed

½ teaspoon salt

½ teaspoon black pepper

½ teaspoon cayenne pepper

HOW TO COOK IT

Preheat the oven to 350 degrees.

Thinly slice—as thin as you can—the sweet onions.

Thinly slice the green onion.

In a tablespoon of bacon grease, sauté the sweet and green onions in a skillet until the sweet onions go clear and the green onions wilt. Set aside.

"This is about as fancy as I get," my mother said.

Lightly grease with butter or cooking oil a medium-sized baking dish, about 9 by 13 inches.

If you use butter, use about half the stick.

Peel the potatoes and slice thinly, no more than ¼ inch, thinner if possible.

Spread a layer of potatoes on the bottom of the baking dish, then, using a spatula, spoon a thin layer of sweet onion and green onion. Then add a second layer of potatoes, and a second very thin layer of the onions. It does not have to be uniform or perfect; it tastes a little better, it seems, if there is some chaos, making little pockets of molten cheese, creamy and crispy. You'll see.

Cover, and set aside.

Shred the American cheese. If it's good cheese and not gummy, it will shred nicely.

Shred the cheddar, but keep it separate for now.

In a skillet, make a blond roux by melting the rest of the stick of butter—a thimble-sized daub of bacon grease melting with the butter will not hurt this process—and stirring in the flour, until it begins to brown. This is not a gumbo roux and does not need to be browned very much at all. Stir in the milk and the mild American cheese, and as it melts, stir in the salt, pepper, and cayenne. You can add more milk, if it seems gunky. You want a consistency like that of a good cream soup. But the truth is, it won't hurt if it's a little thin; it will thicken in the oven. Some people, who like a hotter cheese sauce, will give a good shake or two of hot sauce, but she disdains this, because it can give the creamy taste that whang that the powdered cayenne does not.

As soon as it is good and creamy, pour the sauce over the potatoes and onions. You can give the baking dish a good shake or three to make sure the sauce oozes into the potatoes and onions. Then sprinkle the top with the shredded sharp cheddar.

Bake on a middle rack, covered, for about 40 minutes, or until the cheese is bubbling, the onions are tender, and the potatoes come apart when poked with a fork. Then uncover and cook another 10 minutes or so, until the cheddar on top begins to brown and crisp, and your tongue begins to slap you in the head. Be very, very careful taking this from the oven and serving. It is lava. That said, it is okay to eat a small plate of it, after it cools, just to test it, before suppertime. It might not be good.

NOTE Some people, as a bit of a shortcut, will boil the potatoes for a few minutes first, before slicing and arranging them in the pan, and for scalloped potatoes without onion that may be a good idea, but it upsets the chemistry of my mother's recipe, since the onions will still need to be cooked longer in the oven. If you are a Philistine and do not like onions, just leave them out, and you will have classic potatoes au gratin, or scalloped potatoes, which is still pretty damn good, too.

Pineapple Upside-Down Cake

WHAT YOU WILL NEED

1⅓ cups flour
1 cup granulated sugar
⅓ cup lard or shortening
1 egg
¾ cup whole milk
1 stick butter
½ cup brown sugar
9 to 12 slices canned pineapple (save the juice)
½ small can crushed pineapple (juice and all)
9 maraschino cherries

HOW TO COOK IT

Preheat your oven to 350 degrees.

In a mixing bowl, combine the flour, white sugar, lard or shortening, egg, milk, and ¼ stick of the butter. Mix, however you like, into a smooth batter. My mother believes in using a large spoon, like she is angry at the ingredients. Set aside.

Grease a 9-inch cake pan with the remaining butter, being generous with the butter in the pan's bottom. Dust the butter with the brown sugar, and line the bottom of the pan with slices of pineapple. Then take the crushed pineapple in your fingers and spread it lightly across the sliced pineapple, allowing it to fill in the gaps. The problem with pineapple upside-down cake is, it doesn't have enough pineapple, and all you taste is butter and brown sugar. To be sure, take a few tablespoons of the juice from the can and drizzle it on, which will also help sweeten the recipe.

Finally, place a maraschino cherry, a whole one, in the center ring of each pineapple slice. We think this is a little silly, to be honest, but . . . well, people just expect things.

Pour the batter over the pineapple. Bake from 50 minutes to an hour. Let it cool about 15 to 20 minutes, and carefully flip it over on a large plate.

"It's a whole lot better if you eat it while it's still warm."

In summer, it is delicious cold, from the refrigerator.

Except for my aunt Jo's peanut-butter cake, it is my all-time favorite dessert.

· · ·

They believed a lot of things then. They believed some old women could breathe the pain out of you if you got burned. They believed that if you washed clothes on Thanksgiving it would bring sorrow, and if you had cramps in your feet you should place your shoes upside down under your bed. They believed that a bird in the house, or a night bird's call, was bad luck. These beliefs fade in time, but my mother still won't sweep the floor on New Year's because it is believed to be fatal, it will sweep someone's life away. I still find my shoes upside down under my bed in the guest room every now and then. But of all those beliefs, the one that has endured the longest is the one about the newborn, and the house, and the slow walk around it. "And I guess," my mother said, "it explains ever'thing."

You do not grow up to be just like the person who carried you around the house. You take one thing from them, like the cooking, or maybe two.

"I did cuss some," she said, "back before I found the Lord."

11

SIS

Sis's Chicken and Dressing

Ava

I LIFTED the heavy iron skillet from the oven with a scorched, ancient washcloth she uses as a pot holder, retrieved a steel spoon from the time of San Juan Hill, and pressed it into the golden-brown surface of the still-sizzling, steaming chicken with corn-bread dressing. The crust of the dressing, covered in a glorious sheen of chicken fat, made a crisp, snapping sound, like good crème brûlée. The underneath was moist, creamy, and as smooth as pudding, seasoned with onion, celery, sage, and that rich, buttery chicken broth. The cornmeal mixture was thick, with big pieces of tender leg and thigh meat, the delicious skin left on, because white meat, and especially skinless breast meat, has all the flavor and consistency of an old shoe tongue. The dressing was too hot to taste, really, but some things are just worth a little bit of scorch and pain. People love the cliché, the one about food that melts in your mouth; I wonder how many truly know it?

"Where does this come from?" I asked her, but I guess what I really meant was, *Who?*

"Let me think a minute," she said, from atop a giant leather easy chair. She is a tall woman, but looks like a tossed-down doll in that massive chair; it is too soft, she gripes, and for the first time in her life she naps in the middle of the day. But she disdains spindly rocking chairs the way she abhors bifocals, probiotics, and most physicians. Such things are for old people, she believes. She took off her glasses to remember, put them back on, then pulled them off again. Finally, she closed her eyes altogether. *Ah yes. There . . .*

"Well, hon," she said, "it goes back to that time Sis shot her husband in the teeth."

I knew then that this would take some time.

"Where were the teeth at the time?" I asked, in some weak hope they were resting on a shelf, or on the bedside table in a water glass.

"Well, hon, they were in his mouth," my mother said.

My tiny aunt Juanita, who likes to visit on Sundays so they can walk off down the distant past together the same way they lived it, arm in arm, nodded with more gleeful enthusiasm than seemed appropriate for an eighty-two-year-old child of God. She weighs eighty pounds, her body is brittle and frail, and her steps, in her too-big house shoes, are timid, tiny. But her mind is a razor.

"Shot 'em right out of his head," Juanita chirped.

"False teeth?" I asked, still hopeful.

Both old women shook their heads this time, in concert. My mother looked sad, as she always does when she tells a tale of woe; my aunt was beside herself with glee.

"They was real," said Aunt Juanita. "They was attached to his head."

"Did it kill him?" I asked.

"No," my mother said.

"They was *real* big teeth," my aunt Juanita explained. "This big," she said, and held her thumb and forefinger about three inches apart. In some other families, that might have been a matter for some incredulity. In mine, it was just one more truth that had welled up from a bottomless pool.

"But what," I asked, "does that have to do with chicken and dressing?"

They looked at me like I was simple in the head.

"Because it goes back to Sis, and Sis was one of the best cooks who ever lived," my mother said.

My aunt Juanita nodded, reverently, as if my mother had quoted Billy Graham.

"Who ever lived," she echoed.

"Start at the beginning," I said, a thing I would regret.

. . .

1941

"I wasn't yet five, the first time I seen her . . . well, the first time I can remember it. I remember, 'cause it was the first time I ever went to town." It was well into fall but still warm, because she was barefoot, in a dress cut from a bleached feed sack. Her mother had sewn a ruffle on it, to make it pretty.

She remembers looking at herself in the mirror then, and thinking she looked a little odd. Her hair was as straight and white as corn silk, and cut so short her daddy nicknamed her Pooh Boy, after the little boy in A. A. Milne's drawings, who did, in truth, bear an uncanny resemblance to her. They did not know Pooh was the bear in the story, not the boy, because she could not yet read and neither could he, but they enjoyed the pictures quite a bit. She was a Depression baby, so pale and thin that in old black-and-white photographs she seemed almost translucent, like you could look right through her if you held her to the light.

Her sisters, Edna and Juanita, were fistfighters and fire breathers who would mix it up with the boys and win, or stone a snake, or tease a bull, "but I was little and weak and skeered of the world," so much so that it seemed impossible she even came from a place such as this, from a deep woods populated almost solely with hog farmers, whiskey men, loggers, sharecroppers, and rough, hard women who handed babies off to their oldest daughters so they could pick cotton in the flatland and scrub floors in town.

The farthest she had ever been in her short life was the Coosa River ferry, or the Holiness church, and the most people she had seen in one place at one time would fit under a brush arbor. Now she was bouncing down a ragged ribbon of red dirt in her daddy's battered Model A Ford, rumbling through pines, yellow broom sage, and white waves of cotton, on her way to a great adventure. He always drove fast, like he was afraid that he would miss something, that a thing that happened once in the world might be gone when he got there. When they hit the blacktop, he pushed the pedal to the floor, and the power lines flew by like fence posts, thrilling, as they rushed toward a metropolis of humming looms, ringing commerce, and hot steel.

They were only going to the feed store, to get a load of milled corn for Charlie's Poland China hogs, but the word "town" gleamed with possibility. Rome, Georgia, was not a dusty crossroads where chickens scratched by the fuel pumps, but a real city, with pool halls and Coca-Cola and other great wickedness, not as big as Atlanta, Birmingham, or Chattanooga, but the biggest thing in between. It had risen from the foothills of the Appalachians in the 1830s, inside a triangle of rivers where the Etowah and Oostanaula came together to form the mighty Coosa. Because it was ringed by the low mountains, its founders named it for that City of Seven Hills.

The Cherokee left footprints on this ground. Nathan Bedford Forrest and his lightning cavalry fought the Yankee raiders here (William Tecumseh Sherman burned parts of it to smut anyway, sparing only the churches). Rome would rise from that destruction in time, and by the early twentieth century, its foundries and mills made it the thumping heart of the foothills on the Alabama-Georgia line.

They turned onto Broad Street, so wide that six cars could run abreast between the red-brick and the Art Deco storefronts, two and three stories tall. In better times, there had been an opera house, a symphony, even mansions. The Depression rubbed away some of the gilt, but Rome was rising again, and the old Model A quickly became hemmed in by traffic—*traffic,* in a small Southern city in the dying days of the Crash. On the sidewalk, paperboys in peaked caps and grimy faces, like something out of Dickens, waved headlines of a world heading toward war. The town ladies, their faces painted, shared the sidewalk with severe, disapproving old women in bonnets and plain dresses that swept the earth. Men in straw boaters and suits from Sears, Roebuck, balanced on one leg for a shine.

Her daddy loaded the sacks of corn himself at the feed lot, and they headed home. They retraced their route down Broad Street, the Ford belching smoke and wallowing low on its springs, and had not gone more than a block or so when the old truck shuddered, died, and coasted to a dead stop. It only took one broken-down Ford to bring traffic to a crawl in that swamp of cars, farm trucks, and occasional mule wagons, and the horns began to blow. "Daddy never had a truck that would run real good, that didn't break down every other day, and it broke down right in the middle of town, right in the middle of all them people," she said, thinking back. "And everybody was looking. . . ."

He told her to stay in the cab, then crawled out, flung open the truck's hood, and buried his head and shoulders inside. The truck's starter had been dying for some time, and now it was smoking. This is perhaps her first clear memory of her father, half inside the hood of a broken-down truck, his overalls and boots specked with hot tar from the roofing pitch he used, thin and ragged under a sweat-stained, battered brown fedora. "I kept waitin' for somebody to help him," she said, but the world seemed fresh out of Samaritans.

With one hand on the wheel, to steer, and one on the door frame, he tried to start the old truck by pushing it off. He planned to jump inside once he got it rolling, slam it in gear, pop the clutch, and sail away. But the old truck was just too heavy, and the grade was not in his favor, and his worn-out boots slid on the asphalt as he pushed. The horns hurt her ears; people are brave inside a ton of Detroit steel.

Then, through that dusty windshield, my mother saw her coming. She moved not at a run but at a steady, rapid, thumping stomp, pushing down the sidewalk like a barge in wide white orthopedic shoes, her big arms and wide shoulders straining at her white uniform, the kind waitresses and cafeteria workers wore. Her reddish-brown hair was tucked under a black hairnet, and she cursed the rubberneckers, to their faces, as she came on.

"I'm comin', Chollie," she boomed, in a voice that would pierce fog. She did not slow down as she neared the small crowd gathered beside the car, and the little girl thought she was going to run them down. They parted at the last second like something out of Exodus.

"Hello, Cousin," he said, like he was expecting her. "I am proud to see you."

"Get in, Chollie," she said, "and let me push."

She bent her broad back to it, and slowly, slowly, the truck began to roll. "Try it," she shouted, and my grandfather popped the clutch, and the truck lurched but did not crank, and the big woman cursed Henry Ford for all the misery he had wrought by building such a piece of manure in the first place, and cursed him again for selling it to poor and honest men. Then she pushed harder, pushed until her shoulders trembled from the strain. On the sidewalk, men in suits and ties must have thought it was funny to see the woman manhandle a Model A up Broad Street, and though no one came to help, an even bigger crowd gathered to watch the show. Sis noticed this, and turned her red face to them to curse them more specifically—for being pencil-necked sons of bitches too delicate to push a damn car.

She shoved the old truck a block or more, gathering speed slowly, slowly, till the engine coughed, caught, and roared to life. A cloud of black smut enveloped the big woman, who coughed herself, and turned her steel-gray, drill-bit eyes on the remaining no-accounts on the sidewalk, as if she was daring them to be amused by her. She damned them one last time, unafraid, then jumped on the back of the truck's bed, thick legs swinging, and shouted: "Let's go, Chollie!"

He drove her home—to her small house, on the outskirts of Rome, and they left her waving in the yard.

"Who *was* that, Daddy?" my mother asked.

"That was Sis," her daddy said.

The Model A lurched and bounced across the unpaved road. He would go another year before replacing the starter. For a year, he just tried to park on a hill, or among friends.

"Sis is my cousin," he said.

"She's big, ain't she?" the little girl said.

Her daddy nodded.

"She's a lot of girl."

"She cusses a lot, don't she?"

"Got a mouth on 'er," he said.

Within minutes, they were back in the trees.

He breathed easier in the trees.

"She cooks for a livin'," he said. "She cusses for fun."

"Can she cook good as Momma, as good as Edna?" She pronounced it "Edner."

"She could cook a Lehigh boot," he said, which left my mother mightily confused for a very, very long time. "And you could eat it, by God, with a spoon."

As they rumbled home, he told her the rest of it, told her the legend of a woman loud, proud, and wide, who could outfight most men in a family that included some of the most profane and furious fist- and knife-fighters in the Appalachians.

"It was Sis," her daddy told her, "that carried you around the house."

The next time my mother saw her, months later, the clan from both sides of the river had gathered on the Alabama side, to celebrate a thing that she can no longer recall. But she remembers Sis, how she stomped into the yard with a wooden case of Double Colas on her shoulder, and asked my mother, staring open-mouthed from the branches of a chinaberry tree, where the bleepity-bleep-bleeping ice tub was. She had on a flower-print dress and stockings rolled down below her knees, and carried a purse big enough to conceal a circus midget or a shoat hog. As my mother stared, glad she was high in a tree, Sis rummaged inside, handed her a stick of Juicy Fruit, grinned, and winked. It reminded my mother of a jack-o'-lantern. "Funny," my mother said, "the things you don't never forget. You don't never forget people bein' good to you. Well, I guess some people do."

· · ·

My mother stopped talking then, and sat quietly in her leather chair. Sometimes the story she is thinking goes on uninterrupted inside her head but does not quite make it to her mouth, like how a signal on an old radio with a shorted-out speaker wire will come and go. She does not always bother to start over when she begins to talk again, or even fill you in on the part you missed, like it was your fault for not having ESP, for being unable to read her mind. The frightening thing is, in that silence, my aunt Juanita seemed to be following things just fine.

"You were going to tell me about the dressing," I nudged, gently, "and the teeth?"

"I am," she said.

"Oh," I said, and as I waited for more, the two old women just looked at me again, as if I might be slow.

"Sis was one of the Georgia people," my mother patiently explained, and went silent again, as if that simple designation would tell me all I needed to know. "The Georgia people" is our family's designation for kin born on the eastern side of the Alabama-Georgia line, and it makes them sound exotic, even European, as if they had a different accent or a sixth toe. The Georgia people had descended from the Appalachians in the early twentieth century to work in Rome and Cedartown, Georgia, but they never went completely tame. They were handsome, dark-haired people, but they would rather cuss, imbibe, and brawl than sit in the shade and eat peach ice cream.

"Was Sis a handsome woman?" I asked.

She hung her head.

"No, more square-headed," my mother said, "more oblong."

"But we loved her," my aunt Juanita said.

They described a woman whose body had been machined by whipping giant spoons through pots as big as a fifty-five-gallon drum, deadlifting hundred-pound racks loaded with enough food to feed a platoon, and slinging around fifty-pound sacks of potatoes and flour and meal. She seldom had a job that did not involve the preparation of food, and for eighteen years cooked in the hospital in Rome. "She was *big*—not fat, but big and strong," my mother said. "My God, she was strong. And always playing folly and laughing out loud. She wasn't like nobody else in this world."

She had one of those smiles that pulled people inside a kind of warm circle, the way you feel when you gather around a stove, but when she was angry her face took on a red-eyed, terrifying scowl that would make the dogs run under the porch. Babies, however, loved her; go figure.

But what my mother recalls most was her remarkable language, a cussing of such breadth and depth that kin who never even saw her, who were born a half-century after she passed from this earth, still tell stories of her as if they were actually there when these things happened. Everyone my mother knew, including some deacons, cursed a little bit, in a backslid, mild, biblical way. But Sis knew curses that no one else had ever used or even heard before.

"I won't tell it like Sis said it," my sweet mother said. "I'll say 'GD' and 'SB,' and . . ."

"I understand," I said.

People, in Sis's view, were not just a plain, generic SB. They were a spindly SB, or a wormy SB, or a bandy-legged SB, or just a GDSB. She lived just slightly this side of folklore, and people, of course, built on her legend. "But Sis didn't need no help," my aunt Juanita said, "for people to remember her."

"She saved Mr. Hugh Sanders's life," my mother said.

"How did she save Mr. Hugh?" I asked.

"With a number-2 washtub," she said.

I no longer believed we would ever get back to the dressing.

I did not even believe we would get back to the teeth.

· · ·

It was the damnedest thing, that friendship. One of the most fearsome people in these hills was fascinated by fairy tales, and by the man who told them. "She loved Mr. Hugh Sanders," my mother said, "but ever'body did." Mr. Hugh would become my aunt Edna's father-in-law, but was like family even before then.

Mr. Hugh lived his whole life under the same battered fedora, and his hat had more stories than most men did. The ferryman at the Coosa crossing south of Rome, he was born in an age when old men still went to funerals in Confederate gray, and night riders rode through the pines under white sheets, torches in their hands. Mr. Hugh did his riding on old mules and on polished steel, with the hoboes, and traveled the mountains and far beyond, and found a story at every milepost. He fished, trapped, and hunted for a living as a younger man, and there was not a net he could not knit, a knife he could not sharpen, or a snake or a human he could not charm. But few could remember him as a young man, as being anything but grizzled and gray, with blue eyes that seemed to twinkle when he talked—or maybe we just wanted it to be that way. He lost his wife young, to sickness, and was adopted by pretty much everyone here. "Sis called him 'uncle,' but they wadn't kin. She adopted him, too. She did that sometimes."

People gathered at the ferry to fish and swim and cook their catch. The children swarmed around the old man to hear his tales about bears, deer, birds, possums, and raccoons, which could all talk in his stories, and outsmarted the evil snakes, panthers, and foxes. He sang to them that "the old gray goose is dead," and they wept. Sis sat with the children and clapped her hands.

One day, as he held court, a fierce thunderstorm boiled straight down the river itself. A gray rain fell in sheets, and the Coosa, fed by storm water upriver, surged over its banks, sending the men, women, and children scrambling for higher ground. Mr. Hugh shooed the children away and went to secure his raft, his livelihood. It took longer than he had expected, and he was hip-deep in the roiling brown water when he could finally slog up the bank, toward safety. But the strong wind staggered him, he could barely see, the blowing rain was so thick in the air he could not breathe, and his feet could not find purchase in the slick mud. He fell to his knees once, twice, and the water still rose.

Through the gray curtain of rain, he glimpsed what appeared to be a giant turtle plowing toward him. Some of the Indians believed the whole world rode on the back of a giant turtle, and for just a second he thought maybe he was coming home. But as the apparition drew closer he saw that it was only Sis, waist-deep in the rising tide, with a big number-2 washtub covering her head and shoulders.

She placed the tub over the old man's head and shoulders, like the hatch on a submarine, and, thick legs pushing against the rising river, half dragged, half carried him up the bank. He was finally able to breathe, but the raindrops hammered the top of the washtub like a million sticks on a bass drum, and by the time they made it to safety the old man was as deaf as an anvil.

"You're safe now, Uncle," Sis told him.

"What?" he said.

"You're *safe!*" she shouted.

"What?"

.   .   .

"He said he never did hear good after that," my mother said.

"But he didn't drown," Aunt Juanita said.

"No," my mother said.

They nodded in concert again, and discussed whether it was better to be drowned or as deaf as a pine stump, and concluded that a deaf man could still read the Bible if he chose, and watch *As the World Turns.*

"The teeth?" I asked again.

"Well," my mother said, "it happened at the eatin' table," which *is* kind of funny, if you think about it.

"Tee-hee," my aunt Juanita said.

The unfortunate husband was actually Sis's second, a volatile, short-tempered man. Neither my mother nor my aunt Juanita could recall his name, but they decided it was unimportant to the narrative. He did not leave his mark on local history as clearly and sharply as Sis, but he is remembered for two things: one, he had abnormally large teeth; two, he was mean to her when he drank. They argued often and heatedly, and Sis, routinely and in front of witnesses, threatened to kill him, since cussing him out had achieved little improvement in his behavior. She armed herself for the inevitable.

"But, oh," my aunt Juanita said, "how she loved that man."

He would sometimes hit her when he drank, a thing Sis tolerated once, out of love, apparently. It was so out of character for her that people could barely believe it. But her patience was wearing out, and she warned: "If he ever even tries to lay a hand on me again, I *will* shoot him."

The day it happened, Sis and her man were arguing again at the kitchen table. No one can remember what sparked it, but all agree that what happened next was entirely his fault.

"He should have known better," my aunt Juanita said.

As they argued, he leaned across the table and drew back his hand.

"Better not," Sis told him. "I'll shoot you."

"His name was Carter," my mother said, suddenly remembering.

"No," my aunt Juanita said, suddenly remembering herself, "it was Carson."

"Carter," my mother said.

"Carson," my aunt Juanita said. "I'm sure. They give away some clothes after he died, and they had the name wrote on the inside of the collar—you know, from the dry cleaners'. Carson. C-A-R-S-O-N."

"Well," my mother said, and called him Carter, regardless, from then on.

Anyway, back at the kitchen table, Carson (Carter) cursed Sis viciously, and as he balled up his fist, Sis pulled a snub-nosed .22 pistol from her pocketbook and leveled it at his face.

"I'll shoot you, you snaggletoothed son of a bitch," she said.

"You won't," he said.

"Did you say that I won't shoot you?" Sis said, incredulous.

"I did," Carson (Carter) said.

So she shot him.

Whether or not Sis had been aiming precisely at his teeth as she pulled the trigger has vanished into time. Some people say certainly so, because his teeth sometimes irritated her, but most likely it would not have mattered what she was aiming at, since a snub-nosed .22 is notoriously inaccurate, even across a kitchen table. It would not have mattered if Sis were Deadeye Dick or if she could not hit a bear in the ass with a handful of sand. She just had poor equipment for the job at hand.

Either way, the bullet struck Carson (Carter) square in his bared, snaggled canines, at the precise instant he turned his head. Much of the force of the bullet was deflected, which is a small miracle, but not so much of one that it had God's hand in it. He went to the hospital, cursing and bleeding. Sis went on the lam.

"They kept Sis hid out," my aunt Juanita said.

Later, Sis, incognito, and her daughter, Ruby, went to the hospital to see about him; there was still some question as to whether or not the law would want to know why her mother shot him in the first place. They walked the hall, peeking into the rooms as they went.

"He's in there," Sis said, at one open door. "They've got his damned ol' teeth in there in a glass. I'd know them damned ol' teeth anywhere." Doctors said he would recover, but his teeth were pretty much beyond help.

"But he never did file no charges," Aunt Juanita said. She does not believe that, if it had come to court, there was a judge or jury in all of Floyd County who would convict her.

"If it was me," my aunt Juanita said, "and somebody pointed a pistol at my face and said, 'I'll shoot you, you little SB,' I believe I'd of started backin' up . . . well, a little bit."

Sis went to see Carson (Carter) as he recuperated.

"You shot me, you old bitch," he said.

But because of his wound and his bandages, it came out as: "Uh ougt meah, uh o' mitch."

"Just be glad all I had was that damn popgun," Sis said. "If I'd had me a .38, I'd of killed you."

Oddly, no one can remember what she had cooked that night for supper.

Love would win out in time, and they would reconcile.

"She grieved," my mother recalls, "when he was gone."

I told my mother how much I enjoyed learning about Sis, but still did not understand what that had to do—at least directly—with her recipe for chicken and dressing.

"Because of the pistol," my mother said.

"I don't understand," I said, and she looked at me like I was simple again.

"Because," she said, "it was the same pistol she used to murder Ike."

Like I said, it is a deep, dark pool.

"Sis committed murder?" I said.

She nodded.

"Did she do time?" I asked.

"You don't go to prison," my mother said patiently, "for murdering a *rooster*."

Finally, it was becoming clear.

"Sis's nephew, William, had this rooster—Juanita says his name was Ike—and it was a mean rooster and it would peck Sis," my mother explained. "Every time she went out to hang out the clothes, it would peck her on her legs. She hated that rooster. But it was a pet. I think it was one of those fancy fightin' roosters. Well, William would always eat with them, because she was such a good, good cook. One night, she made a big pan of dressing, and William ate a big plate, and then another big ol' plate, and finally he looked at Sis and said, 'Sis, this is the best chicken and dressing I have ever eat in my life.' And Sis said, 'Well, it ought to be. It's your GD rooster.'

"At least when she murdered Ike, she didn't let a good rooster go to waste." Then my gentle, elderly mother made a make-believe gun with her thumb and forefinger, and leveled it at the television.

"Same gun she used to shoot Carter's teeth out, I believe. One shot. Pew!"

The two old women sat quiet for a little while more, just remembering, though whether they did so together or apart I can't be sure, the one thing I do know is that there seems to be some tonic in it, maybe even a tiny sip from the Fountain of Youth. I think it may be fine to live in the past if that is where your people have all disappeared to, if that is a place where things still make some kind of sense to you.

"Sis was about the best cook we had in the entire family, one of the best cooks that ever was, and we all watched and listened to her and learned from Sis. Chocolate cakes? Coconut cakes? My God. Well, I'm no baker, but she was the finest cake-maker I ever knew. But there wasn't nothin' she couldn't do. Fried chicken? Dumplings? Beans? Cornbread? Biscuit? Vegetable soup? Stew? What a cook. She cooked in the cafés, but that ain't where she learned it. She learned from her people. And what Sis was mostly known for was that chicken and dressing."

"No," my aunt Juanita corrected, "it was dumplin's."

"Dressin'," my momma said.

"Dumplin's," her sister said.

Having done her part to set straight the historical record, my aunt Juanita said she needed to be heading home—she does not drive at night anymore. She began her goodbyes. It takes the old women a long time to say goodbye. They begin in the living room, and say goodbye again in the kitchen, and again at the side porch, and then, finally, once more, in the yard. Only when the door on her blue Chevrolet Silverado pickup slams shut is it official, and even then the two old women talk to each other through the glass—reading lips, I suppose. They have walked a million miles or more off into that shared past, and have never really been apart. Imagine all the joy and heartache, in 160 years. They lived for two decades under the same roof, then lived another four decades, more or less, as next-door neighbors, divided only by a red dirt path, about fifty steps in all. It is a wonder they can say goodbye at all.

"But it was dressin'," my mother said when she came back inside.

Finally, after the biggest part of a day, she began to talk about what makes good chicken and dressing, and what can go wrong if the cook is a chucklehead. She knows because Sis, and her own momma, taught her when she was barely old enough to tie her shoes. One day, Sis handed her a spoon so she could stir. "This way, child," she would say, showing her how to measure salt, sage, pepper, and other seasonings in one big hand, and mix them into the cornbread moistened with buttery chicken broth. As the years and platters passed across their tables, my mother realized that the spoon Sis wielded in her big fist was more like a wand. With a spoon or a pot handle in her hand, Sis Morrison was downright beautiful. What magic there was in cooking. It gave a person such value, such standing. And if it could make a harsh or homely woman lovable, even lovely, then surely it could make a frightened and timid child as brave as a storybook princess.

"Anyway, you start with a fresh pan of hot cornbread," my momma said. "You can't make nothin' good out of old bread. . . . You season the water, and set the chicken on to boil. . . ."

"But," I pleaded, "what happened to *her*?"

"Who?"

"*Her!*"

"Well, son, Sis lived a long time." She cooked and cooked, and the legend of her food grew and grew. In old age, she cooked one last meal for my people, and laid it out before them as if she knew she would be remembered for it, for all time. "There was fried chicken, chicken cooked three or four ways, and pork chops, and potato salad, and green beans, and cornbread and biscuit, and dressing, of course, and cakes—Lord, at the cakes—and . . ." It made my mother almost cry. She remembers how Sis told some bawdy stories, even to my grandmother Ava, and cursed like a stevedore. But we will forgive a great cook almost anything, as I have already said, even in a house with Jesus on every other wall.

"Nobody never told Sis what to do, never told her how to act," said my momma. "Not till she had to go to that place."

Toward the end of her life, her health failing, Sis went to live in a retirement home in Rome. It was a nice place, my kinfolks recall, but for a woman who could sing a hymn and tell a bawdy joke and then punch you in your eye, those pallid days of never-completed puzzles and Kool-Aid must have been hard.

One day, on furlough, the Georgia people took her to see the Alabama people one last time, but she had trouble getting up the steps to my mother's house. One of her kinfolks kidded her about it, and she told him to "go to hell, you old son of a bitch," and threatened him with a pistol she no longer owned. Firearms were not allowed in the retirement home.

In time, she needed help even to stand, a woman still in her rough form but not as sharp, not as clear. She shrank inside her robe, and if she cursed at all it was under her breath. She even started to say the blessing at supper. Night after night, she bowed her head and humbly intoned, like a little lamb:

God is good
God is great

She was just another old woman, it seemed, in a place for them. As she dwindled, the retirement home held a special dinner for the residents and their families. The staff asked Sis, a proven commodity by then when it came to saying grace, to say the blessing for the assemblage. She shuffled slowly and painfully to the front of the cafeteria on her walker, folded her hands, turned her face to the rafters, and began to pray:

Bless the meat
And damn the skin
Back your ears
And cram it in

Sis shuffled back to her seat in the uneasy quiet. Then, one by one by one, the sweet little ol' ladies in their wheelchairs and the ones chaperoned by their walkers began to titter, which was as close as it was ever going to come to jailbreak.

"She passed," my mother said, "not long after that."

The rivers of Rome were prone to flood in the city's early years, so most of the graveyards in and around the city were built up high, some of them even terraced into the sides of the mountains themselves. The history of the South is interred here: Civil War heroes, slaves, freedmen, Doughboys, dam workers, the beloved wife of Woodrow Wilson, and one of the greatest cooks who ever was. My mother closed her eyes for a moment, and I thought, for a second, she might be saying a short prayer to the memory of Sis Morrison.

"His name was Carter" was all she said.

. . .

I still had no recipe. Or maybe I did, and was too dumb to see it. I had the heart and soul of it; the rest was arithmetic. In the end, it took my mother two more hours to translate Sis's recipe for her renowned chicken and dressing, which is my mother's recipe now. She does not believe Sis would mind seeing it written down and shared with the wider world. But if I had heard a big voice call me a GD little SB from the dark rafters as I wrote it all down, I would not have been greatly surprised.

Sis's Chicken and Dressing

My mother insists on dark meat, only. But if you prefer mixed pieces, get a fat bird. The secret to it all is, of course, the buttery chicken fat, and you cannot get chicken fat from a skinny bird. "It's a sin to cook with a skinny bird," Sis told my mother. She is not sure where in the Bible it says that, about its being a sin, but if Sis said it was so, then it had to be in there somewhere, maybe hard up against Deuteronomy.

WHAT YOU WILL NEED

6 or 7 chicken pieces, thighs, drumsticks, or both,
    skin on; or, use a fat baking hen, cut up
1 small carrot, chopped, to season broth
½ cup diced celery, to season broth
1 large yellow or white onion, coarsely chopped,
    to season broth
1 tablespoon salt, for the broth
One 9-inch cast-iron skillet of cornbread
1 egg
1 large sweet onion, such as a Vidalia, finely chopped,
    for dressing mixture
¼ teaspoon black pepper (or to taste)
¼ teaspoon sage powder ("Do not ruin it with sage;
    too much and it's all you taste")
1 teaspoon poultry seasoning (also contains sage)
Butter or bacon grease

HOW TO COOK IT

In a stew pot, boil the chicken, carrot, celery, and coarse-chopped onion in salted water until done, "and tender—it will continue to cook inside the dressing." Chicken drumsticks can be substituted for thighs, but the dish seems to work best with a mix of dark meat. The salt in the chicken broth should be plenty, to season the dressing. Leave the cooked vegetables in the broth. Throwing them out is throwing out flavor. Do *not* waste any of the chicken fat that floats to the top in boiling. It is, truly, like gold.

Preheat the oven to 350 or 400 degrees.

Break the chicken into small pieces, but do *not* shred. Shredded chicken tastes like straw; she does not know how that happens, but she just knows it does. Be careful to discard small pieces of bone and gristle, but do *not* discard the skin. In a large bowl, break the cooked cornbread into small pieces, and gradually stir in the chicken broth and egg, mixing thoroughly until you have a moist, puddinglike consistency. Stir in the chopped sweet onion and the remaining seasonings; then, at the last, gently mix in the broken-up pieces of deboned chicken.

Pour the mixture into an iron skillet that has been greased with real butter. Some of the old women insist on bacon grease; try it both ways till one of them makes you happy. Again, the mixture should be of a consistency so that it almost crawls from the mixing bowl into the iron skillet, like perfectly cooked grits. Bake in the preheated oven until the top of the dressing is crisp and golden brown and the inside is creamy. This could be anywhere from 30 to 45 minutes, depending on the oven. Listen close as you break the crust with the first spoonful. That will tell you if you got it right. . . .

Again, because every stove is different, this dish must be closely watched as it cooks, to prevent it from drying out. Slightly undercooked dressing is still very tasty if it is not too loose in texture, but it may be better to overcook the dressing slightly than to undercook it. Slightly overcooked dressing will be dense and maybe even a little crunchier on the edges but still flavorful. Leave it in the oven beyond this point and it may still have some value, as home plate in a backyard softball game. Remember, all the main ingredients were already cooked to start with.

"Your dressing is going to be crispier in the corners than it is in the middle, and that's just fine," my mother believes. "That's the part I like, that crispy part . . . but I guess you can like any part you want to."

Serve with mashed potatoes or candied yams, fresh green beans or home-cooked collards—canned and frozen collards taste like pond algae—and slaw.

Since dressing is not dressing without cranberry sauce, either make your own or buy a can of the 1950s variety that makes a sucking sound as it slides out of the can. Neither Sis nor my momma would think less of you. We like the jellied kind. Really.

. . .

It has been copied and cloned by so many cooks, so many generations, that people here may not even know they are cooking Sis's recipe. Even my mother has gently tinkered with it across the years. For instance, it was my mother's adaptation to pull the boiled chicken off the bone and mix it, gently, into the cornbread mixture, instead of pressing whole pieces of the boiled chicken into the top of the uncooked dressing and letting it crisp as the dressing cooks. Both have their merits—Sis's original recipe is a prettier dish—but pulling it off the bone and allowing the bulk of the chicken to cook inside the cornmeal mixture means the chicken is less likely to dry out, and the dressing will be further seasoned as it cooks. I have had it both ways and loved it both ways, but even dark meat can dry out a little if the whole pieces are pressed into the top and exposed to the direct heat. I believe my mother's tinkering improved it, but I have to, I suppose.

. . .

We believe that Sis will be forgiven her cussing, that she will be forgiven everything, really, even the shooting of Carson (Carter). We do not count Ike, or all the other birds and beasts of the field she laid asunder over the years, for the sake of a good dressing or a dumpling or a fine meat gravy. And if you do hold such as that against her, then only vegetarians shall enter the Kingdom, and that is a terrible, terrible thought. How awful to spend eternity playing harps, peeling parsnips, and shuffling around in hundred-dollar L. L. Bean house shoes. I think I would rather go where Sis goes, and eat where Sis cooks.

My people tell a story about the great Ever After, one that reminds my mother of Sis. In the story, a rich and selfish man is condemned to hell, and is ushered into an endless dining hall. He sees a great banquet laid out before the assembled people there, a feast of dripping, roasted meats and savory soups and sumptuous stews. The devil's imps file down the table to pass out spoons, but the spoons are longer than the arms of the men and women gathered there. They cannot, as hard as they try, get the delicious food into their mouths, and a great wailing and gnashing of teeth echoes and echoes through the great hall.

Meanwhile, in heaven, Saint Peter welcomes another new arrival, a common and generous man, into a similar great, long banquet hall. The newcomer sees another grand feast laid out before the diners assembled there. But, disconcertingly, the man sees the waiters pass out the same spoons as the ones passed out to the diners in hell, all of them too long for the people to feed themselves. "How, then," the crestfallen man asks Saint Peter, "can this be heaven?"

Saint Peter smiles.

"Because in heaven," he says, "we feed each other."

12

THE SECOND GHOST

Cracklin' Cornbread

*One of my great-uncles, Bill Hamilton, the guitar picker and shoe kicker
who invited himself to dinner, and invited in the Holy Ghost*

THE SEQUENCE of events that led to the miracle on the Dalton Road involved not one but two separate revelations of the Holy Ghost. My grandfather, who was not a churched man, missed the second revelation altogether, because the hysteria and theatrics from the first manifestation made him so mad he left, walking in the dark for a distant crossing, where he swung himself up onto a westbound train.

It was autumn, and one of his guitar-picking, deadbeat brothers-in-law, Bill Hamilton, showed up uninvited for a fine supper of potato dumplings at their rented house in the mountains outside Rome. After scraping the platter clean and licking his spoon, Bill was picking a soulful rendition of "Great Speckle Bird" on his Martin guitar when he suddenly got happy, raised his pick hand to the Lord, and began to shout and praise and prophesy. He sensed the burning specter of the Holy Ghost and welcomed it into the unworthy vessel of his body, and became so overwhelmed with grace he commenced to run to and fro in the Spirit, and inadvertently kicked both of Charlie Bundrum's work boots across the house. One flew under a low, heavy iron bed, where it could not easily be retrieved, and the other seemed to have vanished into thin air, though it would later be found beneath the chifforobe.

Charlie became so angry at that foolishness he gathered his tools and left. There was rumored to be work in North Alabama for a man who could drive a straight nail, and even if there was not, at least he would be gone from these freeloading, guitar-picking, proselytizing shoe-kickers. Ava tongue-lashed him viciously as he walked out the door, leaving her with five children and a washtub full of cracklin' meat to render into lard before the weather warmed.

"It ain't I don't believe in the Holy Ghost," he called to her over his shoulder as he vanished into the night. "It's just that I don't believe He's a'-livin' in Bill Hamilton."

The second revelation, a day or so later, was a good bit harder to deny.

. . .

It happened in the early afternoon. That morning, the air had been chill, hog-killing weather—you never killed a hog till after the first frost—but by the afternoon the air was sticky and warm. The sky was still blue, but she could hear thunder to the west, out over Alabama. Ava, in a severe ankle-length dress and old-fashioned button-up high-top shoes, hunched over a giant bubbling cast-iron cauldron. Her hair fell to below her waist, as black as ten feet down, but in just the past year a single streak of silvery white had begun to snake through. She stirred the pot with a long steel ladle, the handle wrapped in rags to keep it from burning her hands, and when she lifted it from the pot to threaten the children, it smoked in the air.

My mother, still the baby of the family, sat watching from the dirt a safe distance away; the black pot would hiss and spit every now and then, like something alive, and glowed a dull red on the outside. The boys, James and William, watched from the far end of the yard, where they had been banished, too. They were just now in their teens, and tracked in mayhem the way other children tracked dirt; Ava had drawn a line in the clay, and told all her children that if they crossed it and came near the dangerous bubbling pot she would sell them to Gypsies.

"She's witchin' Daddy," James said.

His imagination, and ability to lie, were boundless.

"No," said William, "she's just makin' lard."

My mother was fascinated by her brothers and listened closely to what they said, unless they were tormenting her and her sisters for sport. "They were so mean," my mother told me. "They put me in a sack one time and hung me in a tree."

Ava was not, my mother realized, in fact hexing her man, but did curse him steadily between stanzas of "Victory in Jesus" as she stirred the smoking pot. Of a thousand hymns inside her head, this was her new favorite, and she sang at least part of it every day over every meal she cooked, whether she was joyous, melancholy, or mad. In a house full of Philistines, it was the only church her man and boys were likely to receive.

O victory in Jesus . . .

All the children crept as close as they could. Imagine a thousand skillets, all filled with the best bacon in the world, all going at once, and you might get close to the smell that wafted across the yard, down the road, and into the pines. The children stood or sat as if entranced, and their stomachs gurgled and growled. "My Lord, there just ain't no better smell in this world," my mother told me.

Ava had worked over the hot fire all afternoon, and had all but rendered thirty pounds of cubed, perfect, pure-white pork fat in her ten-gallon iron wash pot. She was trying to fish the last batch of golden cracklin's from the hot, roiling oil when she smelled the rain. She told the boys to run to the house and take their sisters with them, and not to dawdle about it. She did not tell them a storm was coming; she never would have said it that way. She said, in the vernacular of her people, "It's comin' up a cloud."

The first gusts, fierce and sudden, cracked tree limbs along the Old Dalton Road and rushed beneath the cauldron like a bellows. Flames shot into the air higher than her head, and red-orange cinders skittered across the swept dirt of the yard. A few hot cinders landed in the folds of her heavy skirt and in her long hair, which had begun to whip like snakes in the air; as she beat them out with her free hand, she slapped her own face so hard, by accident, she almost knocked herself down. The boys had not moved an inch. If their momma was going to burst into flame, or be carried off into the sky, flapping, by a great whirlwind, they intended to stay right where they were and watch it transpire. Across the yard, they heard the tempo and volume of her voice rise to meet the storm. She sang louder when she was scared.

My Savior forever . . .

She went quiet suddenly and dropped the spoon in the grass. There had been no way to tell how bad it was until it was almost on top of them; there was no dark magic in that, either, no great mystery, only the nature of things in the hills of northwestern Georgia. The high ridges, deep hollers, and thick trees boxed the people in. The storms came rumbling fast and unseen, like a train through a dark tunnel.

Ava took off for the old whitewashed house at a dead run, both hands steadying a biscuit pan heaped high with golden cracklin's, a delicacy as dear as beefsteak, slammed it on the table, then darted back outside to gather her children. She yelled one last time to the nitwit boys, who had finally regained their hearing and some sense, and to Edna and Juanita, the older girls. She scooped my mother, the baby, from the dirt like a good shortstop, and ran again for the door.

The children could see, past Ava's blowing skirt in that open door, what must have looked like the end of the world. The first raindrops hit the roiling hot grease in the giant wash pot with a sound like gunshots. Fire spiked into the air, then geysers of white smoke. The wind shook the thin walls of the old house, and the front window banged loud in its sash. The rented house was ragged and flimsy, and even as she and her children sheltered inside, Ava knew it was like taking refuge inside a cardboard box. She would be afraid of weather all her life, but knew the difference between straight-line winds, which would knock down a tree or break a window, and tornadoes, which would bring Judgment Day, killing livestock and people and leaving the land in sticks.

It was a green sky she dreaded most; a green sky had the devil in it. And even as she counted the heads of her children, to make sure she had not missed one, an odd, pink lightning arced over-head, and the skies changed from black to that dreaded, roiling, dirty green. As they watched, spellbound, a thin, writhing cyclone dropped out of the clouds like a worm out of a rotten apple and began to tear the ridge apart.

There was no car to flee in, no storm shelter to run to. The tall pines around them twisted in the wind, and limbs snapped like Popsicle sticks, and even the hardwoods, the great oaks, began to come apart. The girls clutched at Ava's skirts like they were drowning, and began to sob. The boys were pale, silent. Ava pulled them all close as the storm crossed the ridge, stabbed into the holler, and bore down.

It'll turn, she told herself.

But the tornado did not zig and zag, or climb and fall in the sky. It did not act right. It chewed its way across the valley and down the road in a straight line, roaring like some great machine, and Ava slammed the door shut and made it fast with a slab of board held in place with a tenpenny nail. There was only one window in the room, and Ava pushed her children as far from it as she could.

It'll turn.

The rain hammered the tin roof, and then came the roar itself, more like a machine than a thing of nature. Her children wailed, and she told them to hush, but the truth is, she felt like screaming herself, like beating at the walls herself, from the inside. It was not just the danger but the hatefulness of it, of knowing that the last thing her children might ever feel was terror. The boys forgot to pretend to be brave and stood fixed to her side. The little girls swung on her skirts, about to drag her to the floor.

She had always been an imperfect Pentecostal, mostly because Charlie so often needed a good cussing out, and a certain amount of backsliding was inevitable in the natural world. But it was a religion that suited her, a faith born in breadlines and street revivals, a sect of healers, mystics, and miracles. As the room turned to gloom, she was every inch a Christian and began to pray in the style of her people. That does not mean she gently folded her hands and humbly bowed her head and appealed to the saints. The Pentecostals do not go about God gently. They pray like they are ablaze, in a fire that cannot be doused or smothered but only blown out by a greater one, the way a bundle of TNT can blow out a burning well.

Ava balled her hands into fists and threw back her head and invoked the Holy Ghost, and begged, sobbing, to have it course through her blood and bones and marrow and mind. And as she did, she began to shake. She gathered her skirts in her fingers and whirled round and round, sending her children tumbling or stumbling back across the floor. She bounced, and praised, and crashed to her knees, then thrust her skinny arms heavenward and began to speak in unknown tongues. The skeptics called it theater, religious hysteria, but the followers of the Pentecost knew it was the old language, maybe even the voice of God. It was not guttural or harsh but almost musical, like an antidote, somehow, for the cacophony outside. The children still sobbed, but now their eyes were fixed on her, and amazed. Even the baby, who was being squeezed half to death in the arms of the oldest girl, was rapt.

They noticed, in time, that the shaking of the planks under their feet and in the walls had gone still, and the roar had faded, then died. Ava rose from the floor and opened the door. It was warped from the force of the wind, and she yanked it hard to open it, but there was nothing to see except a gentle rain and a litter of sticks and leaves. The tornado had taken a hard turn, and missed them clean.

Ava dusted off the knees of her long dress and swung the baby back onto her hip. She was bone-white, shaking. She did not seem joyous. She seemed mad.

"Well, I'll be goddamn," she said weakly. "I thought He had us all that time."

It has never been exactly clear why she said it; her children would only guess. Ava, we do know, said what she felt, before her mind began to slip in middle age and after. Her family had retreated to the mountains as the Depression settled on the South like an eclipse of the sun, and they lost a child to it then, to a sickness that could have been cured with a few dollar bills. She had lost so much already, and then here comes an act of God, to take everything else she had. It may be, the way she saw it, He owed her one.

Ava staggered out into the yard to check on the lard, to see what might be saved. The storm had come and gone in minutes, taking the rain with it, but the wind had spread sticks and specks of dead leaves across the cooling surface of the rendered fat. The underneath, she was relieved to see, was mostly clean. She would clean and strain the worst of it later, as well as she could. She laboriously scooped out the leaves and sticks and specks of other trash on the surface. After a while, she felt the eyes on her and noticed the children—all of them—still gathered around her expectantly, waiting for her to levitate, or break into a Tennessee two-step, or turn a stick into a snake. The boys, especially, were still dumbfounded. You could not beat them into church with a singletree, or hold them down for a hymn or a scrap of Scripture with mule harness and logging chains. But that afternoon they had witnessed a miracle with their own eyes, or at least what they believed a miracle to look like.

"Momma turned it," William told his big brother.

James, a born storyteller, did not know what to say. He was used to making up his stories, like the catfish he hooked in the backwater, as big as a Studebaker, that had a dead hog inside when it was hauled to the bank and cut open. Sometimes it was a Duesenberg and a milk cow, but the plot was generally the same. But this? No one would believe this, even if it was God's sanction.

"Momma prayed it away," William said.

The boys decided they would get religion after all, and held revival there under the clearing sky, baptizing each other with wet tree limbs, and would have sung a hymn if they had known any songs except the very bad ones they'd learned from the men down on the river and sang, snickering, behind the outhouse. Then they got bored and just wandered off, to see if the baby would eat a mud pie.

Ava, once she had her wind back, acted as if nothing much had happened; she still had work to do before nightfall, to feed her children. The air had gone chill again, and the sky was glittering and clear, the way it gets in the South only after a storm has blown the thick, wet air away. The children were whining from hunger when she strained and put up the last of the lard and went inside to finish supper.

Earlier in the day, she had put a pot of Great Northerns and ham bone on the stove to simmer, and by evening the beans were about done. Her Charlie had to sell the choice cuts of the hogs he raised then—the loin and chops and fresh ham and shoulder—to pay his debts. But there was still fatback, and soup bones, hog jowl, and pig's feet, cuts that would become delicacies by necessity. The cornbread was the centerpiece of this meal, though.

By kerosene light, Ava mixed up her meal, salt, and soda, then stirred in cold water. When the consistency was perfect—not too thin, not too thick—she stirred in two handfuls of the fresh, crisp cracklin's. She poured the cracklin'-cornmeal mixture into her iron skillet, which she greased with freshly rendered lard, and put it on to bake. She sang over it, of course. It rises better if you do. Everyone knows this.

She cubed some potatoes, about the same size as gambling dice, and set them to fry on top of the stove in a little lard, adding a little water now and then so the potatoes would keep tender as they cooked. She took a small onion and shaved it into the potatoes, because anything else is just ignorant, even if you don't like onion. It smelled so good, the children gathered around the stove and watched it all cook, as if they could will the skillet to give up supper a few minutes sooner. It was just dried beans, taters, meal, and the parts of the hog the better-off people would not have. It took a cook to make it into something fine. "I just wisht I'd of had more onion," to add another layer of flavor to the beans, Ava told her children. "If I'd had a extry onion, I'd of showed y'all sumpin'."

It is a recurring theme in our family history. We were always, as a family, one onion short.

The cornbread came out a light, golden brown, thick with cracklin's in the middle; the cracklin's had gone almost liquid except on the top of the cake, where they were crisped like bacon. Some people used egg as a way to enrich the taste and give it a spongier texture, and some used buttermilk for taste and texture; Ava disdained all this as getting fancy, as trying too hard, and expensive, besides.

She cut the cornmeal into cake slices, and James and William snatched it off the stove and ate it right there, flipping the hot bread from hand to hand and trying to suck air in around the hot mouthfuls to cool it. She threatened to beat them, but she just didn't have the wind, and broke off a little bit of crust for herself. The bread itself tasted of that rendered pork, and here and there were chewy, tiny pieces of the skin. They ate it down to crumbs, and only then set in on the beans and the potatoes and a little surprise Ava had in the oven: some roasted pig's feet, all fat, cartilage, and goodness. Charlie loved pig's feet, which was mostly why she cooked them that night, so the children could tell him how good they had been. Ava knew how to hurt a man.

But it was the bread that they would remember. It is difficult to explain the luster of a cracklin' to someone who has never had a good one. I can't write pretty enough to describe it; you just have to taste it. The best way to appreciate and understand a cracklin' is to hold a still-warm nugget between your thumb and forefinger and gently press them together. The essence that oozes out of the cracklin' is all that is good about Southern cooking, literally rendered into a speck of happiness. That was what Ava and her children tasted in the hours after the storm, when it turned out the End of Days was not upon them after all.

Over in Calhoun County, Charlie stood in line to be picked for construction and roofing crews, and at night he camped in the pines with other men who came to chase work at the army base, dining on canned Vienna sausage and pork and beans. He kept his tools close by his side, in case the police came to roust them for vagrancy, but at least no one was getting happy around the campfire and booting beanie weenies all about the place.

Charlie, when he was drinking and sometimes when he was not, said the Lord could be slow to deliver the common man, if He delivered him at all. This was why that freeloading Bill Hamilton made him so mad, him a-pickin' in a Tampa beer joint one week in his checkedy sport coat, then preaching and dancing and acting a fool when he came home hungry, his pockets turned out. There ort to be a limit, he liked to say, on how many times a man could backslide and still get to come back to the Lord. Charlie paid his own way, and did not ask for help from anyone, even from beyond the firmament. When his children told him what had happened, what their momma had done when the storm was about to get them, he merely nodded his head. Ava was certainly touched by something, he always said, so why could it not be God?

· · ·

It is one of the ways we keep the calendar down here. We remember with food. In my uncle William Bundrum's mind, the storm and that wonderful cornbread would always be linked, so that you could not tell about one of them without telling of the other. But, then, at our table, it seems there was a story in every plate, and a plate in every story, except maybe artichokes. Nobody liked to remember artichokes.

For years after Ava passed, we held a great feast the second weekend in June to celebrate her birthday. We gathered behind her little frame house next to my aunt Juanita and uncle Ed's, which had been closed up tight after her death and would never be lived in again. It was her house. I often caught myself glancing at the windows, as if I might glimpse her there, as if she were merely waiting to join her party when she damn well wanted to.

In the yard, a swaybacked picnic table creaked from the weight of the food piled on top of it, in aluminum foil and wax paper and

Tupperware. There were four kinds of pan-fried chicken, barbe-cued chicken, fried pork chops, barbecued pork chops, barbecued center-cut ham slices, deviled eggs, baked beans with slab bacon, green beans with salt pork, pinto beans with ham, three types of potato salad, fried squash, sweet corn on the cob, creamed sweet corn, sliced red tomatoes, cucumber and Vidalia onion, pickled pepper, macaroni and cheese, macaroni salad, three kinds of coleslaw, carrot salad, casseroles beyond counting, homemade rolls, coconut cake, brownies, chocolate cake, blueberry-and-cream-cheese pie, strawberry shortcake, still-warm biscuits, and a sweating mound of cracklin' cornbread covered in aluminum foil.

That made my uncle William think of the miracle of '41, and that is where he told it to me that first and only time, a square of that cornbread balanced on a paper napkin on his knee. He broke it in two—cracklin' cornbread somehow tastes better if you can see the inside—then pulled forth one of the nuggets of pork fat and ate it with such genuine relish that *I* could almost taste it. "Nobody made cracklin' bread like my momma," he told me, "but this is pretty good, son." It was his mother's recipe from that night, almost seven decades later, rendered and baked by one of her children, or grandchildren; we're not quite sure.

It was early in the new millennium, and he was in his eighties then, tall and thin. The wicked little boy had vanished inside an easy old man in a brown-checked felt fedora with a golden feather jutting from the brim. He told the story the way he did everything else, smooth, cool, and steady, as if the jerks and snatches that disrupted and impeded other men's lives had nothing to do with him. He talked easy, and walked easy. He had poured steel before he retired, running a giant crane mounted on railroad tracks at the big plant in Gadsden, Alabama, tons of iron and other men's lives in his hands. It was not a job for a twitchy man. He retired in his sixties and walked off into the autumn of his years, in Hush Puppies. I asked him, that day, why he'd never told me that story before, in all those days at our house, at all those suppers, and he just shrugged and said, in that easy way, "Well, I guess I just never thought of it, son."

The miracle has dwindled, I suppose. My uncle James, the great storyteller and liar, might have told and retold it many times around campfires or on riverbanks, as a jug went round and round, or as he stood on the sidewalk outside the Food Outlet in town to chat up the widow women. But my aunts say it would have been indistinguishable, in time, from all the other tales in his unlimited repertoire, and likely passed unnoticed. Still, it seems to me that such a miracle should be more revered, more robust than that, not allowed to fade like a newspaper left in the back window of an old Chevrolet.

But sometimes, my uncle William wondered if there was maybe more to it, not less, than first appeared. His mother, in that time, stood in contrast to the people of her mountains. In a land of hard manual labor and deprivation, she could read Shakespeare. She quoted Scripture from thin air, and spouted poetry, though her education had ended before high school. She knew lore, and myth, *and* her Bible. Her mind was not yet tortured. Her mind was beautiful, and even as she began to decline we all saw glimpses of it, in the stories she told. What must she have been like in '41?

William was not a churched man, either, but he saw what he saw that day of the storm. He was also his mother's son, however—smart, and hard to bamboozle. And every now and then, he wondered. With the End of Days upon them, Ava would not have wanted the last thing in her children's minds to be fear. Ava, in those terrible seconds, might have tried anything to spare her children, in what she must have believed to be their last seconds alive, even if all she could do was cast some kind of veil, to fill their eyes and ears with something, anything. Maybe it does not even have to be one thing or the other; maybe, my uncle William wondered aloud, it was both. "Momma," he said, "was smart."

It's easier, better even, just to say she turned it.

"It's a better story," he said, "ain't it?"

I told him it was a pretty good story either way.

My uncle James, all bones and elbows, ambled over from the picnic table, and took a seat beside us on the concrete stoop of my grandmother's house. He had lost most of one ear somewhere along the way, and wore the same khaki work shirt he probably wore in '53, with sawdust in the cracks in his leather work boots older than me. There is nothing on God's earth that old man could not build with a hammer, a handsaw, and an apron full of tenpenny nails; people said he could have hammered together a stairway to heaven if he had not had to stop every fifth or sixth step to try to quench an unquenchable thirst. He stopped swinging a hammer as he passed eighty, and spent most of his time flirting with every slow-moving woman in town, laughing at his own outrageous stories, and slapping his own knee. It was said he had taken to hanging out at the city cemetery, not out of any great melancholy over his impending demise, but because that was one more place the widow women congregated.

They were greatly different men, the brothers. But even if you looked down on them from space, you could tell they were Charlie Bundrum's boys.

"How you been, Uncle Jim?" I asked him.

"Oh, son, it's been awful," he said.

"What's wrong?"

"Well, son, I've quit lying."

"It's been hard on you?" I asked.

" 'Bout kilt me," he said.

"How long you been quit?" I asked.

" 'Bout fifteen minutes," he said.

My uncle William just smiled ruefully. He had seen it coming. After so much time, all the foolishness is a little thin from use. They shook hands across me—the last time they were in the same place at the same time, at least that I can recall. I asked James if he remembered the day Ava turned the storm, and he said he did, of course, said it was a sight to see, son, and then it occurred to him that he had not yet had any coconut cake. He shuffled off to get a slab of it, saying he would be right back. That was ten years ago.

My mother, so young at the time of the storm, only knows what she saw from behind her momma's blowing skirts. "The Bible says the Lord touches people in desperate times," my mother said when I asked her what she believed. "Momma had the Holy Ghost when she was young. It's a sin to have it, I believe, and not make it known."

It may be that we just like to imbue our old people with something more than they are. But someone else will have to say that out loud; my people, truly, would never feed me again.

My uncle William died just a few years after that birthday dinner. A stroke almost killed my uncle James but instead just took some of his memories, the true and the untrue. He is in his nineties now, and still terrorizing nurses. He has resumed lying, I hear. No reason to make things harder than they are.

The other day, I saw him driving. I didn't know he still had a license . . . like that ever mattered.

"I fish all day and I hunt all night," he tells anyone who will listen.

"What do you hunt, Jim?" the gullible ask.

"Why, women, son. Women."

I thought I might ask him again someday about the miracle on the Dalton Road, but most likely I will not, will just leave it as it lies. If I wanted another taste of it, I would have to look for it on a plate.

. . .

But that, too, had all but faded from existence. Of all the recipes my mother tried to translate for me, the one for good cracklin' cornbread is one of the most ambitious and difficult for modern-day cooks, give or take a mean snapping turtle, which can maim you, and poke salad, the poisonous weed. Cracklin' cornbread is not complicated, only time-intensive, and of a world, and a mind-set, so very different from now. Still, as much as anything she shared with me about her cooking, it promised a genuine taste of the past. "Oh, I cooked it over the years," my mother told me. "You just wasn't nowhere close, and so you didn't get none of it." I asked her if she might try again, since I had obviously not been sold to Gypsies, either. But she told me some dishes get to be antiques after a while; the world spins on without them, and the days grow too short for a dish that takes so long and takes such care. She said she would try, though, if we could find the essential ingredient: fresh, perfect, pristine pork fat.

She said it was increasingly hard to find decent cracklin' meat unless you raised and butchered your own hogs, something we did for the last time a few years ago. It had to be pure, white, glistening fat, sometimes still attached to a clean white skin, and sometimes with a thin—barely there—streak o' lean. The lean would burn in rendering, and too much would destroy the delicate process. When she tried to get it at the grocery stores, the young butchers looked at her as if she had asked for wildebeest.

A good butcher shop *might* have it, she said, but most of our butcher shops have vanished in the rural, blue-collar South, and certainly in the poorer counties, even the most rural ones. How odd, that the only people with access to cracklin' meat, the poor folks' delicacy, would be the ones in the country club, the carpet-baggers, the ones least likely to realize the true value in a slab of unadulterated fat.

You can buy precooked cracklin's in groceries, she said, but those are a packaged mess. They quickly go stale, and have an underlying taste and smell reminiscent of a smoldering city dump. I held a package up to her once from the meat cooler, and she made a face of unmitigated revulsion.

We had all but given up. Then, one day in the early fall about three years ago, we got lucky. We had gone to a butcher shop in the country called Valley Meats, in the community of Alexandria, in northeastern Alabama, to buy a pork roast, some salt pork, and some good sharp black-rind cheddar cheese. The shop had its own slaughterhouse, and killed, carved, and packaged pork for the few farmers who still raised their own pork. It was a go-to place for fresh chops and spareribs and thick-cut bacon—not that awful thin stuff that crisped up like burned tissue paper. As we walked into the small shop, the butchers were loading pounds and pounds of beautiful cracklin' meat into brown paper sacks, for an older gentleman I did not know.

I have never seen such avarice in my mother's eyes as when she looked on all that pork fat. She has not flirted with a man for twelve lustrums, but I think she would have winked at the old man if she thought he would share one of those bags of pork.

"Is there any left?" she asked the butcher.

"No, ma'am," said the young butcher, "I'm sorry to say."

She looked like she was going to cry. The young butcher ducked into the back—to hide from her, I believed. He came back a few minutes later with twenty or so pounds of cracklin' meat that had been reserved to mix with scraps to make sausage, or to be sliced and salted, but I guess he just could not break the old woman's heart. As I carried it out, I believe she would have skipped if she had not been afraid of hurting herself.

I asked her if we would have cracklin' bread for supper that night, but she said she needed a day at least to think about it, and maybe even pray over it. Cracklin' cornbread—real cracklin' bread—is a two-step process. Anyone can do the second part, the cornbread, but even a seasoned cook has to take care with the first. "It ain't complicated to make cracklin's," my mother explained, "but you can burn the house down if you ain't care-ful. That's why Momma did it outside." The secret is to make it in smaller batches, resulting in smaller fires. "I'd do it in the yard now if I had a good iron wash pot. But you can't find them no more, either."

In her youth, the job was done by the oldest, wisest, and most trusted, the same elders who laid out the rows of the gar-den and took ticks off babies and said the prayer at Thanksgiv-ing and Christmas. She had to watch the rendering process for years before she was left to do it by herself, in her teens, when she was deemed mature. It is not a job for a chucklehead, and the most experienced cooks burned themselves rendering lard; more burned the lard, just by turning their attention from it for even a scant moment.

"You *cannot* do this and not pay attention," she warned, one more time. From the doorway, I watched her cut the meat up into two-inch cubes, with unerring precision. "They don't have to be perfect size, or perfect square," but they were. She carefully set the heat, added the perfect amount of water, and for hours tended her pot, stirring every few minutes, patient, vigilant. She stared into the pot for a long time, but I doubt if that was all she saw.

Cracklin' Cornbread

The cracklin's are not the main purpose, traditionally, of rendering lard, only a tasty by-product. When the last of the cracklin's are rendered, let the lard cool in the cooking pot until it can be safely removed to store, and use it to make biscuits, or grease a cornbread skillet, or fry good eggs. It can also be used to add a touch of flavor to green beans, greens, dried beans, or other vegetables—in fact, use it for anything you want to taste good. My people do not refrigerate lard, claiming that changes its flavor.

Ask the butcher for cracklin' meat specifically, what some call fatback. Ask for pure white meat, with no more than a trace of lean, or—better—none at all. The skin can be left on, but for best results trim it away, my mother believes. Skin will make cracklin's chewier in the cornbread. Some people like that. "Some people don't know better," my mother says.

WHAT YOU WILL NEED

(FOR THE CRACKLIN'S)

6 to 8 pounds cracklin' meat

1 cup water

HOW TO COOK IT

Cut the cracklin' meat into cubes, about 2 inches square. They will shrink considerably as the fat is rendered.

Empty the cup of water into a thick-sided 2-gallon pot—this will help prevent the cracklin's from burning as the first of the fat begins to melt—and set over medium heat. Add the cracklin' meat, and cook, stirring at least every few minutes, until the water is cooked out and the fat has begun to render in the bottom of the pot. When the water is cooked out and the rendered fat has begun to pool, reduce the heat to low or at most low to medium, just hot enough to keep the rendering process going, and continue to stir.

Do not leave the cracklin' meat unattended, or unstirred, and do not try to rush the process by using higher heat, which will cause burning or uneven cooking. This is a slow, slow process, taking hours. You render the pork fat. You do not fry the cracklin's. If the hot fat spits at you unduly, lower the heat slightly.

Timing varies greatly, depending on the fat itself, and not all the cracklin's will cook at the same time. The cracklin's will be done when they float to the top; they should be a light-golden color. They will burn quickly at this point, so fish them out as they rise to the top, and allow the rest of the meat to continue to cook. If a cracklin' is dark brown, it has cooked too long, like overcooked bacon. *Do not* salt the cracklin' meat as it renders. Do not introduce any foreign matter, such as cayenne pepper, into the still-cooking cracklin's, no matter how good an idea it might seem at the time. It will only corrupt the process and taint the lard.

"Don't use *no* seasoning," my mother warns. "The cracklin' has got all the flavor in the world in it."

Every batch is slightly different. Do not be alarmed if it takes hours to complete the process—even between 4 and 6 hours for larger batches—or disappointed in the skimpy amount of cracklin's you take from the cookpot. Two gallons of cracklin' meat will produce only about a quart or so of cracklin's. That, too, will vary.

They will keep, unrefrigerated, for days, and can be refrigerated and even frozen, or home-canned if sealed in canning jars. If they are going to be eaten as is, taste them before you season them in any way. They require no salt, but can be salted to taste if you are the kind of person who ignores perfectly good advice, or even dusted with cayenne or other spices, if you insist. But my mother says only a Philistine would ruin a good cracklin' with "a bunch of junk." If no one is watching, and you do not feel the need to comply with your physician, eat the still-warm cracklin's one after another, like M&M's.

Now, if you have any cracklin's left, you need to concoct some cornbread. Follow the cornbread recipe from Chapter 3, but stir in 1½ cups cooked cracklin's. It will cook the same.

Most people do not butter cracklin' cornbread before eating, because of the fat in the nuggets that permeate the bread. Eat it hot, as hot as you can stand it.

Serve with practically anything: vegetable soup, potato soup, beans, greens, turnips cooked with butter and onion, or any fall or fresh vegetable. There is no need for meat, my mother believes, if you have this. The bread is the main course. My mother eats a few cracklin's with her beans and greens, like a side.

For a true feast, serve with pinto beans simmered with fat ham, homemade potato salad, and collard greens.

· · ·

It is romantic, I guess, to say that some old people are the last of their kind. But I think my maternal uncles are like that; I never expect to see their like again. I will always remember the last time I saw them together, and how my uncle William, before he walked away in his comfortable shoes, told me of one last miracle, one that occurred when he still had his used-car lot over in Gadsden, a broad-shouldered city downriver from Rome.

It was late summer, and he was cleaning out a used car for resale. As he did so, he heard an ominous hissing sound from a back floorboard. He thought it might be a snake—sometimes people booby-trapped their cars with snakes and even mean dogs—but the hissing seemed to be coming instead from inside a left-behind diaper bag. He opened it, carefully. But all he found inside was a half-full baby bottle, the milk or baby formula left to ferment—and pressurize—for days in the Alabama heat. "I picked it up to look at it," he said, "and the nipple shot off and hit me in the eye."

I told him that did not seem like a miracle to me.

"It was a miracle," he said. "It didn't put my eye out."

13

BITTER WEEDS

Poke Salad

From left to right, Edna (holding her daughter, Betty), Juanita, Momma, Jo, and Sue

1942

SHE WAS FIVE NOW, so Ava let go her hand and allowed her to wander a little from the path, to circle through the trees and the falling leaves or run off to chase rabbits and shadows, because the first cold snap had come and gone and driven the serpents into the earth. But the lesson had continued with almost every step, with almost every tree, bush, and creeping vine, even if Ava had to call the child back to her side every few minutes to teach and show. The path, an old deer trail under a great canopy of hardwoods and thick pines, meandered to the edge of a small abandoned pasture, given over now to knobby gray cedar fence posts, rusty wire and thick blackberry bushes, the wicked, ironlike vines now fading to brown in the cooling days. The child ran out into the clearing, careful of the stickers all around her, and stopped cold in front of a cluster of green plants that towered above it all. The tallest of the purplish stalks was eight feet high, and as thick as her leg at the base, its leaves fading from a dusty green to a purplish red. The plants, at the end of their growth cycle after a long, hot summer, were crowned now with hanging clusters of berries so deeply purple they gleamed almost black.

"Poke salad," the child recited. "Good to eat *if* you cook it right, if you *know* . . ."

She reached up to a cluster of berries. They looked almost fake, as if they were painted on, and shone, unnaturally, in the fading light of the day. Children died, seduced by those berries, like something out of a dark fairy tale.

She pulled back her hand.

"The berries is poison."

She could not yet read or do her arithmetic. But she knew.

" *'Specially* for babies."

A pair of cardinals, a bright-red male and a dusty-red female, burst into the air.

"But not birds," she said. "It don't hurt no birds."

Ava, who had walked up close behind her, had not been worried.

The child's first steps had been across the kitchen floor, then, not long after that, in these thick woods and abandoned pastures and other wild places.

"It's too late to eat now," the little girl said seriously, as if she were the one teaching now, " 'cause the berries is out. You don't pick it once the berries is out, when the leaves turn to red."

"Best not to eat it no-how, not this late in the year. . . . Best to eat it in the spring, when it's tender," Ava said, still teaching. "You can cook it in the summertime if you have to have somethin' for the table, if you're careful, but not late in the summer, and surely not now, in the last warm days." The child tried to tell her momma that she knew all this, that she was not a baby anymore, but her momma told her to hush, and listen.

Even in spring, Ava told her, you had to know exactly what you were doing when you picked and cooked poke salad. The plant's toxins were always there, and grew stronger as the summer slipped by. As the plant matured, the toxins concentrated, especially in the stems and stalks, and the closer to the taproot you got, the more intense the toxins became. "You don't use no part of the stalk, and you don't never, never use no part of the root," Ava said, "no matter how hungry you are." The berries, which appeared in late summer or fall, were always poison, though some old men, holding to the old ways, ate one or two ripe, dried, or pickled berries once a week or so, for kidney or stomach trouble. But even one berry could make a child very ill. Ava told it, all of it, in words the child could understand. It was best to pick it, instead of hacking through the main stalk, and even then you had to be careful, because the toxins could be absorbed in your skin and cause a nasty reaction, like poison oak. You could, however, if you were careful, use the juice from the berries to dye clothes; it ran a blood red when the berries were crushed.

The lessons went on and on till they were part of the child, like the color of her hair or eyes, or the shape of her face or length of her bones. This was a science lesson, really, and a mostly accurate one, though their knowledge was doctored sometimes with folklore, but even in that there was some truth if you knew how to sift it from the nonsense, if you were lucky enough to be born into a ragged dynasty of people who knew, and had always known. Some of it, a little, had been instilled in Ava by her own people, but most of it had been passed down from the mean old man—still teaching, from the grave.

Ava showed the little girl the stripped-clean vines of muscadine, scuppernongs, possum grapes, and small black wild cherry, and she cursed the jaybirds, cardinals, and crows for their gluttony. They followed the vine of a hog potato to its root, and dug it from the ground just so Ava could tell her child it was poison, too. She used a small pair of scissors to snip some highland cress—they pronounced it "creases"—and pulled some wild onion, the crushed blades rank and strong on their hands; it sweetened, like most onions, as it was cooked. Ava would fry it, blades and all.

"A wild onion's got a flat side to the blades," the child recited, again. "Wild garlic don't. You can't eat no wild garlic." Both would turn a cow's milk into an abomination if cows ate the green blades, so, before you hemmed in a cow, you walked the pasture, searching for onion and garlic, and pulled it up. It had been one of the little girl's first jobs, to toddle through the pasture and pull the wild onion.

Together, they searched the hillside for sassafras, to make tea, and ginseng, to sell for cash money, and rabbit tobacco, to roll in old newspaper and blow into a baby's ear to ease an earache. "It's yit too green to smoke," Ava said. By winter, it would be dry and brittle on the thin stalk, and ready to pick.

They did not hurry as they went. Ava knew there would be a full moon to see by on the walk home; she knew things like that. She pointed out that some of the leaves on the shrubs and trees had turned their undersides to the sky, a sign of rain or bad weather, and a bad winter coming, for sure. It was not yet dark, but a screech owl, like a woman screaming, sounded in the dusk, and small birds huddled together on the ground. Signs. Signs upon signs—to make haste, to make ready, to gather as much as you could as fast as you could, before a hard winter set in. When the weather turned, it would snow, or sleet. Ava knew that, too, because there had been a ring around the moon.

As the sun began to slide over the lip of the ridge and the hollers began to pool with dark, they stood side by side to watch a grouchy gray squirrel high in the fork of a water oak, chattering, scolding, accusing, and the little girl asked her momma what in the world they had done to him. She knew her momma would know; it was as plain, all this, as a printed sign in a grocery store. You just had to learn how to read it, and there was no school for it except a walk in the woods.

Ava pointed to the squirrel's nest, and to a hollow where he had stored his food. "He's fat as a little pig—see how fat he is? He's gettin' ready, and he's mad that we're gonna steal his food he's put up." A gray squirrel's tail can be a scrawny, ratty thing, but this one's tail was bushy; that also meant it would be an early winter. They got the same message in the bogs when they stopped to listen to an odd, high trilling, so loud the little girl covered her ears. It had been bone-dry; the grass was burned brittle where it had not given way to dust. Now the frogs were crying for rain, but with the rain would come the cold. The woods said so.

They came upon a gray possum, portly himself, eating his way up a small persimmon tree. If you find a persimmon tree, Ava explained, there will always be a greedy possum not too far away, and this one had eaten, it seemed, half a tree of ripe persimmons. They kept their distance from the creature—Ava had never trusted possums, which were inscrutable—and they just watched it feast on the pulpy, waxy fruit. "It's how you know they're ripe, for a possum won't eat no persimmon if it's not ripe," she lectured the little girl.

"What," the girl asked, "if you ain't got no possum?"

Ava searched around them on the path, among the red and

yellow leaves. She found a fist-sized rock, judged its weight scientifically, squinted carefully through her thick spectacles, and let fly. She missed the possum, and the tree, and a good part of the mountain beyond. A few tries later, she still missed the possum clean, but rattled enough of the branches in the persimmon tree to send the possum climbing even higher, yet with no great urgency. Ava knew the woods, but did not trust a possum not to leap on them like a jaguar. Her woodscraft had an odd gap in it as to possums. They watched each other closely, the woman and the marsupial, as Ava sidled up to the persimmon tree and pulled a piece of fruit.

"If you eat it 'fore it's ripe," she said, teaching, "it'll twist your face up."

The little girl nodded solemnly. She knew.

"But this 'un won't," her momma told her. "It's good and ripe."

Persimmons, she explained, are only safe to eat right before they go bad, and you only have a few days, a few safe days, to eat them. You wait until the fruit changes in color to between a yellow and a dull orange, but the main way you tell is by the texture of the skin. It will begin to shrivel, to wrinkle, near the stem, and there may even be a few specks of black there. If the skin of the fruit is smooth, it is too soon, and a single bite will numb your lips and gums and draw your face into a knot, or at least that is how it feels.

"Look, child," Ava said, "an' I'll show you somethin' purty."

She broke open the small fruit with her fingers, gave it to my mother to eat, then took a small paring knife from her apron pocket. She opened the flat seed, and in the white of the inside, in the last light of the day, was the tiny, perfect imprint of a knife or fork.

"Don't tell me there ain't a God A'mighty," she said.

·   ·   ·

My mother's education had actually begun four years before, before her first intelligent thought, before her first step, long before her first memory. She wonders now if maybe the first things she ever witnessed were that cool, dark path through the great trees, or the red carpets of wild strawberries, or the fluff of watercress that clung to the banks of the clear streams and the brown, slow-moving creeks. It may be that the first sound to register in her mind was birdsong. There are worse things to believe.

On another walk, Ava showed my mother the heart plant, which wasn't edible or valuable in any practical way, but when you pulled it from the earth, to transplant the plant, with its purple heart-shaped leaves, to your own yard, there was a perfect little brown jug on the taproot.

"I guess it ain't worth nothin'," she told her daughter, "but it's purty to look at."

On another, she broke open a smooth green maypop, to reveal the soft white edible pulp, and a surprise, a tiny ballerina that you could spin between your thumb and forefinger, to make her pirouette. She showed it to my mother year after year after year, till one day, in pure delight, the little girl's imagination allowed her to see it, really to see.

My mother knows, as an old woman, that it might not make much sense to some people, how her momma tried to explain this riot of life in the deep woods to someone year after year after year, especially to a child who could only hang there and drool, or toddle behind her. But I guess it is what Ava did for her girls instead of playing Mozart, or singing lullabies to them in the womb. And in time, of course, it did sink in. This is why, when you asked her all her life how she knew a thing, she would simply parrot those words: "Well, I've always knowed." But it only seemed that way, after so much time.

Her sisters sometimes trailed behind them on the path like baby ducks, half listening to their mother talk. They had heard it all before, too, beginning, as my mother had, when they were in swaddling clothes, till it was all imprinted in their minds. By the time they started school, they knew the secrets of the hawthorn plant, and the value of a kudzu blossom, and how to make a salad from the dandelions. And it continued, that education, until they were twelve or thirteen.

Some of it, maybe, was less than sound in its practicality. She had them gather spiderwebs, which could be rolled into a ball and swallowed to ease asthma, and wild-cherry-tree bark to make a tonic. The children drew the line at searching for a skunk, live or dead, though it could be rendered down to oil and used to cure pneumonia. The girls decided that if the choice was death or a teaspoon of skunk oil, they would ask the Lord to carry them home. Besides, there was no assured way to kill and retrieve a skunk without paying a terrible price. You could shoot it from a quarter-mile, but some poor fool still had to go put it in a sack. So we forfeited the miracles of skunk.

She taught them, in the warm weather, to watch every step they made, to listen, and even to smell the air, because of all the fears in the woods there was none so deep as that of snakes. A water moccasin had a stink, a musk, and so did a big rattler, and they all made a rasping sound, moving through the dead leaves or the dry grass, and she retold the story again and again of how her husband was thrown from the mule and almost killed the day he shot the mountain hog, and he never even saw a snake.

You could smell a den, a tangle of snakes, for yards and yards. Ava was terrified of snakes; she knew that black snakes ate the poisonous kind, and rat snakes did nothing but good unless they got among your hen's eggs. But she had also been raised inside the folklore of the Appalachians, and spent her whole life waiting for a coachwhip snake to roll into a circle and chase her, spinning like a bicycle tire, down the path, then, upon catching her, whip her to death. And so her children believed it, too. It was ridiculous, of course . . . but it did make them watch where they put their feet.

Ava could not even imagine a time when the world would change so much that all this knowledge would be of no value, of no practical use. So she passed it down, as any great fortune would be handed down. The thing my mother remembers most was not what her momma said but the way she said it, how she always spoke so, so softly in those woods, as if it really was a kind of secret, and to give a loud, rude voice to it might somehow make it all just disappear.

And maybe, as odd as it seems, that was so. My mother can walk a day, a week, across her land, and not find a maypop, as if the tiny dancer inside was something she's just imagined, all this time. The wild plums, which used to hang like yellow-and-red Christmas lights, have all but faded from her land. She always gets happy to find one at the roadside. The wild strawberries, the size of small marbles, no longer cover the ground, as if they were just some kind of folklore, too. Even the trees, the great canopy, fell to the earth in time, hacked down and trucked away, leaving only thick, impenetrable tangles of new growth, briars, and weeds.

I think that we have just mucked up the land, that it really was fragile, tenuous.

Only the poke salad, it seems, has endured. Poke salad is forever.

A weed so closely associated with poor Southerners that they have written songs about it, famous and obscure, poke salad not only survives but thrives, flourishes, as impossible to eradicate as kudzu or chiggers. Modern-day farmers call it a nuisance plant, but in the worst of times it was the poor man's salvation, rich in vitamins and minerals and good for the blood. "Spinach is the closest thing I can compare it to," my mother says, "and everything that's good about spinach is in poke salad. Poke salad is good food.

"Poke salad," she said, "is a miracle."

It contains, in varying amounts, vitamins A, B, C, and something called vitamin K, whatever that is, and beta-carotene, niacin, thiamine, and riboflavin. It includes the minerals iron, calcium, magnesium, potassium, and more, if you can unlock it from the toxins that are also part of its chemistry.

"Poke salad," she said, "is medicine."

They pronounced it "polk salat," and spelled it that way, too.

It sustained them in the deprivations of the Civil War, when war widows here in the foothills of the Appalachians went begging door-to-door for bread. It nourished them in the lingering darkness of Reconstruction, and again in the Depression. Poor women and men would return to it even into the modern day, when the food stamps ran out, or when the first of the month was slow in coming. It had always been what there was, when there was nothing else.

Poke salad identified the poor like a brand. People with money would never fool with it in the first place; they would never take the time. It could only be eaten safely if it was picked correctly— only the leaves and small stems—and rinsed repeatedly, boiled, rinsed, and squeezed, and sometimes boiled again, and finally fried, to extract the last of the poisons, a process that could take hours. That knowledge was bound to the poor by their hard history, and only they knew how to pick the lock on it; if anything belonged to them in this world, truly belonged, it was that damn weed. You would see the better-offs sometimes in the wild, picking watercress, wild onions, dandelion, and the other edible weeds that grew among the useless things, the ragweed, the Johnsongrass, but you rarely saw a rich woman in the roadside ditch neck-deep in poke salad, unless she was looking for the hubcap off her Oldsmobile.

The wealthy relinquished it, gladly. You asked permission of the wealthy to hunt their land, or fish it, or pick plums or scuppernongs or crabapples off it, but you just took their poke salad. You could steal a chicken and be shot in the back, but no one that we knew of ever filled some poor fool with buckshot for stealing a weed off their land, or even off the state right-of-way.

Now and then, I will still see an old woman tottering along the roadways, stuffing it into a burlap bag, and I always slow down to make sure it is not my mother, and sometimes it is.

I told her she should not be walking the roads, picking weeds.

"I can if I want to," she said.

It is as if she continues to eat it, in better times, out of some kind of fealty.

"Naw," my momma said. "That ain't it. I eat it 'cause it tastes good."

It is not only eternal, but boundless. You could overfish a pond, even a river, and thin the deer and the rabbits, and even strip the banks of watercress and other growing things, but you could not pick enough poke salad to make a dent. Poke salad flourished in heat, and drought, and floods, and was spread broadly across the land, every fall, in the droppings of birds. In winter, it simply withered down to the root, and returned with the spring, growing as tall as ten feet. If you wiped away a pasture and put in a subdivision, it would grow in the ditch. It did not need topsoil, only the poorest, stingiest red dirt. It grew in cow pastures, in the deep shade of pine barrens, in overfarmed, abandoned cotton fields, and seemed to flourish particularly over sewage lines.

"Every time we moved, to every house, there was poke salad," my mother said. "It's everywhere. It ain't particular."

It has remained part of my mother's diet all her life, though the more I learned about it, in my middle age, the more that troubled me. I had liked it about as much as I liked any mushy, spinachlike green, but I never bothered to know its chemistry. It grew in our backyard, but we knew, even as toddlers, not to eat the berries; that was as far as my mother bothered to explain it to us, us being useless boys. But I would learn, much later, that there was no part of the poke salad plant that was not dangerous, poisonous.

Historically, there has been no modern-day epidemic of fatal poke salad poisonings in the American South, but the danger was not just some rural legend or folklore, either. In the nineteenth century, children routinely became sick and some even died from eating the berries, which could cause paralysis of the respiratory system. Grown-ups mistook the tuber, where the poisons were concentrated, for a radish, turnip, or parsnip, and some even took the name literally and ate the poisonous weed raw in salads, or poorly cooked. Those who ingested the improperly cooked plant would foam at the mouth and suffer severe cramps. Their hearts would hammer in their chests, and then they would convulse and be unable to breathe.

"They didn't know what they were doing," said my mother, dismissive.

As she lay in the hospital during one of her many visits in 2016, she grumbled day after day, "If they'll just let me out of here, I'll heal myself. . . ."

As soon as she could walk more than a few yards, she ventured to the edge of the pasture with a brown paper sack, to search for the first tender leaves of the spring. She found a mess of it, and spent half a day or more just preparing it for cooking. Poke salad does not require a cook; poke salad, I think, requires a chemist.

"If you eat poke salad three times in springtime, you won't have a cold in the winter," she said.

"I guess not," I said, "if you're dead."

She did not find me amusing. She told me a story of a day she and my aunt Juanita had taken a walk in those woods when they were still little girls, to test their knowledge of the wild things. It was summer, and the place was a riot of insects and creeping, living things. The leaves from last fall still carpeted the path, but the hot, wet air held them close to the ground. They made almost no sound as they walked, and that is why they were almost on top of the snake before they saw it. They saw the ground seem to move, shift, before their feet. Half hidden by the leaves, a massive eastern diamondback, coiled in the middle of the path. The rattles hummed, and its tongue flicked at the air, tasting the heat. They could not tell how long it was, coiled—the big ones were longer than a man was tall, and as thick as a man's arm—but it took their breath away. They could smell the musk in the close air of the trees.

They froze. The snake did not flee, did not move, except to writhe inside its own circle of coils. The great snake and little girls faced each other on the path.

They tried to remember how far such a snake could reach, and decided it did not matter. They did not have the courage to stare into those eyes any longer, anyway. It was said that a snake could charm you with its eyes, and maybe that was not folklore, either, not altogether. Maybe it just meant you went stupid, in terror, till you fell, or stumbled, and it got you. The two little girls held hands, and, together, leapt backward, pushing hard with their legs. The snake struck out but came up short. They ran back a few steps, but did not run home.

"Why not?" I asked my mother,

"It was our trail," she said, and shrugged.

Both little girls picked up rocks. It was a mountain trail, and there was no shortage of rocks.

"Wait a minute," Juanita said. "It's a big snake."

They piled up a mound of rocks, big rocks, some so heavy they could barely lift.

Together, standing less than ten feet away, they rained the rocks down on it, and one of the first big rocks, by luck, struck its head; it began to writhe, crazily. They moved closer and kept throwing, always aiming for the head, and struck it again and again, until it was still. Knowing of the dishonesty of snakes, they bashed it some more even after it seemed to be safely dead.

"Then we covered it up with rocks, just to make sure . . . and so we wouldn't have to look at when we walked back home."

They went on their way, and headed home when it was getting dark. As they approached the mound of rocks, they saw the snake's battered head, rising, rising, as it worked its way free.

"What did you do?" I asked.

"We killed it . . . some more," she said.

This is what you do with the poison in poke salad. You kill it and kill it and kill it, kill the poison in it, "and then it won't hurt you a bit."

·   ·   ·

The precautions, the consideration of poke salad, must begin long before you cook it. If you are not a careful person, you should probably stick to kale.

"Remember, you can only eat it in the spring or the earliest part of the summer, when the leaves are young and tender, and for sure way, way before the berries, the seeds, grow on the stalks," my mother warned. It is safer not to pick the poke salad at all from midsummer on, because that is when the toxins will grow stronger in all parts of the plant as it matures. My mother eats it only in the spring, when the leaves are at their most tender, and the toxins—if the dish is properly prepared—not likely to harm.

Even picking the plant can be dangerous. Some people are more sensitive to the plant's natural defenses than others. To be safe, wear gloves to pick and strip the leaves, and watch for snakes.

"I admit," she said, "that you ort not fool with it if you ain't sure of yourself."

I reminded her of the last snake she'd killed. It was in the garage, and she had spotted it on the concrete slab.

"It was just a little 'un, but it was a copperhead," she told me when I came home.

She had dragged it out onto the driveway with a rake, and chopped it up with a shovel. She was proud of herself, and took me outside to show it to me.

On the driveway, killed all to hell, was a rubber worm that had slipped off the hook of one of my fishing rods.

"I saw it wiggle," she said.

"It's designed to," I said.

To her credit, it was the same color as a copperhead.

Kind of.

"Don't tell nobody," she said.

"I won't," I said.

I gently mentioned that a woman who can't see well enough to judge a copperhead from a bass lure might be better off not handling toxic weeds. She made me no promises.

Poke Salad

WHAT YOU WILL NEED

1 mess of poke salad leaves (a mess is at least an old-
fashioned brown paper grocery-bag-full, packed
down, though how much a mess is depends on
whom you ask)

½ to ¾ cup bacon grease or the drippings from fatback
or hog jowl

½ tablespoon salt

½ teaspoon sugar

2 eggs

HOW TO COOK IT

In the sink, in a large pan of at least 1 to 1½ gallons of water, wash the poke salad leaves thoroughly, and drain. Repeat this process at least three times, till the water is perfectly clear. If it is not clear, keep doing it. There should be no bits of stalk or stems in the poke salad, only the leaves.

In the large pan, cover the poke salad leaves with water and boil over medium heat 1 hour, until the leaves go tender. The water will be dark green at this point. Drain the leaves into a colander, and use your hands, once the leaves have sufficiently cooled, to squeeze the juice from the poke salad. Be sure to dispose of the first batch of cooking liquid, thoroughly rinse the cookpot, then return the poke salad to the pot, cover with fresh water, and bring to a boil again. Discard that liquid, and rinse the cooked leaves at least three more times, till the water stays perfectly clear. If the water still has a green color, you have not done it right. Some people skimp on this, God rest their souls.

In a large skillet, melt the bacon grease or drippings and add the poke salad, salt, and sugar. Cook for about 5 minutes over medium heat, then, over low heat, stirring continuously, for as long as an hour, until the leaves almost disintegrate—till, as my mother says, "the poke salad is almost the same color as an iron skillet."

When you are almost ready to take it up, stir in the two eggs. They will cook to a soft scramble in less than 1 minute.

"You can eat it plain, but I think the eggs add a little something," my mother says. It has been compared, by some chefs, to eggs Florentine. Really.

You can also add a slivered green onion or chopped small white onion, if you wish, as you boil it.

"But I don't like to mess with the old recipe," my mother said. "It's very, very good with cornbread."

The finished product is not pretty, and that should not concern you. It always looks like you left it on the stove too long. But, then, if you're cooking poke salad to impress somebody, you need to reconsider your life.

"It would impress me," my mother said. "Used to be, you went to somebody's house, you got poke salad. Now they give you . . . well, nothin' good." I asked her if she would trust anyone else's poke salad not to poison her, and she said probably not, "but it would be nice to be offered."

I will have to wait a long, long time before I bring up poke salad again in her presence. Nothing makes her angrier than having to answer a question twice, or three times, because of someone's incredulity. She thinks incredulity and snobbery are the same thing, and I guess there is sense in that, sometimes.

I asked one last time why she worked so hard for what amounts to a plate of perennial ornamental weeds that must be washed, squeezed, washed again, and again, and again, and twice- or even thrice-cooked, to render them safe to eat, especially in a time when she does not have to do this anymore to have a plate of fresh greens. She pretended to be intent on a Western she had seen seventeen times already. "Matt Dillon don't get killed in this one, either," I said. She never answered me, really; some people, as she likes to say, "can't be told nothin'."

In the late 1960s, Tony Joe White finally carried poke salad into the popular culture with his famous ode to the weed.

"Never heard of him," my mother said.

I sang it to her, badly.

Down there we have a plant that grows out in the woods
And in the fields looks somethin' like a turnip green

"Never heard it," my mother said. "Are they makin' fun of us?"

I believe, truly, her devotion to poke salad is a kind of fealty to those days when it was all there was, but, unlike squirrel stew or baked raccoon, she sees this as an everyday staple, like turnip greens or collards, and not a novelty to shock the Yankees. I expect to see her, come spring, again walking the ditches that border her property, a brown paper bag folded under her arm, searching for a good crop of weeds. I guess I will have to go with her. I suppose, if we see a rattler or a copperhead, I will hand her a rock and remind her whom that ditch belongs to.

14

STILL HARD TIMES
FOR AN HONEST MAN

Vegetable Soup in a Short Rib Base

Juanita and Mom

1942

SHE SAT ON THE PORCH of the old house and watched her daddy load his truck, and wondered if this might be the day he finally lost his mind. First, staggering sideways under the weight, he dead-lifted her momma's big cast-iron wash pot, the same one she used to render lard and boil clothes, onto the flatbed of the truck; it weighed more than he did, and he had to cuss it up there the last inch or two. He followed that with a broken-handled boat paddle from his bateau, a battered, leaky, galvanized two-gallon bucket, a large head of white cabbage, three feet of concrete reinforcing rod, a rusted ax blade with a missing handle, a two-foot-long ladle, a big can of Rutler's tomatoes, three big flat rocks he had scavenged from the fallen chimney of a burnt-down house, a paper bag with roughly equal parts salt, sugar, and black pepper, one gallon of moonshine, a double handful of potatoes and onions tied up in a tow sack, and a fifty-pound pine knot. Almost as an afterthought, he skewered the cabbage with the steel rod and jammed the rod into a crack in the wooden bed of the Model A Ford, like he was planting a flag.

She got up and walked inside the house.

"Daddy's gone crazy," she announced.

Her momma did not even turn around.

"Mmm-hmm," she said.

Her daddy said, at least once a day, that he would lose his mind someday, that Ava would drive him to it, and because my mother was not yet six years old, she took him seriously. She watched, waited, and wondered just when that would be, but she was uncertain if she would even know when it did happen; she was not altogether sure how crazy real crazy was. Several of her kin acted strangely, singing spirituals or cursing the open air or sobbing about long-dead kin before wandering off into the dark, and this does not even include the ones on a good drunk.

Some were already ensconced in institutions; others were still walking around in the small towns and wide places in the road, carrying on whole conversations with dead relatives and Franklin Delano Roosevelt. Her momma's people went crazy fairly early in life, so my mother, figuring she needed one sane parent at least to hold things together, was determined to watch for anything unusual in her daddy's behavior. After several false alarms, it looked like the dreaded day had come.

She went in search of someone to tell who might be surprised.

"Daddy's gone crazy," she told James and William.

"Prob'ly just had some liquor," James said.

"No," she said, and told them about the truck.

They meandered into the house.

"Daddy's gone crazy," the boys told their mother.

"Knowed it," Ava said.

Whatever her husband was planning that late afternoon, Ava was against it, sticking to her rule of being against everything if proposed by a man. Ava could nag a man right down to his knees, nag him through the floorboards and down into the ground, where a man would cover himself up with the earth and lie an eternity, just to be safely away. But, grumbling, she did what he asked her to do that late afternoon. She cooked two skillets of fresh corn-bread, and slipped that into a clean flour sack.

"Don't you take the children to be around such people," she ordered as she handed it over.

So, my mother reasoned, it was to be a journey of some kind. Charlie compromised, and said he would take only my mother and the hellion boys. They were in their teens by then, but still burr-headed nimrods and constantly in trouble.

"They griped because Daddy took one of the 'babies,' but I was Daddy's pet, so I got to go," my mother said, thinking back. She thinks it was because he wanted someone to talk to on the dark dirt roads, even if she only understood about every fifth word and mostly just nodded her head, and talking to her brothers was like conversing with hogs. Her momma, still grumbling, swung the curly-headed baby, Jo, up on her hip, as if she was afraid her lout of a husband would kidnap the baby sister, too, for his mad adventure. Then she bundled my mother up in two coats, a big girl's sweater that hung to her knees, and two pairs of socks, and she wrapped a shawl around her head so tight my mother thought she would smother long before they got to wherever her momma was so dead set against them going.

"Bums," Ava muttered.

"Hoboes," he said.

"Bums."

"Still hard times," he said, "for an honest man."

He often said that, during the Depression and the years that followed, even as he bootlegged his whiskey behind the veil of the trees, or, once in a great while, slept off a drunk behind bars.

"The children ain't had no supper," she said.

"I'll feed 'em," he said.

She snorted at that, a sound full of all the disdain of men in the whole wide, judgmental world. She told him not to keep the little girl out late or she would call the law on him, but gave him no instructions for the care and feeding of the boys. They could live on rock candy, tree bark, artichokes, and gunpowder indefinitely, and even if they fell off the truck would find their way home eventually, once they missed a meal or two. Nor did she worry about the boys' freezing in the cold wind there on back of the truck, any more than she worried about the pine knot. Elementally, they were roughly the same thing.

Just before he left, Charlie went to the woodstove and retrieved the remains of the previous day's supper out of a small covered pot, the one Ava used to save bacon grease and other leavings too valuable to feed to the dogs or discard. It was mostly beef tallow, the cooked-down and leftover detritus from the fatty stew of beef, potatoes, and onions she had slow-cooked the day before. With six hungry children, there was little of substance left except the grease, but it was flavorful, aromatic, excellent grease, and Charlie took the cooked-down elixir and spooned it into a clean jar. Then, with the boys sitting on the back, the cabbage flying proudly overhead, he and the little girl headed off in the rough direction of the river.

"He better not have took the good bucket," she said to Juanita and Edna, and went inside to make a good, real supper for anyone with the sense to stay home on a chilly night.

Charlie did not draw a safe breath until his taillights vanished beyond the first curve; you were never safe till the lights of the house went dark in the distance or around the first sharp curve, because, even bowlegged, she could run faster than a Model A could roll in low gear. My mother remembers that it was warm in the cab, not so much from the faulty heater in the old truck as from the warmth of the flat-six motor, which rose from the floorboards and through the firewall. At a crossroads, Charlie opened his door and shouted for the boys to come and sit in the cab because it was getting cold, but they were too hardheaded to sit in the cab with a girl, and proceeded to abuse with stones the rare mailboxes they passed.

People like to talk about the emptiness of the great deserts or the endless plains or the frozen places, but a desolate dirt road in the mountain South, in a forest of black pines, can be one of the most lonesome places on earth. There is an almost unnerving dark in the tunnels of trees, where even people who have lived a lifetime here find themselves imagining the silliest things. But as the headlights of the old truck bored into the dark, her daddy began to talk to her, to tell her stories, history, and tales, and even sing a bit. She remembers the song, an old Jimmie Rodgers song from the Victrola, but mostly she just remembers being warm.

> *All around the water tank, waiting for a train*
> *A thousand miles away from home, sleeping in the rain*
> *I walked up to a brakeman just to give him a line of talk*
> *He said "If you got money, boy, I'll see that you don't walk"*

They drove to a clearing not far from Mr. Hugh's ferry, not a desolate place but one where the distant lamplight of shacks and whiskey fires glittered all around. Charlie gave the boys a hatchet and told them to cut two sturdy limbs, four feet long, with a V-notch at one end, then told them not to wander off and drown and threatened to kill them if they got into the whiskey, something they were prone to do. With my mother's help, he gathered dead wood for a cook fire big enough to roast a bull calf. He placed flat rocks at three points on the ground, one for each of the iron pot's three sturdy legs, and set it level or close to it, then piled the wood under and around the pot. Within easy reach of the fire, he sank the V-notched limbs deep in the ground, and, removing the skewered cabbage, laid the iron reinforcing rod into the notches. Then, with a steel S-hook, he hung the steel ladle to one side. It seemed like a whole lot of work, the boys grumbled, to hang a damn spoon, but Charlie was peculiar about his utensils. He told them only an animal lays his utensils in the river mud, and that left my mother wondering what a possum or raccoon or squirrel or such would need with a ladle in the first place, and she would ask him that, someday when the mean boys were not there to make fun of her and pull her hair. Charlie sent the boys to the river with the bucket to fetch water, and with another warning, not to drown each other. The Coosa was cleaner then; a man could cook with it. It has not run clean in my lifetime.

It had been cold but dry, and the dead wood along the river would catch fast and burn quick. He would not even need the fat pine he had brought. He sent the boys to gather greener wood, for a slower burn. Then he began to wipe the ax head clean with a cloth. It looked like one of her momma's dish towels, cut from a flour sack. She would raise holy hell about that for sure if she missed it.

"Can I light the fire, Daddy?" William said.

James punched him in the arm hard enough to break bone.

"I'll light it," James said, as if it was his birthright.

"Not yet, boys," Charlie said.

The Coosa is a deep, muddy, silent river, a place for big catfish and fat bass and glittering crappie, not a rocky stream where the water tumbles over the clean stones and the trout jump in clear water as cold as ice. The Coosa does not rush, or gurgle, or splash. The big brown rivers only whisper to us here, as the deep currents push south to the Gulf. Charlie told the boys to stop fighting and be by God quiet for a change, if such was even possible, and took a seat on the ground, his back against a fallen tree, to listen. I am told he did this all his life, sometimes wandering far off into a field or deep into the woods to sit and listen and just be in a natural way. Sometimes he drank, but mostly he just sat and breathed. He loved his wife, but she did not come with an "off" switch, and talked nonstop for three decades, talked him right on out of the world. When the babies came, the peace was busted for good. But here along these banks, once he got the two dumbasses settled down, a man could hear himself think, or sing, or just be.

He sang when he cooked, or pounded nails up on a roofline, or when he was sitting on the porch watching the lightning bugs, or out in the driveway, leaning on the fender of his truck, a pint fruit jar of liquor in his fist. He had a fine, strong, clear voice, and his little girl pretended to sing with him, " 'cause I didn't really know the words then. It was one of them records we had, the ones that warped and melted."

Well I haven't got a nickel, not a penny can I show
He said "Get off, you railroad bum" and he slammed the boxcar door

In the distance, off toward Alabama, he heard a train whistle blow.

"Light it now," he said.

·   ·   ·

"Why did you bring such a big pot, Daddy?" my mother asked him.

"We'll have company here, child, d'rectly," he said.

The time of the hobo was at its end in this country, some people said, and good riddance. They said the Great Depression was banished to history. A New Deal had been dealt, and a big war was driving the history of the nation now. But in the mountain South, the recovery was slow to take. Men still rode the boxcars in search of something better than soup lines and chain gangs, from the white sand of the coast to the rail yard in Chattanooga, up the Eastern Seaboard, and into the dusty West. What they had found, often, was more chain gangs, more hardship, but, here and there, the kindness of a stranger.

Charlie chased work on the rails himself, across five counties and five hundred miles, roofing, tearing down barns for scrap lumber, digging wells, digging ditches, anything for meat and beans. Now and then, he would sit in his truck at a lonely crossing as an endless string of freight cars bumped past him, loaded with coal, or timber, or nothing. And he would glimpse, through the door of a freight car, a group of men with smutty coats and grimy faces, the lingering hoboes, chasing the myth of some promised land. Once, he saw a young man sitting cross-legged atop a freight car, staring straight ahead like a sultan, like he owned the rattling steel beneath him and all the land it would transverse. Charlie would never ride one so far as that.

But show him a man who claimed he never thought about running away and he would show you a liar. For a long time, after the death of the child, he wished he could follow that whistle to a place where a man's labor was still worth something, maybe follow it to any place as long as it was a long way from here. He never could, of course, because of the faces looking back at him around that rough kitchen table, and he didn't expect anyone to pin a medal on his overalls for it, but he did mention it, as the years passed by, and he never looked down his nose at the men who had no such anchor and just drifted, floated, as if the lines that held them close to something had been cut clean away.

My mother wondered, briefly, how anyone would know to gather here at this place, at this precise time, which her belly told her was almost suppertime. Surely, the aroma did not waft so far. Her daddy told her later it was the fire. Men were drawn to a fire on a riverbank or a railroad track or a mountain ridge or any other lonely place, drawn to the promise of food or a bottle or just company.

Charlie built his bonfire near a known stopping-off place, where such men got off to scrounge for food, or buy liquor, or just build a fire and spend a night away from the railroad bulls. He had, over the years, made a dollar or two selling whiskey at this spot, for it was a natural fact that a man would go hungry and ragged and homeless but would not go thirsty, and though a man can beg food and clothing along the tracks, a drink usually meant cash on the barrel head. But Charlie hadn't run off any liquor in a while; he had only the single gallon, which he left in the cab of the truck with his Belgium shotgun. He did not often drink in front of his children, though he had wobbled into the house with its taint on his soul.

The iron wash pot was beginning to smoke. Charlie took the old ax head, polished clean now, and tossed it into the empty pot. It rang like a church bell. His daughter tugged at his coattail.

"Why . . . ?" she asked.

"It's just what you do," he said.

It might have been a stone, or a horseshoe, or a nail, or anything, really, anything that would be the base, a kind of seed, for a meal to grow from, even a rock; some people called it stone soup. Every culture in every land had some version of the story of a cook or a lonely traveler who somehow coerces others, with only a hunk of iron or a rock as a starter, to contribute a potato here and a carrot there, culminating, in time, in something delicious, hearty, and complete, from nothing edible in itself.

It would have made a better story if Charlie had coaxed a fine pot of soup from the ax head alone. If he had believed in the fairy tales, he would have let the iron be his only contribution, and let the passersby do the rest. But Charlie hedged his bet. Vegetable soup without some kind of savory starter was no soup at all, so he brought the tallow. It was a method that would endure in our family until the modern day. He hedged even more by bringing the canned tomatoes, which provided the liquid and the overriding flavor—tomatoes overpower everything—and the cabbage, which is the soul of good vegetable soup here in the foothills. He had promised Ava, after all, that he would feed the children something good.

He emptied in the tallow, first, with the detritus from the beef and potatoes and onions, and as it hit the hot iron it began to sizzle, and a delicious smell almost leapt into the cold night air. He stirred it around a bit with the paddle, then, when the fat had liquefied in the bottom of the big iron pot, he opened the big can of crushed tomatoes with his pocketknife and added it to the pot, to begin the stock. He added some river water to keep it from burning, and added freshly quartered potatoes and halved onions, and began to chop up the cabbage with his big pocketknife.

Over the next half-hour or so, as the soup began to bubble, the raggedy men came walking up, one or two at a time. They smelled the elixir on the breeze and helloed the tall man and children around the fire. Children were not unusual in such settings; this was still Steinbeck's America, where whole families traveled as far as their overloaded trucks would go, then just existed, along rivers, in fields, wherever their inertia placed them. Charlie told the men to sit, as if the weeds and the river mud and the washed-up trees were his living room, till there were about six or seven in all.

"What's in the pot, brother?" they asked him, one by one.

"Ax-head soup," he said.

The younger men were puzzled, but the older men were not. Most of them carried some kind of bag or knapsack, and one by one they sidled up to the light of the fire and rummaged around inside for some kind of contribution. No one rode the rails without something—a can, a sack, something scrounged, stolen, donated, or purchased with a few hours of pushing a broom or sinking a post or just listening to a preacher shout about the lake of fire. Some had a few winter vegetables, a turnip or a carrot or two, which they handed to Charlie to wash and cut up. Others had a can of corn, or lima beans, or peas. One man—an old man who looked like he had lived two lifetimes on the L&N—said he had some snuff, was all. Another man had been hoarding a second head of white cabbage, and the raggedy men were glad of that, because even a fool knows you can't have good soup without enough cabbage to sweeten it, and cabbage cooks to nothing. Charlie dumped in the mixture of salt, sugar, and black pepper, and stirred.

His little buddy Jessie Clines lived in a tumbledown shack on the river's edge, and, like Charlie, he earned some side money making liquor. Charlie saw him come shuffling up in his old army clothes, toting absolutely nothing, but smiling in that lost way he had. He was not what you would call a sharp man. Mr. Hugh, the ferryman, rode up on his mule; he did not believe in cars, and hoped to live long enough to see that stinking, rattling fad fade completely away. He brought a jar full of hot peppers, and more vegetables. That meant the ingredients in the pot were cooked in varying times and to varying textures, and even though my mother did not know it then, she was witnessing another secret of the thing: the layers of flavor and texture in what seemed such a haphazard dish. There was not much science to it, as to doneness; if the last turnip or potato tossed into the pot was done, the first had to be.

The men sat against the trees and the logs thrown up there by the flooding river, and watched the fire and smelled the soup, and my mother sat in her daddy's lap and listened to the strange men talk. Even William and James sat still for a while to hear. It seemed that the men had all lived versions of the same story. It had been romantic when they left, to ride free and easy through the country, beholden to no man. But the fact is, the poverty followed them like a hound, and the rails were just a prison on wheels, and sometimes it seemed that the freedom they thought they had attained lasted only for the time it took to vanish around the first blind curve. They found the steel road to be dangerous and inhuman, prowled by railroad bulls who beat them bloody with ax handles and shotgun butts and even killed some of them, without consequence, because nobody did time for killing a bum. They had endured frostbite and starvation, and in the end, when they got where they were going, they discovered it was not even there. There was no promised land. California was a terminus, nothing more. Canada was cold. Mexico was starving, its own self.

"Florida was purty," Charlie offered. He had ridden there with his tools, south to the Gulf of Mexico. He swung a hammer there till the work ran out, then rode the train back home.

"Ay-yuh," said a man in an accent none of them had heard before. They all agreed Florida was pretty, but a man could starve to death picking grapefruit. You couldn't even steal enough grape-fruit to live on. It was the only thing on God's earth a man could eat, eat a bushel, and get even skinnier.

"Et a thousand," Charlie concurred.

The soup simmered as the wood turned to coals, and Charlie got up every now and then to stir it with the broken boat paddle. The oil from the starter would bubble up to form a thin orange film on top of the red soup, and Charlie scooped up a potato and judged it done. The soup could have simmered a little more, but these were hungry men. Some of them had tin plates or cups and spoons in their bundles, and some just drank it from the tin cans the vegetables had come in. When everyone had a serving, Char-lie passed out the squares of cornbread Ava had cooked, and the men thanked him as if it were steak. Some of them had not had good cornbread for years.

As the level of the soup dwindled, the ax blade became visible, and the old men, especially, smiled about that.

"Best soup I ever et," said one of the men.

"Ay-yuh," said the man who talked funny.

"I wisht I'd brung some coffee," Charlie told them.

"Coffee's dear," one man said.

"Right dear," another man said.

By the end of the evening, there was nothing left of the soup but that lump of steel. Charlie wiped the ax blade clean; he would whittle a new handle for it someday, when he had the time. Ava was hard on ax handles; her aim was off a bit, and she broke an ax handle for about every cord of wood she cut. That caused the men to reminisce about great wood-chopping and wood-splitting women they had known; they agreed that Canada, probably, had the best female wood splitters on God's green earth. They supposed it had to be that way, up in the tundra.

That got them to talking about cold weather; it seemed all of them had been frozen to death at least once. One man said he had died in North Dakota, but was resurrected, like Lazarus, when thawed on a southbound train. We do not know for sure that James was inspired by such lying, but I bet he was. Charlie questioned the man as to why he went to North Dakota in the first place. The man said he got drunk in Chicago, and if there was more to it he did not say.

It was the most of the world the children had ever heard of.

"It was like school," my mother said.

Then, in the most remarkable generosity his children could recall, Charlie fetched the gallon can of whiskey from the truck and unscrewed the lid. It would have been an even better story if he had simply handed it over to the men as a gift, but liquor is liquor and thirst is thirst. Instead, he turned his back on his children and took a long, hard pull, *then* poured all of the men a swallow in their cups or cans. He did not say anything except to wish them safe travels and a good night. Then he swung my mother to his shoulder, called the boys to heel, and headed to his truck. The boys lugged the pot, complaining. When they got to the old truck, Charlie reached into the bed and heaved the pine knot onto the ground.

"You can sell that, or trade it," Charlie said to the men. "People always need fat pine, and they'll pay or swap you for it," and the men nodded that it was true, and thanked him as he pulled away.

My mother does not remember much after that, but she is pretty sure the tall man sang them home. She tried to tell her momma about it all, about the ax-head soup and the resurrected man and all the rest, but her momma's heart had too many flinty places in it then, and her story could find no purchase. Over the years, though, thinking back, she believes it was the beginning of a notion she would have seized on the night of the tornado if she had not been too small to know what was happening around her.

It was the notion that there are few hard times on this earth, few sadnesses, that cannot be eased with good savory food, not just solid food that could fill your belly, but food with taste that filled up something else. It was not an original notion, not a profound or poetic one, unless it was your belly, and your soul.

.   .   .

My mother would no more put an ax blade, a nail, or a stone in her soup pot than she would a concrete block or a live skunk. But in many ways she has followed that simple recipe from the riverbank all her cooking life, and, like her daddy, she finds herself spooning it out to passersby and freeloaders and ungrateful children. I suppose we are all hoboes on soup day.

My brother Sam seems to have some kind of built-in sensor to alert him to the days she makes soup. I tell her she needs to call him when she mentions she is going to make it, and she just shakes her head, as if that is the height of foolishness and wasted time. At suppertime on soup days, his red Chevrolet truck will come idling up the driveway. He will say he needed to fix some fence, or work on the tractor, but what he does mostly is eat soup. He can eat a half-gallon of vegetable soup and a quarter-skillet of cornbread or half-box of saltine crackers, without the mildest distress.

But there is no radar involved, either. I learned, a little disappointed, that he knows she is making it a full day before, because it takes two days to prepare properly, holding true to the traditions of the dish, and two days is too long to keep a secret out here, true or not. I had a flat tire on my silver '74 Firebird in front of the

Gamecock Motel one summer afternoon in 1979, and everybody in town knew what I was doing.

The modern adaptation of our family's vegetable soup remains a recipe for two suppers, not one. It relies, perhaps less than any dish in her repertoire, on exact ingredients or cooking times; it's a dish that every cook will perfect in time, with practice. "And even if you mess it up, it'll still be pretty good," she said.

Her modern-day recipe, which goes back just sixty years, begins with a simple supper of beef, potatoes, and onions the day before. Any cheap, fatty cut of beef will do, from utter scrap or flank steak to soup bones or oxtails, the fattier the better, but her favorite is the leftovers from her short ribs, potatoes, and onions. Brown the beef a bit, then cook slowly until tender. Add potatoes and onions, salted and peppered to taste, and cook them until the potatoes are fork-tender. Serve it with green beans or peas or any green vegetable of your choice, and the eternal cornbread, and something cool, like slaw, for contrast.

Do *not* discard the leftovers of the beef dish, even if all that is left, as with Charlie's soup starter, is the beef tallow in the bottom of the pot, or bones. "I just call it the grease, or the leavin's," my mother said, "but I reckon that would scare some people, wouldn't it?" The trick is to use that essence of beef fat and the detritus of the cooked potatoes and onions as a kind of starter, to enhance the next day's soup. "You'll have all that good flavor boiled down already. It makes it so much richer," she said, even if the amount is inexact.

She stresses the great flexibility in this, and if there is more leftover beef, potatoes, and onions than you believe you need to provide that seasoning, use it anyway, to strengthen the flavor. The more you have of the tallow, the richer it will be. "But even a few tablespoons of that beef flavor will make a big difference in the taste of the soup," she said. Plain vegetable soup is bland.

Refrigerate the starter. "The next day, you're ready to make some soup," she said. It can hold a day or two, but do not wait longer than three.

"Why don't you just add some beef to the ingredients, some stew meat, the day you make it?" I asked. She and Sam were sitting down to have a bowl of soup. Sam just stared at me as if I had been adopted. He does that a lot, now that he is old and grouchy.

"I was not adopted," I said.

"One of us was," he said.

"It's a perfectly fine question I asked. Why don't you just use fresh beef for the stock the day you cook the soup?"

My mother shook her head.

"Because then it would not be soup," she said.

She waited for me to read her mind, gave up.

"Then," she said, "it would be *stew.*"

She handed me a bowl.

"We don't do stew."

"What's wrong with stew?" I asked.

"Nothin'. I just don't do it like that."

I started to tell her it seemed like semantics to me, but this was one of those discussions that just circled around and around itself, till, one day, you were sitting on a porch with a blanket on your legs, still mightily confused. The eventual conclusion was that there was just something about the way the flavors in the tallow intensified, condensed, between one day and the next, but the main reason, she said, "is 'cause we've always done it that way."

I asked her if she could just use beef broth, or even chicken broth, as a base.

She did not deign that worthy of the breath it would take to reply.

Here is her recipe for vegetable soup, and if you put fresh beef in it the day of, that is your own damn business.

Vegetable Soup in a Short Rib Base

WHAT YOU WILL NEED

2 large potatoes, diced (not too finely)

2 medium onions, diced

2 large carrots, thin-sliced

1 head white cabbage, coarsely chopped

Beef tallow and detritus ("leavin's")

1 quart canned tomatoes (home-canned are best, because she believes you can taste the metal in commercially canned tomatoes)

1 quart tomato juice

One 11-ounce can white shoepeg corn

1 can limas

1 can young English peas

1 teaspoon salt

½ teaspoon black pepper

½ to 1 teaspoon sugar (to taste)

½ teaspoon chili powder (no more)

½ teaspoon Tabasco sauce

HOW TO COOK IT

In a medium pot, boil the chopped potatoes, onions, carrots, and cabbage—using just enough water to cover—until the potatoes are tender but still firm and not mealy. They will continue to cook in the soup pot, as will the cabbage, carrots, and onions. Set aside, and do *not* pour off the liquid.

Spoon the leftover tallow and detritus into a large soup pot, and add the potatoes and onions; heat until the tallow liquefies, being careful not to burn it. To the starter, add the tomatoes, tomato juice, and second round of cooked potatoes and onion, and the carrots and cabbage. Then add the canned vegetables and the dry seasonings and Tabasco sauce.

Cook over medium-high heat until there is a good roiling boil, stirring, then reduce heat to medium, and simmer, still stirring, for about 10 to 15 minutes. "You got to cook the taste of the can out of it" if you were unable to procure home-canned tomatoes or juice, my mother believes.

The oil from the starter will collect on the surface. "Keep stirring it back into the soup," she said. *Do not* spoon it out, no matter how much of a Philistine you may be.

Then simmer for at least 1 hour, continuing to stir occasionally. Do not be afraid to add salt or pepper to taste. It's your damn soup.

Serve in thick ceramic bowls with cornbread or cornbread muffins (some people like sweeter muffins with this, for contrast).

"It's better in winter for some reason, but in summer you can make it with fresh corn and green beans," she said.

"Is that better?" I asked.

"It is in the summer," she said.

Rather than try to plumb the depths of that logic, I just had a big bowl of her soup, and told her it was the best soup I had ever had, which was probably true. It needs to be eaten hot, so that the oil pools in circles on the surface of the rich tomato broth. I remember how my uncles used to blow on every spoonful. My brother Sam looks like them, looks like my grandfather, and my mother says that watching him there at the kitchen table, blowing on that soup, eating it with such relish, is better than a time machine.

As with most of our stories, there was a point or two that still puzzled me, like how he could be so angry at a preaching, free-loading brother-in-law one night, yet show such generosity to total strangers. I guess he just truly disliked that brother-in-law.

But one thing puzzled me even more. I wondered why my grandfather, who had not gone crazy that day, skewered the head of white cabbage with the reinforcing rod, and flew it from the bed of the truck.

Sam, who has a logical mind, helped reason that out.

"Well," he said, "it was a flatbed truck."

I still didn't see.

"It was the best way," he said, "to keep it from rolling off."

I am not so logical, and from all that I have heard of the man, I am not certain that he was, either. I think my grandfather needed a flag of some kind, a banner, to declare his brief independence from a sharp-tongued woman. What better flag is there in hard times, for an honest man?

15

THE PIE THAT NEVER WAS

Chocolate Pie, Toasted Coconut Pie, Buttermilk Pie

Aunt Jo

1943

HE HAD ONCE been a go-getter, Old Man Rearden. In a time when men slunk around and cooked their whiskey in the secrecy of the pines, he said to hell with all this sneakin' around, and cooked his liquor right in his own house. He pretty much dared the rest of the world to come in his front door and take it, if they had the guts and the gunpowder. The Volstead Act wasn't doodly to him, nor its repeal, 'cause he hadn't never made no damn legal liquor anyway. G-men, gunfire, dynamite, bloodhounds—all of it—he survived.

There were a lot of good reasons to bake such a man a pie.

First, it was just the nice and neighborly thing to do. The Bundrums had moved back and forth across the state line a half-dozen times, and now they were back in Georgia, in a place near the bluffs that rose from the big river itself. Old Man Rearden and his clan were the only neighbors for miles. He was the patriarch of a large and troublesome mountain family, which included several dense and violent boys held barely in check by his quavering voice and trembling hand.

Second, he was a true ancient, thin and frail, and not believed to be long for the world. He mostly just sat on his porch in a wheelchair—the first one my mother ever saw—and watched the river ease by from the high bluff, the breeze lifting his thin hair. The very sight of him was so forlorn, so melancholy, it lingered in Ava's mind long after they went to his house to say hello, and it made her want to do something to ease the old man's receding days. "Momma's tongue was sharp," my mother said, "but her heart was soft. There wadn't nothin' wrong with my momma's heart when she was all right."

And, third, things had not gotten off to a good start with their volatile neighbors. They were trying, at the time, to rebuild relations, after Charlie purposefully shot one of the Rearden boys' women through both bosoms with a .410 shotgun. It may, though, be worth readdressing that she was, at the time, trying to cut him with a big butcher knife, and that she was a large woman, and the wound not fatal.

"Momma was tryin' to mend fences," my mother said.

There is no sounder way to do this than by toting someone a homemade chocolate, coconut, or buttermilk pie, even if that fence was knocked down occasionally with a shotgun blast.

One pie would suffice for badly hurt feelings.

This seemed more a two- or even three-pie conciliation.

My mother stood in a chair, well back from the stove and its bubbling, molten, sugary delightfulness, and watched her momma cook not just for the usual reasons but for détente. More and more this was becoming her routine, to watch and learn, unless, of course, there was a new kitten, or a grumpy ground-hog under the floor, or an apple tree to climb with Juanita, or a daydream that needed daydreaming. But pie was not beans, or biscuit, or frying bacon, or anything so everyday. Pie was glorious. Pie was, well, *pie.* And sometimes there was even a spoon to lick.

To bake them, Ava not only drew on the skills she had learned from Jimmy Jim, who might have been the finest logging-camp baker who ever lived, but went back even further in her memory, to her own, gentler people, who were masters of cakes and pies baked for blue ribbons, dinner on the ground, and other niceties she had all but abandoned when she married the rough boy and his rough ways. She did her best to remember her own grandmothers, who were pure pie-making fools, and their recipes, but with Jimmy Jim's voice in her head, she cut in a little more butter, or shook in an extra dose of cocoa or vanilla, every time.

The ingredients were simple for the chocolate pie. She made not a traditional pie dough but something more like a biscuit dough for the shell, cut in cold butter and vanilla flavoring, and used rich, whole milk instead of buttermilk, then rolled it out to about an eighth of an inch. In blatant defiance of Jim's spirit, she had Charlie craft her an excellent rolling pin—really just a smooth club, but a rolling pin just the same.

"My momma never saw a bought pie shell, not till she was old," my mother said.

The filling was simple, too, just sugar, a little flour, egg yolks, good dark cocoa, some vanilla flavoring, and, of course, more butter, baked until the filling set, till the molten chocolate formed a little skin and then cracked. Those little fissures did not mean she had failed; they meant it was ready.

She never even considered a meringue, though she knew how to make one. She was too vain, anyway, for a meringue.

The way she saw it, the lovely dark brown of the cocoa and the golden brown of the toasted coconut and the glistening custard of the buttermilk pie were things of beauty; meringue, to her, tasted exactly like what it was, egg whites and sugar, and when cooked tasted a little like you had fluffed up some ground-up Blue Horse notebook paper and smeared it across a perfectly good pie. She would just as soon throw a rag over it as spread that tasteless mess across a good pie.

"Meringue," she would say, much, much later, "had to have been invented by rich folks, to hide somethin'. Or they had them egg whites left over from the fillin', and they hated to see 'em go to waste. It's how they got to be rich folks," she always said, "squeezin' a penny."

She sent the first chocolate pie to the old man, still warm, by her own boys, James and William, accompanied by the Reardens' youngest boy, Rodney, who was about their age. They had become good friends and co-conspirators.

"We didn't have no trouble with Rodney. It was Jerry whose woman it was that Daddy shot," my mother said, for the record.

The next day, Ava went to work on the coconut pie. She and Charlie still had little money for luxuries, but they splurged for a real coconut, and Charlie used a hammer and nail to poke a hole in it. Ava offered some to the children, who made a face, and she drank it with great relish at her kitchen table—not from the shell itself, like a heathen, but from a teacup.

Charlie split the drained coconut into two neat halves, which is a trick in itself, and Ava worked the biggest part of an afternoon to reduce the snow-white inside into what she needed for a pie. She took a thick, sturdy steel spoon that had been worn down to something close to an edge from time and use, and scraped and scraped and scraped at the concave inside, drawing a flake, a sliver, from it every time. And when she got tired she would pass the spoon and coconut to my mother, who kept it up till they had not a pile of finely diced coconut, but a fluffy mound of those tiny slivers.

When she had a good double handful set aside, she mixed up what amounted to a simple but butter-rich vanilla custard, and as soon as it had thickened a bit, she stirred in the coconut, taking care not to put in too much. A person wanted a pie to be smooth and creamy, not chewy, unless it was a thick chess pie or some such. Before she put it in to bake, she sprinkled on some more of the coconut, so it could toast.

She did not prepare a meringue for that one, either. Again, she sent the still-warm pie up the bluff with the boys, to present to Old Man Rearden, and rested, content that she had used all her skill to bridge the violent rift between the two families.

On the third day, she began the more complicated buttermilk pie, creaming her sugar and butter, then spiking the ingredients with just a half-cup of thick, chunky, whole buttermilk. It baked to golden perfection, and after it set for a while in its own perfection, she sent it up the hill.

Sometimes she cooked a pie for her children, but sometimes there was not money enough for pie for everyone, and it seemed more important to keep her husband from being killed in retribution than it was to have a houseful of happy children with pie on their faces.

She did not stop with those three pies. Every week, without fail, she made three pies, chocolate, coconut, and buttermilk, and had them delivered to the old man. She did not expect a thank-you note, not in a world where half the inhabitants did not read, but the day after the third pie, without fail, she got her pie tins back from Rodney, scrubbed clean.

It was an act of God that brought them all face-to-face. A storm had blown fiercely across the bluff and had sent Old Man Rearden's wife, whose only name was apparently Old Lady Rearden, tumbling into a flooded slough, where she almost drowned in a foot of water.

"She was real short and real fat," my mother said in explanation.

Ava, when she got word, rushed up the bluff to see about her, only to discover that Old Lady Rearden was not even close to drowned, only wet.

The storm had not chased Old Man Rearden from the porch, and no one had apparently deemed it necessary to roll him inside. They were an odd bunch, the Reardens.

"How do, Mr. Rearden," Ava said.

"How do," he replied.

"I hope you enjoyed your pies," she said.

"Ain't had no pie," he said.

"But every week for a month, I sent you three pies. . . ."

"Ain't had nary a pie," he said, and turned back to watch the river.

It did not take a great sleuth to track down the thieves. The boys had carried them down to the river, eaten them down to the last crumb, washed the tins in the river, dried them on their shirts, and hidden them in the bushes until it was time to return them to Ava, after a day or two.

"I guess they ate 'em with their hands," my mother said, "since we didn't seem to be missing no forks."

If Old Lady Rearden had not been blown into the ditch by the storm, they would have gotten away with it forever, or until Charlie moved the family again, which would be soon.

The saddest part was that Old Man Rearden did not believe that there ever had been any pies to start with, taking the word of his pie-stealing son, Rodney.

This, of course, made Ava mad, so, instead of immediately going to work to repair what had become an even wider breach between the two families by crafting a few more pies and carrying them up the bluff herself, she and the old man just faced each other across the holler, jut-jawed and belligerent.

She tried, unsuccessfully, to beat the pie stealers in her own household, but James and William were about eight feet tall by then and hammered together from what seemed to be saddle leather and two-by-fours, and they just laughed when their tiny mother tried to beat them.

Their daddy would also have tried, but by the time he stopped laughing they had stolen the truck and had a good head start.

"I think, before we moved, Momma might have sent him just one piece of pie," to show the old man what he had missed, and what he might have enjoyed if he had been more gracious.

.   .   .

In my mother's time, the pies were prepared much the same way as these recipes, except for the shells. My mother does not like change, but the ready-to-bake pie shell is one she can live with.

Chocolate Pie

WHAT YOU WILL NEED

1 stick unsalted butter

2½ tablespoons cocoa powder

3 tablespoons flour

1 cup sugar

¼ teaspoon salt

3 egg yolks

2 cups whole milk

1 teaspoon vanilla extract

One 9-inch pie shell

HOW TO COOK IT

This is not a fancy chocolate pie, just a rich, good chocolate pie. There was no such thing in my grandma's time as fancy pie. If you had asked someone for French silk, they would have thought you were talking dirty.

Preheat the oven to 350 degrees.

Let the butter soften as you prepare the ingredients. In a bowl, mix the cocoa, flour, sugar, and salt. Beat the egg yolks, and combine all the wet and dry ingredients in a pan or double boiler. "Be sure not to forget the vanilla flavoring—some people think 'cause it's chocolate they won't need that."

Cook over medium heat for about 5 minutes, stirring constantly, then reduce heat to medium-low, and stir in the butter one big piece at a time—she likes it in fourths—as the mixture thickens. When I asked why she does it this way, my mother's only answer was " 'Cause it smells good."

When the mixture has thickened, pour it, still hot, into your pie shell.

Bake at 350 degrees for at least 10 to 12 minutes, and maybe as long as 15 minutes, depending on your oven.

The chocolate filling does not have to crack when it's done, but it should not worry you if it does, and perhaps it could even make you a little happy. Though it won't be the prettiest dessert you've ever made, it gets prettier as you cut into it.

Do not top it with anything.

The two boys, when they were little, seemed to have a hard time keeping chocolate pie on the inside of their mouths, even if they were just licking the spoon.

Charlie would come home from work and see them besmirched with chocolate up to their cheeks, even their eyebrows; he'd shake his head at the wonders of procreation.

Odd, he would say, how the two boys would one day be able to steal a half-dozen or more chocolate pies without a trace.

Toasted Coconut Pie

WHAT YOU WILL NEED

3 tablespoons flour

1 cup sugar

¼ teaspoon salt

3 egg yolks

2 cups whole milk

1½ teaspoons vanilla extract

1¼ cups scraped or flaked fresh coconut

One 9-inch pie shell

HOW TO COOK IT

Preheat the oven to 350 degrees.

In a bowl, combine the flour, sugar, and salt, and stir in the beaten egg yolks, milk, and vanilla flavoring, but not the coconut. Pour into a medium pan and, over medium heat, cook until it just begins to thicken; then stir in the coconut, saving about a good tablespoon. Cook another minute or two to thicken it a bit more, then pour, while still hot, into your pie shell. Sprinkle the rest of the coconut across the top.

Remember, this is just part of the cooking process. If the mixture has cooked so much it will not pour out of the pan or boiler, congratulations, you have custard, not suitable for pies. Remember, too, to be careful handling the pie shell filled with the hot mixture.

Bake at 350 degrees for about 15 minutes, till it turns a golden color and the coconut on top is toasted. Golden brown may mean the pie is a little too done, and perhaps a little too dense, but, again, that depends on the oven.

"Some people like a thicker pie," she said. "I wouldn't throw out one, if it got a little . . ."

"Dense," I said.

"Gummy," she said.

"Come to think of it," I said, "I like a gummy pie."

She nodded, pleased to be right again, for the fourteen billionth time.

Buttermilk Pie

WHAT YOU WILL NEED

1 stick softened butter

1½ cups sugar

3 eggs

3 tablespoons flour

½ cup whole buttermilk

½ cup whole milk

1 teaspoon vanilla extract

½ teaspoon ground cinnamon

One 9-inch pie shell

HOW TO COOK IT

Preheat the oven to 350 degrees.

Making this pie is a little more tedious: you need to mix the butter and sugar thoroughly; cooks call this creaming, but my mother calls it "mixing it up good." Then you stir in the eggs—you will not separate them for this—and flour, and mix them thoroughly. She does not use a mixer for this; she whips it with a fork.

Stir in the buttermilk, milk, and vanilla, dust the top with the cinnamon, and bake at 350 degrees for about an hour; then lower the heat to medium-low, and bake another 15 to 30 minutes.

You can try the old method of sticking a knife in its center, and if it comes out clean it's done. But if it's golden brown on top, it's likely okay, she believes.

· · ·

None of which did Old Man Rearden a damn bit of good.

In one last attempt as a peacemaker, she started sending him soup. After threatening her boys with severe beatings, which they mostly snickered about, and having her husband threaten them with severe beatings, after which they solemnly promised to do better, she started sending the old man home-canned quarts of her fine, short-rib-based vegetable soup. She sent him one a week, every week, because he had told her once that he certainly enjoyed a fine soup, and it was something he found much easier to enjoy—his own teeth had not survived life's journey to its natural end.

Even though her husband and the Reardens were still officially at feud, she risked a visit to see Old Man and Old Lady Rearden, and to apologize for an unfortunate incident involving her children and a fat hen they had nicknamed, unfortunately, Old Lady Rearden.

Old Lady Rearden the hen had perished in the yard from unknown causes. She lay in the yard with her legs sticking straight up in the air, which reminded the children of the time Old Lady Rearden the human had been washed down the ditch and wound up, in much the same awkward position, in the river mud.

This loss, of the chicken, had sent the children wailing through the yard, lamenting the death of Old Lady Rearden at such a volume that it carried across the ridge to the Rearden cabin; it momentarily disturbed Old Man Rearden, who had to wheel around and check, just to be sure, and even caused Old Lady Rearden a second or two of consternation, as she checked herself.

"I am sorry the children was rude," Ava said.

Old Man Rearden nodded that it was forgiven.

"Did you enjoy your soup?" Ava asked.

The old man just blinked.

.   .   .

"I guess James and William just threw the jars in the ditch," said my mother. "Momma's soup was so good you could drink it, just drink it cold. I guess it didn't matter none. We were movin', anyway."

16

RIBS IN THE DEAD OF NIGHT

Spareribs Stewed in Butter Beans

Jo

1945

FIRST OFF, we might as well agree that three o'clock in the morning is a bad time to take a hog for a drive.

"I remember the night it happened," she said. "It was pitch-black, not a bit of a moon"—just right for sneaking off.

"I remember it because it was the night I swallowed my marble."

I asked why she'd had a marble in her mouth to start with.

"I kept it in my mouth for about three years," she said, and she was serious. "I pretended it was a jawbreaker. When people would ask me what I had it my mouth, I would say, 'Oh, it's my jawbreaker.' It didn't taste good, but it never wore out."

Sometimes there is just not much to say.

My people were movers. Some people are disdainful of that—usually landed people who hacked a piece of dirt out of the forest primeval in the time of Andy Jackson and then stuck with that land through war and flood and disappointing progeny, generation after generation. These are the same people who are prone to say, with understandable pride, that their great-grandfather died in the same bed in which he was born. It seems a dull way to end up, to me, unless you had a hell of a good time in between. But maybe that's just my grandpa's restless spirit whispering in my ear.

He held his family together not with an ancestral home, with neat, straight rows of crops and barbed-wire fence and indisputable property lines, but with spinning rubber and steel, as if the very motion of that old truck was a kind of gravity that kept his people from just drifting off into space. My grandfather did not sit on the same porch in the same swing and use the same fan to swat at the same ancestral flies. But he did move his family eight times in one decade, in the same beat-up, rattling Ford. There were nine of them now, in the caravan. The last child, Sue, came in '44.

"Mostly, we lived a-comin' and a-goin'," my mother said. "I don't know if we ever moved in the daylight." They crossed state lines so much, they couldn't recall which one they resided in.

He had no love in his heart for a landlord, no gratitude, and no sympathy. So it made sense to him to quit on a place not on the day the rent was due, but on a day it was a month past due, more or less; if you could somehow stretch that to a full two months past due, well, why not? But, to get away with it, you could not drive away from a place under the harsh glare of a debtor's sun. You had to slip away in the deep dark, between 2:00 and 4:00 a.m., when the landlord was in his bed, breathing easy, dreaming about ledgers and lockboxes and tinkling coins.

They had left their place outside Rome under the Big Dipper, to move to a place in northern Calhoun County, Alabama, with no discernible name. "They call it Pleasant Valley now, but there wasn't no Pleasant Valley then—it was just a place on the way to Webster's Chapel. I guess it don't matter. We wadn't there too long, no-how." A year or so later, he moved them from there to a place outside the town of Jacksonville, Alabama, called Carpenter's Lane, where they stayed another year or so before Charlie began to fret. It was always just a matter of time before he moved them again. Part of it was that the work would, sooner or later, dry up, but the man was just born under a wandering star.

In the early fall, before the first frost, he announced that they would be moving to a house not far away, near Boozer's Lake. He was a full month behind on the rent on the Carpenter's Lane house, and they needed to be long gone before the landlord came by at dawn, jingling his damn pockets. The two houses were, in truth, only a few miles apart, but the hope was that, by the time the jilted landlord figured out where the Bundrums had relocated to, it would be too much trouble to seek recompense.

"We didn't have much warning," my mother said. "Sometimes he would just tell us the day of, and we'd be gone."

There was a finesse to it, disappearing a family, a houseful of furniture, and the livestock. Start packing too early in the evening and the landlord might happen by to collect or say hello, and catch them with a half-loaded truck in the yard. Start packing too late and they might not be done and gone by first light; landlords were notoriously early risers, as most well-off men tended to be. The idea was to leave the place bare, clean, and swept—because they were not hooligans—but with no forwarding address.

The secret to a successful clandestine move was rounding up enough serious muscle to pull it off quietly and smoothly. They did not own much furniture, but what they had was hardwood and heavy, and there was the giant wash pot to load, and the chop block, and the anvil, and . . . James and William usually did the heavy lifting, but they were in the army for this move, drafted at the end of World War II. This was a problem if you had to move a milk cow, a massive hog, and a four-hundred-pound chifforobe.

Charlie called on a brother, Joseph. Joseph could lift a Studebaker's rear end clear off the ground.

"But nobody called him Joseph," my mother said. "They called him Babe. He was a big ol' rough-looking man, not a good-lookin' man like my daddy, but not a bad-lookin' man, either. He was strong, real strong, and had a lot of reddish-blond curly hair."

I asked her if they called him Babe because he was the baby brother, or had a baby face.

"No, hon," she said. "They called him Babe because . . . Well, a lot of people said he was a ladies' man. Women would holler at him, 'Heeeeeeyyyyyyy, Babe.' "

She thinks now it might have been the curly hair that did it.

"I remember he always had one of them little-bitty Coca-Colas in his hand. Daddy would say to him, 'Them things are gonna kill you.' " He was often making liquor at the time.

But he was a good man to have on a moving night, and by 2:00 a.m. he and Charlie had emptied the house on Carpenter's Lane, transported its contents to the new house, and gone to work on the livestock. They pushed, shoved, and threatened the milk cow onto the back of the truck. Ava and the girls caught and penned the chickens—one or two always headed for the high country and could not be gathered up, so sometimes they had to sneak back to the house in the dead of another night and steal their own fowl—and rounded up the dogs and the spitting, scratching tomcat.

Charlie told the children, as they clambered onto the back of the truck to ride beside the cow, to be careful not to hurt themselves on a sharp, broken piece of bumper that jutted straight out from the rear of the Model A. He had torn part of the bumper away in a wreck, and meant to hammer it into a less lethal protrusion when he had some time, some help, and a heavy sledge.

All that was left, after dropping off the cow and one or two of the children, was a massive four-hundred-pound hog, snuffling ominously in the dark. "Daddy was fattenin' it to kill, and it was *big,* but it wasn't yet hog-killin' time, so we had to move it, too," my mother said. "You didn't kill no young hogs back then. People couldn't afford to kill a hog before you fattened it out. The meat from one of them fattened-out hogs was . . . Well, son, it was just wonderful."

She rode back from the house near Boozer's Lake with her daddy, Juanita, and Babe. They could see the ghostly white of the hog as it circled the hog pen, agitated, as if it knew something was amiss. Charlie backed the truck as close as he could to the gate, which was just hammered-together scrap lumber, and put down a sturdy homemade ramp. But trees and underbrush made it impossible to back tight up against the pen, and the men feared the hog might take a hard left or right turn, escape, and maybe even hurt one of them. It was impossible to put hands on the hog to guide it, for it was a biter; they thought about putting a rope on it, but it seemed to have no neck. The best plan, the men decided, was just to shoo the hog straight from the gate to the ramp, using long poles to keep its tusks from their legs.

"That could work," Babe said.

But the hog did not want to help. It circled and circled the pen, gathering speed, and when Babe swung open the gate, the massive hog shot through the gap and flew out but somehow missed the ramp altogether. It ran headfirst into the jutting piece of broken iron bumper with a force that rocked the old truck back and forth on its springs, and fell dead.

"Well," Babe said.

My mother was so mesmerized, she swallowed her marble.

"I couldn't talk real plain when I was little. I don't know why, I just couldn't. I walked up to Momma and said to her, 'I have swallered my marble.' But Momma didn't understand me, and thought I was sayin', 'I want some water,' and she kept givin' me water and givin' me water. I like to drowned."

I asked her if maybe she could talk fine all along but sounded funny because she always had a marble in her mouth; she said that had never occurred to her, and that perhaps that was so.

"Anyway, I didn't have my jawbreaker no more, that night we moved. I'd done swallered it. I don't know what happened to it after I swallered it. I mean, I guess . . ."

I told her, from meanness, it might still be in her, and that troubled her a good bit. But her pronunciation, she pointed out, did improve.

Either way, the hog was down, and unlikely to rise again. Charlie bent over it, unsure what to do. He had never had to check a hog for vital signs before. Hogs had always come in two clear and uncontrovertible states: alive and snuffling, and sausage. He nudged it with his boot. Then he nudged it harder. After a while, it was clear the hog was done for, at the worst possible time, at the worst possible place. How do you tiptoe out of a place, how do you slink, with a four-hundred-pound dead hog?

It had to be bled, at least, before they could travel with it, and they would have to winch it up on a stout limb to do that much, and all their tackle was already at the new house.

Charlie walked over to the truck and took a seat on the truck bed.

"Well . . . I . . . will . . . just . . . be . . . damned."

"He was so discouraged," my mother remembers. After a few minutes, his chin cupped in one hand, he crawled back into the truck and went rattling off in the direction of the new house. He came back sometime later with rope, his tool belt, a pair of wick-edly sharp butcher knives, a handsaw, a hacksaw, a hatchet, and as many washtubs and buckets as he could quickly find. He would use the truck to raise the hog.

"Let's get to it," he said.

To my mother, watching from the shadows, it was like being "in a monster movie." She pronounced it "mun-is-ter."

They built a fire, but tried to shield it as much as they could in the trees. "They butchered that big hog right there, in the dead of night," my mother said. "They hoisted it up and cleaned it, and scalded it, and scraped it, and cut it up into hams, and shoul-ders, and ribs, and bacon, and cracklin' meat." Charlie and Babe worked mostly in the dark. They did not try to perform the more complicated butchery, but loaded the meat into the tubs and pails and hauled it to the new house to be carved, salted, ground, and rendered. By dawn, there was nothing left to show there had ever been a hog there, or, for that matter, a family. There was almost no scrap. The soon-to-be chitlin's, the lights, the liver, and even the head would be turned into souse, or hogshead cheese. It was still a wild place then, and as soon as they drove away for the last time, the night creatures would erase all evidence.

"Leave me out about seven or eight of the ribs for supper tonight," Ava said as the men carried in the tubs of pork. "And cut 'em in two. We'll have somethin' good." She said there was no reason the poor hog had to "suicide itself" for nothing; they might as well derive some joy from its passing.

"Why did it suicide itself, Momma?" my mother asked, sud-denly talking much plainer. (The only thing they could figure, but not till many years later, was that it was the shock of the hog's vio-lent death that shook loose more than the marble.)

Ava just shook her head.

.   .   .

There was no ice box, so the rest of the meat had to be salted right away, or smoked. It took all day to salt the bacon and fatback, hang the hams, grind and season the sausage, and cube the cracklin's. As Charlie and Babe worked with the fresh pork, Ava baked a pan of biscuits and breaded and fried the liver for a late breakfast. "You always cooked the liver first," my mother said, "because it would spoil the fastest." There was no great joy in the Bundrum household over smothered pork liver; the children were not picky eaters, but it took a lot of gravy and onions to smother the viscosity of a big slab of pork liver. Her daddy and Babe ate it down to the bare platter, and had three or four biscuits apiece. Ava did not spoil her children much, but she promised them something better for supper that night, if they would only be patient.

My mother followed Ava around all afternoon, waiting for her to begin their feast. But all Ava did, at first, was put a pound of butter beans on to boil. Butter beans—what some people call large limas—are a staple here, usually served with cornbread and fried cabbage or potatoes. They are seen as inferior to the banquet bean, pintos. The butter bean, when blandly prepared, is chain-gang food, waxy, about as fancy as chalky black-eyed peas. But prepared and seasoned by a good cook—especially by one with some four hundred pounds of fat pork at her disposal—it was a much different prospect.

"Daddy brought Momma the ribs from that big hog, and the end of them ribs—the big spareribs is what people would call 'em now—was as big as his fist, with a lot of meat, and real, real fatty. Momma had Daddy cut the ribs in two, in half, and she just dropped them into beans. Momma cooked 'em about two, two and a half hours, and when she took the lid off her pot and tried to lift one of the ribs out, the meat just slipped off the bone. The pork fat had melted into the beans, and pooled on top of the butter beans, and that juice was just clear as water." The only other seasonings had been salt, a little sugar, and a small diced onion. Her momma fried cabbage, and boiled potatoes, and made not cornbread but a pan of hot biscuits, some of which she set aside, buttered, and served for dessert with blackberry jam.

"Easy as pie," my mother said, of the meal. "I mean, *easy*."

The great Johnny Cash was said to have spent long hours contemplating whether or not pigs could see the wind. He was also said to have emptied more than a few pill bottles as he contemplated this. But if pigs can indeed see the wind, then who knows what they might think about, what they might scheme or plot, there in the middle of a dark night. I don't believe the hog on Carpenter's Lane suicided itself. I think the pig was just making a run for it; whether they can see the wind or not, they apparently cannot see in the dark.

Spareribs Stewed in Butter Beans

WHAT YOU WILL NEED

1 pound butter beans
8 to 10 meaty pork spareribs
1 small onion, diced
1 tablespoon salt
½ teaspoon sugar
7 to 8 cups water (or more if needed)

HOW TO COOK IT

As with pintos, you have to set some time aside for picking through the butter beans. Find a good chair, and tell your worrisome, telephone-addicted kin that you are getting a CAT scan and will not be able to talk for a while. The beans should be white to cream-colored; remove and discard anything suspicious.

It is not necessary to soak the butter beans beforehand, though they will cook faster if you do. The whole point of this dish is to cook it slowly, slowly, and let the simple ingredients and flavors mingle.

This is an easy dish. In a large pot, combine all the ingredients, and bring to a good boil for just a few minutes. Then simmer for about 2 hours, being sure to stir occasionally. The rib meat should be tender, if not falling off the bone, and the beans should be soft but not mushy, though some breakage is unavoidable. You can make them more creamy by taking a potato masher or large spoon and breaking up some of the beans, or even adding milk or cream at the end, as many people do with white beans, but my mother thinks this is foolish. Cook 'em right and they'll be perfect in texture.

If you have a good butcher, or are good with a saw and have good insurance, you can cut the ribs in two before cooking (they are more convenient to dish up and cook if cut in two, but some cooks prefer whole ribs, for the way they look on the plate).

Do not pepper the beans beforehand. Pepper to taste, plate by plate.

Some chefs believe in searing the ribs in a little fat, along with the diced onion, before adding them to the beans to slow-cook. We are not them.

"There just ain't no need. The pork fat is where the taste is, and the fat will render into the beans, drop by drop, as it all cooks together." Amen.

Serve as Ava did, with potatoes and cabbage. A modern-day version, which my mother swears by, is slightly lighter and provides a delicious contrast. Substitute a purple-cabbage-and-carrot coleslaw for the fried cabbage, and maybe some collards or turnip greens. My people see no sin in eating potatoes with beans, even starchy ones like butter beans. Whole generations of my people would have considered a meal too delicate without two or three starches served side by side, but since it is unlikely you will rise from this meal and go lay some railroad track or dig a mine shaft, you can do as you wish.

. . .

"Get me some good ribs and I'll make it for you," my mother told me of the dish, so I did, and it was of course as delicious as it sounds. It reminded me of a dish I had in a French restaurant in New York, a cassoulet of beans, ham, and sausage. It was called

French country food, and cost about fifty dollars. Nothing with "country" in its definition should cost fifty dollars, but it was delicious, too, almost as delicious as what my mother made for ten dollars and change. But no one told me a single story as I ate it there on the Upper East Side, or at least not any stories about depressed pigs or missing marbles, or anything that really stuck in my mind. I think things taste better with a story on the side.

I remember, after I had finished and paid the bill, that there was not a cab anywhere in that part of Manhattan, and as I moved down the chilly sidewalk I had to admit to myself that there was one great advantage in a nice anonymous French pig. The whole time I was at dinner, I not once had to worry about what that pig was thinking at the end. But, then, I don't speak much French, anyway.

17

CLEMENTINE

Fried Chicken, Fried Chicken Gravy (Water Gravy),

Fresh Green Beans with Golden Potatoes

Juanita, upside down

MY PEOPLE would not, despite what some of my kinfolks have claimed, step over a dead body to get to the supper table. They would, however, drag one out of the middle of the road and leave it in the weeds to get back to the house on time if my grandma was frying chicken. This has occurred.

. . .

Ava came out onto the porch with a handful of shelled corn in her apron pocket, and murder in her eye.

"We'll have chicken tonight," was all she said.

She did not have to say: *And don't be late.*

It was implied.

Fried chicken did not mean merely chicken, fried, but a feast of hot biscuits and chicken gravy, and her famous green beans slow-cooked with golden potatoes, and more. It was perhaps her holy trinity of food. The chicken they fried had little to do with what passes for chicken in the modern day, which is barely food and tastes of what seems to be chlorine and cardboard and fish meal. In my mother's day, and on into my childhood, fried chicken was one of the meals our great cooks used to show off, to bring comfort to the bereaved, to appease a landlord, or to show their undeserving families that they still loved them in spite of everything. It was a meal you thought about all day, a thing you could almost taste in its promise.

No one fried a chicken like Ava Bundrum, except maybe Edna, her oldest girl, or Sis Morrison, of course. My mother, though barely in elementary school, was learning the secrets already. My kin can debate good fried chicken for hours, but agree on a few points. Seasoning should be spare, and breading light; more important was that good, clean taste, and the juiciness. The crust should be almost no crust at all.

Though cold chicken is a delicacy in itself, Ava insisted that her chicken be almost too hot to touch as they all sat down to eat. To be late for it, to let such a blessing get cold, from carelessness or poor planning or even a broken timepiece, would be an abomination, akin to spitting in church, or talking loud while fishing for bream, or interrupting an old person in mid-story. It was still *good* if it cooled a bit, just not the delicacy it was if eaten in the fifteen to twenty minutes after it was lifted from hot, spitting grease. Sooner than that could result in lasting injury to the fingertips, lips, and tongue.

Ava said they would have supper at six.

And don't be late hung on the very air.

The household had changed a lot in the second half of the decade, in the postwar years. Charlie had found steadier work, building barracks at Fort McClellan in Calhoun County, where the war and the Cold War had spurred years of new construction. Edna had married a navy man named Charlie Sanders, which had drawn the beloved storyteller Mr. Hugh Sanders, his father, into the family in a more official capacity; everyone agreed this was a good thing, even if the curly-headed, lantern-jawed son-in-law should somehow turn out not to be. James and William had married but not gone much farther than out of sight, still close enough to come to eat, invited or not, four or five meals a week.

That morning, Ava had seen her husband glancing at the dirt road like it was a magic carpet.

"If you go loafering today," Ava warned him, reading his mind, "take some of these children."

Ava was just beginning to show tiny flashes of the dementia that would descend in middle age and force an occasional Jekyll-Hyde transformation in her character. It made her hard to live with when it descended, and everyone learned to walk soft around her when it did. Sometimes, though, it was hard to tell if it was the light touch of madness, or if one of her nitwits had merely made her justifiably upset.

Charlie was unreliable when it came to a sit-down meal. They had learned not to wait on him as he lingered at the lumberyard, telling tales; he would stop at a crossroads and talk an hour if he happened to see some kin on the road, and sometimes white whiskey was involved. But Ava registered every missed meal, every tardiness. She might cuss and gripe for three full days, and everyone suffered when she finally lost her temper. There would be no biscuit, morning, noon, or night. There would be no beans, just cornbread and buttermilk three times a day. They could live on maypops and artichokes for all she cared, and she would be so hard to live with no one within the house would have much appetite anyway.

In those days, it was not a matter of turning a switch on an electric stove, or lighting a pilot light. To prepare a meal meant chopping and splitting wood, building a fire, and—in summer— cooking within an envelope of heat that was damned near unbearable. A simple pound of butter, with milking and churning, was a half-day's work. A bushel of green beans took an hour or more to pick, and more time to snap. And to procure and clean and cook a chicken—well, a chicken was a by God endeavor.

His usual nonchalance would not be tolerated today.

Ava told him she would watch the youngest girls, Jo and Sue, and Charlie gave his Juanita and my mother, Margaret, a choice: would they rather take a ride with him, which meant a whole afternoon of stories and maybe some penny candy or a bag of parched peanuts, or stay home and help their momma cook supper? Juanita almost knocked my mother down getting to the truck. Juanita, even as a little girl, was a bony tomboy. And though she would become a good cook herself one day, she saw no reason to worship cooking, or study it, or act a fool over it. A lot of bony people, of course, are like that.

It was different with her little sister. My mother loved to watch her momma cook, loved to help, or at least get in the way. It was not only because she loved to eat, but because she loved the artistry and science in it, even if it was just a pot of beans boiling on the stove. So much of what old Jim had preached had turned out to be gospel. They saw it now, saw the difference in a cook who loved to eat and a plain old person who loved to eat, and she loved to see a meal come together, fire by fire. At this point, she had been little more than a spectator, just a little girl allowed to stir a bowl of dressing, a hindrance shooed out of the way whenever a hot pot was carried across the room or a skillet was spitting from the stove.

"You're too little yet," Ava told her, year after year.

"Well, I'm bigger than Juaniter," she said. She meant "taller."

"I won't have you burnt," Ava said, and that was that.

"Only a fool works around a hot skillet with children hanging on them, or if their mind ain't on it," the old man had once told her, more as a warning than advice.

"So I just watched," my mother said, "but I loved to watch. At first, I had stood in the chair, and then behind Momma but a little off to one side, so I could see, but not so close that she'd bump into me with a hot skillet or a hot pan. But I watched."

This day was a true conundrum for her. The chance to go loafering with her daddy was the one thing that would keep her from her momma's side, keep her from the kitchen. She would have stayed, stayed and continued her education, but this was chicken day, and as much as she loved to eat it, chicken meant more than just the artistry, just the craft. Chicken meant mayhem.

Her little heart could not bear what was to come, there in the yard.

She crawled into the seat of the truck beside her sister. They left Ava standing in the yard, surveying her victims, a bonelike rattling of the dry, crushed corn in her apron pocket.

.　.　.

Once the bloodletting was done, and the nasty hell of cleaning and plucking, she went to work on the finer parts of the perfect chicken dinner. She prepared the meal methodically, so as to concentrate on the frying process without distraction.

It was summer, and she had already snapped a mess of beans. (I will not live long enough to get into exactly what a mess is. When I asked my mother, first she said, a little irritated, "I don't know, just *enough.*") Ava put her beans on to cook, and added some fatback, and quartered some white potatoes. Then she patted out her biscuits, but did not put them on yet to bake; she set them aside, covered with a towel, to put them in the oven at the perfect time, so they would come out when the chicken was ready to put on a plate.

She cut her chicken up with almost no waste. Instead of ending the process with just two legs, two wings, two breasts, and two thighs, she had liver to fry, and gizzards, and backbone, and the neck.

She did not soak them in buttermilk. She did not marinate them in anything. These were true free-range birds, raised on corn and whatever in the yard they could peck. They had never been fed a speck of fish meal, which exudes from modern-day mass-produced chickens. They had never been dosed with hormones, or antibiotics. They were big in the leg and thigh but small in the breast, and they tasted clean.

She laid the chicken out on a clean pan and, after making sure the pieces were moist enough to hold on to the meager seasoning, sprinkled each piece—top, bottom, and side—with salt and black pepper. Then she took a handful of flour and dusted each piece— top, bottom, and sides. That was all.

Some people liked to mix their flour and seasonings in a brown paper bag, add the chicken pieces, and shake the hell out of them, but Ava saw that as the waste of a good bag, and too much shaking for a married woman.

She used a twelve-inch skillet, the biggest one she had, but she had cooked a whole chicken in a smaller one. She put about two inches of lard in it, and got the lard hot enough to roil and spit but not burn, then moved it to the side of the woodstove, to let it moderate a little bit. That was all the science she needed. Then she carefully, carefully placed the pieces in the hot grease. . . .

. . .

Charlie and the girls were having a grand time toodling around Calhoun County, Alabama. First they got some parched peanuts from an old man at the side of the road, and that made them thirsty, so they drove to the Mill Branch, which was not haunted in the daylight and not yet polluted with horror stories. Charlie plucked a crawfish from the clear water, examined it, let the girls examine it, and turned it loose. It backstroked away, as fast as a bullet. The Mill Branch in daylight was like a park in the middle of the wilder woods, a place that just seemed to belong to everybody. People brought their children to wade in the frigid water, and turned their radios to anything with a steel guitar. They would put their RC Colas and Nehi grape sodas in the cold water to chill, and buy foot-long hot dogs and hamburgers in town and drive all the way to the Mill Branch to eat them in the shade of the trees. The girls could smell the chili, mustard, and onions on the breeze, reminding them that suppertime was nigh, and Charlie said he guessed they needed to be heading home.

Halfway there, he remembered they needed chicken feed and meal, and he told the girls he would run into Green's Store real quick, and they would be home in plenty of time. His intentions, his girls believe, were good.

Since the beginning of time, old men had gathered in front of Green's Store in warm weather to chew tobacco and spit and lie, and talk about crops and work and dogs and guns, but not wives, because a man had to have some relief. They would compare knives, and argue about whether it was going to rain or just act like it. They talked about who was in the hospital and what their prospectus was as to living or dying, and whether or not they were on the prayer list, and whether all the prayer in the world would do some of them any good. They talked about state government, and whether they could survive that banality and dishonesty for one more year (but would, perversely, send the same people down there to Montgomery every term, over and over again, till they were indicted or died of old age or someone saw their car parked outside a place they oughtn't be). They would brag on old trucks, and look suspiciously on any man who got a new one, because why in the world would a man want a nice truck just to haul manure and stumps and sticky grandchildren? They talked and talked, and sometimes they did not talk at all, but would spend long minutes gazing off into the gently swaying Johnsongrass, or at the passing cars, or clouds, which got them to forecasting the weather again. The loop of conversation seldom changed, just the timbre of the voices, as old men gave up their seats on the bench to other old men, who clicked smoothly, effortlessly into place.

Charlie loved to hear old men talk.

He would have made an excellent old man.

"My mule was laying down this mornin', and that mule don't never lay down in the mornin'," one old man said, from his place on the bench.

"What's that mean?" another old man asked.

"Means it'll rain," the first old man said.

"No," another old man said, "means it won't rain."

This took some time to untangle. By the time Charlie had heard the old men decide for the second or third time that it would probably *not* rain, prostrated mule or no, it occurred to him that the end of the world as they knew it had come and he had not even noticed. It was nearly six.

He hurried the children into the cab of the truck, and they sped away.

My aunt Juanita, being older than her sister, told the official narrative from there.

"Daddy drove with his foot flat on the floor," she said. "He drove fast most of the time anyway, but I mean he had it in the *wind.*" The old truck roared and trembled, and her daddy, who usually drove with one bony wrist hooked over the wheel, gripped it now, white-knuckled, with both hands, downshifting on the big grade on the Nisbet Lake Road.

They were not people who thought only of their bellies, and

food was not, despite its great importance in their lives, their only luxury. They twisted the crank off the Victrola and danced themselves half to death, and picked a mean banjo, and when the work was caught up they sat by that slow river and told stories of luster and passion and high adventure, painting pictures of their world and hanging them on the air. But Ava would have worked half a day on their supper, and the state of Alabama was not big enough for the man, or the children, who brought it all to naught.

Juanita remembers how he barely even slowed down as he made the hard left turn onto the Cove Road, and stomped the accelerator again, the tires sending a plume of red dust into the air, like a wake. The big trees on both sides of the narrow road crowded in and formed a ragged canopy overhead, and as they flashed from shade to sunlight again and again, the light almost blinded them.

Six o'clock had come and gone, and now it was just a question of whether or not Ava had noticed. They were within a mile of home, Juanita said, when it happened.

"Daddy was still just a-flyin', and here she come, walking right out of the trees and growed-up weeds there at the side of the road, and"—Juanita took her palm and smacked it, hard, with one tiny fist—"and daddy hit her."

She stopped talking then, as if out of respect.

"Hit who?"

"Clementine Ritter . . . Daddy run over her."

"My God," I said.

"It was awful, hon," she said.

"My God," I said again.

"She was my friend."

My mother nodded in sympathy.

"What did y'all do?" I asked.

"Well," Juanita said, "we piled out of the truck and run to see, but she hadn't got knocked to the side. She'd gone right under the truck. Daddy'd run over Clem Ritter's head with his truck tire."

"My God," I said.

"Her head was all whomp-sided," she said.

"I couldn't look," my mother said. "I had to cover my eyes."

I truly did not know what to say.

"What did y'all do?"

"Well, son, there wasn't nothin' to do. Daddy picked her up, and slung her off into the weeds."

I think a full minute went by.

"You didn't do anything?" I asked, stunned. "You didn't check to see if she was breathing, or try to go for a doctor, or . . ."

"No, son. I done told you. Momma had supper done."

She said Charlie drove them home, and they went inside to eat. It was a glorious meal, and Ava was hardly angry at all, though saddened by the news of Clem Ritter.

"But . . . Y'all didn't even report it?" I asked.

"No, son, we didn't have to. Along about dark, we were out in the yard and here she come, just staggerin' and weavin' up the driveway, her head still all whomp-sided. . . ."

It was another long, long minute before she bothered to tell me that Clem Ritter was a dog.

· · ·

I should have guessed. I should have recalled Ike, the unfortunate rooster that Sis threw down on with her snub-nosed .22, and how long it took my people to bother to tell me that Ike was a fowl. The sad thing is, my aunt Juanita was not even trying to put me on. Clem Ritter *was* her friend, her best friend.

"Clementime Ritter—we called her Clem for short," my aunt Juanita said. "I guess she was one of the ugliest dogs I have ever seen. I can't remember exactly how we got her, but it might have been in the mailbox. The Bonds—they lived right down the road— was bad to put stuff in our mailbox to scare us, and I think we might have got her out of the mailbox.

"I didn't have no name for her for a long time, because she was my dog and I wanted to give her a good one. I think it was two or three years before I did. I named her for a woman I read about in a magazine, in this story about this woman who suspected this other woman, Clementine Ritter, was runnin' around with her husband. And one day the husband played like he was goin' fishin', but he didn't go fishin', and he went and hid with Clem Ritter in the haystack. The wife heard 'em gigglin' in the haystack, and she killed 'em both. I think she shot 'em. I don't know how we got that magazine—I'm sure somebody gave it to us—but I think maybe it was one of them *True Crime* magazines. And, anyway, I liked the name Clem Ritter. She was just an ol' mutt dog, ever' color you can think of. But she was my dog. She got all right, after a while, but her head was whomp-sided for a real, real long time."

All I could think was, only my aunt Juanita would name her dog after a villainess in a crime magazine.

"What happened to her?" I asked, but should not have.

"The insurance man run over her with a store," my aunt Juanita said.

I decided to wait this one out, too.

"Dee Roper was the insurance man, but he drove one of them rolling stores, like a peddler's truck, in his second job, and he run over Clem Ritter out right past the mailbox," she explained.

"Momma cussed him out, said, 'You have kilt our dog, you SB,'" my mother recalled later. "He just stood there and took it. He never said a word."

"She had a hard life," my mother said, and I believe she was talking about the dog.

"It was a good supper, though," my mother added, after a while.

"It was," Juanita said.

. . .

No one mourned the chicken. My mother remembers mostly the crust, how crisp and thin it was, ranging from a dark brown to almost black in some places, and the crumbs that fell away were tiny, powdery. Ava cooked it over, at most, medium heat, or what would be medium heat on an electric or gas stove. My mother watched her cook it that way, perhaps, a hundred times, pushing the bigger pieces, the thighs and breasts, to the center of the skillet, and the legs and wings to the outside. She put the gizzards in about halfway through—gizzards are like eating a jai alai ball no matter how skillfully you prepare them—and then, finally, the liver, which they considered a delicacy. She remembers that her mother made water gravy, and if there had been no chicken at all there would have been reason for joy with that gravy spooned over hot biscuit.

"We always had fresh tomatoes in the summer, and Momma would slice 'em thick and salt and pepper them, and I think we had fresh cantaloupe, too. But the best thing on the table was those green beans cooked with Irish potatoes. You could see the fat from the pork shining on those potatoes, and in those beans."

Juanita was upset about Clem Ritter's injury, but not so upset she did not eat.

Clem Ritter got the scraps, her whomp-sidedness affecting her appetite not at all.

It was a good day in the end, the sisters agreed.

. . .

If our people really did fly a banner over their cooking, this plate of fried chicken and delicious sides, not the pig, would probably be stitched upon it, if they ever actually took a vote. But, like the cracklin' cornbread, good fried chicken, for such a common-sounding thing, is hard to duplicate in modern times. It has to do with the awful decline in the flesh of the chicken itself.

Ava's chickens did not live in their own filth for a lifetime. They were cooped sometimes, to protect them from marauding foxes and occasional coons, but mostly they roosted in the trees.

There is something right and peaceful about that, in the setting sun, when a chicken rises to its roost for the night, unless, of course, you are trying to eat it.

Modern-day chicken is so inferior that she almost never fries chicken anymore. When she does, it is a celebration of something, or because I begged her really, really hard.

"Buy a whole chicken," my mother said, "and if it comes with the good stuff, cook all of it, the gizzard, and liver, and back, and neck, because all those pieces will flavor the other pieces, make it taste . . . better." What she was trying to say was: deeper, richer. "Leave the skin on," she said, in a way that made me think that, if you skinned your chicken to make it healthier, you should be slapped.

Think about it. Anyone who thinks paring a little skin off a piece of fried chicken will somehow turn it into health food is probably the same person who orders a Diet Coke with a cheese Whopper. Surrender to its goodness, and eat like a gerbil for two days after that if it makes you feel better, in recompense.

"Folly," my mother said, but the way she said it made it sound more like "dumbasses."

Here, as close as we can get, is the modern-day incarnation of the feast my grandmother prepared on the day my grandfather ran over Clem Ritter's head.

Fried Chicken

WHAT YOU WILL NEED

1 frying chicken, whole

2 to 3 cups flour

1 teaspoon salt

1 teaspoon black pepper

1 to 2 pounds lard (enough to form at least a 2-inch
    pool in the skillet)

HOW TO COOK IT

Cut up the chicken at the joints, being sure to save the liver, gizzards, back, neck, or anything else, even if you are not sure what it is. Or, have a butcher do it.

Salt and pepper the pieces, lightly. Using your hands, dust the damp pieces—top, bottom, and sides—as completely as you can with flour. Do not dredge in egg wash, etc. The point is to have a light, barely there crust.

Cover and set aside.

In a large cast-iron skillet (though some people swear by a Dutch oven for this), heat the lard over medium-high heat until it liquefies and heats up, but do not turn the heat so high that it begins to smoke. Lard is not as forgiving as modern-day cooking oils. Gently, carefully drop in the chicken pieces, let them crisp for a moment, then reduce the heat to medium. Do not worry about turning the chicken before you reduce the heat.

Here is where my mother's recipe and her mother's differ from most. Some people cook only a few pieces at a time, to make sure the chicken crisps correctly, and turn the chicken only once. My people do crowd the skillet, trying to leave just a little room between the pieces; a little room between them will be enough to let the hot oil do its job. Over medium heat, cook the chicken between 30 and 40 minutes (stoves vary), turning it four times. I am not sure what the science of this is; I guess it's just because my mother says so. In between gyrations, cover the skillet with a lid—again, being careful, because steam can build up in just a few minutes.

My mother places the bigger pieces in the middle of the skillet, and the wings and legs on the outside.

Add gizzards and livers about halfway through the process. Some people cook livers only a few minutes, but my mother has such a fear of undercooked poultry—it's a cultural thing—that she crisps the organ meats a little more than necessary. A crispy liver is pretty tasty, though.

This is not a complicated endeavor, my mother says. If you don't know whether your chicken is done, remove the thigh, cut into it, and look, being careful not to burn yourself or burn up the rest of the chicken. You can stick a meat thermometer into it if you have one and know how to use it, but in this you are on your own. We have never used one.

My mother just uses a fork to turn the pieces and lift them from the skillet, but she is more adept than most of us. I recommend tongs, good ones that grip securely. Hot grease is unforgiving. I know.

Let the chicken cool at least 10 minutes; the thighs retain heat, and I've seen them smoke when I took a bite, even after 10 minutes.

NOTE She knows many people say crowding the skillet will result in soggy chicken. "I don't crowd it. I make sure there's just enough space. It'll taste better, having it all cook together, white, dark, livers, the bony pieces," my mother says; this is what Ava always believed.

NOTE Some of you will be unable to bring yourselves to fry chicken in lard. It is not a sin to feel this way. My mother often fries her chicken in cooking oil, usually vegetable oil. Some people swear by peanut oil. Some swear by Crisco. The process is not much different, though very smart people will go on and on about burn ratios and such. I do not associate with them. Neither does my mother. She still cooks it in lard about a third of the time, for the sake of history.

Fried Chicken Gravy (Water Gravy)

WHAT YOU WILL NEED

2 to 3 tablespoons flour (may take more)
½ teaspoon salt
½ teaspoon black pepper (at least)
3 cups water

HOW TO COOK IT

My mother has no recipe to make a small skillet of gravy. The above amounts will yield a skillet-full of chicken gravy, which has a remarkable dual purpose. It is a true delicacy for humans, but also an excellent, economic method, with the leftovers, to feed a yard-full of dogs.

The chicken, thinly coated with dry flour, will not soak up as much of the lard as you think if you cook it right, and the chicken fat and skin will add a lovely taste. There may be 4 or 5 tablespoons of fat left. While the skillet is still medium-hot, sprinkle in the flour, salt, and pepper, and stir until the oil is thoroughly incorporated. "Just say 'mixed up good,'" she said. Do not fish the crispy bits from the skillet before doing this; they are where the flavor resides.

Stir the browning flour until you have a nut-brown color. If the flour is still raw, the gravy will have a chalky taste. Be careful, though, not to burn it.

Stir in the water. Gravy is forgiving. The gravy will thicken, if you leave it on the heat.

You can use milk instead to thicken it. Milk gravy can over-thicken and become chalky, gunky, so be careful of the heat. But I prefer milk gravy, and on this my mother and I will never agree.

No matter what gravy you choose, eat it over biscuits, maybe speckled with a little more black pepper, with sliced tomatoes or sliced cantaloupe on the side, and set some biscuits aside, buttered, to eat with jelly or preserves, as Jim advised so long ago.

Fresh Green Beans with Golden Potatoes

This was perhaps Ava's finest dish, my mother believes, because of the distance she carried the simple ingredients. No one seems to understand why her recipe for this basic thing turned out so much better that others'. It just did.

WHAT YOU WILL NEED

3 large golden potatoes, or 10 or so small red potatoes
1 small piece salt pork, fatback, or smoked pork,
   or 2 slices bacon, for seasoning
Small amount bacon grease
1 to 1½ cups water
2 to 3 pounds fresh green beans, any kind
1 teaspoon black pepper (that sounds like a lot,
   but green beans do well with black pepper)
Salt (to taste)
1 white or yellow onion, coarsely chopped

HOW TO COOK IT

Quarter the larger potatoes. New potatoes should at least be halved, so they will cook evenly. Red potatoes do not have to be peeled, but we do it.

In a medium-to-large pot, cook the seasoning meat in a little bacon grease until some of the fat renders into the bottom of the pot, but not until crisp. You are looking for just a little brown on the edges. It will taste better this way.

Add the water, green beans, and other seasonings. Cook over high heat until the water comes to a good boil, then lower the heat to medium. After about 10 minutes, add the potatoes, and cook for about 30 more minutes, allowing most of the water to cook out, and till the potatoes are tender. The beans will be done, no matter what. Green beans are forgiving.

. . .

Ava never forgave Dee Roper for killing Clem Ritter with his mercantile.

"She always called him that SB Dee Roper," my mother said. "I thought it was part of his name."

My mother turned twelve in April '49. Her time as a spectator in her momma's kitchen was done now. She was not the oldest daughter in the house—still learning, certainly—but more and more she did the cooking herself, if Ava was working in a cotton field, or visiting relatives, or just mad at Charlie. At such times, Ava refused to have anything to do with his sustenance, and the children suffered by association. "It was cornbread and buttermilk," my mother said, "if Momma was mad at Daddy."

Juanita's early indifference to cooking and eating, so like her mother's early attitude, had not changed, so there was no struggle for control of the kitchen.

On days when the kitchen was bequeathed to her, to her alone, my mother found a peace there, a kind of quiet. She had studied her mother, and her aunts, and the men, like her daddy, who were at home in the kitchen. It is not so much that they instructed her in any active or organized way; she was more like a dancer watching better dancers go through their steps, over and over again.

They still had no electricity, so there was no modern stove, and no refrigerator. The cooking was still done on a heavy iron woodstove with a square baking box, the oven, attached to one side. Her daddy chopped most of the wood, but if he was chasing work, Ava and the girls chopped it themselves—about an hour of work, and a lot of bloodshed, to fuel the cooking of two or three meals.

She was no better with an ax than her momma was. A scarred, ancient cupboard against one wall held the plates, spoons, spices, and a drawer-full of scarred, pitted knives. The kitchen table had a road map of nicks and scrapes and ancient, mysterious stains, and had been hammered back together after more than one sorry, drunken relative had crashed into it or onto it, or been thrown across it. But my mother looked at it and imagined the food she would place on it, one heavy iron pot at a time, and knew that, wherever they dragged it, through the foothills or along the dirt road, "hon, I was at home."

18

TOMATOES WITHOUT TASTE,
TOMATOES WITHOUT END

Ham and Redeye Gravy

over Fresh Diced Tomato

Aunt Edna and her oldest daughter, Betty

1950

HAM STEAKS with a disc of creamy marrow in the middle, served with fried eggs and hot biscuits, all done right, "don't need no extras," my mother says. But now and then she just likes to show off a little bit. She opens a piping-hot biscuit, covers it with a beautifully ripe diced tomato, salts it a little, peppers it a lot, and dresses it with an elixir made from the hot grease mixed with a few tablespoons of brewed black coffee, stirred together in the sizzling skillet. I cannot really explain why this is so delicious, exactly. I only know that it is.

But almost every time, she apologizes. It is brought down, brought low, by the poor quality of the tomato.

"Ru'nt it," she says.

Every tomato, for fifty years or more, has had something wrong with it.

"Not fit to eat," she says.

She was not always a snob as to tomatoes. As a child, she toddled down rows without end, the tomatoes as big as her head, green turning to orange turning to red. As a young woman, she pulled them by the bushel, one bushel as near perfect as the next, so that you could reach in with your eyes closed and get a pretty one. But that was a long time ago. I asked if maybe she was just a lot harder to please now, as an old woman, and she told me no, you don't get so old you can't tell magic from mush.

The last truly good tomato was probably in . . . Well, she cannot quite recall. "But I was still a girl. . . . We had 'maters then, son," she testifies. Since then, she has stared with contempt at untold baskets of tomatoes in country stores, corner groceries, supermarkets, curb markets, on the tailgates of rusted pickup trucks, and even at unharvested fruit hanging from the vines in other people's gardens, and sniffed. She actually sniffs—in disdain, in frustration—as she looks them over one by inferior one.

I cannot count the times she has stood at my elbow as I paid some cashier or vendor or poor farmer what seemed a reasonable price, as she mumbled about what a shame it was that an old woman could be so lowly bamboozled, hoodwinked, and treated like a dog. I have learned never, never to let her pay with her own money; if she counted out her hard-won Social Security for inferior tomatoes, she would gripe till Kingdom Come. At least she has never discriminated. She has openly disdained beefsteaks, Big Boys, Heatmasters, Sunmasters, Sweet Millions, Mountain Masters, and Boxcar Willies. She does not give a damn.

It is understandable that she would feel that way about supermarket tomatoes, which are not actually food, and most likely ripened somewhere on a truck between here and Homestead, or Mexico, or in the hold of a tramp steamer. A supermarket tomato is food the way a frozen burrito is food: of last resort.

But in the Deep South, in the hot summertime, you would think an old woman could at least ride past a good tomato every now and then, at the rustic curb markets, or on the backs of trucks parked at the side of the road, their springs sagging with watermelons, sweet corn, cantaloupes, and green and ripe tomatoes. You would think that on the back of some raggedy '74 Dodge, on some forgotten crossroads somewhere south of Sylacauga, the perfect tomato would be waiting, or at least one that that did not make her queasy or mad.

No.

"Oh, you can get one that tastes like a tomater a little bit, one of them pink things that makes you think to yourself, 'Well, it's better than no tomater a-tall.' That's what I always say to myself: 'It's better'n no tomater a-tall.' "

As with many things, she blames the men who walked on the moon.

"They ought not have done that," she said. "Our weather's just not right anymore. It used to rain every day in the summer. You can't tinker with nature and expect everything to just be *all right.*"

When she was a child, her people watched the moon, listened

to the wind, smelled the rain. Then some fool goes and just walks all over it.

But whatever the reason, there are almost no real tomatoes in existence anymore, ones that are fit for human consumption (though they are still adequate, she allows, for hog feed). They are mealy, which is the worst sin a tomato can carry, or spotted yellow, or hard-fleshed, or artificially ripened with "chemicals and poisons," apparently in tanning beds. They are too ripe or too green or scarred or blemished or wormy, or, she is almost certain, radiated by the government. The thing is, worminess is about the best you can hope for. "You can cut a worm out," she said, "and go on." When she does find what seems to be a good tomato, it is an impostor, a poseur, and when she cuts into it at home it is unspeakable.

The thing is, she is so disappointed in the quality of the tomatoes that the vendors, whether in a big produce section or standing beside their trucks, agree with her, and tell her they will try to do better.

"They just ain't real good, are they?" she says, sniffing.

"No, ma'am, they surely ain't."

I usually just stand there, uncomfortable.

Sometimes these men grew the tomatoes in their own gardens, sweated over them, stooped over them, prayed over them.

"Well, give me that basket there," she finally says, pointing at one that looks just like all the rest of them.

I have seen it happen all my life. The only decent tomatoes she gets are from our kin, from my brothers, who raised her a garden at various times, or her nephew Mac (who is not really her nephew but might as well be), or other kin who come by bearing bags and bags of tomatoes, mostly for her to can. But for slicing and eating, those, too, are less than ideal to a perfectionist.

I asked her, finally, if she could ever remember a passable tomato in the last, say, decade.

"Why, sure," she said, and waited for me to read her mind.

"When was that?"

I watched her pick through them in her memory like it was a curb market she had happened by, gathering, sorting, discarding, and arriving, finally, in only disappointment. "I'll need to study on it a little more," she finally said. After a while, she just said no, there were none, after all. She loves tomatoes, and eats them every day in the summer, sliced on her plate or in sandwiches or with her cornbread and buttermilk, and enjoys them as much as she can, given such poor quality. But she knows there is a good one there, somewhere, in the weeds.

. . .

The song was perhaps the last one on earth I expected her to know. We were driving to the doctor's office that morning; it seems like going to the doctor is what we do. We go to the heart doctor, the toe doctor, the eye doctor, the urologist, the general practitioner, the doctor who treats her for what she calls only "the bad word," and the dermatologist she nicknamed "Dr. Butcher." He, oddly, is one of her favorites. "He's nice to me," my mother said, "but quick to cut." I do not listen to the radio as we drive, because it will rob us of time, and time is our hobgoblin. She tells me stories as we ride, and does not have to hurry, because she lives forty-five minutes and one drive-through sausage biscuit away from the closest specialist. I do not want her to have to shout over Creedence Clearwater Revival. But I had that song in my head as we rolled through the cotton fields and soybeans and brittle, rustling corn, and the corn made me think of my grandfather's liquor, and that made me think of chain gangs, and . . .

When you wake up in the mornin', when the work bell ring
You go marching to the table, to see the same old thing
Knife and fork upon the table, ain't no pork up in the pan
And if you say a thing about it, you get in trouble with the man

Then, right on cue, the old woman next to me began to sing . . .

Let the Midnight Special shine her light on me
Oh, let the Midnight Special shine her ever-lovin' light on me

It should not have surprised me. Everybody from Lead Belly to Burl Ives recorded that prison anthem, and her daddy, of course, knew every vagabond and chain-gang song ever recorded. But it just sounded strange coming from her. I gave her a few more minutes, a few more stanzas, to let the story take shape inside her head. There is always a story—or stories, swirling in and out of each other, leading nowhere, everywhere. This time, like so many times, it led into the field.

Yonder come Miss Rosie, how in the world did you know?
Well I know her by her apron, and the dress she wore
Umbrella on her shoulder, piece of paper in her hand
Well I'm callin' that captain, "Turn a-loose my man"

"I think it was '49, or maybe '50. I know 'cause James and William had done got home from the army."
"What was?" I asked.
"The last time I had some really fine tomaters."

· · ·

It had started in wintertime, with a curse.
Sunday was a day of feasting for the Bundrums—not after church, because damned if Charlie Bundrum would swing a hammer six days a week to feed chicken to a preacher. No, they feasted in the early morning on Sunday, when every preacher in the world was occupied. "It was the one day we eat better than *anybody*." My mother somehow always made me think of Dickens when she talked about this, about their early-morning journey to procure the elements of their meal. She made it sound like a feast of kings.
Funny how you can see a thing so long after it is over and done with, even if it happened a lifetime before you were born. But she

has always had that skill, to make me picture people in my mind, painting me a picture not only of the physical world but of the feelings behind a thing. She made me see the little store and the glassed-in case with the coiled sausage and fresh hamburger and red steaks, made me see my grandfather there outside the glass, like he had coin in pocket to buy the whole damn store.

He was painfully thin, his health failing even then from a lifetime of hard living, but as hard as an old bone. His Sunday clothes were his everyday clothes, and they sagged and bagged over his body; his work boots were filmed in red mud. The known world was covered in red mud. To my mother, then, he looked like an old hammer handle, worn and cured, "but so thin. I guess it's one of the reasons I loved cooking for him. I thought, if I could just make real good food, I could make him okay."

It was always the same Sunday-morning conversation, there at the butcher shops in the working-class neighborhoods in Jacksonville. "What have you got that's good?" Charlie asked.

He preferred to deal mostly with kinfolks, so he would get an honest answer. Fortunately, two of his cousins by marriage, Ed Young and Y. C. Bonds, ran neighborhood groceries.

"Y.C. was married to Mary Emma, Uncle Babe's daughter—you know, it was Uncle Babe who helped butcher that hog in the dead of night. Sometimes Daddy had to get Y.C. out of bed on a Sunday morning to open up his store. Ed Young was married to Lois Bundrum. They sure had some pretty children, but that's account of Lois."

He would ask them if they had any T-bones—they cost a dear thirty-nine cents apiece—and he would nod his head as if he had actually been considering T-bones but was not altogether set on them. Then he would ask about fresh ham, or streak o' lean, not salted but fresh, the lean streak a bright pink.

The cousins, by marriage or not, treated the thin man in the ragged overalls with respect; Charlie Bundrum was the kind of man who would help you drag your ox out of the ditch, metaphorically and otherwise, and earned friends. Sometimes, if times were hard, he decided on the fatback, and sometimes it was the beautiful freshly sliced ham, which had a ring of fat an inch thick circling the lean, its center eye creamy with marrow. "I remember us having beefsteak for breakfast," my mother said, "but not a lot. I remember Momma frying chicken. But usually, if Daddy cooked breakfast for us on a Sunday, it was pork."

One winter morning, after selecting and procuring the meat, he went looking for a winter tomato. His hopes were not high; it would have to be a world traveler, that tomato, if he found one at all. The hills of northeastern Alabama and North Georgia had real winter, miserable ice storms, and sometimes even troublesome snow, so any fresh vegetable had to come from someplace the winter didn't go. My daddy's cousin Carlos was named for the logo on the side of a wooden crate of Mexican produce, I guess because his people were just so happy to have something, anything, that did not come from a can.

It was a different time then, a time before people ripened their vegetables with chemicals, so the well-traveled tomatoes might be edible, if somewhat jostled or bounced around. If they looked passable, Charlie would take two or three of the ripest ones. They had to be dead-ripe for the delicacy he had in mind.

He would leave the store trailed by his girls, the meat, wrapped in clean white butcher's paper, under one arm. At home, he would stoke up the fire on the woodstove and reach for an iron skillet that had rarely if ever been exposed to soap and water.

"Daddy always cooked the meat and made the gravy," my mother reminded me, as if this was something I should not get wrong, like Scripture. "And Momma always made the biscuits and the coffee. They cooked together, side by side."

The pork, either ham or thick bacon or crispy fatback, would be cooked to crisp perfection, but not petrified.

"Daddy was an expert," my mother said.

The biscuits would be immaculate, each rising to a perfect dome, with just the slightest dusting of browned flour.

Ava took over the skillet and fried perfect eggs—not too runny, not hard and tasteless. The white had to have the last speck of runniness cooked out, while leaving the rich yellow to run liquid.

If you think that's not an art, by God, try it some time.

Then she relinquished the skillet to Charlie once more, for his famous redeye gravy, which he prepared with the care of a chemist. But the winter tomatoes, as he had expected, were at best so-so. It was not that he didn't make a good redeye gravy, because the gravy itself was excellent. It is just that, on a humdrum tomato, it was not good enough to satisfy her daddy, my mother says. "We waited all week for that breakfast," my mother said, "and Daddy wanted to be proud of it. He wanted it to be good, for us."

This was their luxury, but without luster.

"Come summer," Charlie said, "I hope, by God, we're drowning in 'maters."

. . .

And it came to pass.

"Daddy always planted a big garden, not really even what you'd call a garden, but a great big field," my mother said. That spring, he broke ground for seven or eight long rows, "as long as a chicken house," she recalls. He hitched their horse, Buck, to the plow, so every foot of it was hard-won. Charlie worked every evening after work and into the night, lining up his rows with white rags tied to stakes, so he could make them out in the moonlight. Charlie believed he had to plant more than seemed necessary, to ensure, in the end, that he and his family had enough to carry them through the summer and early fall, and enough to can for the winter. The drought would destroy some of them, or storms would obliterate them, or hard, soaking rains would bring them down under their own weight. The caterpillars would feast on them, or the birds, or any one of a dozen wild, furry things, and sometimes, because of things no man or woman could figure, they just wouldn't make.

"He planted so many he couldn't stake them, planted so many he had to just let them grow on the ground," she said. "Tomatoes will make fine on the ground, but you lose a lot more, to the cater-pillars and such, and some will make but make ugly, and good for nothin' but piecing up and canning."

Charlie was either ahead of his time or else behind it, but he refused to doctor his garden with the primitive pesticides of that time, and used no chemical fertilizer beyond some cow manure he had worked into the red clay in late winter or early spring. Red clay is not rich bottomland, but it will make tomatoes, squash, okra, green beans, watermelons, cantaloupes, and more, espe-cially if you can awaken the soil with some kind of fertilizer. Charlie planted them all, but he put more rows in tomatoes than all the rest combined, just to be sure. Then he stood at the edge of his field and waited for nature to do its worst.

But the droughts did not come. The dust did not blow, and the ground did not crack, and when the wind came it seemed to pass high over the plants, which snaked along the ground and sur-vived, whereas staked tomatoes were knocked down. The rains, when they came, were gentle for this volatile corner of the earth. Every afternoon, it seemed, brought a thunderstorm and a soak-ing rain, not enough to wash the world away, just enough to sink deep into the ground before blowing itself out or moving off to the east.

The pestilence descended, as it always does, but Charlie and the girls moved through the fields flicking the green caterpillars off to the ground and stomping them. The birds descended, too, but they fashioned a scarecrow out of old pie tins and a raggedy shirt. It was not scary at all, but apparently the crows were too busy laughing themselves silly to eat the family's crop, and the plants bore fruit.

My mother was twelve years old that summer. She remembers walking through the field with her daddy and Juanita as the first tomatoes changed from orange to deep, delicious red. Her daddy pulled one each for her, Juanita, and himself, and they ate them there, passing the saltshaker back and forth. The tomatoes tasted clean, with that tart bite of acid, and were juicy but not watery, the way some store-bought tomatoes can be.

"We'll have 'maters this summer, by God," he said.

The tomatoes made early and in a great bounty. On Sunday, as the first crop ripened to perfection, he drove his girls to town and they made a great ceremony of selecting slabs of ham a half-inch thick, though it is unclear which cousin by marriage he bought the meat from. He prepared a perfect redeye gravy, and Ava baked a pan of perfect biscuits. And as he drizzled the gravy over a perfect tomato, he sang.

If you're ever in Houston, well, you better walk right
You better not squabble, and you better not fight

Or the sheriff will grab ya and the boys will bring you down
You can bet your last dollar, Oh! you're prison bound

"I still think it's the best thing, about, I've ever eat. He'd take the grease from that fried ham—that clear, hot grease—and spoon in fresh-brewed black coffee. He'd spoon it in till it was about two-thirds coffee, one-third of the fat. Then, he'd take a tomato or two—they had to be dead ripe—and dice 'em up, and use a little salt on 'em and a lot of black pepper. He'd take two of Momma's biscuits and open them up, and pile that diced tomato on top. Then he'd spoon that mixture, that redeyed gravy—nothin' but coffee and grease and the leavings of the fried meat from the bottom of the skillet—onto that tomato. And that hot grease, it causes that tomato to kind of wilt. I don't know if that's the right word for it, but it does, and . . . Well, the trick to it is, you have to eat it right then, or it's not fit to eat. But if you eat it right then . . . Lord.

"Fresh ham will make good grease for it. Salt ham is too strong sometimes, or too salty, but fresh ham is fine. But that white, streaked meat is fine, too, for this. Even good bacon will make good redeye gravy, but mostly for this you need fresh pork, not smoked, because you don't want sugar or maple or other stuff in it. It messes it up."

Her daddy diced every tomato himself, and, working quickly, prepared every serving of the gravy, because if it was not scalding hot it would not work, would not wilt the tomato or properly ferry the juice down into the biscuit.

He would make a double portion for himself. They ate it together at the small table with those fried eggs—not cooked hard, not too runny, just right—and the fresh ham or whatever fresh pork they'd chosen. If it was ham, he would take a Case knife and remove the marrow from the circle of bone, spread it on a piece of fresh biscuit, pop it into his mouth, and close his eyes.

"The thing you got to have to make it taste right, besides the perfect tomato, is that perfect biscuit," my mother said, because a gummy biscuit or a mealy biscuit, or one constructed from old flour, would ruin it. But that, as they say, is another story. She knew how to make biscuits by then, but not the perfect one, not quite yet; her momma had still not trusted her with such an important mission.

I asked my mother where her father learned his redeye gravy. It sounds like the kind of thing Jimmy Jim would have relished, but she believes her father learned it from his mother, the former Mattie Mixon, the gentle, long-suffering woman with the broken spine who perished in Jim's exile. Mattie's only real joy in her life came from the stories she told her children and the good food she cooked for them, and her journey was hard and mean every day she opened her eyes. When people say, at a death, that someone found peace, this is what they mean. Some people would say that was not much of a life, but not my mother. Even if a person's only legacy is one lingering taste, "Well, that's somethin', ain't it?"

.   .   .

But in the field, the tomatoes continued to make, and make, and make. . . . They made big, and round, and now, looking back on it, it seems like they all made perfectly, without blemishes. The family could not pull them fast enough to keep them from growing to maturity, going ripe, and rotting in the field. Maybe if the tomatoes had been coarse-skinned or blemished, they could have let them lie, or fed them to the hogs, but they were too pretty, too luscious for that.

Charlie went to work in the field as soon as he came in from work, just to slave over the bounty he had wished for, and Ava and their daughters worked all day, some days, and still failed to keep up with the curse of rich soil, and the right amount of rain, and the perfect sun. They needed help.

"James had come home from the army, and Charlie Sanders was back from the navy, and I can still see 'em walking through the fields on either side of these big washtubs, totin' out just tub after tub after tub," my mother said. "Edna and Momma went to work canning them, and they canned quart after quart, worked themselves to death. We borrowed jars, and bought jars. We traded 'maters for jars, or a full jar for three empty jars." To leave them to rot was unthinkable; it would be like burning money on the ground.

They ate tomato sandwiches on white bread, with mayonnaise, salt, and pepper (this, with a cold glass of milk and a few potato chips, remains my favorite simple summer lunch). They sliced platters of them to eat with everything. They ate them with white milk gravy and biscuits, and fried them, ripe as well as green. "You do it just like fried green tomatoes, but you choose one that's turning, not soft yet, and it's good," my mother said. They tried, literally, to eat away the surplus.

They gave tomatoes to kin, and friends, and to passersby they did not know from Adam, and still they made. They put up a sign that just said:

MATERS
FREE!

Ava, who was literate and then some, added the exclamation point as a call for help. It was a point of pride to Charlie that almost none of those tomatoes rotted in the field. The walls in the house were lined with bright-red quarts of canned tomatoes, and green tomato pickles, and even these they had to give away. Finally, the season passed, but as the summer faded into fall, now and then a rare, red tomato, like a mockery, still showed itself in the withering vines. People who had worked a lifetime in the red dirt said they had never seen anything like it, and it became another of those very small legends in this part of the world. I guess maybe it was because there was not much else to talk about, this far out.

Finally, fall turned the plants to brittle sticks, and winter dusted them with frost, and it was almost a relief. Charlie again herded his girls into the butcher shop to select their breakfast meat from behind the counter of the little groceries. There was Juanita, Margaret, Jo, and the baby, Sue. For a second, just a second, his eyes rested on the sad little bin of winter tomatoes. He told the girls they would have ham and eggs, and milk gravy on their biscuits, and maybe some hot buttered grits, but not a tomato, not again.

"I can still taste them," my mother says now, and there has never been a single solitary one to compare to that time—not to any one tomato, or any basket or bushel, but to the thousands of dead-ripe, perfect ones in that long-ago field. All she can do is keep trying, one biscuit, and one gravy, at a time.

Ham and Redeye Gravy
over Fresh Diced Tomato

Smoked ham steaks can be substituted as a shortcut, if you are a Philistine, or just very busy, my mother concedes. Salt ham can also be substituted, but the flavor will be strong. You won't get enough grease from the ham alone to make the gravy.

WHAT YOU WILL NEED

4 medium to large tomatoes
1 tablespoon lard or bacon grease
4 slices fresh ham, about ½ inch thick (do not trim fat)
About ½ cup brewed black coffee
Salt and black pepper (to taste)

HOW TO COOK IT

Dice the tomatoes, about 1 tomato per serving, and set aside.

In a 9-inch skillet, or larger, heat the lard or other fat until it liquefies, being careful not to burn it, then fry the ham until the fat is crispy.

Set the ham aside, but keep it warm.

Carefully stir the coffee into the still-hot skillet, trying as best you can to keep it to that ratio of two-thirds coffee to one-third ham fat.

Heap one of the diced tomatoes over an opened fresh hot biscuit. Sprinkle with salt, and more liberally with black pepper.

Then spoon on the redeye gravy, at least 3 or 4 tablespoons, allowing the hot grease and coffee to wilt the tomato slightly. The redeye gravy should trickle through the tomato, carrying its taste down into the biscuit.

Eat immediately, with ham and eggs.

NOTE Some people like to pour the mixed coffee and grease into a bowl first, before serving. But this may be a mistake, since the redeye gravy will grow cold quickly, and leave you with an abomination. Timing, again, is everything.

· · ·

"What I learned from it," she said, almost seven decades later, "was how things can go together that ought not go together, like how that meat-grease-and-coffee mixture could wilt that tomato just the right amount, but how you salt it first, to begin the process of wilting it, to get it all goin'. Daddy showed me. Daddy showed me it was all right to be particular." She will not apologize for her standards, on good tomatoes or anything else. She has not had a really good slice of ripe cantaloupe since that monkey came back to earth.

19

DIDELPHIS VIRGINIANA

Baked Possum and Sweet Potatoes

My aunt Juanita and uncle Ed, after the possum scare
and before their marriage

1953

SHE DOES NOT KNOW what woke her. She only remembers opening her eyes and seeing, down the hall, the silhouette of her father in a straight-back chair, staring into the dying coals in the fireplace.

It was the middle of the night, and he was usually fast asleep. He went to bed early and was not a restless man.

"It scared me a little bit," my mother said, thinking back.

She wrapped a quilt around herself and walked softly into the front room.

Her sister Juanita snored softly in her bed near the fire.

"Daddy?" my mother whispered. "How come you're up? Is something wrong?"

"It's Juanita, hon," he said softly.

"What's wrong with her?"

"I'm just scared to go to sleep," he said.

"Lord, why?"

"Well, she eat that whole possum for supper," her daddy said, deadly serious, "and I ain't never knowed nobody eat a whole possum and live."

The truth is, he had never known anybody to eat a whole possum at all, and certainly not anyone who was roughly the same size and weight as a lemur. In her bed, Juanita snored peacefully on.

"I guess it don't seem to have hurt her none," he said after a while, but they sat up anyway.

"She had been terribly ill for a long time," said my mother, thinking back. "It was ulcers, and, oh, hon, she suffered. She hadn't eat nothin' solid for so long.

"Till that possum."

I asked her if the possum saved her sister's life, but she said she didn't believe so.

"But it didn't do her no harm."

. . .

The possum was an important element in the diet of my people; there is no denying this. But it is included in this book only because I love my aunt Juanita. That may have to be enough.

My mother does not believe many modern-day chefs will attempt a recipe for baked possum and sweet potatoes, and the truth is, she never particularly enjoyed the process of preparing one, but it was subsistence cooking when she was a child. Its oil, rendered in cooking, was considered to be serious medicine, used to ease arthritis in the old, and was even rubbed on the chests of coughing children. Why would it not be medicinal from the inside out? But to my mother, it is no kind of delicacy.

"I'll talk about it," she said, "but I don't like it."

I asked her what a possum ever did to her.

"If I can't enjoy what I cook," she said, "if I can't enjoy eating it, I'd rather not cook it."

"If I had me one right now I'd cook it," said my aunt Juanita, slightly insulted. "I might not could eat a whole one, but I believe I could eat a whole lot of one."

The Virginia opossum, *Didelphis virginiana*, walked with the dinosaurs. It is a semi-arboreal marsupial, which means it lives mostly on the ground but can climb trees if it so chooses, and carries its young in a pouch, like a kangaroo. It is not lovely, at least in its adult form. It has beady eyes that glow red, a white face, pointy snout, prehensile tail, silvery hair, and fifty teeth. People have been bad-mouthing the possum for as long as Europeans have walked this land.

"An opossum hath a head like a Swine, and a taile like a Rat, and is of the Bigness of a Cat," wrote John Smith of the Jamestown Colony, in the early 1600s. "Under her belly she hath a bagge wherein she lodgeth, carrieth, and sucketh her young."

But fairly early, the hungry colonists discovered they could also eat them.

My aunt Juanita, in '53, was just doing her part.

. . .

"She was nineteen years old when it happened," my mother said, thinking back. "She was keeping house for the Ropers, the same Mr. Roper who run over Clem Ritter with his store. I reckon she forgave him. I don't know for sure; Juanita could hold a grudge. Juanita was helping to take care of Mr. Roper's mother-in-law, who was old, while Mr. Roper was out peddling in his truck. I can't remember her name, the mother-in-law. Juanita would stay with 'em during the week and come home on the weekend. She'd ride with [cousin] Leonard Bundrum, who was not much to look at. . . . Well, to tell the truth about it, he was so ugly you almost couldn't look at him, and he took up with a girl that was as ugly as he was. She had a million freckles. Daddy nicknamed her 'The Speckled Beauty.'

"Anyway, Juanita was bad to have ulcers, and her and Mrs. Roper ate a whole dishpan full of popcorn one night and the ulcers busted in Juanita's stomach, and she was awful, awful sick. Edna would always take us home with her when we got sick—she was just like that—and she took Juanita home with her, and tried to get her better. Juanita lived for months, it seemed like, on cream-of-tomato soup and soft crackers, but she wasn't gettin' no better. Juanita had always been skinny, but she was losing weight. I'd go sit with her. We were all worried. She just wouldn't, couldn't, eat anything solid. Finally, she come home, but she wasn't no better.

"Well, she said she might could eat some fish if it was bland, and Daddy went up to Guntersville with his snag rod and fished for them jack salmon, and brought 'em home in his coat pockets. And Momma boiled 'em in a kind of stew, and Juanita ate that, day after day, and they gave her some strength, but she still wasn't gaining any weight back. And then . . . well, I ain't sure where that possum came from."

Her mother baked it with sweet potatoes.

"I ate a sweet potato," my mother said, "but I was careful not to get no possum on it."

The flesh crisped a golden brown, and ran with a clear grease.

"It was the best thing I've ever eat," my aunt Juanita said. "But it's not true I eat a whole one. I saved a leg for Momma."

When she finished, she got up from the table, walked to her bed, and went to sleep without pain.

"I slept like a baby," she said. "I didn't know you could eat yourself well with possum."

Still, her sister and daddy stayed up all night, just to be sure.

"It was a big possum," my mother said. "We're talking two or three pounds, cleaned."

"And a half-loaf of bread," my aunt Juanita said.

"Not only did it not hurt her, but she was okay after that," my mother said, "and she never had any more trouble with her stomach—well, not till she was in her old age."

I asked them both why people did not eat more possum.

"Well," my mother said, "you can't just hit one with the car and run over and get it."

"They eat carrion," my aunt Juanita explained.

My mother merely closed her eyes and shook her head.

The procuring, sanitizing, and preparation are a part of our folklore and history, but a thing "ever'body just can't do," my mother said.

"But it's worth it," Juanita said.

My mother just looked sad.

. . .

As a boy, I wandered the mountains of home with a stone-dead flashlight and a flapping tow sack in my hand, following the bobbing light of my big brother, Sam, who followed, unerringly, the music of the dogs. It was so cold it burned through the legs of my jeans, but on a cold night the scent was plainer, cleaner on the ground, and the dogs locked on to it for miles, and sang it back to us across the dark.

There was Joe, in front. He was a coon dog, mostly, but he would lower himself, when he was younger, and run a possum or two if he felt like it. He was at least as smart as most of the people who followed him across that landscape, and if he didn't like the other dogs he ran with, he would just go lie down back in the truck and refuse to associate with any riffraff. But if he felt like it, when he struck that trail, nothing could shake him.

"That dog hunts for hisself," my brother explained to me. "He's got personality, and it's best not to make him mad." He was ferocious when he caught his quarry on the ground, but would not fight other dogs; he would just look them over and show them his backside as he walked straight away.

Personality was what he had instead of ears. A lifetime of battling mean boar coons across the landscape of the Appalachian foothills had left him without those, and left his body a slab of quivering muscle, crisscrossed with white scars. He was basically a black-and-tan coonhound, my brother believes, and a little feist, and some cur dog, but what he had more than anything was that intelligent nose and that beautiful, singsong voice. You could hear him two mountains away, hear that lovely sound.

I gave up hunting long before my brother and my cousin Tommy and others still followed those dogs across the ridges and deep into the hollers, but I will always remember that sound, how it shifted when a trailing hound struck the trail, and became even more urgent when a dog had treed.

Joe ran in front, trailed by Low Booger, a black-and-tan with a low, low voice. Next came Belle, a gyp, with a lovely, ringing voice. Other, lesser dogs, young and unproved, trailed behind. It was how they learned, said Sam.

"There was one that would tree backward. He would strike a trail and follow it the wrong way, so he'd run away from the direction the possum was goin', and the trail would just get colder and colder . . . and then have to double back and follow it the right way. Always found the possum. Just took a while."

The possum is not exactly a racehorse. It can move fast for a creature that seems to lack the capacity to run; it just seems to toddle quickly.

"They ain't like a coon. A coon will go up a big tree, go up high, but a possum will just climb into any ol' bush it comes to," he said.

It is believed that a possum has a fine memory and can remember a persimmon tree, recall its location, years after it feasted there. You would think, my brother said, they would remember a slightly better tree to climb.

"Sometimes all you had to do was shake the branches and it'd fall out on the ground. You had to hold the dogs back, because a possum ain't got no chance against a dog.

"But usually they'd sull. Don't nothing else in the whole world do that, that I know of."

When a possum sulls, it feigns death. It keels over, its legs go rigid, its lips pull back from its teeth, and a foul odor from its anal glands wafts from the body. The fainting is an involuntary action, not a conscious strategy. The idea is that a predator will lose interest in the unappetizing corpse and not eat it. After a half-hour or so—sometimes as long as three hours—the possum will come to and toddle off.

They do not always sull. A possum, especially one cornered in a stump hole, or a hollow tree, may fight back, and bite with its fifty teeth. "They got real brave in a hole," Sam said.

"But it wadn't unusual to have six or seven possums in a sack at the end of a night," Sam said. "We'd sell to the old people, for a dollar or two apiece."

I asked him if he had ever eaten possum.

"Not voluntarily," he said. "When I was little, they fed it to me. They fed me a lot of things when I was little. But I wouldn't eat one now. I know what they *do.*"

They eat plants, and fruits like persimmons, but they also eat frogs, and eggs of any kind, small rodents, and pretty much anything good and dead.

"When I was a little boy, there was a sinkhole in the middle of that big pasture by the house, the one where Mr. [Paul] Williams kept his cows. It was a real pasture, there at the edge of the lake, and I used to love to go to the pasture, but I didn't go to that sink-hole but once. That was where Paul would take the cows that had died, and the possums . . . well . . ."

"Cows?" I asked

"Yep."

"Possums goin' every which way."

"Sweet Lord," I said.

"Yep."

So you cannot just catch a possum and cook it, said my aunt Juanita, utterly unshaken. You have to cage it, and feed it for a week or so, on fruits or grains like corn, until you flush the nastiness from its system. "You have to clean 'em out," Juanita said, and as you do, you fatten it, like a goose.

It is, in many ways, a miracle food. The flesh is oily, greasy, yet still low in cholesterol.

"Possum is good for you," my aunt Juanita said again, for what no one believed was the first time.

I asked my mother if she would walk me through the process of cooking a possum and sweet potatoes. She said it would be better to talk to Aunt Juanita about that. I have never seen my mother relinquish her authority in the kitchen so fast in my life.

There are two methods. My aunt Juanita prefers the traditional one.

Baked Possum and Sweet Potatoes

WHAT YOU WILL NEED

1 whole possum, cleaned

4 or 5 sweet potatoes, peeled

¼ teaspoon salt

½ teaspoon black pepper

HOW TO COOK IT

Preheat the oven to 350 degrees.

In a big pot, cover the possum with water and bring to a boil; then simmer over medium-low heat for another 2 hours.

Remove the possum and place it in a roasting pan. Line the possum with sweet potatoes.

Bake, covered, for another 45 minutes to 1 hour in a moderate oven, uncovering for the last 20 minutes or so. If you want crispier possum, bake uncovered for about 30 minutes.

Alternative Method

WHAT YOU WILL NEED

Same as above

A clean hickory board, about 1 inch thick, 8 or 9 inches
     wide, and about 12 inches long

HOW TO COOK IT

Boil the possum for 2 hours, as in the traditional method.

Then, in a large roasting pan, place a clean, water-soaked hickory, cedar, or apple-wood board.

Rest the possum on the board, and line with peeled sweet potatoes.

Bake for 45 minutes, leaving it uncovered for crispier meat.

Remove from the oven, and let stand for 20 minutes. Then, using oven mitts, carefully lift the board, with the possum and sweet potatoes on top, allowing the oil to drain off into the pan. Carry the board, possum, and sweet potatoes to the back door. Fling the possum and sweet potatoes into the yard.

Eat the board.

"I don't think that's funny," my aunt Juanita said. People have damn near frozen to death, she reminded me, to procure a good possum.

Her late husband, my uncle Ed, passed away in the spring of this past year. When they were newly married, just a few years after the possum-eating incident that caused my mother and grandfather such concern, Uncle Ed went hunting with my brother and some other boys on a night when the temperature dropped to twelve degrees, to catch his Juanita a possum. It was a fine hunt, and with Joe in the lead, the dogs treed several fat possums. But, following the dogs to one last tree, my uncle lost his footing on a rickety bridge and fell into a freezing creek, losing his grip on a whole sack full of possums. My brother Sam jumped into the frigid stream to help lift him out. Uncle Ed had bad legs, broken in a truck accident when he was a child, and was floundering. The other hunters retrieved the possums, which were not drowned, and together they finally got Uncle Ed to the bank. By then, the boys were, most of them, wet and freezing and as wretched as my uncle, and faced miles of cold travel to get home. But the blue-collar Southern man has a beautiful stoicism about him as to hypothermia, or maybe that is just the effect of the hypothermia. He does not panic, at least so as you can tell, or whine. My uncle Ed acted, Sam recalls, like the prospect of freezing to death in the Appalachian foothills in the deep, dark dead of night was mostly just inconvenient.

"Well, boys," said Uncle Ed, shaking, turning blue, "I guess we've got about all the possums we need. We might as well go to the house."

They walked through the night, their clothes freezing into slabs of ice on their bodies, their faces burned red by the cold, the dogs whining around their legs.

The old dog, Joe, was nowhere around.

He knew foolishness when he saw it, and just went home.

· · ·

I have a brave palate, I believe.

I have eaten a snail, which remains, to me, just an excuse for garlic butter. I think you could substitute a lot of things for snails, maybe even a piece of chewing gum, and be just as happy. I love tripe, of any variety, and lived on pig-tripe burritos in downtown Los Angeles for the better part of three months. I will eat souse, though it is a physically unattractive commodity. I love marrow, of any kind. I have eaten boiled octopus, though I wish there were a way to stop it from jiggling so much. I have eaten snake, and alligator, and once bought a street chicken in Haiti and ate it on the street, fried in what I am pretty sure was transmission fluid. I will pick the lock on a blue crab, or whack it with a hammer if need be, to get at the goodness inside. Blue crabs, stone crabs, lobsters, all bottom-feeders, are just the possums of the sea.

But the Southern land possum has little to fear from me anymore. I have eaten them, when I was younger. My uncles used to tell my girlfriends we ate possum every Christmas, which cost me the affections of at least one horrified member of the choir at the Saks First Baptist Church. Or it could have been my mullet, which was luxurious. But I do not believe I will eat possum again, at Yuletide or otherwise. It is not the oiliness, or the stringiness, or the flavor of it. The flavor is not objectionable, though it does not taste like chicken, either. I just won't eat it again, for sentimental reasons.

A few years ago, in warmer weather, I saw a mother possum toddling across the ridge on my mother's mountain, a half-dozen babies clinging to her back. When they get too large for the pouch, they crawl out and cling to their momma's fur, and she carries them that way, sometimes for miles. It is one of those sights on this earth that just make you glad to be alive.

I guess cattle do, too, grazing across a lovely pasture.

But giving up possum is a damn sight easier than giving up short ribs.

20

STAIRWAY TO NOWHERE

Real Biscuits, with Sausage, Ham, Fatback,

Fried Potatoes, Spanish Scrambled Eggs

Sam, in the beginning

PEOPLE WHO grew up in empty places have a feeling about trains, and the farther out they lived, the deeper the feeling seems to be. I have heard old people talk about it, about how they felt when they heard that whistle off in the dark. Up close, it could take their breath away, so fierce it seemed to have shape to it, the way a strong wind looks in the falling leaves, or heat shimmers on a blacktop in the hot summer. From far off it was a lullaby, or a long goodbye, or just a mystery that would never be solved, because trains have not stopped here, or anywhere close to here, for a long time.

My mother does not hear any of that. When she hears a train whistle, or the distant clatter of the cars across the rails, she thinks about old men and new babies, and a stairway to nowhere, and cats dancing. And she thinks of biscuits—not slow and easy, as she would prefer to make them, but rapid-fire.

By now, she had mastered most things in the family repertoire, "ever'thing *but* biscuit. Momma would trust me to do most things by then, but she never turned a-loose of that biscuit pan. I guess biscuits was too important. The old people always said, 'If the biscuit's good, you can forgive or forget just about anything else.' But it would be a while before I'd get my chance with that by myself."

Even by her eighteenth birthday, she was still somehow unworthy. Oh, she had the knowledge, and knew the ingredients and the arithmetic and could even tell, as her ancestors could, if a biscuit was done or almost done by its smell alone. She knew buttermilk-based, sweet milk–based, and combinations and variations thereof, and had stood by her mother and the great Sis Morrison and other legendary cooks, learning.

"But till you could make biscuit with your own hands, by yourself," my mother said, "well, you just wadn't much cook a-tall." It may be that her momma never got over the days when she had to scrape the bottom of the flour barrel, when every pinch was precious, too precious to be entrusted to the apprentice as long as she was able to do it herself. It may be, as she saw her daughter's talents bloom, she was a bit jealous, and held this specialty back, for herself alone. Great cooks, like any artists, can be that way, and Ava was a jealous creature. She was known for her biscuits. No one made biscuits as crispy on the bottom and light on top as she did, holding tightly to her father-in-law's artistry and opinions, decade after decade.

Either way, my mother had to follow a lonely train track to a forgotten hotel in a forgotten place to prove she could, with her own two hands, bake that Southern essential. There is, as in all things, a story in it.

"I remember it was wintertime, and it was cold. And me and Juanita like to of got hit by the train. . . ."

She and Juanita, who was fully recovered from her possum debilitation, rode their bicycles partway to Tredegar, that little ghost town where Jimmy Jim had recovered the diving cow, then walked the track the rest of the way. They went there to visit their big sister, Edna, who had moved to Tredegar with her husband, Charlie Sanders, and her growing family. She had just brought her fourth daughter into the world, and had to take to her bed, to rest.

"I'd begged her to name that baby after me, and she did. She named her Wanda Marie. My middle name is Marie," she told me, in case it had somehow slipped my mind. She would have gone anyway, to help, but now she was bound to.

"Juanita planned to go home and I was going to stay, to help look after Edna and the baby and the other little girls. There was just the oldest, Betty, and Linda, and Libby then, and now another girl. Charlie Sanders never had no luck with boys."

My mother always enjoyed walking the tracks. "I used to could even walk them rails when I was young," my mother said. "You should of seen me, just a-gettin' it down them rails. I almost never did fall."

At the end of the trek, they would have to cross the infamous trestle. The revered Mr. Hugh Sanders, who had retired from the Coosa ferry and lived with Edna and his son Charlie, had already warned them twice not to dawdle on the trestle, and to listen close before crossing the span and run like blazes when they did, whether they heard a train or not. The very nature of the trains, he told the girls, had greatly changed.

"She's a diesel," the old man had explained, not some lumbering steam train, and she moved so fast she could be on you like death itself if you were not watchful. There would be no clickety-clack of old-fashioned iron, or great plume of smoke, to warn of her approach. She would come in a great rush on slick steel rails, and the roar would be just a few cross ties ahead of the gleaming engine, "and God help you, children, if she catches you on the trestle."

The trestle has not changed, still a relic from the bygone South, a tall, creosote-soaked structure, and too long, end to end, to outrun a train if it caught you in the middle.

The day after Edna's child's birth, the sisters were pushing their bicycles across the trestle when they heard the whistle—not a whistle at all but a blaring horn. And, just as Mr. Hugh warned, the train came in such a rush that they had not even heard its engine when they started across, and suddenly could *feel* it, in the rails.

"It like to got me and Juanita, on that bridge," she said. They guessed at the direction of the train, which was obscured by the trees, and, their bicycles bouncing along the cross ties, they sprinted for the near bank. It was too far to jump even if there had been deep water in the creek—it would have killed them—"and we seen it comin' at us just as we got close to the bank, and jumped for that, and slid down them gravel.

"Could you imagine me running a track now?" she asked me.

I thought it was a trick question and just said, "Sure."

She remembers rising from the gravel, shaken but unhurt, and watching the train flash past, car after car. It was a passenger train, "and you could see the people in the seats inside, and I guess they could see us, but they didn't wave. It didn't matter. If they had waved, they'd of done been gone by the time they did."

The trains had not always passed Tredegar by. Once, in the years after the Civil War, there had been a thriving little settlement there, and even a train depot, loading dock, and hotel—grand for its time, two stories tall, with a wide staircase. It had mostly all rotted down and been reclaimed by the forest, all but the old hotel. It was here that Charlie and Edna made their home, in this place everyone else in the world had left behind.

"The second floor had just about rotted apart, so my daddy and Charlie Sanders tore the second floor off the hotel, and they put a new tin roof on that first floor, and Charlie and Edna made that their house," my mother said. "They did a pretty good job of it, too."

They left the grand staircase in place, "but it didn't go to nowhere. It just went up. Edna put her canned stuff—her canned tomatoes, and her soup, and pickles, and pepper, and her jelly and jam and fruit—on the steps of that stairway, and, oh, hon, it was so pretty." Two or three times a day, a train would blast past the old hotel, just a few feet away, and the jars, like the lights on a jostled Christmas tree, would tremble on the steps of the staircase.

But the most magical thing in the old hotel that afternoon was in the kitchen, hardwired to the wall. She cannot recall the brand name—she thinks it was probably a General Electric—but it was white and chrome and brand-spanking-new. It was the first electric stove she had ever touched, and it seemed oddly out of place in that old structure reclaimed from the past. And right next to it was a real refrigerator, not an ice box, but a thing that hummed and growled, and when no one was looking she opened the door and just stood there, staring at the aluminum ice trays. It was not the first one she had ever seen, only the first one she had ever touched.

"Charlie Sanders had a good job at Fort McClellan—hon, I think it had something to do with 'lectricity. Mr. Hugh took care of cows for Mr. Boozer, who owned a bunch of land there, and they had sweet milk, and buttermilk, and real butter."

"Edna was in the bed with the baby, and I got to do the cooking . . ." with all those wonderful tools.

"You'll have to watch Grandpa about the milk," Edna told her from the bed. "I got to noticin' that the milk was comin' in short, less than it should have been, and I snuck out to the barn, where he was supposed to be doin' the milkin', and there he was, and him a grown old man, squirtin' the milk from the cow's udder straight into the little kittens' mouths—I mean, a whole bunch of it. And he was just laughin', and the kittens were just a-dancin'. . . ."

Charlie Sanders was still something of a puzzlement in the family. He was a tall slab of a man, dark, grinning, and blue-jawed, with tight, curly hair, a sportsman who took hundreds of deer and thousands of fish, who did not stop at one drink of liquor ever in his lifetime and loved to laugh out loud. "He had devilment in him, but Charlie Sanders's heart was all right, and he would have give you anything that he had," my mother said. He said what was on his mind, and if he had ever been embarrassed by it, or regretful of it, no one could recall.

He had inherited his father's ability to tell a story, and when he had heard about a contest to write a slogan for Carnation milk—the winner got five dollars—he rushed into the kitchen to tell Edna.

"Edna, get a pen and paper. I'm gonna win us five dollars."

"Oh Lord," Edna said.

He recited:

Carnation milk is the best in the land
Because it comes in such convenient little cans
No tits to squeeze, no hay to pitch
Just punch a hole in the little son of a bitch

It did not win.

"But them was very convenient cans, you know, because they was little. So he had that part right," my mother reasoned.

Around dark, the little girls and Charlie announced that they were hungry.

"Well, I can cook anything," my mother said boldly.

"I would like some biscuits," her brother-in-law said.

"Biscuits," the little girls echoed.

Her heart fell, but she did not confess.

"I guess people would think it strange that a good cook—a good cook down here, I mean—hadn't never made a biscuit."

Charlie Sanders said they had fresh sausage, and some ham, salt pork, potatoes, and eggs in the kitchen. They wanted breakfast for supper—a common thing then.

"Which y'all want?" my mother asked.

The two men and three little girls just looked at her.

They were hungry.

They wanted all of it.

"You can let Daddy make the biscuits," Charlie Sanders said, as if he somehow knew that my mother was untested as a baker. Mr. Hugh's wife had died young, and he had raised his sons by himself, cooking every meal they ate. He, too, was one of the best cooks in the family, or in any family at that time.

"No," Mr. Hugh said. "Let the child make them."

He shrugged into his coat.

"Besides," he said, "I got to do the milkin'."

A line of cats and kittens followed him to the barn.

My mother went to work. She shaped a half-dozen sausage patties, less than a half-inch thick and as big around as a Moon-Pie. Then she took a hunk of ham from the refrigerator and sliced it into squares and triangles, also slightly less than a half-inch thick. Anybody could make a ham or sausage biscuit, but the salt pork presented a problem—it would be too salty unless it was thoroughly rinsed and soaked. Fortunately, Edna was not the kind of cook to leave anything to chance. She had already done this, and wrapped it in clean wax paper, and put it in her refrigerator. My mother sliced it, too, a little less than a half-inch thick, cut away the skin, and wound up with a slice about five inches long. "It was purty meat. Didn't have hardly no lean on it."

Finally, she sliced three or four large white potatoes into half-inch-thick wheels. She would fry the fatback in one skillet, to render the good lard in which to fry the potatoes, and fry the sausage in another, while the biscuits were baking, so that they would all still be hot to the touch when served.

Then she turned to the flour barrel.

"I knew what to do. I'd watched it a hundred, maybe a thousand times, but biscuits are just tricky. There's women, good cooks, famous cooks, that's afraid of biscuit. There's old women ain't never learned to make no really *decent* bread." She had come to think she might be one of them.

By sight and feel, she carefully portioned her ingredients, sifted her flour, then combined the baking soda and salt, and kneaded in lard and butter, working smoothly and gently, not slow but steady.

She took about a handful of lard and worked it into the flour first, till the mixture was crumbly in texture. "I made them the way the old people do. Careful. It's pretty much like surgery. The dough has to be just right."

Then she slowly added the liquid, a little at a time. "I would have rather used buttermilk and water, a mix of it, but they wanted me to use sweet milk. That works good, too."

"I patted 'em out with my hands; I don't cut 'em, the way a lot of people do. It should be just thick enough to form a dome, and I feel the flour as I do it. If the flour's old, I can feel it, and if the flour's old, the biscuits won't rise."

She laid them out in a blackened pan from before the Civil War, a pan Mr. Hugh's mother had made biscuits in, and her mother before. She greased it with a little lard, and wondered how many times that had been done, how many thousands of biscuits had been baked there.

It was about then she noticed she had an audience. Charlie Sanders and the three little girls stood watching her, the little girls big-eyed and solemn.

They knew their momma was the best cook in the world, and

their grandpa, and their daddy was no slouch. They had doubts about this interloper.

"I guess they *was* hungry," my mother said.

"Quit bein' so easy," Charlie said. "Get rough with it."

He moved in beside her and reached for the dough.

"Scrub your hands," she ordered him, and surprised herself at how grown-up she sounded. "I don't like nobody in my food but me, and for certain not without clean hands."

"I done done it," he said.

But she was amazed at how fast, and sure, the man worked. He had learned from his daddy, and from cooks who made biscuits in the mess halls and the galleys of ships in the navy, for hungry sailors; he had made them for whole shiploads. There was no time to dawdle in an arena like that; they'd throw a slothful cook overboard, he believed, feed him right to the sharks.

"He did not make the prettiest biscuits, but he made 'em fast," she said.

What she learned, making them at his elbow, was that every biscuit did not have to be perfect or uniform on the outside. It was the chemistry, not the aesthetics, that mattered. If you had good flour and fresh ingredients, and took the biscuits from the oven at just the perfect time, well, "it didn't make no difference if you had a ragged biscuit or two in the batch."

As they baked, she fried the sausage till it was crisp around the edges, the ham just enough to give it some brown, and the fatback till it was crispy, then fried the potatoes in thick chips, till crisp on the outside, almost creamy inside. As they finished, she split biscuits and slipped sausage in some, ham in others, and stuffed some with a strip of fatback and a single round of potato.

With the eggs, she tried something a little different. She diced a smidgen of hot pickled pepper, sprinkled it all into the hot fat, and soft-scrambled the eggs on top of it, folding in some government cheese. But she could have sautéed a crocodile and no one would have noticed, not with a platter of sausage, ham, and fatback biscuits on the table.

"I didn't want no real hot, just a little taste in them cheese and eggs," she said.

It all disappeared, and this made her happy: "Edna's kids was used to eatin' good." The dessert biscuits, buttered and jellied, were delicious. They disappeared, and the house went to sleep around her. Mr. Hugh told her the biscuits were better than he could make, and if it was a lie it was a kind one; the old man, of the same generation as Jimmy Jim, could cook anything, on a stove or over a campfire.

It all seems a small thing now, a thing of little drama, but she would never forget it, "because it was my first biscuit." A million biscuits later, she still remembers everything about that night. You can never tell what people will care about.

"And I went home and told Momma I could make the biscuits, too, from then on. But she kept makin' 'em in the mornin', for years and years and years, but she would let me make 'em in the evenin' time. I guess them biscuits was less important."

When people ask me now what makes my mother's biscuits so special, I try to explain the best I can. The bottoms are crispy, not soft, and golden brown and domed on top, not discs, like cut-out biscuits. They have to be eaten hot or the bottoms will go from crispy to hard; if you are traveling, like to a family reunion or on a road trip to the Gulf, you can wrap them in foil, or in a towel inside Tupperware, which will make the bottoms go soft. This is not as good as hot biscuits, but passable.

But, piping hot, there is not a better biscuit in the whole biscuit-eating world, not in the fanciest bed-and-breakfast in Charleston, or on the greatest battleship among all the ships at sea.

The crispier bottom is a platform, it seems, for all the good things to come, all the things you can pile on top, like bacon or little triangles of country-fried steak, or a resting place for redeye gravy or sausage or gravy or chicken gravy.

In a lifetime of uncertainty and woe, you smell them wafting through the house in the morning, and you just kind of know that everything is going to be all right.

. . .

"The recipe is the same, more or less, as with the little biscuits we used in the butter rolls. Now, like before, I won't try to tell the people to make 'em how I make 'em, but I'll tell 'em how they ought to make 'em, you know, for them, so they won't make no mess. . . .

"The first thing you got to have is a big bowl, to make 'em up in. A glass or ceramic bowl is good. I admit I did mix 'em up in a big ol' plastic bowl, but I forgot one time and set it on a hot stove eye, and it didn't burn all the way through but it was fixin' to burn all the way through. I threw it out, because it had the imprint of the stove eye on it, and it reminded me what I'd done, and I didn't like that.

"Anyway, you need a big bowl, one that'll hold about three pounds of flour. You won't use three pounds, ever, but it's good to have room to work."

The recipe has changed, as ingredients have changed. She has relented, and uses Crisco sometimes when she cannot find or make good lard, and always self-rising flour. She still makes them the old way sometimes, mixing her flour and soda, working in some good lard, but she makes biscuits every day she is alive, if she is able, and she admits, shamefully, that she has bowed to expediency.

Here, in her words as much as was possible, is my mother's recipe.

Real Biscuits

WHAT YOU WILL NEED

4 tablespoons lard or Crisco

3 to 4 cups self-rising flour (you will only use as much
as needed)

¾ cup buttermilk

¼ cup water

HOW TO COOK IT

Lightly grease a biscuit pan with lard, big enough to hold anywhere from nine to twelve biscuits. Cover with a cloth or paper
towel, and set aside. "Remember, the biscuits will have lard (or
Crisco) in them," my mother said.

Sift the flour, all of it, to screen out any trash.

In a large bowl, repeat the process from Chapter One, creating
your flour bowl to hold the wet ingredients, being sure to leave at
least 2 inches or so of flour in the bottom.

First, with your hands, squeeze the lard into pieces into the
bottom of the flour bowl.

Carefully pour in most of the buttermilk and water.

"I put mine in all at once, instead of trying to pour in a little
at a time, and work it, and pour in more, and work it, and pour
in. . . ."

Gradually work the flour into the liquid and fat, as before.

Remember: "You don't want sticky, and you don't want dry.
And you have to really work it in or you'll have one greasy biscuit
and one hard, dry biscuit. You may waste a pan or two of biscuits
till you learn. You want to be able to roll them into a ball, firm
enough so they will hold their shape."

Again, do not worry about waste. You can sift the leftover flour
back into your bin.

You should end up with a nice semi-firm wad of dough.

Pinch off a piece of dough, she said, "one that will fit easily in one hand—but I've got small hands."

Roll it into a ball, then flatten only slightly, carefully, in your hands. The biscuit will be more a patty shape, but will rise into a dome as it bakes.

Place the biscuits on the greased pan. Do not crowd them or the edges will not brown right. As with the butter rolls, spacing is important here.

"It doesn't matter about the size. All mine are not the same size. Some people roll them out and use a cookie cutter so they'll be the same size, but I like the dome, and you can't get the dome unless you do it like this."

Preheat the oven to 450 degrees, for 10 minutes.

Place biscuits on the middle rack. Bake until golden brown.

"How long, in minutes?" I asked her.

"I got no idea," she said. "It's like cornbread—I know by the smell."

Normal people cook them around 15 minutes.

The best thing to do, as with all things she cooks, is to pay attention. If the top of the biscuit is good and brown, the bottom will be crispy, and the middle will be soft, fluffy, but done.

"It all depends on the stove. All stoves ain't equal. They cook slower when they get about wore out . . . kinda like me."

Sausage

WHAT YOU WILL NEED

1 pound, more or less, seasoned fresh pork sausage,
    hot or mild
1 tablespoon lard
Yellow mustard (to taste)

HOW TO COOK IT

Frying a sausage patty may sound simple, but if you have had as many bad hotel, restaurant, and fast-food sausage biscuits as we have had in this sad life, you might understand how easy it is to serve up a pitiful sausage biscuit, and how low the standard is.

This need not be exotic; fresh store-bought pork sausage is fine. Some people like to grind and season their own sausage from fresh pork, sage, red pepper, garlic, and other fine seasonings, and some people still sew all their own clothes and think JCPenney is the devil.

We are not aiming to be backward here, but you want plainly seasoned country sausage, not more exotic varieties intended for more complicated recipes, like lasagna and so forth; it should say so somewhere on the wrapping. You can choose between hot or mild. But even mild country sausage can be a little spicy, so hot sausage may be too much, overpowering.

There is a trick to frying it for biscuits. The thickness is everything. You do not want a thick hockey puck of sausage for this, though that is probably a poor standard of measurement in a place where it can be eighty-six and humid on Christmas Day.

Pat it out in your hands. You want a patty just a little bigger around than your biscuit, "because it's gonna draw up a little bit." It needs to be, before cooking, just a little less than ½ inch thick, my mother believes.

You do not want a big thick biscuit and a sad, tiny scrap of sausage, so that all you get is a mouthful of dough. Keep that in mind as you prepare both meat and bread.

The sausage begins, of course, with an abundance of fat, so you will not need much fat in the skillet ahead of time. "Use just a little lard, just a little, so it won't stick," my mother implores.

She likes to get the skillet hot, over about medium-high heat, so you get that nice sizzle and maybe just a bit of crisping, and in her defense, if you do not put a little fat down first, you will leave a skin of sausage on the skillet bottom when you try to turn it. After a few seconds, reduce the heat to medium.

Fry until the pink edges begin to take on color, just a few minutes, and turn. The sausage should be brown and just the slightest bit crispy. Now do the same to the other side.

Timing is everything in this. If either the biscuits or sausage gets cold, this is ruined. Split the biscuit completely, ease in the patty, and top it with the rest of the biscuit. Serve immediately.

My mother believes you can add just a hint of yellow mustard to the top of the patty, but this is a matter of taste.

NOTE If smoked sausage is your passion, split a 4-inch section of smoked sausage and leave it connected by the casing. Fry on both sides till the casing is crispy and the other side has just a bit of brown, then lay, casing side up, on your split biscuit.

Fast-food biscuits, which have become an essential form of sustenance in the modern-day South, combine big, thick, doughy biscuits and thin discs of rubbery pork sausage. Most likely, the patty was precooked, and just warmed over. Just as you cannot equate restaurant beans and greens with real food, do not make the only sausage biscuit of your life one from a drive-through.

That said, on a lonely highway in the early morning, with a thousand miles to go, even a fast-food sausage biscuit is better than no biscuit at all.

Ham

WHAT YOU WILL NEED

1 pound smoked ham
1 tablespoon lard
1 dash black pepper

Slice into pieces no more than ½ inch thick and about 4 by 4 inches. Ragged shapes are excellent for this, so the pieces do not have to be square. In a strange way, the more ragged, the more appetizing it looks. Try, if you can, to leave a little fat on each piece.

This is already cooked, so just fry in the lard till you have a little brown color and the edges of fat have crisped just a bit, or at least gone clear. As it cooks, sprinkle with a little black pepper.

Smoked ham, when skillet-fried, can go a little tough, so do not overcook or it will be a miserable ingredient for a ham biscuit.

Some people like salt ham for this, but store-bought salt ham is unreliable and errs usually in a saltiness that makes you think of salt pork served on a chain gang, or on sailing ships in 1792. It is not just the saltiness of the ham, but the chemical tang.

Fatback

WHAT YOU WILL NEED

1 pound fatback or streak o' lean
1 teaspoon black pepper

HOW TO COOK IT

Whether to use pure white fatback, which my mother calls white meat, or streak o' lean is a matter of taste, but since this dish will be rendered and cooked slow till crisp, crumbling, the lean can get brittle and seem overcooked and taste strong. She prefers pure white fatback when she can get it.

If you can find freshly slaughtered pork, as for fatback—hog jowl will also work in this—use it, but my mother often has to make do with store-bought salt pork, usually presliced. This cannot be cooked by frying or baking till the salt has been at least partially boiled out.

If you have to slice it, those slices should be about ¼ inch thick, and between 3 and 4 inches long. Cover the salt pork with water, and boil for about 15 minutes; let it cool till it can be handled. Lay the slices on paper towels, cover with another layer of paper towels, and "pat the water out."

"Then you just fry it till it goes crisp—you know, crumbly."

I think this is my favorite biscuit, a piece or two of white meat cooked crisp, a circle of fried potato, and a dab of mustard. "And you have flat got somethin' good."

Fried Potatoes

This is not the basic Southern recipe of cubed potatoes, which resemble large hash browns. It is, instead, more like a thick potato chip, crisp outside and soft inside.

WHAT YOU WILL NEED

3 or 4 medium-to-large white potatoes

3 to 4 tablespoons lard

1 teaspoon salt

1 teaspoon black pepper

HOW TO COOK IT

Peel the potatoes, and slice them between ¼ and ½ inch thick. No one is giving out a ribbon for this, so you do not have to be exact. But if you cut them thicker than ½ inch, they will never get done.

This may sound as if it should be easy. It is not easy. In a large skillet, over medium heat, get your fat hot, and ease in the sliced potatoes. They may try to stick, from the starch, even if you have good lard.

Cook until they turn golden, the outer edges are crisp, and a crisp golden sheen begins to form on the rest, then turn. Repeat the process. The thinner parts may crisp through, like chips, but this is fine. You want the middle still to have some soft, creamy potato, for contrast.

Of all the things my mother prepares, this is in my Top Ten.

"It ain't that hard," she said, after I told her I believed it was. "Cut 'em just right, cook 'em with patience, and drain 'em on some paper towels, so they won't be so greasy, and you'll have something fine."

Spanish Scrambled Eggs

This a slightly fancier version of the eggs she cooked that night.

WHAT YOU WILL NEED

6 eggs, beaten

1 teaspoon salt

¼ teaspoon black pepper

¼ teaspoon cayenne pepper

1 tablespoon good bacon grease

1 small onion, diced

1 blade green onion, slivered

½ cup mild cheese

HOW TO COOK IT

First, season the eggs. Add the salt, pepper, and cayenne to the eggs, mix them in, and set them aside.

In a large skillet, heat the bacon grease over medium-high heat until it goes clear, then set the stove to medium. Add the onion and green onion, and cook until they begin not just to go clear but to crisp a bit.

When just the slightest bit of caramelization is showing on the onion, stir in the eggs and then, quickly, the cheese, scrambling them into the other ingredients with a large spoon. You do not want a smooth omelet here, and you will not be flipping anything. We like our scrambled eggs a little on the soft-scrambled side.

"But why 'hot Spanish eggs'?" I asked.

She told me it was because, at the last second, Charlie Sanders shook in a big dose of hot sauce—it was just the kind of thing he would do.

"But why 'Spanish'?" I asked.

She just shrugged.

Why not?

.   .   .

"It is not a simple thing, to make biscuits in a hurry," she said, thinking back to that supper. "Edna could do it real fast, but that might just be because she was married to Charlie Sanders."

My mother would rather be careful, steady, as she is in all things.

"But I'll tell you somethin' you may not believe. Even though I'm old, I think I'm faster than I used to be. I mean, I'm faster at makin' a good biscuit."

I told her to be careful not to get sideways, moving so fast through her kitchen.

If she found any humor in that, she did not say.

There is probably more attention paid to the eccentricities of biscuits here than is necessary, but it is hard to exaggerate how much they meant to the people. When I was a little boy, I actually used to agonize over precisely how to eat those biscuits.

Should I eat them plain, with my grits and eggs and sausage and bacon or ham, or butter them and maybe spread on some muscadine jelly, or cherry, or grape, or maybe some apple butter, or fig preserves? Gravy, of any kind, complicated things. How could you choose between heaven and a higher one?

"Why," she told me more than once, "don't you have 'em both ways?" And as our people have done forever, she would ask how many buttered biscuits we wanted for dessert, and she would butter that fine second battery of biscuits, and slip the pan back into the warm oven as we ate our breakfast.

I wasted a lot of time as a little boy, wishing I were somewhere other than right here. All children do, I guess. I have been a lot of places, and I have never found any other place where you had a hot, glorious homemade biscuit for your breakfast, and then had a better and even sweeter biscuit for dessert.

. . .

My mother stayed with her big sister and her family for a few more days after Edna was back on her feet. Childbirth was not something she liked to dawdle over, but she appreciated the help, and bragged on my momma's food, on all of it, especially her biscuits. It may seem a small thing now, but when one of the truly fine cooks in the known universe gave her blessing on biscuits, the last of the great delicacies, there was not so much victory as relief. My mother got back on her bicycle and pushed it, bouncing, across the trestle—at a dead run this time from beginning to end. But the train was not running, and she felt foolish at the other side.

She had no written proof. She had no ribbons from the county fair, for pies or cakes or pickles or jams. No one wrote a story about her in the paper. The word just spread, among family and friends on both sides of the state line, and that is what she would be known for, something attached to her name like a blood type on one of those stainless-steel bracelets they sold at the drugstore. She was a beautiful girl, and a kind girl, but what she would be known for, more than anything, was this:

Margaret Bundrum was a good cook.

I asked her once if she ever wanted to be something else.

"Well," she said, "I always wisht I could dance."

21

PEOPLE WHO COOK

Buttermilk and Cornbread Patties

Mom, in her thirties

THEY DANCED UP A FOOL at Darby's Lake. The bands, mostly local boys who worked in the cotton mills and steel plants, played mostly old, traditional country, and some bluegrass, but now and then they would risk salvation by whipping a little "Lovesick Blues," and even some of that new stuff, that rock and roll. They might even have jiggled their legs a little bit as they picked, but if they had shaken it like that boy Elvis, the police would have dragged them off to jail and gone to hunt for an exorcist.

"I never danced," she said, "but I watched 'em dance. I loved to watch 'em dance."

It was largely square dancing, and some wild boys could do a mean buck dance, the way her momma and daddy used to dance when they were young.

"They had little boats out there, little boats you could ride in, and paddle around. But I never went in any of them, neither. I guess I was shy."

She would go with her sisters, stand in the back, and tap her foot.

In all her years, she never learned a step.

"I was busy, son," she told me—usually in the kitchen.

She learned to cook because she loved the craft, but also because, as the family changed in her teens, there was no one else. Her daddy was ill, and her momma was losing her battle against an early-onset darkness that some people might call dementia, but we just referred to, politely, as "not all right," in the same kind way that a drunk is "not all right." As the older girls left and her momma wavered between eccentricity and something worse, there was no one else to cook for her momma and daddy, or for her little sisters, Jo and Sue. Even before her teens, she had been *the* cook. You miss a lot, standing over a stove.

She still went to Darby's Lake when she turned eighteen, but not to listen to the music. "I went to clean house and cook for some people," she said, to help make a living for her people. She cooked for others, for strangers, and at suppertime she went home to her momma and daddy's house in the woods, catching a ride with whatever kin she could. She walked a lot when there was no other way to and from work.

There was no school to miss. They had moved so many times, it had been impossible, year after year, to rejoin her own grade, and as she slipped behind, she finally just gave up, which broke her heart.

"I went to work over there to Darby's Lake one time, to this old man's house, an old army man named Major Bryant. I never heard him called nothin' but 'Major.'" She went to cook and clean, and as she worked she noticed the young people drifting toward the lake, to swim, and dance, and ride in the little boats.

The old man, who was a nice old man, saw this.

"Why don't I cook for you?" he said.

He cooked good cornbread, and a big skillet of potatoes and onions, and stewed cabbage, "and, I mean, it was good. He could cook some awfully good food. And he poured me the biggest glass of milk."

Most people were nice to her when she was in their houses. They seemed to like her food, and sometimes they let her take food home to her people, though it is a point of pride with her that there was usually little of it left. She cooked country food, the same food that these people who could afford a housekeeper had grown up on, cooked either by their family or by the hired help who came before her. But none of them had ever cooked for her before that day.

Her rides had all failed to show. She remembers walking home in the dark, for hours, walking into the quiet house, late.

Her daddy was standing over the stove, frying hoecakes, singing softly. The rest of the house was in bed.

I had not been in Washington
Many more weeks than three
I fell in love with a pretty little girl

She fell in love with me
Fell in love with me

His old truck was broke down, he said, or he would have fetched her.

"Thought I'd make us some supper," he said, "while I waited up."

She took me in her parlor
She cooled me with her fan
She whispered low in her mother's ear
I love that gamblin' man
Love that gamblin' man

He crumbled fried cornbread into two glasses, poured in cold buttermilk, put in a dash of salt and pepper, and stuck in two blades of fresh green onion and two spoons.

It was funny how such a simple thing could be so good. They sat on either side of a lantern and ate, talking quietly, because they did not want to wake the others.

She had met a boy, she told him, a good-looking marine from the mill village, and though they had known each other only a little while, they had talked about getting married someday. But then who would cook for y'all? she wondered aloud. He told her she was not the only good fry cook in that little house, by God—and he smiled—so everything would probably be all right.

He said he would take the mill-village boy fishing, to see if he was any-'count, and maybe just to threaten him a little bit. There was something about being in the middle channel of the Coosa, in a rocking, raggedy boat, with whole trees floating sideways in the current, that tended to give a young man religion.

Her daddy was still sitting there when she went to bed; he did not rest well anymore, and there was a foreboding in the house in those days, as both her momma and daddy changed. Things would never be the same as in the hundred or so kitchens, it seemed, they had all gathered inside before.

She went to sleep thinking how there were some people in the world who danced, and some who cooked, and how it was the first time in such a long time when she went a whole day without cooking something for someone. She had walked ten miles that day, from one kindness to another.

. . .

"I do forget things," she told me, a lifetime later, "but I still love to cook. . . ." And I realized then that I had asked her a thousand questions over the past year about how she learned to cook, but rarely if ever asked her why, while others went out to learn a step or two.

It was easy enough for her to answer:

You do not forget the best days of your life.

"I remember how Daddy and Momma used to cook together on a Sunday morning, and when they'd cook they'd sing. . . . Daddy would sing honky-tonk songs, stuff from the pool hall and the radio and the records we played on the Victrola, and Momma would sing about the Lord, but sometimes she would sing about that other stuff, too, you know, stuff from the *world* . . ."

Daughter oh dear daughter
How can you treat me so
Leave your dear old mother
And with that gambler go
With that gambler go

". . . and Momma would make the bread, the biscuit, and make the good coffee, and Daddy would cook the meat and the gravy, and fry the ham or the streaked meat or sometimes even some country-fried steak when he could get it, and he would cook the redeye gravy, or water gravy, or the white milk gravy. And they would slice ripe tomatoes to eat with it if they had 'em, or slice a fresh cantaloupe, and it was all just *so good,* hon, because they took such care with it. And, oh, hon, it was just the most happiest time. . . ."

Buttermilk and Cornbread Patties

WHAT YOU WILL NEED

1 cup self-rising cornmeal

3 cups buttermilk or whole milk

2 tablespoons lard or bacon grease

1 dash black pepper

1 dash salt

2 blades green onion or small white onion, chopped

HOW TO COOK IT

In a bowl, mix your cornmeal and 1 cup buttermilk till you have a nice thick batter, like pancake batter.

Heat your lard or bacon grease in a 9-inch iron skillet, and use a large spoon to ladle out a single dollop for each patty. Four will suffice for 2 servings. Fry until the cornmeal browns and gets a little crispy, then flip, and do the same to that side. Size and thickness do not really matter. You want a crisp outside and a creamy inside.

Being careful not to burn your fingers, crumble the hot cornmeal into a glass, cup, or bowl, then pour on some buttermilk. Do not drown it. Eat immediately, topped with chopped green onion or white onion. Some people, like me, also like it with whole milk, but Momma disapproves.

The trick in it is to be able to taste the hot cornmeal and cool buttermilk together, the bitter and the sweet.

22

BLACKBERRY WINTER

Wild Plum Pie, Blackberry Cobbler

Aunt Sue, the baby sister

1956

WE HAVE a time here called blackberry winter, which is as pretty as it sounds. It comes in the late springtime, when the cold weather should be well and truly past, March and April have come and gone, and another endless summer is weighing down. The first thick, humid days are on us already, and the bleak landscape of the mountain South again covers itself in heat and green. The buzzing, whirring things, the wasps and mosquitoes and all the rest, descend.

But then, for just a few days, it all seems to shift, change, into a last breath or two of cool. "They call it blackberry winter because it comes after the blackberries bloom. It'll turn almost cold, like wintertime. It'll just last a little, little while, and then it's over, and it's summertime."

This was Velma's season. She would sit in her kitchen on A Street with my mother, drink her unusual coffee, and plan the desserts she would craft from blackberry islands and plum trees that grew in the mountains around Jacksonville, Alabama. "I used to sit with her at that big ol' long table, and we'd talk about what we'd cook once it all come in. I loved that ol' woman. Now, *that* was a cook."

One thing she could never figure out: one of the best cooks she had ever met did not brew her own coffee, or at least she did so strangely. She put instant coffee in a percolator, let it cook and cook, going from its weak beginnings to something darker, stronger, and drank cup after cup.

She made immaculate pie crusts from scratch, and picked her filling from the trees, yet she got her coffee from a jar.

"But it was good coffee. She could even make instant coffee taste good."

"How?" she asked her once.

"Boil the hound out of it," Velma said.

·   ·   ·

My mother married a man who would rather have a cheese sandwich on white bread than a home-cooked meal. Now, what are the chances of that?

"Some people just don't have no luck," she said, but that was not altogether true. With the husband came his momma, who shared her wisdom, and was perhaps as close to an angel as my mother knew. She made the best desserts in the foothills.

She might even have saved her and my big brother, with a wild-plum pie.

Velma was everybody's angel, if they were hungry. She fed half the mill village, year after year. People still talk in amazement about luscious meat loaves, and pot roasts with potatoes and onions served in pans you could wash a baby in, and skillets of cream gravy she was not even able to lift, and pies, my God, the pies, baked not in puny tins but in great trays. Her husband, Bobby, a small man, could have had a nap in one of those trays.

"Some people don't like their mother-in-law, but I loved mine." They worked side by side in her kitchen and prepared a thousand chickens, baked, fried, whole lakes of buttery dumplings, and creamy pots of beans that seemed to have no bottom, and in summer they stirred skillet after skillet of fried green tomatoes and squash and okra and a dozen other things Bobby grew in a garden that seemed to have no boundaries. Only the seasons could mark its beginning and end. They lived in big, ramshackle houses in the country or little mill houses in town, for their wealth was hidden inside Velma's oven.

"She knew how to season, like they said Grandpa Bundrum could season, but I got to see Granny Bragg work in person in the kitchen, and I never really got to see him. It didn't matter none if it was just supper for her people or a whole army," my mother said. "She cooked hog liver and onions in white milk gravy and people lined up for it . . . and people don't even really *like* hog liver. But they liked it if she cooked it, I'll tell you that. You got to be a blame good cook to make people like something they don't like."

At dinnertime or suppertime, depending on her shift at the cotton mill, first cousins, second cousins, kin twice-removed would come walking down the alphabet streets to the house where she cooked a massive meal every single day, somehow finding time between her shifts, where she kept a never-ending thread spinning for eight or twelve hours a shift, perched on an upside-down Coca-Cola box so she could reach her machine. Sometimes her man and boys did not show, because they'd rather drink than eat, but even so there was almost never an empty place at her long, long table.

No one knocked. No one asked to sit down, because no one who behaved had ever been turned away, and if they were close kin she even fed the ones who acted a fool.

"It was mostly cousins that come in, but not all the time." Sometimes Velma would look up to see an expectant young man she did not even know, holding a knife in one hand and a fork in the other, as if he had been sitting there every day of his life.

"Ari and Roland was first cousins, and they would come in that front door and be set down at that ol' table even before the screen door had a chance to hit," my mother said.

Velma's face was etched with worry and her eyes were set in dark circles, for she lived and cooked in the heart of a storm that could, in a second, sweep away all her efforts and best intentions. But the two things she knew best were food and the human heart. When my daddy was long, long gone from my mother and their sons, her heart, and kitchen, were still open to my mother, and to us.

"I learned how to season from Momma first, but Velma knew things other people didn't know," my mother said.

What my mother learned mostly was desserts, but not delicate, light, creamy desserts. No one made cobblers of such breadth, depth, and taste as Velma Bragg, "and the thing of it was, they were just so, so simple." No one made a richer pecan pie, or finer layer cake. But the one dessert my mother would always remember was a labor-intensive delicacy from the distant past, one most of the world had forgotten or just given up on, because it was too much trouble.

"But she made one for me," my mother said.

. . .

My big brother was due in the early fall of '56.

"I was just so terrible sick when I was first expectin' your brother, and I thought I was goin' to die. I couldn't eat nothin', not even bland stuff like bread or taters, and I was so weak." All her mother's home remedies had failed.

"This ain't good for the little 'un," Velma said.

"Well, what can I do?" my mother said. "I can't even think about food."

"I'll study on it," Velma said.

They were snapping beans, in the relative cool of the porch in an Alabama summer.

"I'll need some plums," Velma said after a while.

The very idea of a sour wild plum made my mother gag.

"I'll need a gallon or two, for a decent pie."

The next day, she worked her shift inside the bone-splitting shake and clatter of the mill, and in the late afternoon she and my mother walked into the pastures just outside town, to search for the wild-plum trees, which used to be easier to find. It was the season for plums—a small red-and-yellow fruit about the size of your thumb, and you had to race the birds for them sometimes. They grew in front yards and cow pastures, and even in the ditches at the side of the road. Velma put down an apron and had my mother sit in the shade on the grass while she picked the fruit deftly from between the thorns. Thorns were nothing much to Velma; she made a living sticking her fingers into the whirring teeth of a hungry machine.

Then she walked home with my mother and did something

that, as far as anyone knew, she had never done. She cooked a pie she did not share. It was a gift.

First she sat on the porch, to catch the breeze, and squeezed the pits out of a million or so ripe plums. This took hours to do.

"I saw her make some other'ns for people with the seeds still in 'em, like a cherry stone, you know, under the crust . . . for people she didn't like."

She called it a wild-plum pie, but it was more a cobbler, a simple dish. She mixed the red-and-yellow plums, a gallon or two, with cups of sugar, and set them in her refrigerator overnight "to make the likker," as she called it. The next day, she poured them into a baking dish, tossed in an ungodly amount of good butter, covered the lake of fruit with a latticework of rolled biscuit crust brushed with melted butter, and baked it until the fruit bubbled up between the strips of golden dough. Then she brushed the dough with butter again, because there really never is enough good butter in this world, and handed my mother a massive spoon.

There was something about it that broke through my mother's illness, and she ate about a quart of it.

"I ate it for days, and days, till it was gone . . . and then she made me some more. I don't know how she knew. I guess, if you cook as much as she did, you knew everything."

She regained her appetite overnight, and her health, and the last few weeks of her term were nearly without incident. It was almost like there was some kind of magic in it. "But I had my strength back. I don't know how she knew I could eat that when I couldn't eat nothin' else. But Velma knew everything. Let me tell you, that old woman was smart."

She made blackberry pie, pretty much the same way, and a cherry one, and peach, and apple, but these she called cobblers instead. She made them in the summer and early fall from fresh fruit, and from home-canned fruit in the winter and spring, altering only the sugar content in the recipe. We do not know why she called some things cobblers and some things pies, but if Velma had wanted to call them flying saucers, that would have been fine with my mother and fine with me.

She would make it for us one day, but not often, because of the tedious nature of removing the seeds, but she made up for it with blackberry cobbler with a buttered biscuit crust, every time we begged.

Wild Plum Pie

WHAT YOU WILL NEED

2 to 2½ cups wild plums
1¼ cups sugar
1 stick butter
1 recipe biscuit dough (page 50)

HOW TO COOK IT

First pick some wild plums. Big store-bought purple plums will not do, but some markets carry something close to the wild plums we picked when I was a boy. If you pick them wild, be careful of the thorns.

Remove the seeds, or pits, or stones, whatever you call them. This can be done by breaking them and squeezing the seeds out over a bowl, so you can catch the juice. There won't be that much, but that's where the flavor is.

Throw the seeds into your yard. With any luck, you'll have wild-plum trees someday.

The day before baking, combine plums, skin, pulp, and juice with the sugar in a sealed container. Overnight, it will make what Velma called the "likker."

Pour this into a medium baking dish, and dot it with chunks of cold butter. Use about ¾ stick of your butter, and save the rest to melt and brush on your crust.

Preheat the oven to 350 degrees.

If you have a favorite pie crust, you may want to use it here, but Velma's latticework of biscuit dough, rolled out no thicker than ¼ inch, is hard to beat for taste and the beauty of the dish. Velma would slice strips about an inch wide and weave them across the top of the pan. But the secret, she always said, was the butter.

Be sure to butter it twice, once before putting it into the oven, and again when you take it out. Use your remaining butter for this.

Bake at 350 degrees till the crust is golden brown and the juices from the plums and sugar have bubbled up and at least partially glazed the crust.

There are other options for the crust, both of which taste very good. A solid crust, slashed diagonally a half-dozen times to create vents, will cook up softer, less crispy; some people like that. Be sure to butter this crust, too.

The other, a drop crust, is the one my mother likes for blackberry cobbler.

"There ain't no bottom crust on this," my mother explained. "The cooking fruit and butter will be under direct heat," and this creates a filling that a traditional pie, she feels, cannot compare to.

"I've had bad cobbler," she said, "and every one had a soggy bottom or a tough bottom. Better to have no bottom a-tall."

You'll notice that there are no spices involved in this dish. None react well with the wild plums, which have a tart, clean taste. Velma knew not to mess it up, but Velma knew everything.

Blackberry Cobbler
(with Traditional or Drop Crust)

WHAT YOU WILL NEED

2½ cups freshly picked blackberries

1 to 1½ cups sugar

1 stick butter, melted

1 cup self-rising flour

1 cup whole milk

1 dash salt

HOW TO COOK IT

As with the plum pie, combine the sugar and blackberries, and store in the refrigerator overnight in a covered dish, to make the "likker."

If you want a traditional crust, follow the biscuit crust recipe, as in the preceding recipe, either in lattice form or vented crust. Or create a simple wet drop-crust by mixing the flour, milk, and a dash of salt, and pour over the fruit.

My mother likes to create islands of the batter, leaving little rivers of the blackberry filling. This will allow the edges of the drop crust to crisp a little, and allow the fruit to bubble through as it cooks. But before placing it in the oven, drizzle about half the melted butter over the top. When it's done, repeat this.

The same recipes work well to make apple, peach, cherry, and other traditional fruit cobblers.

Some people like to top their cobbler with vanilla ice cream. "But if you got good cobbler, you really don't need to try to make it no better."

.   .   .

She lived more than a hundred years. She did not teach my mother all she knew, of course, because we shared only a sliver of her century of life, and there just wasn't time. "But I got a lot from her," my mother said. The last meal Velma cooked for us was when I was almost grown. That last time, she cooked a Southern breakfast of sausage, eggs, biscuits, and one of those massive skillets of gravy she could no longer lift. At the end, her fat cat, whose name I cannot recall, leapt on the table, and I wondered why she did not shoo it away. I realized that she could not see it. She had cooked mostly by feel as her vision failed. She was one of the best cooks in the world, too, even in the dark.

TILL IT THUNDERS

Turtle Soup

Charlie, with a big river cat

1958

THE MEN ON THE RIVER just called the creature "that Ol' Mossy Back," for the century of green moss and algae that had gathered on the rock-hard carapace that armored his back. The ones who had seen him up close, and were more or less sober, said he was as big around as a truck tire, and had to weigh close to a hundred pounds, give or take a jug or two. They said the great shell covered only a fraction of his body, leaving his head and muscular limbs exposed; it was more like a shield, a thing for battle, than a moving box to cower within. His head, on the end of a thick, serpentine neck, was the size of a softball, and his stubby tail was crowned with primeval scallops, like those of the dinosaurs he had outlasted and left entombed in the earth. If you somehow snagged him with a rod and reel, he would dig his sharp, hooked claws into the bottom and, his powerful legs pulling, drag you along the riverbank or into the current itself, until the line—or the rod—snapped in two.

He was said to have dozens of hooks embedded in his leathery skin, going to rust, like something out of Melville. But no man had ever laid a hand on him, even those who had dared. Here in the foothills, in the easy, brown current of the Coosa, he reigned at the top of the food chain, eating anything and everything that drifted within range of his lunge, which was always a little farther than expected, and as quick as that of a striking snake. His jaws, tapering to a hooked beak, could snap a broomstick in two. Even accounting for myth, he was a great and terrible thing.

No one knew, at least not then, how long his kind could live, but it was believed to be forever, and it was said that they never stopped growing. Even the lesser of the species could go to thirty or forty pounds, far too big to fish for in any gentlemanly fashion, or even with a three-pronged hook fixed to the end of a pool cue, the apparatus my grandfather Charlie used for giant catfish. You could catch the smaller of the snappers in a homemade trap, or foul-hook them with a snagging hook, but to take the big ones, a brave man had to descend into the murky pools of the Coosa and lay his shaking hands on that shell.

The college boys down here, the ones sober enough to pay attention in biology class, knew him as *Chelydra serpentina,* for his snakelike neck. The greatest of them, the mossy back, had been alive for at least four generations of men, but most people knew him only as a shadow in the water, or glimpsed the top of his ridged shell, or that wicked snout lifting from the water. Once or twice in a man's lifetime, he might see the creature crawl atop a half-submerged tree to bask in the sun, as if to assure people that he was indeed real, and that he was still here. My grandfather, who knew this river like his own tears, had seen him many times.

But the next day, not only would the creature be gone, but the snag, the dead tree, would be, too, broken free from the mud of the bottom and vanished overnight, to roll in the current and reappear downstream, miles and miles away, or to disappear for good, snagged underneath the surface, to rot. So, when a fisherman claimed he had seen the creature, he could not even point precisely at where it used to be, and his people would josh him unmercifully for making up such a whopper of a tale.

But that did not mean that they would not listen to it, again and again. Most of the wild and woolly things in their rich past were gone by 1958. A man might see a skulking bobcat, like a ghost, or step on a snake, but the woods and the riverbanks were losing their mystery, their monsters, as my grandfather's life wound to a close. The last bears had been run to ground, and the last of the panthers had vanished into the Smokies or the swamps far to the south.

The mossy back was what was left.

When they swam in the river, my mother and her sisters watched for him in the murk, in water the color of coffee with cream, and over the years, every nudge against their leg, every sighting of a big snapping turtle on the bank or on a floating log, became *him*. And maybe that was the way of it: that the great snapper was them and they were him, all of them living inside the same enduring myth. But you dared not say that to my grandfather; he intended, before his days were done, to catch him, and eat him.

"Think of the pot of soup," he often said, "that rascal would make."

. . .

My mother and the handsome man had their baby boy, my big brother. When Sam was a toddler, they practically lived on the river with my grandfather, with pretty much the whole clan. As people would get off work on the weekend, you would see their cars pull up to the bank, and if the water was high, my grandfather would ferry them across to a small, sandy island in his homemade boat. It was their island, the Bundrums' island. That was understood.

"We used to camp on it and stay for days—you know, one of them islands where the current had pushed up the gravel and the sand over time. The water was muddy and the banks were muddy, but the island was clean, and we rowed out in Daddy's boat, and we built a fire, and we cooked and camped there and went swimming there," said my mother. My brother Sam learned to walk in that gravel and sand, and toddled, literally, in my grandfather's boot prints, dressed in a pair of blue leather cowboy boots, a blue cowboy hat, and a gun belt with a matching pair of six-shooters riding high on his waist. The pistols dragged in the sand as he walked, because he had legs as fat and short as a Quaker Oats box (and still does). He swears he remembers it, remembers the island of sand and the old man and the slow, brown water pushing by.

He also swears he remembers catching, with his grandpa, a smaller monster, a snapper only about the size of a hubcap, not some slow box turtle or terrapin, harmless and helpless when you flipped him on his back. When his grandpa flipped this one over, it used the strong muscles in its long, wrist-thick neck to flip itself back onto its feet, and then it wanted to fight. He and his grandpa watched it escape to the river, because, his paw-paw said, he didn't like to mess with the little 'uns.

His paw-paw was just about done by then. He seemed to be shrinking away, almost folding inside himself. He still sang and laughed and drank and lived out loud, but to look at him, knowing what he had once been, would break their hearts. He did not take giant steps anymore, and staggered sometimes, even when sober. He had always been skinny, but now he was truly bones, and the best cooks in the world could not keep flesh on them. "I tried, God knows I tried," my mother says now. They literally searched the landscape for things he might eat, anything that would give him strength, or just hope.

The place he had been happiest in his life had been here, along this river, and in his last days he haunted its banks, surrounded by his children and grandchildren and cousins and kin.

"He always said he could live on the water someday," my mother said. "He almost did, one time. He found us a house on a creek. . . . Now, why can't I remember that creek's name? But we didn't move there. I guess somebody got it first. But he meant to.

"So we went to the river, pretty much every day he wasn't workin'. It was free to go to the river. Nobody really owned the river back then. It was where we went when we had something to celebrate."

Charlie fished from before dawn till after the sun had slipped behind the hills, using a pale-green closed-face Zebco 202, like every other workingman on earth. But sometimes he just let his bait float, forgotten, on the currents, just watching the water, as if expecting, with every glance, to find some new miracle there, or some old one.

He had seen the mossy back as a young man, and as an old man, taunting him from the middle of the river or on some distant snag. Years passed, sometimes, between sightings, but he never stopped looking for him, and in his last days he walked the banks and the sandbars with my brother stumbling behind, both guns drawn. It may be that my brother saw the mossy back, too, but he cannot say for sure.

"I was too little," he said, "but it *seems* like I did."

The old men who lived along the river—hermits, drunks, muskrat trappers, whiskey cookers, men on the dodge, and one or two addled old men who had forgotten who they were hiding from or what they were hiding for—conferred with him about the creature, heaping on their own histories, stories, and lies. He had been spotted as far north as the headwaters in Rome, as far south as the railroad bridge in Gadsden—which would have been a trick, seeing as how he would have had to crawl around a hydroelectric dam. They all swore that the creature had bitten clean in two a big fish they were trying to land, or had dismembered a close personal friend of theirs.

No, others would argue, they knew for a fact that ol' so-and-so lost that finger in basic training at Fort Benning, or maybe the cotton mill in Leesburg. That sometimes led to one man's calling another man a damn liar or a son of a bitch who did not love the Lord, and sometimes knives were pulled.

It was not a thing Charlie wanted his grandson to see or his family to be around, so he would sometimes move on down the river or tell the men to settle down before he cracked some damn heads, but it was useful information, still. If nothing else, it kept the story alive for another day, and there is such value in that. It made the campfire brighter, and the old quilts warmer, to believe that monsters still walked their earth.

. . .

This, too, was one of the happiest times of my mother's life. In the evenings, my grandfather built a big cook fire on the clean gravel of the island; some nights they ate like poor fishermen, and some nights they ate like kings.

"We eat sardines and crackers and sliced onions, and Daddy would buy wedges of hoop cheese in a black rind—good sharp, hard, perfect cheese—and I don't know why it tasted so good, but it did. You won't get me to eat no sardines now," my mother said. "We had Vienna sausages—Daddy put hot sauce on 'em—and pork and beans, and he always had candy in his overalls for Sam."

I told her of a passage from the Southern writer Marjorie Kinnan Rawlings, from *The Yearling,* where one of the rough-and-tumble Forrester boys, content beside a campfire, said he would rather eat cold biscuit in the woods than cake in the indoors. And my mother said yes, that was the way it was, but she still wasn't going to eat no more sardines for the rest of her natural life.

Other nights, they ate like sultans. On the campfire, they fried crisp hoecakes or flapjacks and stirred up big cast-iron skillets of potatoes and onions. They made Brunswick stew—they called it camp stew—from pork, chicken, and sometimes rabbit or squirrel, and concocted a spicy fish stew from the succulent crappie they pulled from the river, or from the big river catfish my grandfather caught along the bottom or sometimes took by hand, feeling for them under the overhangs and caves at the muddy banks.

This process was called, for reasons that have never made much sense to me, "noodling." A catfish noodler felt under the banks until he located a catfish, and tried to get the fish to clamp down on his hand or arm. The catfish had sandpaperlike teeth inside its mouth, and though its bite might abrade the flesh of the hunter, it was unlikely to do more lasting damage, unless it somehow dragged the noodler underwater and he drowned.

Cleaning them was troublesome, and you could tell novices from their festering puncture wounds. The catfish were booby-trapped with sharp, poisonous spines, and too slick to get a good grip on. My grandfather had not been a novice for a long time. He would pick out a tree on the river's edge, and nail the catfish to it by driving a tenpenny spike through its skull, then, with a pair of of pliers, snatching the entire skin off the flesh with one fierce downward jerk. Then you filleted them, to fry over the fire in big iron skillets and smoking kettles, or cut into chunks for soup. My grandfather was partial to soup. He could devour a gallon of it, people said, even as he began to fail.

He preferred turtle.

"I'll have turtle yit," he swore, "before I die."

After supper, they told their own lies and stories, about bootlegging and faith healing and run-over dogs, "then we wrapped up in them old quilts," my mother said, "and we went to sleep. I thought about snakes, I guess, but not enough to keep me up." They went to sleep sometimes while the thin man was still talking, as if he knew there was not enough time left to relive all the wondrous things he had witnessed. I am older now than he was then, and am only beginning to understand how fearful that can be.

One day, when the weather had begun to turn and the first few red leaves had begun to color the banks of the river, they saw him. It was him, wasn't it? It had to be him. He almost seemed to pose on a gray, weather-beaten snag not far off the bank, the sun on his back, his beaked head raised as if to sniff the breeze for dinner. He feasted on water moccasins, other turtles, birds that pecked along the banks, ducks that he took from under the water, bullfrogs, and small and big fish of every kind. But for almost an hour he just posed there, the moss on his black shell drying to wisps of dark green, and Charlie Bundrum told the grandchildren to hush and be still and just watch.

Finally, the creature slid into the water and disappeared, like the submarine he was, only to reappear farther downstream; he seemed to be heading for the bank, not far upriver from where they stood. My grandfather made up his mind. He hurried after him, moving more or less parallel, trying to guess where the creature might reach the mud bank.

If he could catch him in the shallows, by God, if he could just get a grip on him, away from those jaws . . .

He watched, helpless, as the snapper, with just his shell and his snout above water, moved into the shallows and headed toward the lip of the bank and . . . disappeared. Charlie had forgotten about the caves. As the river rose and fell, on a timetable decided by the power company's hydroelectric whim, as the currents carved the mud from the banks with every rising tide, this created dark overhangs and deep holes into the banks, just the kind of places where a monster would dwell.

Charlie marked, in his mind, the spot on the overhang where the snapper had disappeared, and found a place upriver where he could more easily enter the river. He waded in his overalls and work boots to the place where he believed the turtle to have disappeared. But when he got there, he found not just a hollowed-out overhang but a dark hole, a true cave, one that extended several feet into the bank. He had to go on his knees to fit inside the opening, his head just above the waterline, the roots from the trees above poking through the ceiling of mud, so many and so thick he had to push through them, like a bad dream. He had to crouch chest-deep, but there was enough light filtering through the roots to see he was wedged into a space as deep and wide as he was tall, about six by six feet. If the snapper was here, he was certainly just underneath him, in the tea-colored water.

He was a brave man, everybody said, but his heart lurched just a little bit when he felt something heavy brush against his leg.

. . .

My mother had seen her daddy and the other men hunt for turtles this way before, "to just reach under the water and feel for them, and grab them by the tail—the smaller ones, I mean—and throw 'em up on the bank. Some men took their shoes and socks off and used their big toe to feel with." Her daddy rejected this as undignified, and said that, though a roofer could get by with nine fingers, he needed all his toes, to level his feet and keep him from leaning too far to one side and falling off the roof.

The snapping turtle does not like to be handled. If you had the poor sense to grab the turtle on either side of the shell, the snapper would simply snake his long neck around and bite you, though it seemed impossible; the big ones truly could easily dismember and maim a man.

But older turtle-hunters had learned they could grasp the sides of the shell just in front of the back legs, which was just, just out of reach of the snapping jaws. You could, sometimes, get a grip on the tail and carry a turtle that way, but if you let him swing too close to your leg, he would bite you there, too.

"The old saying was that if a snapping turtle bit you it wouldn't turn loose till it thundered," my mother said, but she could not recall if she had ever actually seen a turtle clamp down on anyone, or if it happened to occur in a thunderstorm. The truth is that when a turtle clamped down it tore away at the flesh where it bit—the beak was made to do that—and then just bit again.

This was what my grandfather was feeling around for in the dark.

·   ·   ·

Charlie had never been a smoker—he took his tobacco as snuff, when he took it at all—but he was not the man he used to be, and lost his wind quickly. He was already weary, and he had not yet put a hand on the thing. The technique was to keep your hands flat, your palms and fingers more level, instead of just letting your fingers dangle like bait. At first, all he felt was water, silt, and mud.

Finally, his fingers brushed the top of the hard shell. If he had touched the head, or touched too close to the jaws, he might have been maimed.

He felt, quickly, lightly, carefully, for the seams in the carapace, hoping the turtle would not thrash away, and gently slid his fingers around the rim of the shell till he felt it go smooth. He froze. The front part of the shell, the part closest to the head, was smoother and more even on the sides and front. His hand was moving toward the mouth. He reversed and slid his hand in the other direction, until he felt the edges of the shell taper and become more jagged, spear-shaped. This was the area behind the back legs, over the tail. He could not grab the short legs. The claws were like fishhooks.

He took a breath and grabbed for the prehistoric tail—hoping he had a good grip—and hauled backward and up, trying to back out of the hole as quickly as he could at the same time, and somehow keep the creature off the bottom, to keep it from getting a grip in the roots and mud. For several long minutes, they pulled against each other, till, finally, he felt the creature lose its grip, just a little, and he dragged it out into the sunlight. The turtle arced its neck around and its beak snapped at the water and air. Charlie kept moving, fell twice, went under, but dragged it through the water and then along the bank, till he got his legs under him and tried to lift it out of the water by its tail.

"And I was losin' my holt," he later explained, so he slid one hand down to the shell in front of the hind legs, then quickly grabbed the other side. He lifted it bodily out of the water—the turtle snapping at his knuckles, just out of reach—and he staggered to the bank.

His people had gathered there. They did not cheer or slap hands. You did not cheer groceries.

My mother did not see any romance in it at all.

"What's happenin'?" people asked.

"Daddy caught a turtle," she said.

It was as big around as a washtub, and so heavy he could only stagger up the bank. Still, he knew. He could not so easily have bested, or even lifted, the real Ol' Mossy Back. The snapper had gone into that hole a legend, but came out as something less. It was still a fine turtle, but it was just a damn big turtle.

"Is that him?" all his kin asked him, one by one.

He just shook his head.

It was supper, was all.

· · ·

They killed him quickly. Charlie did not let anyone poke the snapper with a stick or tease it. He held out a branch as thick as his wrist, and as the snapper struck out, to sink its beak into the wood, Charlie beheaded it with one quick swing of his roofing hatchet. He cut the bottom shell away with a sharp knife, and the top, and threw the entrails into the water, to be devoured by the catfish.

It has been said by my people that there are seven types of meat in a turtle, but my mother believes there are only two primary kinds: clean-tasting white meat, and a fishier-tasting abomination closer to the hindquarters of the beast.

"Stay away from the tail. There's meat in it, but it has a terrible taste," she said. Some people ate it, she said, and made a face.

The recipe, like most camp cooking, leaned heavily on things that could be carried in a burlap bag. The meat was cut into chunks, and boiled in an iron pot in a tomato-based broth with tomatoes and onions, with a strong dose of hot sauce and some chili powder. Like the creature itself, the soup had bite. The turtle, cleaned, had only about six or so pounds of usable meat, and made three gallons of rich, hearty soup. Rich people would have put sherry in theirs, but no one around that campfire had even the vaguest notion of what sherry was, unless it was one of the Johnson girls.

As they ate, they talked about the mossy back that had gotten away, but no one—not one soul—questioned whether that had indeed been him that my grandfather had followed into the cave. He just slipped by my grandpa somehow, just eluded him, by an inch or less, there in the murk and the mud. There must have been two turtles in that hole, they reckoned. That must have been how it was, my grandfather said, more or less.

· · ·

The snappers are smaller now. They are not endangered or threatened; it is just that the real monsters seem to have passed into antiquity, in the way the great billfish have been snatched from the oceans. Even a ten-pound snapper will bring the kinfolks out now, to watch it crawl across the ground or chomp down on a stick. My mother still gets one or two smaller turtles every now and then from well-meaning fishermen, but she lets my brothers clean the carcasses. There are just some things an old woman should not have to do, and cleaning a turtle is a lot of work for a couple of handfuls of meat.

"It's not like cleaning a chicken. It's hard to tell how much meat you'll wind up with when you first start cleaning a turtle, but you need about a good pound or pound and a half to make a good soup," she said, though the basic recipe is much the same, whether you have a pound of meat or three pounds.

"The thing you have to remember about turtle meat is that it's tough, even if the turtles ain't real big, and you have to cook it a long, long time to get it right. For a soup, you want it to cook till it comes apart, like the pork in a Brunswick stew. It can have kind of a sweet taste. If I'm gonna eat it, I'd rather eat it fried, but Daddy liked turtle soup, so that's what we're gonna do."

Turtle Soup

WHAT YOU WILL NEED

1½ to 2 pounds turtle meat

2 slices thick-cut bacon or salt pork, cut into fourths

1 tablespoon salt (at least)

1 teaspoon black pepper

1 small head white cabbage

1 quart crushed tomatoes (home-canned is better)

4 to 6 medium potatoes, coarsely chopped

2 large onions, chopped

1 quart tomato juice (home-canned, if possible)

½ teaspoon hot sauce

1 tablespoon chili powder

HOW TO COOK IT

Cut the turtle into chunks. "The size don't matter so much,'cause it's gonna come apart as it cooks," my mother says.

In a large pot, render the fat from the bacon or salt pork, and set the meat aside. Place the turtle pieces in the pot, and brown the outside just till the skin begins to crisp slightly, turning once. Do not use flour to coat; this recipe does not require a roux. Do not try to cook the meat through; the turtle will cook to pieces in the liquid ingredients.

Cover the browned turtle with water, and bring to a boil. Add the salt and pepper, so they can cook into the meat, then simmer the turtle for 2 hours or so. "Turtle meat is tough. You want it to cook till it's fallin' apart. You may have to add water, but don't drown it. You want to let the water cook out, leaving you a good, strong base."

To the pot, add the cabbage, and the bacon or fatback. Then, after about 5 minutes, add the tomatoes and other ingredients, wet and dry, in any order you wish. Cook over medium heat until the potatoes are soft and the onions and cabbage begin to come to pieces—½ hour or so is more than enough—then reduce the heat and just let simmer for at least another 20 minutes. The potatoes might melt and fall to pieces if you let it simmer longer, but my people like it that way.

Though it seems an uncomplicated process, it can be hard to get right, she believes. "You have to taste," she said.

Taste for salt and pepper, and add accordingly, but gradually. If it lacks kick, add more chili powder first. If you really like heat, add a dash or two more of hot sauce, to taste, as it cooks.

"If you douse the cooked stew with hot sauce after it's done, it won't taste as good. All you'll taste is the hot sauce."

Serve with potato salad and cornbread muffins or some good buttery crackers. She likes Captain's Wafers, instead of the pasty and chalky saltines.

"Rich folks' crackers," we call them.

. . .

To be honest, I am not wild about turtle in most incarnations. But the soup I appreciate. It doesn't taste like anything else, and you can almost taste the passing of time in this, too, maybe even taste the river itself. I know that may be romantic, but if you remove the backstory from food you remove the secrets, and even the taste somehow, we believe. In the same way, I believe that looking at that river is the closest I will ever come to really seeing my grandfather.

The rich folks, of course, mostly own the Coosa now. Their mansions and vacation homes ring the lakes and backwater and even line the main channel, but every now and then, if you can somehow block the Tudor mansions and two-story boat docks from your mind, you can almost imagine it the way it was. It is still littered, here and there, with fallen trees, and on those snags rest the terrapins and the wading birds and the other wild things. And every once in a great while, you will see that broad, flat creature, his great shell sloping from front to back, the dark, bony carapace scummed with moss.

I heard a bunch of dumbasses say once they liked to shoot the big snappers, for fun, and watch their bodies sink to the mud. I think my grandpa would have punched them in the mouth. Some people down here just need to be hit in the mouth now and again, or at least sent to bed without any supper.

It has been years since I saw a truly big snapper in the river, one of those monsters we used to tell about. The last time, I was close enough to see the ripple of fish in the current, and when they came too close I saw the creature slip off his snag into the water among them and disappear. He was probably not the legend, either, not the Ol' Mossy Back of my grandfather's time. But it is nice to believe that he could, as the legend claims, live forever. I guess he would be about as big as a Fiat by now.

As my grandfather grew ill, and the visits to the river dwindled and finally stopped altogether, my brother Sam went looking for him, in the footsteps of other old men.

"We lived in a house on the Cove Road," my mother said, "with Momma, and every day a farmer, Mr. Leon Boozer, would bring his hands to our well—we had good cold water—and they'd eat their lunch there. I think it was Lige Smith, and Ernest Smith, and Otis Meade that was his hands then. Well, for some reason, Sam always liked to be around them old men, and he would sit out there with them and even follow them around—he was still just a little-bitty boy and still just waddlin' around—and they would give him part of their lunch to eat. I think it made him feel like he was real big, you know, grown-up, to eat lunch with the men.

"And one day, Ernest's wife had cooked 'em all some turtle to eat. Her name was Thannie Matildie Tiffany Jane Sharon Susan Charlemagne Smith. It was real long, but that was her real name. I ain't sure why she needed a name that long, but that's what it was. Anyway, that ain't the point of it. . . . The point of it is, she made them that turtle to eat—I believe she fried it—and they gave it to Sam. I reckon they thought it would be funny to see the little boy eatin' turtle, like he would make a face at it or somethin'. But he just eat it all up, ever' bit of it, and he told 'em that, awwww, shoot, that wadn't nothin' to him, to eat no blame turtle. His paw-paw used to give him turtle all the blame time."

"My paw-paw caught a turtle one time," he said.

The men smiled.

"He caught the biggest turtle they was."

That was not the truth of it, of course, but legends get started with less.

"You got any more of that turtle meat?"

24

OFFERINGS

Smothered Cubed Steak

My big brother, Sam, and little brother, Mark

1958

THEY SAY a poor man makes the paper only twice in the Deep South, unless he breaks the law or plays football. The newspapers record the happenstance of his birth, and the inevitability of his death. If he was not an important man, or at least born to important people, it is unlikely that, either time, a great deal of ink was spilled. A lot of great men have lived and died down here inside a paragraph or two.

When I was a boy, I read of a great Grecian king, and how there were even greater kings than Agamemnon, but there was no one to sing about them in glorious tomes.

I wish I had been around, wish I had been working at some old Underwood, when my grandfather passed. I would have written the hell out of his obituary; I would have drained a tanker of ink, and killed a lot of trees, over his memory. I would not have used any fancy or flowery words, or maybe even any big ones, because I don't really know that many big ones that I can spell, and would not have cluttered his memory with foolishness like that, anyway. But I could have come close, I believe, to a glorious tome. My people deserved it.

But they didn't need me.

They didn't even need the newspaper.

The word went quickly, sadly out, as if on some kind of dark wing, and by the evening of his death, a glowing string of headlights crawled slowly up the Cove Road, to park amid the ragweed and Johnsongrass along the blacktop, till they strung out for a quarter-mile or more. There were old Chevys with a single headlight and electrician's tape holding on the taillights, and ancient Fords on bald tires, and a Nash Rambler that wouldn't go in reverse. There were pickups with logging chain coiled in the beds, curling in rust, and probably a crushed can of PBR or two. There were Buicks and Oldsmobiles, big, heavy cars hung with chrome and wicked tail fins. There were all kinds of cars, because a good carpenter and roofer makes all kinds of friends, rich and poor. Few men are more appreciated than one who can keep the rain off your head and run off a little good liquor now and then. And a good talker to boot? Of course they would come, by the dozens.

The men came first, deacons, backsliders, and unapologetic sinners, old men with ancient black broadcloth suitcoats over their newest overalls, prosperous men in suits from the Sears, Roebuck catalogue, and young men in ducktails and rolled-up blue jeans and shiny penny-loafer shoes, side by side, heavy tool belts clanking against their waists, good lumber on their shoulders. With Winstons and nonfiltered Camels dangling from their lips, they sawed, hammered, planed, and sanded smooth a simple pine coffin, with no velvet or satin, for this was for a workingman to lie on, a man like them, and they would not insult his memory with such things. But every board was cured, and the seams were watertight, and the joints were true. You could not slip a sheet of notebook paper between them, it was said, you could have dragged a silk scarf across it and not snagged a splinter anywhere.

They helped the undertaker lay him out in the front room, in the blue suit and white shirt he had bought to go see James when he was in basic training over in Mississippi. They folded his big hands over his breast, and it was odd, for such tough men, how gentle they were with him.

"It's all I could stand to look at, was his hands," my mother said. They were big, scarred, and as rough as sandpaper, the knuckles bulging from where he had broken them against the heads of foolish men, the fingers cut a thousand times by fishhooks, razor-sharp hawkbill knives, and a few million nails.

"People loved my daddy," my mother said.

Maybe that is true of any good man on such a day, even any man at all.

But it was true of him the day before he died, and the day after, and all the days to come.

Like most of the houses Charlie Bundrum had rented, almost

all his life, this one was hidden in deep woods, far off the little country road, "and we didn't have no porch light," my mother said. As the dark fell, Ambrose Parris ran a drop cord onto the porch and rigged a bright light on it, so the people who came after they got off from work could find their way to him through the trees. Ambrose knew his way around electricity.

The men moved to the porch, to stand and smoke, and let the gentler people fill the house. Hubert Parris was there, and Bill Hulsey, Earl Woods, Claude Bundrum, Hoyt Fair, and big Fred McCreeless, who wept like a child. The McFalls came, came by the carloads, from the big house out by the curve of the railroad track. Charlie had been friends with all of them, and though they looked just alike, that army of blond-haired people, he could tell them apart from across a thousand acres. Even my daddy was there, reappearing as if by magic and as sober as a church, and he wept, too; he said the only man he had ever truly respected was lying yonder, dead. He told how my grandpa could grab your hands and look in your face and tell you, looking at you, what you were worth. It was an awful thing at first, but my daddy did not stop taking Charlie's hand, and he never stopped offering it, because sometimes men did change.

There were other men, many others, who came to help, to observe the traditions, and to register their respect—carpenters, electricians, steelworkers, farmers, cattlemen, landowners, and movers alike.

"Did not any women come?" I asked my mother as she talked of that day.

"They came later," she said.

"Why later?" I asked.

"They were busy," she said.

"At what?" I said.

"They were cooking," she said.

In her kitchen by the railroad track, Mrs. Ethel McFall cooked all day. One car would not hold all the food Mrs. Ethel had cooked, but, then, she was used to cooking for an army, since there were

McFalls beyond counting on the Roy Webb Road. But she and her brood were just a few of the people who carried food up the trail to the house on the Cove Road, following Ambrose Parris's beacon. In dozens of kitchens, as far away as Rome, the old women cooked for the mourners who would fill the house, because it mattered that you came, and it mattered if you walked up to the door with a big pot in your hands.

Louise Bundrum came, and Margaret Bundrum came, and other kin from Jacksonville, and Elsie McFall, Bobby Jean Bragg, and Mrs. Vivian Woods, whom my grandfather and Aunt Juanita had nicknamed, for reasons no one knows, Petunia Perkins. "There were so many, hon, I can't remember 'em all," my mother said.

They moved slowly, carefully, through the grass to the porch, so as not to spill their offerings, and passed up great platters of meat loaf, fried chicken, and pork roasts, mounds of biscuits and still-warm discs of cornbread, and deep pots of pinto beans and Great Northern beans and black-eyed peas. They carried mounds of fried potatoes still in the skillet, which could be warmed up without fuss. There was potato salad, stewed cabbage, stewed squash, and mounds of slaw, and a few hundred or so deviled eggs, and platters of sliced onion, sliced tomato, and pickles, what they called "the green plate." They passed up coconut cakes, and pineapple upside-down cakes, and, of course, cold and baked banana puddings, and chocolate pies, and a blackberry cobbler as big as they had ever seen. Velma Bragg sent a peach cobbler as big as a wagon.

They brought coffeepots, and filled, perked, and poured as fast as it could be made, and washed the dishes like the little house was a meat-and-three, and refilled the plates almost immediately, because the two things they understood best in this world were work and food; food had always made life worth living, so how could it not ease, at least in the slightest way, the pain of a good man's death?

"And I couldn't eat a bite," my mother said. "Me and Juanita just sat there," as the kind people came one by one to tell them how sorry they were, and they mechanically shook hands, were patted a thousand, two thousand times, but there was really nothing to say, because how do you make sense of it when someone puts out the sun?

She cannot remember where Jo and Sue were; it could be, as was custom, the children were with kin, to shield them from all this, or it may be they sat with their momma on the side of her bed; odd, how she cannot recall.

She remembers, though, being so hungry, yet sick to death at the same time. They had not eaten for a day or more, and as the old ladies pushed plates of food at them, they took them, and thanked the ladies, and then just set them aside, to pile up beside them as the crowd grew larger in the old house.

People formed a line to pay their respects to her daddy in the front room, then filed into the bedroom to say how sorry they were to Ava, who had not moved from where she sat on the edge of her bed for two full days, and could not look on her husband at all. She blamed him for this, too, blamed him for dying, which to her was just another form of loafering, just another time he ran off and stayed gone too long.

Every kindness just reminded them, all of them, about what was missing.

It was unbearable.

Earl Woods, who ran the gas station in town, saw my mother and Juanita there, looking so lost, next to those stacks of plates of cold food, and went to find his wife.

A tall, thick man, he knew his way around under the hood of a Pontiac, but also seemed acquainted, at least a little bit, with the human heart.

"Them children ain't had nothin' to eat in a long time, and they ain't gonna eat nothin' here, not with all these people, not with their daddy in that next room," he told his wife, Vivian.

"Well, let's take 'em home, then, Earl," she said impatiently, as if he could have cut to the chase and saved them all some wind.

Vivian, a short, wide woman, cleaned doctors' offices and other buildings to make money, but was known as an excellent cook.

"I can whup somethin' up," she said.

They herded my mother and Juanita into their car, and left the crowd and the specter of death behind, for just a while, in the trees, and as Earl drove he talked nonstop about their daddy, and confessed he had told some great whoppers over time.

It was Earl who had spread the story of Charlie Bundrum the great fisherman, who would catch jack salmon so fast he did not have time to put them on a stringer, so he would just slip them into the big pockets of his ragged old fatigue jacket and cast again, and again. Some days, he would get a little drunk, and Ava would find, sometime later, a fish in a left-hand pocket. And once, Earl said, Ava washed the old green jacket and heard a thumping in the washing machine; when she looked inside, the water was swimming with fish. "And your poor momma, bless her heart, had to stand there and pick them fish out of that washing machine." It wasn't true, of course; maybe it was a little better than true.

And Vivian Woods told how, when she would walk to work, Charlie Bundrum would drive by in his old truck, loaded down with shingles and buckets of tar, and shout out to her, "Heyyyyyyyy, Ol' Lady Perkins," and people around her would look at her funny, because her name was not Perkins a-tall.

"But your daddy named everybody, I guess, so that's who they was, who they got to be after a while. Didn't matter what your momma and daddy named you. Just mattered what Charlie Bundrum named you . . . though I do believe it was Juanita who named me Petunia. Petunia Perkins. My Lord."

"I remember him doin' that," my mother told her, " 'cause I was in the truck with him, and off you went, your dress tail just a-flappin' . . ."

"I was Pooh Boy," my mother said, after a while.

"I was Snag," my aunt Juanita said.

"I know," Mrs. Woods said.

They drove to their small house in town, and the girls sat at the kitchen table and listened as Earl told stories of the day their daddy chased off some ruffians with a roofing hatchet and a Belgium shotgun, while Vivian scrounged in her refrigerator for something she could cook in a hurry.

"How 'bout some cubed steak?" she asked.

She made up some biscuits in record time and put them in the stove, and went to work on the main—and only—course. She had some small, cheap cuts of beef, like flank steak, and she took one of those hammers that look like medieval torture devices and beat it till it was a ragged sheet of meat, beat the mortal hell out of it, till you could almost see through it, then salted it, peppered it, dusted it with flour, and laid it in the hot grease.

When it had browned and was smelling so good, she turned it with a fork, then quickly added a few tablespoons of flour, a little more salt, and a big dash or three of pepper, and stirred all this around the steak until it browned, then poured in some milk to make a nice gravy, being careful not to let it get too thick.

Some cooks would take the cubed steak out of the pan first, make the gravy, and then return it to the pan, but a real smothered steak had to stay in the pan, Vivian believed, to add the tiny little taste of the beef itself to the milk gravy. It was, of course, hell to stir it all up. The crisp bits of the breading and black pepper gave the gravy its taste, she believed, and the sisters realized that they were hungry for the first time in a long, long time. They ate their steak and gravy and biscuits at the little kitchen table, with Earl and Vivian Woods leaning against the counter, talking and talking and talking about their daddy in life.

The steak was so tender they could cut through it with the edge of a fork.

"I'd be riding down the road, and your daddy would see me, and he would flag me down or I would flag him down, and we would stop right there and talk, you know, 'cause there might not be a car comin' for a day and a half, and if there was a car we'd pull over to the side of the road and just talk an' talk, and I can't tell you one blessed thing that me and that man talked about. . . ." And he talked and he talked, but not about how he would miss her daddy, not how sorry he was. He talked about what a pure joy it was to be close to him, as if he would walk into that kitchen at any moment and be welcome to what was left.

But there wasn't anything left.

They ate till they were full, till they realized, looking at their clean plates, that somehow life had gone on, after all.

. . .

She does not have to beat the hell out of it anymore, like Mrs. Woods did.

"You can buy it in any store now—cubed steak—done beat up and tenderized pretty good. You can still whack it some if you want to, though," she said.

"You don't have one of them meat hammers," I said.

"Got too old," she said. She thinks maybe she might have sold it at a yard sale.

Now and then, she would like to whack it again, though, for Earl and Vivian Woods.

"They've both gone on, too," she said.

I told her there were some cultures—in Asia, I believe—who whack a bell to honor their ancestors, or to summon them, or something.

"I guess this is kind of like that," I said, and she said she reckoned so.

. . .

Smothered Cubed Steak

WHAT YOU WILL NEED

4 tablespoons flour

¼ teaspoon garlic powder

1 teaspoon salt

1 teaspoon black pepper

¼ teaspoon cayenne pepper

3 tablespoons lard or Crisco

4 to 6 pieces cubed steak (done beat up), about a ¼
   pound or less, each

2 tablespoons finely diced onion

2 cups whole milk

HOW TO COOK IT

In a bowl, mix the flour, garlic powder, salt, pepper, and cayenne.

In a medium or large skillet, melt your grease over medium heat. Lightly dust each steak front and back with your seasoned flour, and carefully lay them in the grease. Let them sizzle for a second or two, then reduce the heat to medium-low and cook slowly till they are golden brown; turn, and cook the other side till golden brown.

When they are almost done, add the finely diced onion, and let it cook a minute or so—not crisping, just going clear. Reduce the heat to low. Use 2 tablespoons of the remaining seasoned flour for your gravy. Stir it in, and brown it to a nice tan, being sure to scrape the bits of crisped flour from the bottom as you do, allowing them to mix into the roux. Then slowly pour in the milk, stirring as you do. You do not want the gravy to be thick, just a nice medium. Do not worry if you tear up the steaks. It does not matter.

Serve with biscuits, mashed potatoes, and sweet peas or green beans. We like this with baby limas, too.

It makes my mother a little sad every time she cooks it, of course, but not enough to make her stop cooking it forever. I guess, like in all things down here, it's just the gravy, the gravy that reminds you how good life can be, even in mourning.

"Gravy," Charlie Bundrum liked to say, "is a reason to live."

.   .   .

When the great Mississippi writer Willie Morris passed away, I stood in his kitchen, surrounded by people who loved him, with a plate in my hand. There was fried chicken, of course, and potato salad, casseroles, and tomato sandwiches with mayonnaise and black pepper on white bread, and I do not believe they were trying to be ironic, or rustic. There was a big banana pudding, and coconut cake, and so much more, the feast that follows a Southern funeral. There were authors there, and college professors, editors, poets, and, I believe, at least one governor, but the tradition and the love behind it were the same as in the house where they laid my grandfather out. Willie Morris loved such as that, such custom, and believed, fervently, in ghosts.

And I thought of a night when I sat across from Willie in his study, and listened as he, still half drunk, read some pages I had written about my people, about my own grandfather. He snapped the book closed after a while and told me that I was right to believe how important it was to record their stories. They would last inside those stories, but they would *live* in the language, if the language was worthy of them.

"I say it's the language," he said.

I had not known there was a difference, but I understand it now.

Earlier that night, he had eaten a big plate of catfish, French fries, and hush puppies, and drunk whiskey from a brown bottle, and bounced into both sides of the door frame as he meandered to the car. It struck me, later, that I had never met a great man, or even heard of one, who was perfect, and certainly not one who could hit both sides of a doorjamb on the way out of a restaurant, or this world. A few years after the funeral buffet, I wrote a story about his passing, and, like an undertaker or a coffin maker, I used all my skill, such as it was, to sing of him as gloriously as I could in a thousand words or so. He deserved ten thousand at least, but deadlines are deadlines. I guess we all cook what we can.

The people who carried those pots up that dark trail to my grandpa's are mostly gone now, and even some of their names are forgotten, but not their kindness, or their recipes. That was their language, I suppose.

25

GOVERNMENT CHEESE

Cheese-and-Sausage Pie, Macaroni and Cheese,

Grilled Cheese Sandwiches with Pear Preserves or Muscadine Jelly

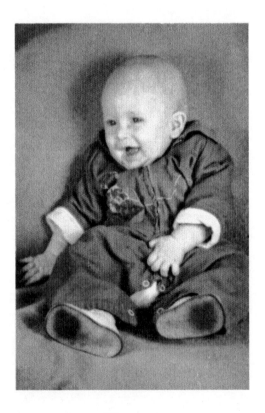

Me, early on

1959

I CAME INTO THE WORLD as a five-pound block of government cheese. Well, the whole truth is that a block of cheese was
mistaken for me, across a busy town square. My mother was, it
should be said, making a run for it at the time.

"Don't matter the circumstance," I told her. "It ain't nothin' to
be proud of, to be mistaken for cheese."

"But it was *real* good cheese," she said.

. . .

I had not known, as I began this book, how often larceny would
figure into the narrative of our recipes. It is a little sad, I suppose.
I could wish that were not so, but I could also wish for a Duesenberg and would still be tooling around town in a Toyota.

My mother was involved in theft only three times in her long
life, though it is doubtful you will see her name on the post office
wall. She stole only one thing on purpose, which is not a bad
record for eighty years; in the other two robberies, the thievery
was foisted upon her by fate.

"I did steal an onion," she said, coming clean. "I did it. I did.
But you be sure," she warned me, "not to make it seem worse than
it was."

She appropriated the onion when she was just a child. She
and Juanita were walking home from picking cotton. They knew
they were having beans and cornbread for supper, but were out of
onions. "Beans and cornbread are not complete without onion of
some kind. I mean, it just ain't right, you know?"

It matters little if it is raw, pickled, white, yellow, green, tame,
wild, or minced into relish or chowchow. "But we did have *num.*"
It was on the edge of a field that had already been harvested, so it
was a left-behind onion, left to rot. They stood over it a moment,

torn, then pulled it and skipped home. "But, you know, it always kind of bothered me. Only thing I ever stole . . . Well, only thing that I *meant* to."

The second time, the one involving cheese, was mostly beyond her control. I was there when it was perpetrated—well, kind of. It was not my fault, either, but I suppose you could argue I was complicit, in accordance with the laws of the state of Alabama. If a bank is robbed, for instance, everyone inside the getaway vehicle is guilty. And since she *was* the getaway vehicle, since I had not yet actually been born into this world, I was still in on it, and essential to the caper. It started with a blue maternity dress.

"I remember buyin' it 'cause I wanted somethin' pretty to wear to town. It was the only maternity clothes I had back when I was havin' you. I saved up for it. I remember the top, the shirt, was solid blue, and the skirt had little designs on it. I think it was flowers. . . . No, it was checks. Little blue and white checks. I always wore it to town that day, the days we went to get commodities. It was always a big day."

People told her how pretty the dress was, and the old ladies always asked when the tiny blessing was due, and what she would name him or her. She said the baby was due in July, or maybe August, and though she was still wrestling with the decision she thought she might name it Ricky if it was a boy, for Desi Arnaz, who played Ricky Ricardo on *I Love Lucy.* This caused the little ol' ladies to walk away, uncertain. Why in the hell would a woman in the foothills of Alabama name her baby for a Cuban bandleader?

It was one of the times when my daddy had gone on the lam— this time it would turn out to be for two whole years—and my mother and big brother had gone to live with my grandmother again. She took in laundry, and worked as a cook and a maid in other people's houses, but still qualified for a smidgen of government assistance. She got a little card in the mail, testifying that we were indeed poor by a reasonable standard, and once a month she and my big brother, Sam, traveled to town, to the recreation center in Jacksonville, to pick up our dole of government food.

My people called it "our commodities," from the wording on the little yellow card. It was always a grim day when she and my daddy reconciled, because she had to give up the commodities if she took him back. It was not, my kinfolks believed, a fair swap. All in all, they'd rather have the cheese.

"It never occurred to me to feel bad about taking our commodities; we was doing the best we could," she said. But she did notice, in time, that the country people who came to town to take their allotment came in freshly ironed dresses and starched white shirts and their newest pair of overalls, as if to say, if anyone was watching, that even though they were standing in line for charity they were not begging for it. This is why my mother was proud of that one good dress, and why she wore it to stand in that line.

For my people, commodity day was the single most satisfying aspect of being poor. It was not a check, or food stamps, but the actual bounty of the republic. The foods and the portions would shift over time, but in those days you got five pounds of yellow cornmeal, five pounds of plain flour, a two-pound can of good peanut butter, five pounds of rice, two two-pound cans of a processed mystery meat that tasted suspiciously like Spam, powdered eggs, powdered milk, a whole cooked chicken in a can (still one of the most amazing things my big brother says he has ever witnessed), a big can labeled "cooked pork chunks," and, per household, one five-pound block of blessed pale-yellow cheese.

She used the flour and meal for her biscuits and cornbread. The thick peanut butter, so dense you could barely spread it on a slice of bread, remains the best peanut butter I would ever taste; she used it in fine peanut-butter cookies, and on thick sandwiches with her homemade jelly. She used the whole canned chicken with dumplings and in porridge. She simmered the pork chunks, which were too salty to eat any other way, in beans and soups, and mixed the rice with butter, sugar, and cinnamon for delicious rice pudding; unlike the flatlanders and the swamp people, we did not eat rice unless it was in a dessert. The Spam-like meat she fried, mostly for breakfast; we were told the Hawaiians did it that way, which made us feel very cosmopolitan.

"It was—all of it—as good as you'd get in the store," my mother said of her government surplus.

But the cheese—well, the cheese was something else altogether.

It was not like that stuff you buy in grocery stores, that fluorescent-orange, gummy, petroleum-based cheeselike film wrapped in its individual plastic envelopes, which always remind me of the cellophane on cigarette packs. The government cheese was firm and dense and had *taste,* a mild, clean, but still . . . well . . . *cheesy* taste. It was so good that the old people still recall its flavor to this day; when they take a bite of the store-bought stuff, they make a face like a bug flew in their mouth.

It was not rich folks' cheese, not an earthy goat cheese or a pungent Stilton or a rich Parmesan or such, not even the sharp, hard cheddar that my grandfather loved to eat on the riverbank with his saltines. But, then, the government cheese wasn't supposed to be exotic. It was, as purveyed by the government, an excellent source of protein and calories and vitamin D for the great unwashed; the fact that it tasted good, that it made other things taste good, was unintended, a happy mistake.

Other people, people who had the misfortune not to be poor, coveted our cheese. My brother's friends always asked my mother for a toasted cheese sandwich, which was three times as thick, buttery, and cheesy as a pedestrian grilled cheese. Sometimes, getting fancy, she spread on some fig preserves, or a little grape jelly. She doctored hot biscuits with a triangle of the cheese. It melted beautifully, creamily. She used it to make the best macaroni and cheese, which we consider a vegetable here. She mixed the cheese into creamy grits, and delicious scrambled eggs, and excellent molten, bubbling scalloped potatoes, which might be one of the most decadent dishes I have ever tasted. She laid it on hamburgers, a quarter-inch thick, and cut it into cubes to mix into the batter for Mexican cornbread and hush puppies.

She loved good black- and red-rind cheddar, which we called

"hoop cheese," loved its sharp taste, "but cheddar don't melt good, and ever'body knows it." In some dishes, she added a little sharp cheddar to the mild American cheese for contrast.

But the best thing she made, my big brother believes, was a kind of cheese-and-sausage pie, a simple and admittedly greasy thing she made for her children every time she picked up the commodities, to celebrate their largesse. Sometimes our other, close-in kinfolks gathered on the days the commodities were distributed, like it was Labor Day or Independence Day, and my mother and aunts made a half-dozen pies, sometimes more. There are worse things to rally around, I guess, than a loaf of good mild cheese.

It may seem an odd thing, but word would spread, and people would even bring their own pie shells and pork sausage; my mother was the arbiter of the cheese, and so a very valuable member of the clan. They would bring a hand-cranked ice-cream maker, and would flavor the ice cream, sometimes with a can of peaches in heavy syrup, or fruit cocktail. They brought guitars, and played the music they had grown up on—gospel, mostly, like Hank Williams's "I Saw the Light."

The pies came out of the oven four at a time.

To hear my big brother talk about them, you would think it was the best time of his life. I think that has less to do with cheese than with other things; it was a time when he was surrounded by people of great strength and toughness and warmth, when all you had to do to make something of your life was bow your back to it, and things still made some kind of sense.

"I miss them pies," he said.

I suppose, strictly speaking, we broke the law just by spreading the bounty of that cheese to our kin, which the government guidelines specifically forbade, as if that block of cheese were a piece of road equipment. She never sold an ounce of it, but she cut off one-pound blocks and gave it to her sisters, closest friends, or anyone unlucky enough not to be poor, so often and so regular that they, too, began to count down the days of the month to cheese day. In time, she spread our allotment so thin that the cheese ran out long before the month did, and a great sadness descended on our little corner of the earth.

It never occurred to her, she told me, to ask for more. For a people who made illegal whiskey in the pines, and sometimes went a whole lifetime without paying any federal taxes on anything, we were oddly honest about dealing with the government as to cheese. We waited patiently in line, took our allotment—no more, no less—and moved on, being sure to say "thank you."

Besides, the holders of the cheese kept close, close track of it: one box per household.

When the lawbreaking happened, it happened, if not by accident, at least under extenuating circumstances. My mother always took Sam with her, in his Billy the Kid outfit. He had finally gotten tall enough so his guns did not drag in the dirt. He always had some tiny pieced-together toddler-sized wagon with him back then, and he insisted on taking his wagon to town with them, to help with the transport. "Sam come into the world workin'," my mother said.

It was July 1959, just a few days before I was born. My mother was taking in ironing then, to pay the light bill and buy groceries, and the little frame house held in the heat like a chicken house. I've asked her if, considering I was about to come into the world, she might have tried to get some rest, maybe even gone to sit in the shade sometimes, for her sake and mine. She only shrugged; everyone worked then, till their time. I guess I should just be proud that she was not sipping on a Budweiser and smoking a Marlboro; I have friends whose mommas did, and, come to think of it, none of them became astronauts.

The trip to town was always respite, I am told—the cool air rushing through the car window heaven-sent. The city of Jacksonville administered the distribution of the commodities then, in the red-brick city recreation center across from the police station and jail; some days, we could get commodities *and* go see my daddy or one of my uncles or any one of several kin, all at the same time.

That day, the man in charge was Ernest Jones, who had given up farmwork and gone to work for the city. Ernest knew my people, knew the fat-legged little boy with the six-guns and the cowboy hat, and knew their situation. It was clear, too, that the young woman was expecting.

Every recipient got an empty box at the start of the line—or brought a box from home—and it was filled at the table as the person slid it along. Ernest and my mother chatted for a minute, and as she moved on down the table he eased a second loaf of cheese into the cardboard box.

"I can't . . ." my mother said.

"Sssssshhhhhhh," Ernest said. "We had some extry."

She still protested, afraid of what people might say, so he tried, halfheartedly, to hide it under the sacks of rice and meal. He did a poor job of it, though, and she just stood, horrified.

"You'll get me in trouble, you don't go on now," he said kindly, and, feeling like everyone was staring at her, she finally moved on.

"Momma always said if she was ever gonna steal anything she would steal a hoop of good cheese," my mother said, thinking back to that day. "She said that to *ever' body.*" So no one would believe this was not premeditated, since the whole world knew the Bundrums were a cheese robbery waiting to happen.

To make things worse, three-year-old Sam insisted on dragging the commodities in his wagon. It was too heavy for him to pull, what with a ten-pound allotment of cheese in it, so she took out the illegal, second block of cheese, cradled it in her arms like the precious bundle it was, and hurried to the car. With her free hand, she helped Sam pull the wagon, hoping the cheese wardens would not inspect it. It may seem silly now, but it was not silly then.

As they lurched away, she heard an ancient, quavering voice call her name. It was one of the old women who frequented the recreation center, which had a piano for psalm singing, a few card tables for Rook and bridge, and good chairs in which to visit and gossip about the heathen, the inebriate, and the unfortunate. My mother just kept moving, cradling her illicit cheese like a newborn, and tried to keep her back to the old woman.

The old woman called for her to stop. "I want to see the baby," she said.

Apparently, her vision was not superb. My mother just walked on, faster. We jumped into the car and fled, all of us—my mother, my brother, and I. I already had a criminal record, and I do not believe my skull was yet fully formed. I think that might be some kind of gold standard, even for us.

I finally came into the world on the twenty-sixth. I weighed, oddly enough, just slightly more than a block of cheese.

There was no celebration, no gathering of the clan, when I came home from the hospital. There was not one damn pie to mark my arrival. Not only had I been confused with cheese, I was regarded, universally, as being of lesser value. I guess I should be grateful I had yet to be born the day of the cheese larceny. If my mother had been forced to choose which one of us to leave behind, I am not confident it would have been the second block of cheese.

"It was *real* good cheese," she said.

. . .

When I moved away from home and out into the wider cheese-eating world, I was amazed by the snobbery I encountered as to cheese. If you want to see a gourmet's face fall, make him a sandwich with American cheese. "Is there no Gruyère? Sacrilege!"

"Some people don't know what's good," my mother explained.

When the government decided to stop the distribution of the surplus food, in the early 1970s, it greatly affected our lives. When the cheese disappeared from her pantry, many of the recipes we had come to love all but faded from existence. There was simply no suitable substitute for commodity cheese, at least not one that was available to us.

You could still buy sharp cheddar in the country stores, but not a milder cheese of this quality. The store-bought cheese in the supermarkets was flatly inferior, and expensive. Even if you could find a deli or a butcher who sold good American cheese, an inch-thick stack of it cost as much as a steak. Today, a five-pound block of good cheese would cost more than your light bill.

"You can't make bricks without straw," my mother said. "Well, you can, you know, like they did in the Bible, when the Hebrews was in bondage, and Ramses told Moses to make bricks without straw, and . . ."

I told her I knew the story.

But now and then, when we are talking about my mother's cooking, my brothers and I will get to reminiscing about those recipes, and it is almost pitiful to see grown men trying to taste something again, from thin air. The thing my big brother most missed, I believe, was the cheese-and-sausage pie.

"I *will* cook it all again," she promised, "soon as I can find some cheese."

But after about forty years, you begin to wonder. I have tried to bring her a passable substitute, off and on, but she knows at a sniff it is not worthy. We do not have good delis in the small towns and out in the country. In the grocery stores here, the closest to quality American cheese is not even labeled American cheese; it is the sliced but not individually wrapped Kraft Old English cheddar slices, which are really just barely sharp American, and sold beside the sliced but not wrapped American slices, which are also solidly edible on sandwiches and in some recipes. Do not make the mistake of buying the cellophane-wrapped cheese film, which is mushy and may not even be actual food.

But if you live in a place with a good deli, the cheese man will find you some firm, mild American cheese, close enough. Taste it first, however, before you take it home, to make sure it does not taste of suntan lotion or baby oil or something you might use to lubricate your car. It should be mild, but you should know it is cheese. I found some at a good deli and took it to my mother, and in a while that old smell drifted through the house again. Most of the people—the guitar pickers and ice-cream crankers—were missing, but it was the closest I had felt them in some time. You have to do something nice for your big brother now and then, to make up for that time you caught him hung up in a barbed-wire fence and hit him with a rock.

Here is a breakdown of just a few things you can do with good American cheese, once you get over your snobbery:

Cheese-and-Sausage Pie

WHAT YOU WILL NEED

½ cup ketchup

¼ cup yellow mustard

1 pinch black pepper

1 pinch garlic powder

1 pinch onion powder

¾ pound quality American cheese

1 pound fresh pork sausage

3 frozen pie shells

HOW TO COOK IT

Preheat the oven to 450 degrees.

In a small bowl, mix the ketchup, mustard, pepper, and garlic and onion powders.

Cut the cheese into long strips, about ½ inch wide and ¼ inch thick. Set aside.

Crumble the fresh sausage into a skillet, and fry until it is done but not too crispy. Drain the cooked sausage as much as possible, and place it on a paper towel. This is the one time in this whole book of recipes when there is more pork fat available than you probably need.

Gently, gently, brown the thawed pie shells, as if you were making any other pie. When the edges of the shell turn a light brown, take them out. You can roll out some homemade pie shells if you want to, my mother said, "but that may be a lot of trouble for this kind of thing."

With a spoon, spread a thin layer of the sauce mixture onto the bottom of the cooked pie shell, just enough to barely, barely cover. "Don't use too much or it will be soggy. But it'll also help keep the sausage grease from seeping so much into the pie shell."

Onto the surface of the sauce, sprinkle the cooked, crumbled sausage until the surface is well covered, but do not overdo. "Don't use too much or it will be greasy. . . . Well, it's gonna be a little bit greasy, I reckon, but . . ."

Then crisscross the strips of cheese across the top, leaving a gap of about 1/4 inch between them.

Place the pies in the oven, and bake until the cheese melts, bubbles, and begins to brown. You have to let it brown a little—this is where the magic is. Remove from the oven, and let sit for at least 5 minutes. *Do not* let greedy children near them while the cheese is still hot. We know the results of this from grim experience.

Cut into four pieces.

NOTE This dish is especially good for breakfast. For breakfast, forgo the sauce altogether, and substitute fresh sliced tomatoes. You can top the cheese-and-sausage pie with a fried egg, maybe two, or with a layer of soft-scrambled eggs. Serve with buttered grits, salted and peppered to taste, or fried potatoes. For lunch or supper, just abandon any pretense of being healthy; have a second slice, and later try not to think about the fact you just ate half a sausage pie.

Macaroni and Cheese

WHAT YOU WILL NEED

4 strips thick-cut bacon

1 small onion

1 leek or green onion, slivered

About 8 ounces uncooked macaroni (any shape, but
my people are suspicious of anything more esoteric
than elbows)

½ cup or so whole milk

2 tablespoons butter

1½ to 2 cups grated American cheese

1 pinch black pepper

1 pinch cayenne pepper

¼ teaspoon salt (less if bacon is salty)

HOW TO COOK IT

Cut the bacon into pieces no wider than ½ inch. Dice the onion fine. Fry the bacon, and add the finely diced onion and leek or green onion as soon as the fat begins to turn translucent. You want the bacon to be cooked and just beginning to go crisp, but not crumbling. Set aside.

Boil the pasta until it is still firm but done. If I used the term "al dente," someone here would slap me stupid.

Drain the pasta.

Stir into the pasta about half the milk and the butter and return to the stove over low heat; then stir in the cheese, bacon, onions, black pepper, and cayenne. Salt to taste, and stir in the remaining milk until you get a perfect, cheesy consistency. The cheese and other goodness should not pool in the bottom of the pan, but cling to the macaroni.

Serve quickly: it will set up like particle board when cold.

This, of course, is not a traditional method unless you are preparing it for 5-year-olds. But we like it.

You can finish it in a more traditional way, of course, and bake all the moisture and much of the taste from it. You can pour it into a baking dish, top with some grated cheddar or even a sprinkle of something fancier, and bake, uncovered, at 450 degrees for about 10 minutes, and then broil another 5 or so.

My mother sees that as unnecessary. It just bakes the macaroni dry, bakes the taste right out of it, she believes. I know this is sacrilege, and may seem unsophisticated. We do not give a damn.

"People who say they like dry macaroni and cheese cooked in the oven are just puttin' on," she believes, " 'cause they seen it that way in a magazine."

If you feel somehow cheated by not having oven-baked macaroni sprinkled with breadcrumbs, think about your childhood, when your momma spooned it right out of the pot. Which one, truthfully, did you like better?

Grilled Cheese Sandwiches
with Pear Preserves or Muscadine Jelly

The jelly will liquefy, which is why preserves, of any kind, might be best for this.

WHAT YOU WILL NEED

> 2 slices bread, your choice (all we ever had was white
> bread when I was a boy, but this works with wheat
> or honey-wheat or sourdough)
> Butter
> 1 slice American cheese, ¼ inch thick
> Pear preserves or muscadine jelly (or preserves or jelly
> of choice)

Preheat the oven to 350 degrees.

Butter the bread generously, on both slices.

On the bottom slice, buttered side up, place the cheese slice and about 1 tablespoon—no more—preserves or jelly.

Top this with the other slice, buttered side down. Top that with one thin pat of butter—"a little extry," as my mother says—and place in the oven on a baking sheet. When the bread browns, the cheese melts from the sides, and the pat of butter on top has disappeared into the bread, it's ready.

Let cool a minute or two, since the cheese, butter, and jelly or jam will be like molten lava.

If it goes soggy, use less butter and jelly next time. "I'd rather have a lot of butter and put up with a little bit of soggy," my mother said. Some people like to place something on top of the sandwich to press it down. We don't.

Eat it and be glad to be alive, and do not tell your doctor.

NOTE This can also be prepared on top of the stove. The bread will be less crunchy.

NOTE If you prefer a more traditional grilled cheese, make yourself one, but eat it with a dab of jelly or preserves on the side. I like strawberry. I'm just sayin'. Scramble some eggs to go with it, and maybe a few slices of thick-cut bacon, and some grits, for a light breakfast.

26

SOMETIMES THE PIES
JUST CALL YOUR NAME

Pecan Pie

Me and Sam

1964

THIS IS NOT the first memory I have of food. My first memory, I believe, was when I ate the Wet-Nap that came in the bottom of a two-piece dinner from Kentucky Fried Chicken just outside the high-school football stadium in Sylacauga, Alabama, because I believed it was food. The less we say about that, considering that this is a cookbook, the better.

This is only my first memory of my mother's food.

And I thought I would die.

I had already been banished from the kitchen, banished from any proximity to the hot stove and sharp instruments. She made me step back even a few steps farther, beyond the door, in case I should suddenly go peculiar and fling myself into the cabbage grater. I had exhibited some unusual behavior already, even beyond the Wet-Nap incident, behavior that made biting into a moistened towelette seem almost humdrum in comparison. I had, after chewing on it like it was gum, somehow poked a plastic poinsettia berry up my nose, requiring medical attention. The less said about that the better, too—though even that should not be strange for the son of a woman who walked around with a marble in her mouth for about three years. I also went crazy at a lumberyard. That time, they said it was probably just sunstroke.

So I stood in the doorway, at a safe distance, and watched her work. The holidays were approaching, and all manner of fine things appeared as if by magic from that little stove. She did not talk to herself then, but she did sing, and over a lifetime of memories of my mother's cooking, those first days, listening, hold a peace and a warmth I cannot put into the right words no matter how hard I try. I guess the less said about this, too, the better.

Of this day, I mostly remember the smell. Later, much later, I would recognize it as a blend of butter, roasting pecans, melting brown sugar, vanilla flavoring, and more. When she pulled the thing from the oven she showed it to me, a perfect pecan pie, at or near the top of the pinnacle of what a great Southern cook can do with a dessert.

"It has to sit and cool," she told me, "and then you can have a piece."

"How long?" I asked.

"A hour or two," she told me.

I had a peculiar habit, as a boy, of spinning in a circle when I heard something I did not want to hear.

This time, I damn near went into orbit.

"One HOURRRRRRRR!"

That equated to starvation. I would be down to rag and bones, crawling across the floor, faint and quavering.

"Can't he'p it," she said.

"Damn," I said.

"What did you say?"

I think I shrugged.

"Let me get my belt."

She had never actually struck me with a belt, and would never. But I still harbored some fear of the unknown. I fled. If you did not want your children to learn any new words, you should not let them play in the proximity of pulpwooders, or anywhere close to the playground at the Roy Webb Junior High School Halloween Carnival.

One of the first things I had learned about my mother was that, although she had the memory of an elephant, her wrath was short-lived, and a lap around the house or a sprint through the cotton field usually took me out of danger. But the smell of that pie kept me in a tight orbit of the house, as if it were calling my name. I circled and circled until I saw her, finally, step out the front door and head down the short walk to my aunt Juanita's house.

As soon as I saw her reach for the door, I was inside the kitchen, reaching for a knife. I was usually not allowed to touch knives, for fear that I would cut off my own head.

I did not cut a piece. I cut a slab. Half, roughly. Maybe half and *some.*

I did not take a plate. There was something just wrong about stealing a plate. I cradled the still-hot pie in my hands and sprinted across the backyard and took a hard left turn to the horse pasture, and the shed that sheltered a long legacy of poor choices in the selection of Shetland ponies. I settled down behind it, well out of sight, and started to eat.

Lord.

There is nothing else to say about it.

Just . . .

Lord.

I did not wolf it down. I savored it, trying my best to keep the filling from running through my fingers. It was like trying to eat a very savory puddle of mud. I would learn that this why you had to let a pie "set."

I ate it all. I licked my fingers clean. I passed out.

It may be I just had a nap, but when I woke up I had a little trouble walking a straight line, and I think I was seeing double. I think I was mildly drunk, and at the same time talked very, very fast. I had the strength, the energy, of a hundred little boys. I giggled, and I hopped.

I was so drunk I staggered straight into the house, straight into her.

"What did you do?"

"Et some pie," I said, and giggled.

I do not recall being beaten then. I guess she figured that pie theft was in my history, in my genes. I do recall that it was quite some time before I could see right again.

She would have liked to present it to us at supper. It deserved that, not to be wolfed down behind a shed by a nitwit.

She just did what she often did.

She sighed.

"Well," she said, "you can't have no more."

Any more and I'd have floated into space.

Pecan Pie

WHAT YOU WILL NEED

1½ cups chopped pecans

1 cup brown sugar

½ cup granulated sugar

1 stick butter

2 tablespoons flour

2 eggs

1 teaspoon vanilla extract

¼ cup pecan halves

1 pie shell

HOW TO COOK IT

Preheat the oven to 350 degrees.

Mix everything except the pecan halves and the pie shell. If it seems a little thick, you can thin the mixture with about 2 tablespoons of water. Then pour it into the pie shell.

Top with the half-pecans in whatever design you wish, or just eat them.

Bake about 45 minutes, but check it after 40.

Let it set, under guard, for 2 hours, covered only with a clean cloth. Do not cover it with anything airtight. It needs to breathe.

Some people eat this with ice cream, but that is just crazy talk.

"You sure don't want no more sugar," my mother believes. "That's just askin' for trouble."

· · ·

I never had a piece of pie that good again, but, then, my mind was not sound. I believed, for at least part of a day, there was some kind of dark magic in that pie that crossed my eyes and gave me the giggles and set me to staggering and hopping like a fool. My mother said it was probably just sugar; you can get roughly the same effect with a Ding Dong and a large RC. I know. But though I am ashamed to admit thinking this way, it might have been a little better, that pie, because it was illegal pie. I think I know how James, William, and Rodney Rearden felt, so long ago, when they absconded with pie. I remember all manner of morality tales and fables about boys who stole pie, and were hexed, vexed, and haunted, so many and so often that I came to believe that pie thievery must have been a very common thing back then. I would not do it again—it would be unseemly. But sometimes I pass a pie in a bakery, and I wonder. It would probably just taste like pie. "But how will I ever know unless . . ."

27

RED'S

The Hamburger Steak with Brown Gravy,

The Immaculate Cheeseburger

Granny Fair

1965

H E R   N A M E was Irene, but no one called her anything but Granny Fair. She wore cat's-eye glasses with little rhinestones in the sharp corners, and what she could not make out through those thick lenses she ignored. She drove as if her hairnet were a crash helmet, and a '51 Chevrolet were a rocket ship to the moon.

"And she," my mother said, "was my ride to work."

We lived with Grandma Ava then, on the Roy Webb Road. My mother landed a full-time job cooking at Red's, a café just this side of Anniston, on the Jacksonville Highway. She got a white uniform, and a hairnet of her own.

"You ride to work with me, child," said Granny Fair, my uncle Ed's mother, who waited the tables and worked as a carhop there. "You just sit back and rest."

You could hear her coming as far as the highway, pumping the brakes and grinding the gears. She approached every turn like it was a surprise, as if it had, that second, crossed her mind. My mother waited for her at the end of the walk, atremble. Tires smoking, Granny Fair made the turn into the driveway by inches, scattering the loose gravel of our driveway; there she slewed and fishtailed and, finally, ground to a shuddering halt. My grandma had planted a row of buttercups inside some old tires, and though this was not their original intent, they more than once kept Granny Fair from driving straight into the living room.

"I wore out a good pair of shoes on that car, wore a hole in the floorboard, ridin' the brake that I didn't have. I think I rode 'em for a year at least, and I wasn't even drivin' it. I had to 'magine me a brake on my side. . . . I mean, I 'magined *hard,* and I mashed it all the way through the floorboard.

"She'd come up to every red light like she was gonna run right through it," and come to another sliding, smoking stop, half side-ways, scaring the drivers in the cars around her half to death; then she would take off, tires smoking again, as the light turned green. "Wasn't any seatbelts back then. I didn't have nothin' to save me. I was just in the hands of the Lord. I remember she run into the ditch one time and just laughed, and just put 'er foot down and come slidin' and jumpin' out of that ditch and just kept on goin'.

"I guess she was what you would call 'happy-go-lucky.' "

The old woman blistered through the little town of Jacksonville with utter disregard of the speed-limit signs or the parked patrol cars; it was just hard to give a ticket to anybody whose first name was Granny. She left a little more rubber as she headed south out of town, and sailed free and clear almost to the Anniston city limits before she veered into the parking lot of Red's Barbecue without even breaking speed.

"She'd be right up on it—I mean, right up on the building—and she'd lock them brakes down, and the gravel would just fly, and I was so afraid that she would knock out all the windows at Red's, and we'd both get fired. I would get out and I couldn't even move my legs good. I guess I was stiff from fear. I don't think she meant to scare me. I think she just drove that way.

"We worked the day shift, her and me. She waitressed, and did what I think they called curb service, and I cooked. I was always the cook. I liked my job." Or it may be she only thought she did, and was really just glad to be alive. They might have slid and slewed up to the women's prison in Wetumpka and she still would have thanked the Lord to be there, and asked to be let inside, please.

The kitchen had always been a sanctuary, and this one was no different. She walked in the door there and knew it was where she was meant to be.

To her, being a cook in a blue-collar café was the opposite of a dead-end job. This was the beginning of a hundred, two hundred chances to make people glad to be alive.

You could say there was no place like Red's, or say that every place was, and you would be right either way. The forties and fifties might have been the golden age of the American diner, but the sixties, here in the turbulent South, was her time. Red's, a combination barbecue joint, short-order emporium, and meat-and-three, brought her skills as a cook into the twentieth century, without discarding a thing her people taught her.

It was a true Southern café, not just a place for a sandwich and a cup of soup or a bland plate of toast and eggs, but a sit-down restaurant that catered mostly to working people, a place to purchase the home-cooked food that they grew up on, or just a truly good hamburger in the days before fast food taught us to settle for nothing much at all. Mothers and grandmothers might pass from this world, but their food, and their recipes, lived on and on at Red's. You could get a real barbecue sandwich, or a plate of black-eyed peas and hog jowl, or backbone and collard greens, or a breakfast like your momma used to make.

It was a segregated world, and northeastern Alabama in 1965 had high and dangerous walls. Down the highway, in West Anniston, black-owned cafés cooked the same food, the same way, for the same people, same in almost every way but color. For, though the wealthy might eat at Red's or its mirror image just down the road, might come in for a taste of their long-ago heritage, these cafés really belonged to the blue-collar people, who would be born, live, and pass from this world without ever uttering the words "poached" or "soufflé" or even "medium rare." Things came "done," or they came "not done."

She belonged.

But this is not to say she did not dream a little now and then.

Wearing her starched white uniform, she worked side by side with a tall, skinny, fair-haired boy named Shelby Pollard, who cooked like an old woman trapped in a young man's body.

"I remember, on New Year's Day, we all sat down and eat together there. Usually, we were too busy to eat when we were open for business . . . but he had cooked black-eyed peas, and greens, and good cornbread, and he'd cooked his peas with hog jowl, and it had just cooked to pieces, and . . ." He could line up a hundred cheeseburgers on the grill, sear them perfectly, dress them with lightning speed, and make it all taste as if he had doted on each one, like it came from their grandma's kitchen.

His dream was one day to open a café of his own, one like this. He talked about it every day, and when he did, he swore he would hire her as head cook, and they would make good money then.

He spoke with such enthusiasm, such conviction, that she believed him; day after day, over the hot stove and grill, they talked about how it might be, what they would serve. Shelby was the kind of cook she believed her grandpa to have been, unflappable, precise, who never burned, never guessed wrong. He had learned from his people, too, one pot at a time. Other cooks came and went, young men who had drifted out of the military after Korea, or came to serve at Fort McClellan and just never left, cutting themselves out of the world they had left in Michigan, or elsewhere in the Midwest, as if they had clipped themselves from a magazine. The one thing they had in common was that they were all cooks, cooks with experience, not shoe salesmen or electricians who had decided to be cooks when they saw the want ads. It is different now, she believes.

Shelby was different. He had a plan. But always, partway through the dream, the doors to the kitchen would bang open and in would come Granny Fair at a dead run, shouting out orders she might have written down or might not have. She swerved, every time, to the dessert counter, where lines of tiny chocolate, vanilla, and butterscotch puddings had been set out in paper cups for the lunch crowd. You got a pudding free sometimes with a hamburger steak, mashed potatoes, and green beans, or a barbecue sandwich, fries, and slaw, or, if you were Granny Fair, anytime you damn well wanted one.

She would snatch one off the counter, and a plastic spoon would somehow materialize in her hand, and by the time she had made her turn to go back to the dining room it was gone, and she slam-dunked the cup and spoon into the trash can and hit the doors again. The whole trip lasted maybe ten seconds, and maybe three bites. My mother tried to keep count one day, but it was impossible.

"And then, when she come back, she'd get another'n, and in three bites it was gone, too, and when she come back she'd get another'n. It seemed like, every time she came through there, she got one." Management did not care; Granny Fair moved faster than any big woman they had ever seen, and was worth every pudding she consumed. She floated through that dining room on a sugar high, floated from car to car at the curbside, and they would have had to hire three non-pudding-eating waitresses to do that one old woman's job.

. . .

You knew it was a real barbecue joint because they misspelled it, with pride.

The ad, in *The Anniston Star*, told you all you needed to know:

RED'S PIT BAR-B-QUE

Owned & Operated by R. C. "Red" Harrison
(located in)
Harris Trailer Park
Jacksonville Highway
Open 7 days a week,
5 a.m. to 12 midnight
Call 7-2593

She knew her customers, or at least she knew most of their names. It was easy. They were embroidered right there on the pockets of their shirts. This was their place, too.

There was a reason why the phone number on the newspaper ads had only five digits. If you couldn't figure out the rest of it, you were obviously just passing through, and they could do without you. You might try to order tuna salad, or white bread with your pinto beans, or say something mean about Lurleen Wallace. Anniston was the biggest place between Birmingham and Atlanta, but this café was never intended for tourists, though truck drivers and old soldiers were welcome as long as they did not talk on and on about how they did things up north.

It was open from 5:00 a.m. till midnight because Anniston was a twenty-four-hour city then if you worked with your hands, and Red's caught at least pieces of the first shift, the second, and the third, coming and going. The city workers filed in all day, the ones who paved the streets, rode the garbage trucks, checked the water meters, cut the grass, and dug the ditches. The mechanics and the gas-station attendants came at noon, scrubbed clean with Octagon soap up to their forearms or elbows, sitting with the police and state troopers and housepainters and nurses, and with the insurance men in their short-sleeve shirts and clip-on ties. The body-and-fender men all smelled like Bondo, and the secretaries smelled like Evening in Paris.

They still made some steel here then, and trains lumbered through the city loaded with new iron, scrap iron, and slag, which piled into black hills on the west side. The chemical plants filled the air with the complicated aromas of dangerous toxins and money, and people will always take a paycheck over caution, even if it does come powdered in PCBs. People here wanted and needed to work; they did not call the sewing plants "sweatshops," and you could start a revolution here easier than you could organize a union. Sweat and grime and even a little blood and poison were just what a person had to bear up to, to get by. Hell, even war. All they asked was that they not do it all hungry.

The steelworkers did not call themselves that; that was what they called themselves in Pittsburgh. They just "worked at the pipe shop," pouring, crafting, welding, and when they sat down to order, you could see the outline of the black smut on the bottoms of their boots, and the pinprick scars that covered their forearms after years of living in a shower of sparks. They came in at five in the morning and got ham and eggs with grits for sixty-five cents, and it always puzzled her, how a man could wear that smut on his way *to* work. She guessed they took it home on their boots, and brought it back the next day. It was a two-fisted city then, and a two-fisted city needed a place where you and the smut you tracked in were welcome, where you wiped your feet twice and still left the print of a size-twelve Wolverine on the linoleum floor. The waitresses swept it clean when they cleared the tables, just in time for some cotton farmer from Munford to track in a powdering of red dust.

The textile workers always seemed a little off at first, a little numb; she would learn that this was because the vibration, the nerve-racking clatter, and the killing heat took a while to wear off, and they tracked in not smut but lint, missed when they brushed each other off at the end of a long shift. It was always odd to see people come slowly back to life, to smile and laugh and feel. They ate their lunches from sacks, standing beside their machines—bologna and potted-meat sandwiches on white bread—and came here for supper, to celebrate the end of the day. The single ones, and the ones without children, came to decompress over a good cheeseburger or splurge on a hamburger steak. On the weekdays, and weeknights, the working people ate hamburgers. On the weekend nights, in celebration, they had the hamburger steak. They had hamburger steak on their anniversaries, and on their birthdays, and after church. It was the same kind of ground beef, but the patty was bigger, and it sounded fancy.

The couples with children ordered pork, beef, and chicken barbecue at the takeout counter or curbside, for two dollars a pound, and took Red's home with them to their frame houses in the country.

The sweatshop women came in groups of six, eight, more, because there was a sisterhood there. They wore their scars on the ends of their fingers, which had grown back bumpy and even black, from being pierced more than once by the needles. But they painted them, anyway, in bright red. In solidarity, the waitresses gave them an extra pudding, or three, or five. The fortune-tellers came; they looked not like Gypsies, in beaded and bejeweled headdresses, but like grandmothers, in smocks and tennis shoes, and made the drive from Piedmont, which was lousy with fortune-tellers back then.

The farmers came in their overalls. They sat down talking about the weather and got up worrying about the same, and complained about how much they had to pay the crop dusters, who sat three tables away; they always smelled like cotton poison, and even flirted with Granny Fair. The back-shop men came over from the newspaper, and the pressmen, and the sportswriters. The disc jockeys ate there, and the government employees who tended the stockpiles of nerve gas left over from wars long gone, but too dangerous to move.

And, of course, there were the soldiers. So many soldiers.

You could hear them from the parking lot, could hear them all along the Jacksonville Highway, what we now call Highway 21, marching to a cadence on the parade grounds and parking lots and green lawns of Fort McClellan. The fort was too far away to make it out from Red's, but it was as much a part of the atmosphere, the feel of this place, as the thick air and red dirt. They dressed in civilian clothes, but their heads, as slick as onions, set them apart. They were sunburned pink by an Alabama summer, dreaming at night of a cool Wisconsin, or *Wonder Woman,* which they lingered over a little longer than necessary to divine the plot of such a quick read. They ate banana pudding by the bucketful, or chocolate—anything, as long as it was sweet. They tried to act big, but Granny Fair called them, every one, "Sonny Boy," and called us the same.

It made my mother sad sometimes, because most of those boys were leaving straight for Southeast Asia, and though we did not know a lot about the geopolitical situation, we watched the news, and they got blown up there. And it just seemed wrong that soldiers could go from reading a comic book your boys would read to fighting in a war.

There were, especially on the late shift, whole tables of no-accounts, the gamblers and fighters and hard drinkers who had no discernible source of income and had all the time in the world. The whole world, in her culture, could be divided into two groups, the ones who were "no-'count" and the ones who were "some-'count." In between were the guitar pickers, who played honky-tonk on Saturday nights and joined the hallelujah chorus on Sunday mornings.

Jack Andrews, Charles Hardy, and the Couch boys always came in sooner or later, after picking some hot country on the radio station's local talent show, or playing a dance. Guitar pickers always lived in the in-between, in neither one world nor the other, like cats. They wore pearl snap-button shirts and talked about Nashville, and sometimes had to run out, quick, to make their shift at the cotton mill.

I guess, to hear her tell, everyone in the place was dreaming about something.

In the meantime, this was about as good as it was going to get.

People went two, three times a week, because they felt at home. Tracy and Deb Thomas would drive a half-hour or more to eat at Red's. And if they did not eat at Red's, they ate at Star's, just a few blocks away. Same crowd. Same food, more or less.

"In the daytime, they came in their overalls, but on Friday night, they all got dressed up, and still came to Red's," said Deb, who went there to get the food she had grown up on, pinto beans and cornbread, with a big slice of sweet onion. It was a barbecue, true, according to its sign, but the cooks knew their customers.

People would fluctuate from Red's to Star's to others here, sometimes boycotting a restaurant because of a slight or an imagined slight, but rarely because of the food.

"I went to Star's, and I asked the waitress for a piece of chocolate pie, and she told me, 'No, we ain't got but one piece, and you don't need it,'" said Deb. So she went to Red's, and had "good steaks, catfish, slaw, and good fried chicken, and mashed potatoes, and that redeye gravy, oh my God. . . ."

They had it cooked right, once, maybe when they were children. They would not tolerate less.

To make them sit down to a stale bun or a questionable slaw was picking their pocket.

"I don't know when people stopped caring about their food," my mother said. "I don't mean the cooks. I mean, people will just eat what you throw at 'em. It's like they give up on having anything good."

When I was a boy, staying at my lovely aunt Sue's, she cooked hamburger for me, the exact same way. She learned it from my mother, who learned it at Red's. Sue, the baby of my mother's family, died when she was still a young woman, and my memories of her grow dimmer every year, as my own faculties erode. But I know she was the kind of person who made Red's the institution it was, who could run a sewing machine twelve hours for time-and-a-half, take the balls of cotton from her ears, and go celebrate life one good plate at a time. I can still see her sitting there in that restaurant—sometimes by herself, but surrounded by people with whom she felt at home, who asked her how her momma was, and asked her, always, to come and see them, even if she had not the vaguest idea where they lived.

· · ·

"People remember the simple stuff, mostly," my mother said, "but mostly I remember the hamburgers. They'd let me take it home to y'all. Do you remember the hamburgers?"

I think I can still taste them.

It is hard to describe the beautiful simplicity of a good blue-collar Southern cheeseburger of that era. Or, more accurately, it is hard to explain its appeal in a world of massive half-pound bacon cheeseburgers made from elk meat and buffalo butts and covered in Asiago and pork belly and served with a side of truffle and rosemary-scented pumpkin fries and a habañero-infused pickle spear, and a Diet Coke.

The problem is, much of the time, that the aioli went afoul that morning, and the bright-red meat in the middle of the rare patty is just worrisome in the aftermath of a thing called Mad Cow. The thirty-two-grain bun, studded with seeds of an unknown origin (but they appear to be mostly pine nuts), is crumbly, tough, and toasted hard to hide the fact that it is stale; no amount of Bavarian mustard on this planet can make up for the fact that the pink, mealy tomato was pulled green and rode a thousand miles in three tractor-trailers before it finally met the knife, which was likely wielded by a young man with a lip piercing and a hair bun and a full-body tattoo of a carp.

A hamburger patty here was not wafer-thin, not fast-food-thin, but thin compared with the excess of today. It was simply cooked right. It was salted, generously peppered, and cooked till it crisped around the edges. Then it was covered with a thick slice of mild American cheese, which melted into the browned crispiness of the meat on the grill. The bun they laid it upon was fresh, and soft, and they dressed it quickly with a daub of sauce that was mostly ketchup, mustard, black pepper, and a little hot-pepper sauce, and then layers of fresh red ripe tomato, shredded lettuce, dill pickles, and sweet onion. The top bun had a spread, not a gob, of mayonnaise. It was served hot where it was supposed to be and cool where it was supposed to be, not some mushed, tepid mess in between. It crunched when you ate it, and did not run down your chin for effect.

They served it with fries that would burn your fingers, and a little bowl of the best coleslaw in Calhoun County and maybe the whole earth, stirred together that morning by an old woman who had to take off only her wedding band, which was most likely the only jewelry she had ever cared about.

"We mixed it up in big pickle jars, just cabbage, carrot, good mayonnaise, some dill-pickle juice, and a seasonin' or two, and we mixed it up with our hands," my mother said.

Its shelf life—or cooler life—was quitting time. They served no bad, old, questionable slaw here.

The soft buns were always soft, because someone paid attention and threw out the ones that were not, or saved them for the hog farmers. The fries were hot, because a cold potato is insulting to a woman who spent an hour's pay for a burger and fries.

"It was good food," my momma said.

It was the first takeout food we ever tasted. They were just her hamburgers, really, the way she cooked them at home, but because they were wrapped in paper they were exotic, and I still remember the smell as she carried them into the house after she got off work.

I have had a few thousand hamburgers in my life, all over the world, and I am still searching for something even close to this.

The other mainstays were given the same attention to detail, the hamburger steaks, and good chili dogs, and barbecued pork. She was not trusted with the pit—you had to be a hundred, at least, to be trusted with the pork barbecue—but she learned how to build the perfect sandwich from the old men who worked there. She watched another cook chop the perfect blend by combining the tender lean, the inside meat, with the fat and the crispy skin. A fresh bun, one small splash of tomato-based barbecue sauce, and amen. The old men would measure the meat each sandwich got by holding it in one big hand. A scale would have insulted them.

The chili dog was just a simple, boiled dog dressed on a soft bun with homemade chili, a little mustard, and a lot of finely chopped onion. They did not drown it in mustard, which would make your mouth twitch into a knot, like you had eaten a bad persimmon. They did not drown it in chili, which would mean you tasted nothing else, even if it was good chili. People did not want to eat their hot dogs with a knife and fork. They wanted to hold a hot dog like a civilized person, and enjoy it, without wearing it. They did not question its pedigree or its raising or its state of mind, and did not care if it was all prime beef or sawdust and kangaroo, as long as it tasted good and did not make them ill. It was a damn hot dog; you paid your money and you took your chances, and hoped that the butchers used enough spice in the seasoning to give it a little taste. They were made of pork and beef; chicken had yet to make its unfortunate entrée into the equation of the hot dog.

The thing is, unless you opted for the slow-smoked barbecue, you were not buying just the meat. You were savoring the preparation. With the burger, it was the crust on the meat, mingling with the cheese, with the contrast of the fresh, cool vegetables. With the hot dog, the simplest of things, it was its construction. To this day, there are institutions that survive because they held to these simple ideas, of consistency and quality over excess and pretension and silliness, places that have become great, great successes. And then there are the smaller places, like Red's, which just, one day, quietly closed its door, leaving a whole city of people who worked with their hands to sit over their disappointing food and say, "Hey, you remember that food over at ol' Red's? You remember how it . . ."

. . .

The Hamburger Steak
with Brown Gravy

WHAT YOU WILL NEED

1 small onion

1 pound ground beef

¼ teaspoon garlic powder

1 teaspoon salt

1 teaspoon black pepper

About 1 teaspoon bacon grease

¼ stick butter

2 teaspoons flour

1½ cups whole milk or water

HOW TO COOK IT

Dice your onion fine, and work it into the hamburger meat with the garlic powder, ½ teaspoon salt, and ½ teaspoon of black pepper. Form three oblong patties, about ¾ inch thick—no more than about 1 inch thick. Make sure your onion is finely diced, since this will cook quickly.

Melt your bacon grease in a 9-inch skillet and get the skillet hot, then lower the heat to about medium. Lay in your meat. You should get a nice sizzle. Cook it till the pink side up begins to brown through on the edges, and flip. There is no need to season; the seasoning is on the inside.

Cook to taste. The bane of any hamburger steak is a rubbery texture, which will happen if you cook it too long, even if you cook it slow. You want a quick sizzle, to get some flavor; then watch it closely as it finishes. As soon as they begin to crisp good on the second side, remove them and set aside.

Now, again, you have to work quickly. Stir in the butter and melt it quickly, then the flour and the remaining ½ teaspoon salt and ½ teaspoon black pepper, and let the flour brown, a little darker than sausage gravy. Slowly pour in the liquid, give it a good, hard stir, and put the hamburger steaks back into the skillet as the gravy thickens. Do not get huffy. Stir around them, and if you break off a piece or two, that is fine, as with the cubed steak. Thicken to taste. Something nice happens to the hamburger steaks as they finish in the gravy, though it is only for a few minutes.

Be sure, when you put them on plates, to spoon a little extra gravy on the steaks. Serve them with mashed potatoes and green beans, and, of course, good slaw. They go well with any soft dinner rolls, or cornmeal muffins, or even biscuits.

As a child, I believed only rich people ate hamburger steaks. As a grown man, I have found nothing but disappointment, for the most part, in restaurants that believe a hamburger steak is just a hamburger without a bun, and a bottle of Heinz 57.

The Immaculate Cheeseburger

It's just a hamburger, but we would almost dance around the house as children when she told us we were having them.

I would not know for years that she made them that way to stretch the ground beef, to feed everyone in the house, that she sometimes even worked bread into the meat to make it go further.

WHAT YOU WILL NEED

½ head iceberg or romaine lettuce

1 large ripe tomato

1 Vidalia onion

¾ cup ketchup

¼ cup yellow mustard

½ teaspoon cayenne pepper

½ teaspoon garlic salt

½ teaspoon chili powder

½ teaspoon soy or Worcestershire sauce

1 pound ground beef (this will make 4 or 5 patties)

1 tablespoon bacon grease

Salt, to taste

Black pepper, to taste

4 to 8 slices American cheese

4 soft hamburger buns

Handful dill pickle chips

½ cup good mayonnaise

HOW TO COOK IT

Obviously, a grilled burger, cooked outside, is best. But for the sake of history, we'll cook this one inside.

First prepare your sauce and toppings. Shred the lettuce, slice the tomato about ¼ to ½ inch thick, and the sweet onion the same.

In a small pan, combine the ketchup, mustard, cayenne, garlic salt, chili powder, and Worcestershire, and heat till it bubbles a bit. Set aside.

It's time to cook the hamburgers.

The patty is everything. You want a thin patty, no thicker—not a sliver—than ½ inch, and even thinner is better, and a good inch bigger, around, than the buns.

It does not matter if the patties are ragged. It does not even matter if you can see through them in places. The more ragged, the better they will taste. I don't know why.

In an iron skillet, melt a little bacon grease. This will help, especially if the ground beef is too lean. Salt and pepper each side.

Let the fat sizzle a bit, lower the heat to medium, and lay in the patties. It is the crisping that carries the taste here, which is why thin patties can have more taste than a big bloody burger. Cook to taste, but adjust your heat to make sure both sides get some crunch. They will, of course, cook very quickly.

As they finish, cover each with a slice of cheese, or preferably two. This will make a mess but will be worth it, we believe. If you are cooking for a voracious meat eater, just put two patties, separated by a slice of cheese, on the bun. Again, it is the crispness that matters.

To build the burger:

Do not toast the buns. Place the patty—or two—on the bottom of each bun, cheese side down.

This will keep it from sliding around.

On the patty, put a nice dollop of sauce—enough to cover it, but not sloppy.

Then, in this order, add about two pickle chips, one slice of tomato, a handful of lettuce, and one wheel of Vidalia, the whole slice. Spread a little mayonnaise on the top bun.

Serve it with chips or, of course, fries, and a side of slaw.

A root beer does not hurt.

· · ·

"I didn't get to work there as long as I'd liked to have. Me and your daddy got back together, and we moved off—up there to Spring Garden, up above Piedmont—and I didn't have a car, and Granny Fair just couldn't come and get me every day all the way up there," she said. It might have been more than she could stand, anyway, to ride the entire length of Calhoun County with that death-defying old woman in her four-door rocket ship.

"I heard, a long time later, that Shelby got his restaurant, and I was happy for that."

28

"WHEN MOMMA WAS ALL RIGHT"

Tea Cakes

My brothers and me, at the beach with Ava

1966

I WISH you could have seen her stalking those chickens, and her nearsighted.

Oh, she was still able, even still limber, eerily so. And she still had a fine memory of their transgressions. She could remember being pecked, just once, for years and years, and that old woman could hold a grudge. But game chickens tend to look a lot alike, and sometimes she would bait them, lure them, snatch them up, get a good grip, and . . . at the last second realize she had snatched up the wrong bird.

It would have been a grand story if she had then flung it away to run free and gone in search of the right, bad one, but she did not have time to go plucking roosters from the yard like daffodils.

My big brother and I watched with growling stomachs, and fascination.

"She get the right 'un?" I would ask.

"Nope," he said.

A terrible squawk would pierce the air.

"But she's still quick, ain't she?" I said.

"Yep," he said.

But sometimes she would spot the right, bad one as it fled the carnage, or at least the one she believed to be it, and she would go after that one, just as intent, just as patient, till she had it in her grip, wrung its neck, looked a little closer, and . . .

"Damn," she said.

It was a two-chicken day, two iron skillets cooking side by side on her stove, and we were not sorry a damn bit. A great cook can do that to you, can make you bloodthirsty like that.

I do not know if she ever got the right, bad one. Her mind had never been the same after her husband died.

"But Momma was all right when I let y'all stay with her," my mother said. "I never would have left y'all to stay with her if she hadn't been all right."

When I remember my grandmother, it is not the woman in her middle eighties, rocking quietly, a little befuddled, in a chair in a room filled with stuffed animals and the other doodads that the young, for some reason, bestow upon the old. I think of her the way I did when I was a boy, and she was still the most interesting creature in my world. I guess it is a cliché, but she spoiled me, spoiled us, in the only way she could. She cooked, and cooked, and . . .

"Y'all went and stayed with her every weekend when we moved up to Spring Garden, and she fried you a whole chicken every time, and made you chocolate pies, and fried pies, and she made you a sack-full of tea cakes . . . every time."

"There wasn't nothin' wrong with my grandmother," my brother Sam said.

It may be, he reasoned, that "ever'body else was crazy."

She, and her great food, was our sanctuary then. My mother, with our little brother, Mark, running buck wild around the house, struggled to survive a marriage that was doomed, and she sent us on those weekends back to my grandma's little red house, with its mountains of old, cheap purses crammed with prayer requests and empty Juicy Fruit wrappers, and forgotten bags of seed corn, and old radios that were as mute as stone. There were Sears catalogues from the Korean War, newspapers from God knows when, and water bills from 1959.

We were ignorant of a lot, but smart enough to know this was, in many ways, as good as life could be.

We ate, and ate, and ate, and at night she told us story after story, of the past of our people, and the fables built on the natural wonder of the foothills, and the creatures there.

I guess there wasn't anything wrong with her.

In the mornings, she would stand in that tiny kitchen and shake her head.

"There ort to always be some tea cakes," she said.

Only in the Depression, in the worst of it, did she fail in that.

She would bake them the old way, with plain flour, mixing in her salt and soda. A tea cake was a delicate, subtle thing and should not be messed with, lest something be forgotten somehow in the messin' around.

She used the most basic ingredients, just butter, egg, sugar, vanilla flavoring, and such.

"I use buttermilk," she said, "but don't tell nobody."

She always said that, about everything.

Even if she gave me a dollar—"Don't tell nobody."

She made her dough, rolled it out, and used the lid of a can of Bruton snuff to cut them out. Once she had cut all she could, she rolled out the scrap and cut that, and rolled it again, till she could not cut any more and there was just one little wad of dough that had to be shaped by hand.

Every batch had that little, single, ugly cake.

"Why do you use a snuff can?" I asked.

" 'Cause it's sharp," she said.

They came out of the oven soft in the center with a thin brown ring around the edges.

I've used the word "perfect" a lot in this book, I know, mostly to honor these cooks.

But this was perfect.

Well, maybe all but the little ugly one, which she ate herself.

She used a spatula to lift them from the pan, and placed them in a clean cloth flour-sack, or sometimes a pillowcase, and then she hung it on a nail so we could get one every time we walked by till it was empty, till she filled it up again. But she gave the first two off the pan to us, on a real plate, with a little pat of pure white butter. The way to eat it, she said, was to put a smidge of butter on a knife and butter every single bite.

"Why do they call 'em tea cakes?" I asked her.

" 'Cause rich people eat them with tea."

Why, hell, I thought. *We have tea. We have cakes.*

I guess we were rich.

. . .

But, as with most recipes I tried to draw out of my mother, there was a hitch.

She gave it to me without a measurement for flour.

"Enough," she said.

I pleaded.

"Just enough."

It occurred to me that it was no great mystery.

You simply had to do it just like Ava did. Here is Ava's recipe, passed to us by my cousin Jeanette.

. . .

Tea Cakes

WHAT YOU WILL NEED

½ cup butter

1 egg

1¼ cups sugar

½ teaspoon baking soda

2 tablespoons buttermilk

Enough plain flour for a soft dough

1 teaspoon baking powder

1 teaspoon vanilla extract

HOW TO COOK IT

Preheat your oven to 350 degrees.

First, cream the butter, and add the beaten egg, and sugar. Dissolve the baking soda in the buttermilk, and, in a large bowl, gradually work in the flour and baking powder until you have a soft dough. Only then work in the vanilla. Roll out the dough— thinner than biscuit, thicker than pie dough—and cut the cakes out. If you don't have a lid from a can of Bruton snuff, use a cookie cutter, slightly bigger around than a half-dollar.

These will cook quickly. Bake for 8 to 10 minutes, till the middle rises, and the edges flatten and turn brown.

Store them in a cloth sack if you can.

Serve them, if you want, with a little pat of butter on the side.

You could, of course, use self-rising flour, but I wouldn't. Some things were not intended for a modern world.

29

MONKEY ON A STRING

Barbecued Rag Bologna Sandwich

Dressed with Shredded Purple Cabbage Slaw

Me, before running off to join the circus

1967

THIS WAS THE YEAR I ran away to be a circus midget.

My mother had been mean to me for some time, most of her cruelty resulting from an incident in which I patiently waited for my big brother to get hung up in a barbed-wire fence and busted him with a rock.

I had harbored the grudge that led to that a long time, so long I had actually forgotten why I was mad at him in the first place. But he was bigger than me and as strong as a bull calf, and I knew that any revenge had to happen at just the right time and situation, one that would allow me to bust him one but would also give me a chance to run for my life and hide out, probably till I graduated from high school. I think I might have even prayed for it, for the opportunity, which is a little like praying for a good chance to steal a chicken. I had been to church twice that year, once for the Christmas play and its accompanying treats, and again for dinner on the ground, and you would be surprised how much religion you can soak up in such a slight dose.

My chance came that summer, when we were going for one last swim in the creek that ran through Mr. Paul Williams's pasture, before the weather turned chill. Sam was squeezing through the strands of barbed wire when he got snagged, not just on the top wire, but on the one below, too. The Lord had placed a good-sized chert rock right there close at hand, so I took good aim, let 'er fly, and ran like a man on fire.

My mother did not whip me then, either, but she yelled at me, which was rare enough, and asked me what I would have done, how I would have even lived with myself, if I had killed my big brother with a rock while he was hung up in a fence. I told her I did not see what the big deal was, since I missed his head.

I missed his torso, too, but caught his knee pretty good, enough to draw a satisfying amount of threats on my life. It did not even hobble him much. My big brother was impervious to harm or pain; he went a month with a broken arm, and claims he went thirteen years with a tooth abscess, but I suspect he is lying.

I had made a few other piddling mistakes that summer, not really worth talking about. My mother, though, like all mothers, liked to stack the cold transgressions and bring them all up anew, with increasing disappointment. Sometimes, like the time I lopped the legs off a new pair of blue jeans with a pair of shop scissors, she cried. So I just had to quit that place. You make your mother cry, you got to hit the road.

I had loved this road, this yard, this place between the fields and streams and gravel, before I turned eight and became more philosophical about things. The yard, the fields, even the cotton wagons where I played were full of high adventure, even danger. We watched hawks from the roof of the shed, and gently tied June bugs to strings so we could watch them buzz round and round, till my mother, with her great heart, let them slip the string. We ran from red wasps, and spent untold hours poking at dead snakes with sticks, and digging up ant beds, to see the intricacy of the tunnels and life so far underground. My grandma continued to sugar me half to death with red and grape Kool-Aid and Juicy Fruit, and always had a dime for some black-walnut or butter-pecan ice cream.

"Why would anybody even want any ice cream other than black-walnut or butter-pecan?" I asked her once.

"God knows," she said, over a bowl as big as mine.

Then, as if some grand revelation had settled upon her . . .

"Black-walnut *and* butter-pecan," she said, took my bowl from my hands, and refilled it with two big scoops of each.

Like my brother said, there was nothing wrong with our grandma.

But, lately, the magic had just gone out of the place. First grade had been miserable, painful, all bound up, buttoned up, and slicked down. Second grade did not improve, and the teacher had an evil eye, besides. I jumped off the big yellow bus at the end of the day, with Mr. Tom Couch, the driver, telling me to slow my little behind down, and was already peeling off my clothes as I entered the door to the little red house, to get into the short pants and Kool-Aid–stained tank top that allowed a boy to breathe a little bit. But the thing about school was, it was always, always waiting on you, with that evil eye, the morning after.

I was coming off the bus one afternoon, shoestrings dragging in the dirt, when a red wasp, unprovoked, popped me right in the corner of the eye. I screamed and ran to the house, hurling my hated math book into the rosebush, yelling that, on top of everything else, now I was going blind.

My mother daubed on a little wet snuff, so now not only was I blind, but I had snuff and spit in my eye.

Well, to hell with this.

If the magic was gone from this place, this place of creeks, cotton fields, and gentle sloping hills, then I was gone, too.

Then the magic came rolling right down the road.

. . .

It was still light outside the evening it happened. I was propped in my bed in my grandmother's little house, a shorted-out electric fan rattling off and on in the window beside my head, a ragged library copy of *The Hardy Boys* in my hands. The view outside my window was, literally, in black and white: white bolls of cotton and black stalks, as far as I could see. On a moonlit night, they shone not white but a ghostly silver, and as a little-bitty boy I believed I could almost reach out my window and grab a soft handful of cotton and stuff it in my pillow. Now the breeze carried a whiff of cotton poison.

The pickers, I knew, would come at sunrise. The first sound I heard this time of year, every year, was the old trucks limping into the field, and the clang of the tailgates as the pickers stepped down to their labor. My mother and grandmother and aunts would wade into the field with them, for a few dollars a day.

Sometimes, when they picked close enough to our house, the pickers pooled their money and paid my mother to cook a noon meal for them, and they would step from the field and straight to our table, or take their plates to the shade of the chinaberry and willow trees. It was usually just cornbread and beans with a chunk of fatback, but they had been raised too good to ever actually fish that out and left it for the next one, who left it for the next, till, by the time they trudged back into the field, there was still a lonely little piece of pork resting in the empty pot. . . . But even this was good food, and they always praised her as they lifted the straps over their shoulders and dragged their sacks back into the stalks.

I must have drifted off just as the sun began to set. The Hardy Boys had always been a little slow for me; they engaged in almost no fistfights, no shooting, and no cussing whatsoever. There seemed to be few girls, and what few there were seemed to be a little proper for me. It was one of the reasons I loved Westerns. You wouldn't catch Miss Kitty acting all stuck up and talking about Dartmouth.

I woke like a stick breaking, woke to something that shook the floor of the frame house. I woke to a great trumpeting—not of horns but of beasts. Elephants! It had to be. Elephants, at our door!

It was a sound I had heard only in Tarzan movies at the Midway Drive-In, or in a black-and-white after-school matinee on WBRC, on *Dialing for Dollars.* It had to be a dream, or what my people had come to fear and call merely "the crazy come early." Then I heard it again, and again.

I wasted several fine seconds in disbelief, wondering if my mind, as my big brother said it would someday, really had turned to mush. Then, rumbling through the window, came what could only be the roar of a big cat, a lion or tiger, answered by another, and another, and another, then a shrieking of monkeys that could be nothing else, and a roar of what I thought must be bears, and . . .

I tore barefoot through the small house, banged through the screen door, and rushed out into the yard. My mother and two brothers stood in the gravel driveway, openmouthed, as a line of pachyderms as big as dump trucks, their trunks and tails entwined, swayed down the two-lane road.

The sun was setting on a parade, but not the kind the circus brings to a city's main street, with tumblers and clowns and a ringing calliope, like I had seen on television. This was a workmanlike caravan trundling down a country road, as the circus prepared to set up its show in the fallow field across the road from our house on the Roy Webb Road. The elephants, I suppose, had been unloaded, to exercise them, and they were followed by a throng of garish circus trucks painted to promise the wonders of the universe.

The side panels and tarps had been slid back or thrown back, and massive tigers, perhaps the most beautiful creatures I had ever seen, circled inside the bars. A male lion with a magnificent black mane perused me like I was a pork chop—regally, just like they wrote about in books on Africa I had read. Then a riot of monkeys rolled by, still screaming, crazed and rude, and then an honest-to-God giraffe, and more, and more, and . . . I would say it was like a dream, but I had never dreamed this good.

My aunt Juanita lived next door to us, and she stood there, too, with her fat beagle, Mugsy, just as one of the elephants shook the air with a sound louder than any natural thing I had ever known. The obese beagle, who had not run a step in about six years, leapt straight up, turned in the air like a cartoon, and, his spindly little legs already in motion as he touched down, raced for the house. He tore through the closed screen door like it was paper, and hid under the bed. "Hid there for two days," my aunt Juanita said.

Some of the circus people—I could not tell if they were tightrope walkers, jugglers, roustabouts, or telepaths, since they were all in their street clothes—had gotten out to walk a bit, and some of them waved at us as they strolled by. It bothered me a little that I could not divine their status, their celebrity, without their makeup, sequins, and rhinestones; it never occurred to me they might just be pedestrians.

But then came the stars of the circus I knew were stars, walking together, and even in their street clothes they had to be someone special. They were the little people—what we called, because we did not know any better in the late summer of '67, midgets. Even compared with the pachyderms, they were the most wonderful things I had ever seen, and if my big brother had not been there I would have jumped up and down with joy.

They did not do a single trick or stunt, unless you count smoking a Marlboro. They wore denim and khakis, work clothes, just like the men here wore, with fedoras and peaked caps on their heads. One of them, the smallest, had on a ragged gray suit and had rolled the legs of his pants up a time or two, to keep them out of the weeds and red mud, and I heard my brother say, in the practical way in which his mind worked, that it must be hard to get a good pair of pants with legs so short, and my mother told him to hush.

I was a little puny in those days, and we were about the same size, that little man and me. If you had painted me up and put me in a little suit, and maybe a rubber nose and some big ol' floppy shoes, then you could not tell us apart, and I might just have me a career. The idea that I would grow out of it by Christmas, or even by Tuesday, did not penetrate my mind or puncture my enthusiasm.

Then the little man waved at me, looked right straight at me and waved, but in my enthusiasm it seemed to me that he was waving me in, beckoning, inviting me to join the troupe. Only then, as the caravan filed into the big fallow field across the road, did I even notice it was beginning to rain.

. . .

"It was in the paper," my mother said.

"Why didn't you tell me?" I said.

"I wanted it to surprise you," she said.

I almost forgave her everything.

I would learn that this was the Al G. Kelly & Miller Brothers Circus, and it was to open that next day just north of Germania Springs, almost in our front yard. We would not even have to beg a ride from one of our aunts to get there, just look both ways and strut across the road like we were somebody, like the circus was in our front yard all the time. She had saved up for it, she told us, so we could all go. But even better than that, I knew I could sneak away as soon as she turned her back and watch it rise from this brightly painted but road-grimed caravan into what was said to be the second-largest traveling circus on earth; it said so, right in the newspaper. This was not some rinky-dink carnival—you could read the whole story of it as the trucks rolled by—but the largest collection of animal acts on the planet, with two hundred performers and twenty-two acts of world renown, right there in the broom sage.

There would be the great elephant Myrtle, the "Dowager Queen of the Herds," and the Arturo family, renowned trapeze and high-wire daredevils from Austria, wherever that was, who performed without a net. There would be acrobats, bareback riders, fire eaters, lion tamers, clowns, snake charmers, a "trained Egyptian hippopotamus," and, with any luck, a soon-to-retire human cannonball. And I would be that boy I had read about, read about in at least a dozen books, that boy peeking under the flap of the tent.

The rain was coming harder now, turning the red dust to mire. My mother tugged at me.

"Go inside. Now!" she said, but I shook my head like a two-year-old, and she left me there in the rain.

I watched the last of the trucks roll by—how many I can no longer recall—watched, in dismay, as the first of them began to sink into the red mud beneath the grass of the field.

The great trailers hauling the big cats wallowed up to their axles, and a man went running down the line of trucks, yelling for them to stop. The caravan stalled in the rain, and the elephant handler guided Myrtle and the rest of the rocking beasts to the stalled trucks. Mud didn't mean nothin' to Myrtle. Working fast, they put the elephants in harness, and used them, like wreckers, to drag the trucks one by one from the muck. That alone was the most amazing thing I had seen in my life.

Then, in a different kind of disbelief, I watched as their handlers loaded the elephants onto the trucks on the firm blacktop, and watched the trucks, all of them, turn around and head back in the direction whence they came.

I didn't run after them, but I wanted to.

I stood in that rain and cussed the red mud with every blasphemy I had ever heard, and I had listened close. I threw rocks at nothin', and I probably cried. Then I went and sat on the porch, left behind. I would have made a good midget, I believed, for at least a little while. I could have wowed 'em in Albia, Iowa, or Snohomish, Washington, and brought the tent down in Bolivar, Tennessee. I just knew I could.

I sat there a long time, and decided it did not have to end like this.

They would not get far overnight.

Tomorrow, then, when the rain slacked, I'd go find them.

Eight-year-old boys think like that, especially ones like me, who had been dropped on their heads soon after birth. I concede it might have held little promise in the long run, since I grew up to be six foot two, and about 245 pounds, give or take a sausage biscuit. But back then, I was just the right size for the big top, for the second-greatest show on earth, and even if I did outgrow it, I bet there was almost always an opening for a lion tamer, or a human cannonball. I bet they went through those people pretty regular.

I was a runner already by then. I ran away five or six times when I was a boy, but never got much beyond the mailbox, much outside the orbit of the circle drive; still, I got farther than my big brother, Sam, who ran away just once and only hid under the front porch—a pitiful stab at running away, if you ask me. I blame books for my wanderlust, blame them for opening my mind to a world of oceangoing ships and silver wings and open highways, for taking me, camel-back, along the Silk Road, and through the smoke of Gettysburg, and up the creaking stairs of 221B Baker Street. They say you don't miss what you never had, but I believe the people who say such as that never wondered if they would live their whole lives hemmed in by pulpwood roads and rusting dump trucks and, beyond that, row after row of white.

Tomorrow I would slip clean away.

"You want to come in and wash your hands," my mother said, startling me. "It's time to eat."

I do not believe she could read my mind, but sometimes back then it seemed like she could. I started thinking about cows, to confuse her. I used to think that if I would think about cows, just cows, then all she could see, with her mind snooping, was cows.

"I am sorry about the circus," she said.

Cows.

Cows.

Cows.

. . .

I guess, somewhere a long way from here, there are smart children.

There are children whose minds are not hardwired to their bellies.

My mother held me to this red dirt, to this little place, with a stick of rag bologna.

She did not have a smoker, so she made one from the rusted old barbecue grill, and tossed some chips of hickory from the woodpile onto the hot coals. When a lovely smoke roiled through the rusty holes, she laid on the low heat a thick, solid chunk of rag bologna, made from a combination of pork and beef.

I smelled it before I even left the yard, as I headed off down the road to try my hand at show business. I had a plan, more or less. The caravan of trucks had headed south on Highway 21, just a mile or so from our house and parallel with our country road, so south it was. I would have left the night before, but it was raining, and it was dark, and I was eight, and Momma had supper done.

By midmorning I was packed. I had a pocketknife, a half-dozen peanut-butter crackers, and a dollar.

My grandma had given the dollar to me that morning.

"Where you headed?" she asked, as I packed.

"Runnin' off," I said.

She came back a few minutes later with her change purse and unfolded a dollar.

To this day, I do not know if she was bribing me to stay, or just saying *bon voyage*.

And I was gone.

I made it almost all the way to the culvert at Germania Springs, a good hundred yards from the front porch, when the bologna began to sing to me. I decided, a few steps farther on, that perhaps I could run away later.

In the backyard, the rag bologna had begun to sweat and drip into the fire. My mother took a big fork and cut slices from it about three-quarters of an inch thick, and laid them back on the fire. She basted both sides with a good tomato-based barbecue sauce, the same one we used for almost everything, and left them on the fire till the sauce had formed a thick crust and the bologna had begun to char just a little bit.

She laid them on a platter and began to build what may still be the best sandwich I have ever had. She opened up a soft hamburger bun, buttered both sides, and put them on the grill just long enough to warm them and let the butter melt and slightly, slightly brown, but not toast.

She put the slice of bologna on the bun, added just a teaspoon of the good sauce, then a dollop of good homemade slaw, and, finally, the second buttered bun.

She served it with some potato chips and a glass of sweet tea with a healthy wedge of lemon.

Then, when I was done, she made me another one.

That is the beauty and wonder of being eight. I was still ready to travel.

"Got to be movin' on," I told her, like I was forty.

"Momma done tol' me," she said.

Damn! Ratted out by the codger.

"Where you goin', exactly?" my mother asked.

"Gon' join the circus," I said, but my heart really wasn't in it anymore.

"Well," she said, "let's all go."

It turned out the circus had only moved about five miles down the road, to set up at a higher, drier place in the Eastwood neighborhood. My aunt Juanita drove us there in a Chevrolet Biscayne, which was not nearly as romantic as I had hoped the journey would be.

I watched a bear ride a tricycle, which to me seemed like a silly thing for a bear to do, and one he would not do if he was running free in the Smokies, and watched a man stick his head into a lion's mouth, and watched the monkeys fling some poo. That seemed to be the extent of their act. Hell, I could sell them my little brother. He could do that.

I watched a beautiful girl in spangles walk a high wire, and three dozen clowns crawl into and out of a car the size of a Nash Rambler, and the elephants, Lord, the elephants, doing all kind of tricks—sitting on command like a good dog—and that didn't seem right to me, either. It just seemed like they should be eatin' a tree someplace hot. I waited and waited for the human cannonball, but I reckon he had the day off.

The midgets stole the show, as I recall, but for the life of me I cannot recall a thing they did. I waved and they waved back, but if they had planned to recruit me it must have slipped their minds. I guess show business is a busy life, and you don't have time to waste on the wishy-washy. But on the way out, my mother bought me a monkey puppet on a string that you could make dance by jiggling two little sticks, so I forgot about them after a while.

Barbecued Rag Bologna Sandwich
Dressed with Shredded Purple Cabbage Slaw

WHAT YOU WILL NEED

1 to 2 pounds hickory chips

for the slaw

½ head small purple cabbage

1 teaspoon black pepper

¼ teaspoon garlic salt

1 teaspoon dill pickle juice

¾ cup mayonnaise

for the bologna

1 stick rag bologna, about 2 pounds

1½ cups tomato-based barbecue sauce

6 hamburger buns

HOW TO COOK IT

This takes some time.

First prepare the slaw.

This is a slightly different version of the traditional mayonnaise-dressed slaw that we eat as a side. Shred the purple cabbage—do not chop it. You will not add carrots or any other vegetables to this, either.

Stir the black pepper, garlic salt, and dill pickle juice into the mayonnaise, let sit a few minutes, then stir the dressing into the cabbage. You can add or subtract mayonnaise for this, to taste.

Just remember: gunky, soupy slaw is bad slaw, especially for this. You want it to be crisp.

Set it aside.

Now see to the fire.

As blasphemous as this will sound to those who believe that a grill is a holy thing that should only be tended by fourth-generation pitmasters, this process ain't that hard. It is, after all, bologna.

First, take about 1 to 2 pounds of hickory chips—or apple, or maple, or anything pretty much except old cross ties or plywood or formica—and cover them with water until they are soaked through; let them sit in the water for an hour.

You don't even really need a fancy smoker. Just build a nice hot fire with about 1 to 1½ small bags of charcoal in any standard covered grill, and when the coals have faded to a dull red, toss on about ½ pound of the soaked hickory, or a good handful or so. Try not to smother your fire. You just want a good smoke, and a nice medium fire. Keep a squirt bottle of water handy for flare-ups. Let it cook down to dull red coals, then add more chips.

Now see to the meat.

This is not something that will still be good in a week, so only smoke about as much as you plan to serve, and a few slices left over for perhaps the best midnight snack you will ever have.

Rag bologna is not sliced. You want to smoke it in one big chunk, then slice it, and put it on the grill with sauce to finish. You'll probably want slices of about ½ inch per sandwich, so 2 pounds of bologna should be plenty for four to six people, plus snacks. Some people believe only beef bologna is quality bologna, but those of us down here who grew up on a mix of beef and pork may prefer the combination, though it is increasingly hard to find without chicken leavings messing it up.

Your best bet is to go to the deli and ask for a quality bologna, unsliced. If you buy a big tube of bologna from the supermarket, it may have a bright-red casing around it. This is not food. Things will go better if you remove it.

Once your fire is ready, it's time to cook.

Do not rub the bologna, season it, or do anything.

It's bologna. The spices are on the inside.

I've been asked why you don't just slice the bologna and cook it slowly on the grill. The problem is, it dries out. Think of every sad piece of fried bologna you ever stared down as a child. That, but burned, is what you'll likely get if you keep it on the grill long enough to get some smoke.

"It cooks the juice right out," my mother believes.

Every outdoor griller has a technique, and can argue for hours over smoking boxes and such. I think, if you build a banked fire, as if you were going to smoke chicken or a small roast, it will be fine.

Place the bologna on its side, away from the direct heat, and check it every few minutes to keep it from burning. After about 20 minutes, turn it, and then turn it every 20 minutes until all four sides have received some smoke. I know what you are thinking: How does a round cylinder have a side? You know damn good and well what we mean.

It is not the end of the world if it blisters or chars a bit. Just try not to immolate the thing on the direct heat of a hot fire. And continue to watch the flare-ups. There is a lot of fat in bologna.

Smoke it, if you can keep a lid on the inferno, for about 1 to 1½ hours, adding the wet wood chips gradually, so as to keep the smoke coming and not kill the fire.

The heat and smoke, even in such a short time, should have put a nice color on the rag bologna.

It may take less time, it may take more; the truth is, this is not filet mignon. You just want it to soak up some flavor.

Now, being careful not to let the whole damn thing roll off into the grass—this has happened many times—remove the bologna from the fire, and slice it into wheels about ½ inch thick. Place them on the grill, and baste with your favorite tomato-based barbecue sauce. Any good rib or pulled-pork sauce will do.

Grill it till you get a little more crunch and color, and a nice glaze of sauce.

If it looks dark brown and leathery, you have gone too far.

There really is no "done" where bologna is concerned, only overdone. If it has a nice little char on it, and the sauce has bonded with the meat, it's ready. The secret, my mother believes, is in the char, just that tiniest bit. "That's where your flavor is."

To build the sandwich:

The bun is a matter of preference, as long as you prefer it the way my mother wants you to. Texture is everything with this. It needs to be soft and fresh; a crumbly bun will ruin the sandwich. Whole wheat will ruin it. Sesame seeds will ruin it.

Trust us. You want simple for this. That said, we got some potato buns once, by accident, and it was like angels started to sing. Try some good, soft potato buns.

Do not put any extra sauce on the bottom of the bun. This is your foundation, and you want the cooked sauce and char to be in contact with the bun. You want to taste it in the bun.

On top of the bologna, you can, if you must, add just a teaspoon or so of heated barbecue sauce. This, too, is a matter of preference; I add none. The glazed sauce on the meat is delicious, and is easily drowned, masked. I know this sounds high-hat for bologna.

On top of the bologna, add a generous dollop, a heaping tablespoon at least, of the shredded-cabbage slaw.

Top with the other bun, and serve with some good potato chips and maybe another little dollop of slaw, because you just can't ever have enough slaw, and maybe a little bowl of the sauce to dip your chips in. We know how to live.

.   .   .

As good bologna vanished from the diet of my people, so did this recipe. I went forty years or more without a decent barbecued bologna sandwich, till one was bestowed upon me in Memphis, where they understand such as this. You can even get one in the airport. It was pretty damn good.

They charge about six dollars for a bologna sandwich there. I guess it was worth it, to remember my one and only brush with show business, to remember little people in the tall grass, and elephants in the broom sage, and monkeys on a string.

30

EDNA'S ARK

Fried Fresh Crappie, Hush Puppies,

Tartar Sauce

Getting ready for the majors

1967

I GUESS there were a lot of reasons why they built it.

My aunt Edna and uncle Charlie fished the backwater, it seemed, every weekend when the weather was mild. Their daughters, Betty, Linda, Libby, Wanda, and Charlotte, were raised with fishing rods in their hands. It would take a big boat to float them all along the Coosa, and all the fish they could catch. It almost killed me, as a little boy, to ask a *girl* how to rig my minnow on the hook, or how deep to set my float, but I got over it in time. They were their momma's girls, and did not go all squeamish when it came time to bait a hook; they sent a million minnows into the murky water without even a sigh, and, I swear, caught washtubs-full of speckled crappie, the tastiest fish in the Deep South. The family needed, and deserved, a fishing boat of considerable size.

It may be that their reasons for building such a thing went all the way back to that stormy day, so long ago, when the rising water almost claimed their grandfather Mr. Hugh, when Sis Morrison came to his rescue. But you cannot always count on having a big woman around with a number-2 washtub. So it may be that they had never intended to build a boat at all. It may be that they built an ark.

It may also be that my aunt and uncle remembered the island, the spit of gravel in the middle of the river, that my grandfather Charlie went to so often in the last year of his life, a place to cook, eat, and sleep, and listen to the river. What better island than one that floats, that you can sail all the way to Georgia and back, waving as you passed at the old men in lawn chairs on the bank who were pretending to fish?

But I think it had everything to do with time.

Blessed time.

You could slow time on a houseboat.

I believe it with all my heart.

It took years to build the great big thing, or it may just be that it seemed that way, because of the anticipation. It grew from their yard, one weld, one rivet at a time, handmade, resting on two massive steel pontoons. The day they finally hooked a truck to it and dragged it, an hour or more, to the river, was an event like what I imagined it had been to launch the *Queen Mary*. But an Alabama man made these welds and put these rivets in, so it held. It had a central cabin, with a bathroom, a gas stove, and kitchen tables; enough bunks to sleep a navy; a sundeck covered in Astro-Turf, for just lying around; and a wraparound deck, so you could fish in every direction.

It was so tall its upper railings routinely snagged on the low bridges, and you had to wait for the river to lower, at the whim of the hydroelectric gods. But sooner or later it would scrape free, and we would glide on down the river, or up it, never any faster than an old man could backstroke through that current. It was prone to breaking down, but that was only a problem if you were downstream of the dock; upstream, you just rode the slow brown water southward, and tried to run her aground as close as possible to your cars. I cannot recall if she had a name.

Sometimes I would sit beside my uncle and watch him pilot, and it was easy to pretend this was something more, some antebellum riverboat, a floating palace peopled with gamblers and dancing girls and even soldiers sailing off to fight the Yankees upriver, with a great paddlewheel pushing us along instead of a Johnson outboard. The river's backwater straddled the state line, and I was still young enough to be amazed at that—how you could be in one state one second, then cross a ripple or two and be somewhere else.

Now and then, he would see one of those old men on the riverbank, half dozing in their lawn chairs, and sing out to them: "Do you have the time?"

And the old men would answer, every time: "Alabamer time? Or Georgie time?"

And it didn't matter.

The day was as long as you wanted it to be, and some evenings, instead of heading in, we would just find a place to anchor, turn on the electric lights, and fish all night. I remember dozing off at the rail, and awakening to a tug on the line. I would reel in a crappie the size of a dinner plate, glad I had not tumbled overboard.

The only time that mattered was the amount of time it took you to transfer that fish into some hot grease. Our people did not smoke fish, or salt them; they caught them and ate them, and every second in between lessened the pleasure in it.

The freshest fish I have eaten in my life was on that boat, going from the river to the plate in minutes, fried up by one of the best cooks who ever lived, my aunt Edna, who taught my mother the finer points of frying fish.

Of course, you had to catch 'em first.

. . .

The polluters were well on their way to ruining the river, but the crappie were safe to eat. Some of the fishermen used man-made lures, but my people will always believe that a bucket of minnows, hooked so that they will wiggle a little, dangling at the appropriate depth on a bobber, is the tried-and-true strategy. Hook it behind the head, cast, and wait. If you catch one, then you may catch a hundred.

They ran shallow in cold weather and deeper in the summer, but you could still find them in the shade. In the summer, and it seemed it was always summer, you could catch them in the brush, off the ledges, the points, or the creek mouths—a wide, flat, speckled fish with fins on the top and bottom, a pretty fish. There was maybe more sport, and of course more fight, in bass, but most people caught crappie for supper and for fun.

Fried, they had none of the muddy flavor of the bottom-feeding catfish. The flesh fried up clean and mild and pure white, so tender it really did seem almost to melt in your mouth. I've read a hundred recipes or more for crappie, for thick batters and spicy batters and even batter fancied up with whipping cream. My aunt Edna did not believe in any of that.

"And Edna was the best fish cook there was," my mother believes. She filleted them with a knife so sharp we were not even allowed to look at it, as if it could cut you from across the room. Mr. Hugh sharpened it himself; no one born since 1919 should be allowed to sharpen a knife. After the fish were cleaned and the insides were relegated to the river to feed the catfish, she ran the razor-sharp blade once down the gills to the tail, then flipped the fish over and, the flexible blade bending almost level with the tabletop, ran it along the skin. You did not scale crappie.

She sprinkled the fillets with salt, dusted them with unseasoned self-rising cornmeal, and laid them in grease so hot you could feel it on your skin from six feet away. If the grease was not scorching hot, the fish would go greasy and limp. They were done before you could even get anxious. I remember four skillets on the stove at one time, roiling, popping. Edna's daughters, all taught to cook by their mother and each other, cut thick fries, and whipped up hush puppies from cornmeal, buttermilk, white onion, green onion, and cheese.

I remember the hush puppies better than anything, how crisp they were on the outside but creamy on the inside, how the specks of onion and cheese melted together in the delicious cornmeal. They served it all with freshly made coleslaw, a delicious fresh, tart tartar sauce, and gallons of sweet tea with lemon.

My aunt Edna did not ask me if I wanted seconds. She just put it on my plate. It is how I remember her now, with a big spoon in one hand, telling me, over and over, "You ain't got enough. You ain't even got enough to taste." I have never known a person to take more pleasure in seeing another person enjoy food. On the rare, rare occasions when the fish were not biting, she conjured up a hundred or so chili dogs. Again, it is probably just nostalgia, but it seemed even the Igloo cooler was a treasure chest, and the Coca-Colas, the ones made with cane sugar, were so cold they burned your lips and throat.

I wish, all the time, that I could somehow recapture the magic of that place, when time was an ally and not my hobgoblin. Only a boat on the water can do this. The closest I can come, as with the cracklin's, with the pinto beans, with every recipe in this book, is to get a little taste of it, every great now and then.

You can still eat crappie in the clean rivers, but this recipe, and its sides, go well with pond-raised catfish, which are milder- and cleaner-tasting than the muddy river cats, and other mild white fish. But the old people will swear that nothing in this world tastes like crappie.

Fried Fresh Crappie

WHAT YOU WILL NEED

2 pounds fresh crappie

1 tablespoon salt

1 cup self-rising cornmeal

2 cups lard, or vegetable or peanut oil

HOW TO COOK IT

Lightly salt each fillet, and dust with cornmeal.

In a large cast-iron skillet, bring your lard or oil to 450 degrees. If your grease is not hot enough, the fish will be greasy and soggy. With crappie, the crisper the fish the better.

Because you will use your grease more than once at a large fish fry, even our people sometimes use the lighter oils for this. You'll use this grease for the hush puppies.

Cook the fillets till golden brown and crisp. Thicker fillets will take longer.

"Don't use no pepper," my mother said. My people believe that pepper will scorch in the hot oil and leave a bitter taste.

Hush Puppies

WHAT YOU WILL NEED

1 cup self-rising cornmeal

½ cup buttermilk

½ cup water

1 teaspoon salt

1 small onion, diced

1 green onion, diced

¼ cup American or mild cheddar cheese

HOW TO COOK IT

Mix all the ingredients in a large bowl. With a tablespoon—not a measuring spoon, but a steel spoon—spoon dollops into the hot grease from the fish fry. They will not be round balls but more patty-shaped. Fry till golden brown, and turn. You want the outside to be crispy and the inside creamy, as Aunt Edna made them.

Tartar Sauce

WHAT YOU WILL NEED

1 cup mayonnaise

¼ cup diced sweet onion

¼ cup sweet pickle relish

½ teaspoon black pepper

½ teaspoon lemon juice

½ teaspoon cayenne pepper

HOW TO PREPARE IT

Mix everything together thoroughly, and chill.

"Don't be stingy with it," my mother said.

Serve the fish, hush puppies, and tartar sauce with freshly made French fries, and a big dollop of freshly made slaw.

Tiny bones will, even with someone good on the knife, sometimes materialize, so eat slowly, and savor. This is not much of a hardship, for real food.

.   .   .

Fried fresh fish, however she can get it, is my mother's favorite meal. She has had to make do with farm-raised catfish for a long time, which sometimes has a blandness to it, but we have this dream that, in our lifetimes, the rivers will run clean again. We may, someday, even catch a few crappie, but only from the banks. Edna's ark is in rust and ruin now, and so many of the people who rode her back then are missing. But if people can live on in my mother's kitchen, then surely they can live on here, in the slow current, slipping back and forth forever between Alabama and Georgia time.

31

STAGGERING TO GLORY

Barbecued Pork Chops and Ham Slices, Deviled Eggs,
Baked Beans with Thick-Cut Bacon, Jalapeño Cornbread

Uncle John

1969

MY AUNT JO had noticed the hogs were behaving oddly.

As we have already established, hogs are enigmatic creatures. They will run over you, at a full pig gallop, to get to a trough. Put something, almost anything, in the trough, or on the ground remotely close, and they will devour it as quickly as possible, till every scrap, kernel, or crumb is gone. We have kinfolks like that.

Beyond that, who knows why a hog does what a hog does? I have seen them stand still so that you could scratch them behind their ears, and I have run for my life from the same creatures, which apparently thought *I* was dinner. I have been treed by them, to sway at the top of a pine sapling, only to see my uncle John, my aunt Jo's husband, walk into a pen and tell that same monster to do something—to git, or come here—and watch it obey like a lap-dog. You just cannot figure a hog.

But this was something new. These hogs seemed to be drunk off their behinds.

My aunt Jo stood at the fence and watched them stagger across the ground of the pen behind their house in Calhoun County. They did not seem to have the dreaded blind staggers, or fever of any kind, or to be in any distress at all. They just seemed to have a little trouble trotting a straight line. They meandered, and sometimes just got to leaning a little bit, and fell over. But they got right back up every time, to meander off, list, and fall again.

It is hard to tell if a hog is happy, but they did not seem to be *un*happy.

"Your hogs are actin' funny," she told my uncle John.

He stood for a minute and watched.

"Well," he said.

"Well" has more uses than any word in the vernacular of my

people. It can denote surprise, or disappointment, or resignation, or agreement, or defeat, or realization. Or, in this case, all of that.

My uncle John did not raise puny hogs. He raised hogs the size of a Coca-Cola cooler—long, tall, immensely fat hogs, who waddled more than walked across the pens. He was finicky about his livestock, and worked to keep his pastures and pens clean. He did not crowd his hogs tightly together in a pen with a wood floor, but gave them some breathing room, in a hog-wire pasture, which seemed to make them healthier, less prone to disease. Some farmers said a hog would run all its weight off if you gave it room, but not these. He fed them massive amounts of clean corn, then supplemented that basic diet with scraps and especially, if he could find it, breads.

Someday, somewhere, people would clamor for lean pork. Here, then, the more fat on a hog, the "purtier it was," my momma said. "And your uncle John had some purty hogs."

He was generous with that bounty. He gave my mother pounds and pounds of it—of ham, sausage, pork chops, and more—and sometimes he would barbecue all night for family reunions or just birthdays. As news of the enigma of the staggering hogs spread through the family, it caused great alarm.

"What if we don't get no pork?" I asked my mother.

"Well, I don't know, hon," she said.

It was not like we were living out *Old Yeller.* We would not have starved. But we would have damn sure missed a barbecue.

It became the single most-talked-about thing in our lives, more than football, more than work, more than fistfights and pocketknives and even pie. Politics, which was tearing up the outside world then, was not much in our thoughts, at least not compared with pork.

But quickly, thank goodness, my uncle John figured it out.

He did not mean to do it, but he was getting them drunk on sour mash.

It was not the by-product of whiskey making, though some

bootleggers did feed their hogs the dregs of their mash. The problem, as it turned out, was doughnuts.

James Green, who married my aunt Sue, owned the Dixie Cream Donut Shop, and prepared the finest glazed doughnuts, brownies, and cinnamon rolls I have ever tasted. His shop, not far from Red's Barbecue and straight across the highway from one of the main gates at Fort McClellan, was an institution here, too, and we used to stand in the back and watch the hot glazed doughnuts roll out by the thousands, amazed.

There was, of course, some wastage. My uncle John had decided to try an experiment, and feed the leftover doughnuts to his hogs. He knew what eating a lot of doughnuts would do to people, and reasoned, correctly, that it would have the same effect on the hogs.

He combined the doughnuts with the corn, in fifty-five-gallon drums.

"I didn't think about the yeast," he said.

Quickly, the doughnuts, corn, and moisture created what was essentially a fermenting mash, and as he fed that to the hogs, they did get fat, good and fat—and good and drunk. He had the only hogs in Calhoun County who were too drunk to oink and too drunk to care.

But, my God, the meat . . .

· · ·

It bothers me that I cannot remember the occasion.

It may be my uncle John just wanted to see if drunk pork was good pork.

Southerners love to put on airs as to their barbecue, and speak in utter disdain of anyone's method that differs even slightly from their own. I have always found it amazing that such snobbery could exist inside a big ol' boy in a Dale Earnhardt hat, a T-shirt from Panama City Beach, and an apron that trumpets NO ONE CAN BEAT OUR BUTTS. They will tell you that beef is not real barbecue, and will threaten to beat you like you stole somethin' if you even mention a chicken.

I love it all. Pulled pork will always be the ultimate for some Southerners. In the Carolinas, whole hogs turned on a spit, and split hogs cooked all night in great brick pits, till the sweet meat all but fell off the bone, seasoned only with salt, pepper, red pepper, and a vinegary sauce—and sometimes seasoned with nothing at all. In Memphis and Birmingham, great slabs of ribs were smoked to perfection, spiced with dry rubs, and served swimming in sweet sauces. I have been overjoyed to sit down to all of it. There is a lot of bad barbecue out there, of course, but a lot of good survives.

This is only how we did it, among my people. But it remains the best barbecue I believe I have ever had, not just the meat itself but the way it all came together on those picnic tables in the afternoon.

The pits were actual pits, shallow depressions in the red dirt, filled with hickory and sometimes cherry, cooked down to coals that glowed a dull red. The men raised the cooking surface by lining the pit with a single layer of smut-streaked concrete blocks. The pit, as I remember, was as long as a pickup truck, and topped with all manner of grates. There were oven grates, perhaps from those derelict stoves, and once I remember a grate from a construction site, with diamond-shaped mesh. It was all cleaned, cleaned again, rubbed with cooking oil, and then laid across the blocks. The secret was a nice, slow, even fire.

My uncle John, who knew hogs, knew barbecue. This was the perfect pit for the kind of meat he was planning to prepare.

It was mostly fresh ham slices, about one-half to three-quarters of an inch thick, and fresh center-cut pork chops, and sometimes big spareribs, or country ribs, which are really not ribs at all. The ham slices each had a disc of marrow inside the bone, which, if it did not melt out in cooking, might be the single best taste—just a taste—I have ever enjoyed.

The pork was dusted with salt and pepper and laid on the

grate, slightly off the direct heat, and, right away, swabbed with a homemade sauce made from ketchup, mustard, vinegar, brown sugar, and other spices. They did not stir it; as per our tradition, they mixed it up in quart Mason jars and shook the hound out of it.

Once doused with sauce, the meat was covered with heavy foil, to keep some of the smoke in. The idea of coating the meat with sauce so early in cooking was to keep the meat moist, and catch that smoke. You could have cooked it to crispy doneness in an hour, easy, but he moved the pieces around and around on that grill so that they cooked slow, for hours. I used to stand at one end of that bed of coals, at that grate sagging under chop after chop, slice after slice, and think that, no matter how long I lived or how far I roamed, life would never be this good again.

"Me and your uncle Ed cooked all night this one time," said my uncle John, remembering, "and every time I'd take up a big tray of it he'd have some, and he ate and he ate, and when it got to be about daylight, he looked a little shaky and said, 'John, I believe I got to go lay down.'"

This meat was not trimmed of fat—it would have dried out quickly. Every ham slice had at least a half-inch or more of white fat, and by the time they took it off the grill, it would have shrunk to half that, dripping into the fire and rising up again into the meat, thank you, Lord.

There would be stories told, of course, and sometimes guitars picked, and as my uncles tended the pit my aunts created the sides, which would have been enough, more than enough, even if there had been no barbecue at all.

They made deviled eggs by the dozens, peeling, splitting lengthwise, and mixing the yolks with mayonnaise, just a taste of mustard, sweet relish, black pepper, and a dash of garlic powder and cayenne.

They stirred up giant pans of baked beans, mixing pork and beans with diced onion, green pepper, ketchup, mustard, brown sugar, onions, and more, then covering the top with thick slabs of bacon, cooking first covered and then uncovered, so that the bacon melted into the beans and then crisped.

They made a simple potato salad from red potatoes, purple onion, and egg, dressed in mayonnaise infused with garlic powder, and skillets of hot and sweet cornbread made with a little sugar and diced jalapeño. And, of course, there was slaw.

· · ·

You read, all the time, about how sweet pork can taste.

Imagine it, fed on Dixie Cream doughnuts.

It is almost impossible to cook pork chops on a grill and, without resorting to fancy infusion and marinating techniques or trichinosis, serve them with any degree of juiciness. Cook them good and done and they have the consistency of boot heel.

These did not.

The ham was crisscrossed with fat, not quite crisp. The pork chops were delicious. The sauce had specks of dark char in it.

One of the first things you learned in the country was that you could not toss a dog a chicken or pork-chop bone, because it would splinter, or hang in the dog's throat, so I sat on the back steps to my grandma's house utterly surrounded by pitiful, unrequited hounds, at least till I was sure no one was watching, and I fed them gristle and lean but never fat, because the fat was the best part.

I remember walking up to my mother, to hand her my plate, and how she just stood and looked at me, shaking her head. I do not remember this, but she claims I was covered in barbecue and no small amount of pork fat, from my belly button to my eyebrows, and my shirt would never, ever come clean again.

"Was it worth it?" she asked.

"Uh-huh," I purportedly said.

I believe this is an exaggeration.

I believe my etiquette was better than that.

I do remember how the paper plates sagged in the middle, and how, no matter how hard people tried, something would bleed through onto the knee of some Sansabelt slacks or something called pedal pushers, but there was not much that could ruin those days.

The pork was praised, and praised again.

We are forgiving of drunks here, after all.

·   ·   ·

Barbecued Pork Chops and Ham Slices

WHAT YOU WILL NEED

the sauce

2½ cups ketchup

¾ cup yellow mustard

1 cup apple cider

¼ cup diced onion

½ cup Worcestershire sauce

2 tablespoons salt

½ cup brown sugar

1 teaspoon molasses

1 teaspoon cayenne pepper

the meat

4 fresh center-cut pork chops, about ¾ inch

4 fresh (not smoked or salted or cured in any way) ham slices, about ¾ inch

2 tablespoons salt

2 tablespoons black pepper

1 tablespoon cayenne pepper

HOW TO COOK IT

Fires vary, grills vary, times vary—everything varies, in barbecuing for us amateurs.

This is a rough outline, at best.

First, place all your ingredients for the sauce in a jar, and shake it till blended. There is no need to warm it.

Prepare your fire. If you use charcoal, and wood chips for smoke, bear in mind that you will need about 1½ to 2 hours of cooking time. You will need to move the slices, if you are using a small grill, to control your cooking temperature.

Lightly salt and pepper each chop or slice, and swab sauce on both sides. Place on the grill. This will help the sauce cook into the meat a little. You are not grilling the meat, and then putting sauce on it at the last minute.

Be sure to mind the fire closely, and use a squirt bottle to prevent flare-ups. A little char is fine later in the cooking process, but not at the beginning.

Cover as it cooks, but check every few minutes. This is not something you can walk away from, like so many of my mother's recipes.

Swab again with sauce after about 30 minutes, then again when the meat is almost done.

"The thing about chops and ham is, you don't have to cook all day if it's a small batch," my mother said. "Just don't get in no rush, and don't let it fry on the grill, and don't let it get tough, especially them chops, and . . . and don't cook nothing really good on a brand-new grill. I'd rather taste rust than taste paint." Break in your grill on a pack of hot dogs or some hamburgers, and then barbecue.

Over the years, she was almost, almost able to find again that luscious, sweet flavor of the pork.

But, then, all her pork was sober.

Deviled Eggs

WHAT YOU WILL NEED

1 dozen eggs

1 cup mayonnaise

1 teaspoon yellow mustard (no more)

1 teaspoon black pepper

2 tablespoons minced sweet pickle

1 teaspoon dill pickle juice

About 1 tablespoon cayenne pepper

HOW TO COOK IT

This will make twenty-four halves, but if they're any good, it's better to have too many.

Hard-boil, cool, peel, and split the eggs. Remove the yolks and, with a fork, mash and stir them till they are mostly smooth. "It won't hurt if there's a little bit here and there that don't get mashed," my mother said.

Stir in all the other ingredients except the cayenne, and mix it until it goes mostly smooth. Using a spoon, fill the empty whites with the mixture. You do not have to be exact. Dust each one— slightly, slightly—with a little cayenne. Some people like smoked paprika.

They will still be good the following day, but the day after they will not. Eat 'em up.

Baked Beans with Thick-Cut Bacon

WHAT YOU WILL NEED

Two 15-ounce cans pork and beans

1 green bell pepper, diced

1 medium sweet onion, diced

1 cup ketchup

½ cup yellow mustard

¼ cup brown sugar

1 teaspoon black pepper

½ teaspoon garlic powder

¼ teaspoon cayenne pepper

1 pound thick-cut bacon

HOW TO COOK IT

Preheat your oven to 350 degrees.

Search through the pork and beans for the single little cube of pork in each can, and discard—you have your own pork. Mix all the ingredients except the bacon, and spoon the mixture into a large baking dish. You want the beans to be only a few inches deep. For one thing, the larger surface allows for more bacon.

Cover the top of the beans with whole slices of thick-cut bacon, but try not to overlap.

Bake, covered with foil, for about 40 minutes, or until the bacon has begun to render into the beans. Then uncover, and cook another few minutes, until the bacon has begun to take on color. You do not want the bacon to crisp through, like well-done breakfast slices. But if it still seems too limp, just leave it in the oven a little longer.

The fat in the bacon should be almost buttery soft and the beans will be thick and should have taken on the rendered fat, and taste, of the bacon.

Do not be concerned if you can see the bacon fat pooling on top of the beans. This is the point.

"This here, and a skillet of fried taters and a pan of biscuits, is pretty good by itself," my mother believes.

This is not a delicate dish.

You can, of course, cut back on the bacon.

You can.

Jalapeño Cornbread

WHAT YOU WILL NEED

1 cup self-rising cornmeal

½ cup milk

½ cup buttermilk

1 egg

¼ cup diced onion

¼ cup diced green onion

2 jalapeño peppers, finely diced

¾ cup grated sharp cheddar cheese

1 tablespoon sugar

2 tablespoons bacon grease

1 tablespoon melted butter

HOW TO COOK IT

Mix all the ingredients except the bacon grease and the melted butter.

Preheat your oven to about 400 degrees.

Grease a 9-inch cast-iron skillet and, on top of the stove, heat it until the iron is hot and the fat sizzles. Turn off the stove eye, and pour the cornmeal mixture into the hot skillet. Drizzle the melted butter over the top, and carefully place the skillet in the oven.

Bake for about 30 minutes, or until the cornbread browns.

This is, of course, far, far too much trouble for a pan of cornbread, and I have to beg a long time to get her to bake it for me, but I am not above it—not a bit.

She wants it said that she only puts in the sugar under protest. "But it won't hurt if it's in muffins."

. . .

The Dixie Cream was shuttered long ago. The hogs went cold-turkey.

Now and then, we still have good barbecue, but it is not, of course, the same. Well, one thing is. I still cannot eat it without wearing it, though I am better now. I have not gotten any barbecue sauce in my eyebrows in years.

32

THE RUNAWAY

Roast Turkey

Aunt Jo

I HAD ONE JOB. I had to lug the twenty pounds of marble-hard frozen turkey from the checkout counter at the A&P to the Chevrolet Biscayne, without dropping it. You'd think a boy could do one job.

. . .

Everyone else had more than one job during the holidays. My mother had four or five, I believe. She pushed herself hard in the fall, to give us a good Thanksgiving and Christmas. She did not do a lot of shopping, because there was never money for that, but she took in laundry, and still cleaned houses, and cooked for people in town to make a little extra money, so she could "go see Santa Claus." I was eleven and already having some serious doubts about a fat man in red velvet whose sleigh had to be pulled with a tractor down the main drag during the Christmas parade. Then I found out that my mother had to go see Santa Claus at the Mason's Department Store and *make payments* on Christmas. I all but wrote him off. I say "all but" because it is unwise to bad-mouth Santa anywhere close to the holidays, even if you catch him smoking a Marlboro next to his red kettle in front of the TG&Y, and know for a fact he stored his sleigh, in the off-season, in a chicken house out on the Roy Webb Road.

She still found time to cook for us, and her kitchen and the kitchens of my aunts were rich with the smell of pumpkin and sweet-potato pies, pecan pies, peanut-butter cookies, spice cakes, more. They stirred together simple treats from cocoa, butter, and uncooked oatmeal, and made drop-crust cobblers with buttered biscuit topping from the fruit they canned in the late summer and early fall. She made ham and biscuits and wrapped them in foil on a stove that stayed on almost all day, to keep them warm, and Ava made tea cakes and hung them in a cloth sack on a nail, and the whole house smelled of peeled oranges, and chocolate-covered maraschino cherries, which are as much a part of the holidays down here as blown fuses, plastic snowmen, and three-legged reindeer. Outside, in the distance, you would routinely hear the boom of a 12-gauge shotgun—not from deer hunters, but from people trying to blast mistletoe down from the high trees.

Everybody had jobs, multiple jobs. My uncles climbed ladders and nailed up strands of big fat antique Christmas lights, and spent hours, days, untangling wads of wiring that, they swore, had not been that way when they put them away last year. They finally gave up, griping, leaving one forlorn string of lights dangling from the gutters to the ground, to go put up their mommas' Christmas trees.

Even my brother Sam, who thought he was grown, had numerous jobs. His most important task was to go cut our tree, usually off someone's land or the state right-of-way, which might have been stealing, but not the way we reasoned it out. The way Sam saw it, we paid state taxes to pave the roads and maintain that right-of-way, so they were all our trees, in a sense. Whether it was legal or not, he allowed me no say in its selection whatsoever. It was always a cedar, but I have to concede that, though it may not have been beautiful to some people, it seemed—and smelled— that way to us, year after year. I was not even allowed to help drag it home. I did not have sense enough even to drag a tree.

"How come you never let me cut down the tree?" I asked him, later.

"Toes," he said.

I do not know if he meant mine, or his.

I had one job.

I was turkey boy.

.   .   .

I had volunteered as soon as I was big enough to know what a turkey was, and what it stood for. It was not just a matter of selecting poultry for a dinner. Our holiday season began with that great meal, not one minute before. The whole season, a whole Christmas, depended on my mother and me, and the Thanksgiving dinner, the holiday kickoff.

It was not just us. Working people started looking forward to this meal as soon as the weather slipped below ninety-two in the shade, and saved for it, in coffee cans and Christmas clubs.

The turkey was the foundation. It was not unheard of for 911 operators to receive this call:

Caller: "I need help."

911: "Yes, ma'am, what is your emergency?"

Caller: "I need help with my turkey."

911: "What kind of help?"

Caller: "I can't get it out of the oven."

911: "Why not?"

Caller: "I'm old."

Apparently, putting it in there had taken quite a bit out of her.

My mother had turkey down to a science, and an art. First and foremost, it was important not to be premature. You had to wait, and wait, till you saw the first of the Christmas lights illuminate the dark country roads, hung from little frame houses and mobile homes and wrapped around the bare trees, till the city workers strung them from the streetlights on Pelham Road. They had to light our way.

My mother never bought a turkey early, believing that if you waited till the last minute you would somehow get a turkey shipped to the grocery as part of a second or even third wave, which she believed to be fresher, and not one that had been frozen rock-hard since before Halloween. There is logic in it, I suppose.

Sometimes it was a one-turkey holiday season and sometimes a two-turkey one; sometimes we had a big baked ham for the Christmas meal. It often depended on the people my uncles worked for, who gave a coupon for a ham or a turkey as a holiday bonus. But 1970 was a turkey-excursion year, pure and simple, and, as per tradition, I had been allowed to assist in the selection and transfer of it. Mostly, this consisted of bouncing up and down as my mother tried to make up her mind, and shouting, "Get a big 'un!"

I wanted a turkey more along the lines of an ostrich.

She did not, ever, listen to me. She got a puny fifteen- or twenty-pound turkey, and instructed me to carry it to the checkout.

I will be honest. None of them ever really looked like food.

I believe that turkeys just freeze harder than other substances on earth. They seemed to have more in common with bowling balls and anvils than with something a person might, someday, be able to consume. This was perhaps the time when I began to see my mother as some kind of alchemist, able to turn lead to gold. There were fresh turkeys for sale in the world somewhere, just not in our A&P.

She paid for it and pointed me to the car, but that did not mean she would be coming anytime soon. She knew the checkout girl, and the butcher, and three out of every four people in the aisles, and so she had to linger behind and visit as I transported the bitter-cold, rock-hard turkey to the car.

I was eleven, and people did not blister through the parking lot of the A&P. But my being run over by a car was not at the top of her worries.

"Do not run with it," she said, like I was an idiot.

I had tried to run with it when I was five years old, from excitement. I fell, and, between the rock-hard turkey and the asphalt, was damn near crushed to death.

"Do not," she warned, "set it down and wander off."

"What if I . . ."

"*Do not* set it down."

She decided this was all too much for me, and was making apologies and heading for the door when an ancient, a great-aunt or distant cousin twice-removed, cut her off, and she just had to trust me.

I guess I got distracted. As she instructed, I carried the brown paper bag with both arms wrapped around it, but I lingered at the coin-operated rocky horse in front of the building. It was a particularly rambunctious rocky horse, and one that an eleven-year-old would not be ashamed to be seen upon. I considered, for a moment, climbing up on the mechanical pony and taking our turkey for a ride, but I had trouble fishing out my nickel with both arms full of frozen turkey, which caused me to reconsider. I wish I could say things were fine after that.

In that moment or two of indecision, the film of ice around the turkey's plastic wrapping had gone from slick to wet. I felt it through my sleeves, and panicked a little, picturing the thing tearing through the wet bag and crashing to the pavement. I locked my arms around the bag and squeezed with all my might, but a frozen turkey is not proportioned in such a way as to help a boy who was just trying to do his best not to ruin Thanksgiving and, by association, Christmas.

It went the other way, shooting as if propelled by a cannon from the top of the bag, crashing with a sickening, awful sound onto the asphalt, and rolling down the incline of the parking lot.

My mother could not have purchased a turkey from a store with a nice flat parking lot. This lot did not have one downhill track; it had two. The turkey first headed south, then curved more east, or maybe it was east and south, I am not sure. But it traveled like it still had feet.

I caught it, using every curse word I had in my vocabulary, just before it made it to the highway, where I am almost certain it would have rolled to Montgomery.

I just have one thing to say. Whoever makes those plastic wrappers is not paid nearly enough. I'd have thought it would shred, and though I am not saying it was not perforated ever so slightly in a place or two, that wrapper held up and saved the turkey, and—or so I believed at the time—my life.

I ran for the car, set the turkey on the hood to open the door, and heaved it into the backseat. I was sitting there beside it just a few moments later, when my mother got to the car.

"Where's the bag?" she asked.

"What bag?" I asked.

"The paper bag the turkey was in."

I could see it between me and the store.

"Throwed it away," I said.

"Why on earth?"

I shrugged.

We went home. She had three boys. Chances were, in our gene pool, at least one would be peculiar.

I confessed some time later, after Christmas.

"Well," she said, "it was a big turkey, and you wasn't no size at all. We had to give you goat's milk, you was so puny."

That did not make me feel much better. Not only had I failed at my one job, but nobody was surprised.

Our menu on Thanksgiving was always the same. It was as if the ghosts of the great old recipes came together in that kitchen, and I guess in a way they did. There was nothing exotic, nothing new, and it was perfect that way.

That year, there was runaway turkey, cornbread dressing that you could eat cold, standing inside the door of the refrigerator, pinto beans simmered with ham bone, mashed potatoes with little lakes of melted butter, creamed onions cooked in bacon fat, sweet potatoes, green beans, hot biscuits, cranberry sauce, fresh coleslaw, and more, and more. There was a dessert or two, if you were able. It all started with a long, long prayer, because a short prayer was not in our history. I always opened one eye, to see who was not doing it right, only to find that the only one not doing it right was me. Every other head bowed. Every other eye closed.

The turkey was beautiful—golden, partly submerged in butter and juices, and there was no sign, none, that it had been a traveler. I went through the whole meal waiting to bite down on some gravel, but I forgot after a while, over the drumstick. My mother always saved me one, and she saves me one now.

Roast Turkey

WHAT YOU WILL NEED

1 turkey, about 15 to 18 pounds
½ cup vegetable oil
3 tablespoons salt
1 pound butter
1½ cups water

HOW TO COOK IT

Use a real roasting pan with a real, vented lid.

The 911 operator is busy already.

Some people like a few sprigs of rosemary, or garlic, or a dusting of paprika. Some people like a brine. Some people like smoke.

"I like to keep it simple," she said, and she prefers a smaller turkey now, though I believe they would be just as hard to catch once they got rolling.

Once the turkey is thawed, pat it dry. "Then I rub it all over, inside and out, with cooking oil." That seems to cling better than butter. Then she rubs it all over again, inside and out, with salt.

The pound of butter goes on the inside, and the water goes in the bottom of the pan.

"Just lay the butter in there?" I said.

"Just lay it in there."

It will melt, mix with the water, and steam through the body cavity.

She also rinses the neck, gizzard, and liver, and returns them to the body cavity.

"There is a lot of flavor in them."

Preheat the oven to 350 degrees.

"No black pepper?" I asked. I remembered the black pepper speckling the bird as she took off the lid.

"I quit," she said.

"Why," I asked.

"I wanted to."

She seemed disinclined to tell me any more.

"Well, how long do you cook it?" I asked.

"Till it's done," she said.

About halfway through the time she refuses to tell us, carefully remove the lid and ladle some of the liquid in the bottom of the pan onto the bird, then cover it and finish cooking.

She finally relented and told me she cooks an 18- to 20-pounder between three and four hours, till it almost falls apart.

"It won't be pretty, but it'll be good."

Do not bind the legs, do not stuff the bird with lemons, and do not, ever, stuff the bird with breadcrumbs or cornbread stuffing or anything like that. Stuffing the bird prevents the heat, and she believes the flavor, from reaching the inside.

I asked her about using a meat thermometer. She went momentarily blank.

When it is done, there will be a pool of browned butter and drippings in the bottom of the pan.

"Some people use that for gravy, but we don't need no gravy."

. . .

It is the simplest recipe I have ever seen, or even heard of. It may be, of course, that it is no better than other turkeys I've had in my lifetime. It may also be that simple, even simple excess, is just better. I guess, if I was going to be honest, this notion is at the heart of most of our food. I see it now.

I guess I figured that out when I went back through these pages and counted the number of times that "1 stick butter" was the measurement we used, except in this one, where it was "1 pound."

I guess some cooks might even see that method as clumsy or the like.

As a man who has failed even at carrying food, let alone at cooking it, I believe now and always will that what my mother and my people do in a kitchen is nothing short of beautiful, and I get to say.

Because she was still recovering from her ordeals this last holiday season, I had to be turkey boy on my own. All the turkeys were still frozen hard, but they are lighter now. They put them in big, stretchy, plastic nets now—I guess to prevent runaways, but I don't know. She got it into and out of the oven without calling the rescue squad, and everything in those pots and pans was the same, just the same, as if time had stood still. Only we were different, older, and, though I would like to say "smarter," I am not altogether sure. But I made it across the parking lot this time, all the way. My big brother did not say anything, but I think I know what he was thinking: *How far away did you park?*

"We'll have ham for Christmas," my mother said.

I like ham.

You can get a good grip on a ham.

"UNTIMELY FIGS"

Ray Brock's Fig Preserves

He hath laid my vine waste, and barked my fig tree: he hath made it clean bare, and cast it away. . . .

—JOEL 1:7

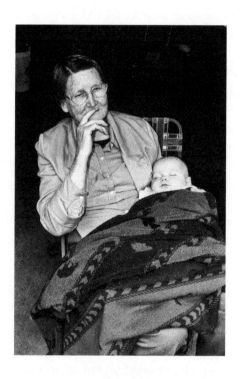

Momma

HER HOUSE may be in order, but she harbors a secret. Her thieving did not stop with that onion, or that cheese. I discovered it, in an empty place on her shelves.

I had come home to visit at suppertime, and asked for breakfast, please. She laid thick slices of sugar-cured bacon onto a battered and blackened cookie sheet, and baked them until they crumbled. She fried a platter of eggs, melted cubes of mild cheese into creamy, buttery grits, just enough to taste, then woke them up a little with some coarse black pepper. She moved from stove eye to stove eye to oven rack and round again, all with that truck-stop shuffle, that café slide, so it would all be done at the same time and come hot to the table. She learned this not from the matriarchs, from the family recipes and traditions, but at Red's café. I came back just a few minutes later to find her lifting a pan of biscuits from the oven. Only one thing was missing: a little taste of something sweet. I perused a row of jellies, jams, and preserves on her kitchen shelves. There was red cherry, grape, blackberry, blueberry, golden apple, rusty red crabapple, others . . . and not one jar of fig preserves. I was hoping for preserves.

I asked her if she had any somewhere, put aside, and she just looked sick. She told me no, said she might not put up any fig preserves for the rest of her life. "I done somethin' terrible, hon" was all she said, and for a long while she was too ashamed to tell me what that was. She said only that she had sinned, and not a piddlin', rinky-dink sin, either. As it turned out, it was a whole tree of it.

. . .

It began with a simple gesture of generosity, from an upright man. Ray Brock has since gone on to his reward, but he left a multitude of people here in the red dirt who speak well of his name; even sinners respected Ray. He was a preacher of the old order who lived in the little mill town of Piedmont, in northern Calhoun County, and had been a friend to my family for most of the twentieth century. He baptized more than a few—some more than once, because the first time sometimes did not take. He prayed for them to be healed at their bedsides in Holy Name of Jesus Hospital, and when it was time, prayed them right on out of this world and, it was to be hoped, into the next. He was a lean, stern-faced, warmhearted Congregational Holiness, who believed in the Holy Ghost *and* human charity, and would not foul his pulpit with politics. He preached of the wages of sin and of the Streets of Gold, and no wiggle room in between. It was up or down with Ray, and not an inch of sideways.

"He even went in the jails, to save people," said Aunt Juanita, who was Ray's friend. "Don't know if it did no good, but he went. I remember one night he got up without a word and walked out of a gospel singing at Community Church—and I mean they were *singin'*—and got in his car and left, 'cause the Lord told him Mr. Hudgins was 'bout to die, and Ray went to his bedside and they prayed and he got Mr. Hudgins saved. Ray told me, 'Juanita, sometimes the Lord just puts it on me so strong, I can't *stand* it.'"

In 1986, the year the great sin was committed, he came by Aunt Juanita and Uncle Ed's house for a cup of coffee.

"Do you like figs?" he asked her.

"Well, not so much," she said, "but Margaret sure does."

"Well," he said, "I've got a big fig tree in my yard in Piedmont that's just hangin' heavy with ripe figs, and I hate for 'em to go to waste, or for the birds to eat ever' one of 'em. Tell Margaret she's welcome to 'em if she'll come and pick 'em."

My mother loves figs more than just about any food in the world. She will eat them raw, dried, and home-canned, whole, in a light syrup, or in gooey dark preserves. I've watched her eat a quart of freshly picked figs, and seen her gaze through the car window at a stranger's fig tree with pure avarice. She planted a dozen trees on her own land over the years, with no luck. She made sure they had sun and water, but they just didn't make. So, she admits, she coveted the figs of others.

"Tell her it's a big ol' tree plumb full of ripe figs, and tell her to get 'em all if she can," Ray told my aunt Juanita. "Tell her not to worry if we ain't there when they come." His sister had been sick over in Georgia, and some mornings he and his wife drove over there to sit with her and were gone much of the day. "Just tell her to help herself, and welcome."

My mother had never been to Ray's house, but my aunt Juanita told her not to fret, she knew how to get there. "But I couldn't go," Juanita said. "I don't know what happened. It may be I had to sit with Momma." My aunt Edna, the oldest sister, who was still driving long after the laws of man should have forbidden it, volunteered to drive my mother to Piedmont purely for the distraction it would provide. Aunt Edna was a constant traveler; she loaded her pistol, checked her blood sugar, got somebody to feed her bulldog, and just went, as far and as often as she pleased. She was not overly concerned with the directions Juanita had, having once heard someone say it was the journey that was important, not the destination.

Besides, she knew Piedmont back, forth, and sideways; it was only about eleven miles north on Highway 21. Ray's house, my aunt Juanita had instructed, was on a quiet street in a quiet corner of a quiet town, and easy to find. She described it in detail; it was a big white house, built when they built 'em right, and had recently undergone some renovations. It would be the white house with the big fig tree in back.

"I told her exactly where to go," Aunt Juanita said.

Aunt Edna had sewn uniforms at Fort McClellan till she worked her way up to where she was telling other people how to sew them, and it was not in her nature to dawdle or meander or lollygag, which, my people believe, is unusual for a government employee. She was still very much the older sister in charge in those days, and drove with confidence and conviction to an old white house, recently refurbished. The paint buckets and ladders were still there. In the back, a fig tree—well, more like a big fat bush—sagged with fruit.

"And I was so happy," my mother said, " 'cause there ain't nothin' better in this world than a ripe fig. I mean, it's in the Bible."

> *And the trees said to the fig tree, Come, thou, and reign over us. But the fig tree said unto them, Should I forsake my sweetness, and my good fruit, and go to be promoted over the trees?*
>
> —JUDGES 9: 10—11

She plucked one, and tasted it. It was firm, sweet, and perfect. Ray, my mother thought to herself, sure knew how to prune a fig tree. The idea was to keep the trunk short and the tree fat and bushy, so that a picker could reach everywhere. You wanted a fat tree, not a tall one, not really a tree at all. Only the mockingbirds and jaybirds could feast on the high figs in a tall tree. Her momma had told her that.

The figs were dead-ripe but firm, and if the birds had discovered them, they had not made much of a dent. She also noticed Edna was nowhere around.

After a few minutes, she saw her walking back from somewhere, carrying a lawn chair.

"She wouldn't think nothin' about just takin' it off somebody's porch," my mother said.

Edna made herself comfortable, adjusted her big straw sun hat, and prepared to nap.

"Ain't you gonna help me?" my mother asked.

"No," Edna said.

"Well, why not?"

" 'Cause I don't like figs," Edna said.

"Well, then, why did you come?"

"So you wouldn't have to walk," Edna said.

With Edna dozing, my mother methodically stripped the tree all but clean.

"I took my time, and I enjoyed myself. I think I even got me some Bruton. It was one of the best days I'd had in a long time. . . . Edna wadn't near as bossy, asleep."

She left only a handful of figs. Edna, who had apparently developed the ability to supervise even when in dreamland, asked her why she was quitting before she was done.

"I thought I'd leave a few, in case Ray wanted a few when he come home."

"You've done stripped it pretty good," Edna said.

"Yeah, but . . ."

"And he did tell you to get 'em all," she said.

My mother took the last fruit.

> *And they shall eat up thine harvest and thy bread, which thy sons and thy daughters should eat: they shall eat up thy flocks and thine herds: they shall eat up thy vines and thy fig trees: they shall impoverish thy fenced cities, wherein thou trustedst, with the sword.*
>
> —JEREMIAH 5:17

Edna nodded, satisfied. She hated to see a thing half done, even if she was only spectating.

"She could also be just the least little bit greedy," my aunt Juanita said, many years later.

My mother went to the car and came back with a pint of pear preserves she had put up that year. She placed it carefully between the screen and the door, so it would be impossible to miss.

She rode home cradling her figs, not quite a gallon. "I was a little bit disappointed. The way they talked, there'd be a bushel-basket-full. I guess I was a little greedy, too.

"But they were perfect. I had meant to eat a few, and then put the rest of 'em up in some preserves. But once I got started, I couldn't stop, and I eat every one of them. I didn't put up even one little-bitty jar, not for y'all, not for *nobody*. They were the best figs I've ever eat."

When my aunt Juanita saw Ray in town a few days later, she asked him how he liked the pear preserves that her sister had left him.

Ray told her he had not seen them.

"Well, Margaret left you some in the door, after her and Edna went to your house to pick the trees," Juanita said.

"Nobody picked my figs," Ray said. "I was expectin' 'em to, but they never showed up. I even waited for 'em, waited for 'em all day, but I never saw them. My fig tree's still just full of figs, 'cept for what the birds got."

"Well," Juanita said.

"Well," Ray said, always the Samaritan. "You tell Margaret I appreciate the preserves anyway, and appreciate her thinkin' about me."

"I wonder," Juanita said, "whose they did get. We can't tell her—it'll kill her. She ain't never stole nothin' in her life," giving her a pass on the government cheese and the onion, too, I suppose.

"I won't tell nobody," Ray said.

"I won't, neither," Juanita said, and called my mother as soon as she got home.

. . .

And the stars of heaven fell unto the earth, even as a fig tree casteth her untimely figs, when she is shaken of a mighty wind.

—REVELATION 6:13

"Dear God, I stole 'em," my mother said.

She and Edna had apparently turned a block too soon, and wound up at the one nearly identical house with a single fig tree.

"That's how you know there's an ol' devil in this world," she said.

"It wasn't my fault," my aunt Juanita said. "My directions was perfect."

"It wasn't my fault," my aunt Edna said. "I follered the directions."

"It was my fault, for trustin' 'em in the first place," my mother said.

She thought, somewhat bitterly, that she should have known better. She had grown up and grown old riding around with them, hopelessly lost.

"We got lost coming home from Florida and went through Heflin twice. We went up and down one highway so many times that the people who lived on it got to know us."

Her imagination galloped away with her. "You think they could put me in prison, for stealing? I mean, nobody would put you in prison for stealing a fig, or a few figs, but a whole tree? They'd put you in prison for a tree-full. They'd put me in jail . . . in Piedmont jail. And I just got deathly sick."

What, she wondered, if there had been people at home who had been there the whole time, watching, faces pressed to the window, to watch one old woman strip their tree of figs while another old woman—the lookout, obviously—had such contempt for the law that she stole a chair and took a nap?

"Is it something they could put you in prison for?" she asked her sisters.

"No," Edna said.

"Yes," Juanita said.

Edna told her it was unlikely the Piedmont police would jail a poor widow woman for stealing fruit, and if they did, it was unlikely they would jail her, the unknowing wheelman . . . or -woman. It wasn't like she left with the tires smoking, she said.

"Edna always just kind of took things in stride," my mother said, "but she wasn't the one going to Tutwiler." Tutwiler is the women's prison in Wetumpka.

What bothered Edna was there was a whole big tree of figs in Piedmont still unpicked, and rotting on the vine. It was not, as we have said, that she enjoyed figs herself; it was the principle of the thing.

"You want to go back to Ray's house and get the rest of them figs?" my mother asked, incredulous.

"Why, sure," Edna said.

"I'd have to disguise myself," my mother told her. "What if the people who owned that other house drove up? They'd think I was doin' it to somebody else's fig tree, and they'd call the police."

She told Edna she could drive her own self to Piedmont and pick the legal figs.

"I don't like figs," Edna said.

.   .   .

"Well," my mother said, "wild horses couldn't have drug me back to Piedmont." She did not go to Piedmont for about fifteen years. Unsure of the statute of limitations, she changed her eye doctor from the one in Piedmont to the one in Gadsden, just in case.

The sisters did feel sorry for her, after a while. Juanita and Edna tried to tell her that she had more than paid for a measly paper sack of figs with her pint of excellent pear preserves.

"Why, you can get seven dollars for 'em in the Smokies, and you know you could get at least five dollars for 'em down here," Juanita said.

I asked why they were worth more in the Smokies.

"Tourists," my mother said.

Ray told my aunt Juanita to tell my mother that she had committed no great sin, because there was no larceny in her heart.

"I got some muscadines there, ripe, if you want them," he said.

Edna said she would be by directly.

"I like muscadines," she said, but could not get my mother to go with her.

. . .

My mother sought solace in her Bible in the days after her larceny, but even in those pages there was no comfort. It seemed as if every chapter and verse threw her crime right back in her face.

Genesis, of course, offered no refuge. She could see, in her mind, Adam and Eve being seduced by the serpent under the Tree of Knowledge of Good and Evil, then stumbling from the Garden of Eden, in sin.

> *And the eyes of them both were opened, and they knew that*
> *they were naked; and they sewed fig leaves together, and*
> *made themselves aprons.*
>
> —GENESIS 3:7

The Piedmont figs went unclaimed, and rotted on the vine.

We needed, obviously, some sort of closure. Every few years, I asked her if she wanted to go back to Piedmont, to the mistaken house with the mistaken fig trees, to apologize to the people there.

"What if they hold a grudge?" she asked. What if they'd just been laying for her all these years? She imagined that jar of pear preserves—empty, of course—sitting on a shelf in the Piedmont Police Department, with her fingerprints all over it. She was too old, she said, to do any serious time.

"And poor ol' Ray's done gone on, and he ain't here to stand up for me. I wouldn't even have a witness."

The experience has not, however, turned her against figs in general.

"I still like the taste of figs. I'd eat some right now if I had some. I mean, I ain't crazy."

But even after all these years, she still has had no luck with cultivating a fig tree of her own, and wonders if that might be some kind of punishment for 1986. It can happen. The Bible says so.

> *I have smitten you with blasting and mildew: when your*
> *gardens and your vineyards and your fig trees and your olive*
> *trees increased, the palmerworm devoured them: yet have ye*
> *not returned unto me, saith the Lord.*

—AMOS 4:9

We do not know exactly what a palmerworm is, but it sounds terrible. I told her that, with all the Lord has to worry about, it is doubtful He sent a plague unto her fig trees. I do not believe plagues are as specific as that, but my knowledge of the Bible is not as broad or as deep as I would like.

"I've mostly got over it now," my mother said, lying. Every time she walks past a pack of Newtons in the grocery store, she feels a tiny twinge of shame. She did not put up fig preserves for years, but she is over that, too. Her only regret is that she did not get to make some for Ray, before he passed. I asked her if she thought of Ray every time she messed with figs, and she said of course she did, and I told her that is a fine way to remember a person.

Ray Brock's Fig Preserves

(Makes at least 3 pints)

WHAT YOU WILL NEED

½ gallon figs (at least)
3 cups sugar

HOW TO COOK IT

"First thing about figs is that figs is something you don't mash, you don't bruise, you don't hurt. You be gentle with figs."

Pick through the figs by hand. Figs should be ripe but firm. If you are unsure, taste one. Make sure to remove all stems. Throw out the ones with bad places: "If you find a mushy one, throw it out," she said.

Wash them all thoroughly.

Place the whole figs in a large bowl, and cover them with the sugar. Use a spoon or your hands to make sure all the figs come into contact with the sugar—again, working gently.

"Let 'em sit in the sugar, covered, overnight," my mother says. "They will make their own liquid to cook in."

Place them in a pot, and cook over low heat, stirring often.

"They'll come apart and make their own syrup. When they've come apart, and almost all the liquid—not all, but just a little—has cooked out of 'em, they're ready."

Being careful not to get burned, which is a hard-and-fast rule for any canning project, "put 'em in the canning jars while they're still hot." Fill almost to the top, to the neck of the jar, but do not allow the figs to touch the underside of the lid. Do not pack the preserves in. "I don't know no better way to say that," she said.

"Be sure to use new lids. You can reuse rings, but not the lids." Figs will absorb the hint of any rust, or any ghost of what was in the jar before, like tomatoes. You can smell tomatoes on lids long after they are thoroughly washed.

You can put the preserves up in pint jars—there may be some left after three jars—but it may be best to put them in ½-pint jars, to cut down on waste. They will keep a year or longer, but in the refrigerator they seem to lose some of their flavor, though none of the sweetness.

Some people use them in cakes, fruitcakes, or pies.

"They make fine Christmas presents. Just put a bow on top," she said.

This same process, she believes, works with just about any preserves, from apples to pears, as long as they are not stolen. But whereas other fruits may need spices, the figs need only the sugar.

·   ·   ·

She really had intended to make Ray some preserves with the figs from his tree, if they had in fact been picked from his tree, and if she had not eaten them all before she found out they were stolen from people she is still afraid to face, twenty years later. If you are those people and you are, by any chance, reading this, do not come after us, or talk bad about us in Piedmont. Remember, we know where you live, more or less.

SPRING

Fresh Field Peas with Pork, Stewed Squash and Sweet Onions,
Fried Okra, Sweet Corn, Fried Green Tomatoes

Ava, in old age

THE KITCHEN still makes her seem young, even after all this time, in the same way that, when she was just a girl wrapped in all those friendly ghosts and drawing on all their wisdom, it made her seem old and wise and skilled beyond her years. But the kitchen is, as she said, all about the past, and the ghosts crowd into it more and more with every passing year. An old person gets a little tired sometimes, living in the past, so deep into that past, even if it tastes so good.

But the garden, now, the garden is different.

The garden is about the future, and hope, and plans.

And, of course, there is the food.

She may look down the turned rows and see her daddy walking there, cursing a never-ending field of tomatoes, but the garden is mostly about new things, and the loose red dirt under her feet actually seems to draw the years from her, through her shoes. She feels that way every spring, just seems to get her breath somehow, when she smells the turned earth, and she can walk across it when it is red, clean, and brand-new, and not a weed—not one— dares to raise its ugly head.

"Red clay ain't the best dirt, and this mountain dirt has got a lot of rocks in it. We picked dump trucks full of rocks from this dirt, and one still pushes up ever' now and then. But mostly it's good, I believe."

She sees the winter as a kind of purgatory, and behaves as if she lives in a frozen tundra, huddled in some gulag. She wears layers and layers of flannel and thermal and quilted everything, and punches at her television, trying to find a weatherman, this time, with a sunny disposition. She would settle for a kind lie, rather than one more forecast for thirty-seven degrees and rain with a chance of something called a "wintry mix," as if it were a party snack. She says, over and over, the same thing: if she can just get into March, if she can just get started on her garden, she believes she would feel all right. It has been that way for as long as I can remember, but it got worse when the years piled up on her, when the sickness surprised her, like a thief.

The devil tried to do her in, finally, by taking her spring.

"I am not going to miss another spring," she said, within days of coming home last summer.

"I'm not going to miss another garden."

It was the weeds she hated the most, of course, or, more, the *idea* of the weeds. She could almost feel them there in her hospital room, choking, covering over the ground, leaving room for nothing good to grow. She lost to the weeds for the first time that spring, and lost much of the year around it. It was just the spring she missed; you could have the winter.

When she came home from the hospital, my brother had laid out a garden for her, and even with a late start he brought in a good crop of the things she loves to cook and eat. But it was not the same. She was too weak to work it with him, or even really to walk it. This year would be different, because it had to be.

It hasn't happened yet. The days are still cold now, as I write this, but I still know precisely how it will be. She and my brother will first lay out her garden in their minds, side by side in the living room, in front of a fire, and they will plan and plant it together, in sweet corn, tomatoes, field peas, green beans, squash, okra, hot pepper, and onions, white and green. Later, they will plant greens, turnips and collards and mustard, and more.

They will talk, and talk, and talk, about seed, and tomato plants, and fertilizer, and dirt. They will talk a hundred hours about the dirt alone, the chemical nature of it, and drought, and irrigation, and flood. They will discuss blight, and caterpillars, and deer, and birds, and rabbits, and he will want to talk about pesticides, and she will tell him not in her garden, buster, and they will argue, but she will win, because we let her win—not in fear but in recompense, for everything that has come before this day. You know what I mean.

They will talk, and talk, and I will not have a damn thing to say. I talk all the time, talk too much, about things I know or pretend to know something about, words on paper, but this is useless and trivial, because when you have finished there is not one damn thing in a bushel basket. It is not important compared with the failing electrical system on the old Yanmar tractor, or the new drain they will cut to channel the rainwater, and whether or not the rains will come at all. Last year, the corn baked in the field. They will discuss whether they will need a new scarecrow, or just stick with the aluminum pie tins they have hung around the garden to scare the birds away. I don't think the birds are scared a damn bit, and the deer are laughing at us, but no one cares what I have to say. They will talk, for hours, about snakes, most of it myth. It still amazes me how people who can tell a false bloom from a real one on a squash plant, who can tell a tomato's heritage from fifty yards away, still believe that hanging a dead rattler in a tree will make it rain.

"You can't do nothin' about the deer," my mother says. "You can't build a fence high enough." My brother Sam nods. You have to figure some loss. The thing is, she does not even really mind the deer, or the birds, or the rabbits; she will swap some green stuff, here and there, to see all that life sneaking through the rows.

They do inventory in their heads, how many tomatoes to cook green, eat fresh, and can. She tells him they will have to be sure to pick the squash as soon as it comes in, and he nods impatiently, because what is he, Momma, a moron?

Watermelons? They almost forgot about watermelons, and cantaloupe, and mush melon. They would have to discuss peas. Purple hulls, or crowders?

"I like watermelon," I say, but no one seems to be listening.

In a way I cannot truly explain, my silence is the best it gets, here in my mother's house. I let all this knowledge, the lore, the traditions, run around me and through me, and I listen to it the way some people listen to that music my mother talked about, that music played and sung in a language people might not understand anymore. Certainly, I have lost it somewhere. But you still know it's pretty, know it has much, much to do with you, with who you are, even if you no longer know the steps, or the words.

"What will you cook," I asked her, "when it comes in?"

"Why, all of it," she said.

Fresh Field Peas with Pork

WHAT YOU WILL NEED

1 cube salt pork (about ¼ pound fatback,
   or streak o' lean, or hog jowl)
1 quart shelled field peas, or any fresh peas
1 teaspoon salt
½ teaspoon sugar
1 small onion, diced very fine (optional)

HOW TO COOK IT

In cold water, rinse the salt pork thoroughly.

Cover the peas with water, and add the fatback, salt, and sugar.

"That seems like it ain't much salt, but it's plenty," my mother said, especially with the salt pork.

Bring to a good boil, and then cook over medium-low heat for about 45 minutes.

You should be able to mash the peas easily with a fork. Do not cook them to death, or the hulls will separate and you will have mush.

Some people like to add garlic, or black pepper.

"You don't add black pepper to fresh peas," she said.

I knew better than to ask why.

The peas will have a fresh, nutty taste, better, cleaner, sweeter, and less starchy than dried peas. They taste new.

Stewed Squash and Sweet Onions

WHAT YOU WILL NEED

8 small, tender summer squash

1 large sweet onion

1 slice bacon

1 teaspoon salt

½ teaspoon black pepper (optional)

½ teaspoon sugar

½ stick butter

HOW TO COOK IT

Slice the squash into wheels about ¼ inch thick.

Dice the onion.

Cut the bacon into small pieces.

Cook the bacon in the pot until it renders a little, but do not cook it crisp. Add the squash, onion, salt, pepper, and sugar, and add just enough water to cover.

Cook over medium heat for about 30 minutes, till the water has cooked down, the squash is tender, and the onion has gone clear and soft. Add the butter, and cook another 10 minutes or so, adding just a little water if needed. Do not add too much or you will ruin it.

"Some people put too much sugar in the squash . . ."

I waited for it.

". . . but I don't."

Fried Okra

This is not a wet-battered fried okra. Nothing my mother cooks from the garden is battered that way. It defeats the purpose of fresh food, she believes.

WHAT YOU WILL NEED

1 pound okra, small, young, and tender

½ to ¾ cup cornmeal

1 teaspoon salt

½ teaspoon black pepper

2 tablespoons bacon grease

HOW TO COOK IT

If you are picking okra, or selecting it at a curb market, small is better. Pods even as big as your index finger may already be getting tough, and if you have ever bitten into a piece of okra that seems like a piece of thin bark off a chinaberry tree, you know what we mean.

Cut the okra into pieces of about ¼ to ½ inch. It is fine to keep the tips, but discard the stem.

Add just a little water to the bowl of cut-up okra, toss the okra in it, then pour off the rest of the water.

Add the meal, salt, and black pepper to the bowl, and, with your hands, mix it in good.

Heat your grease in a cast-iron skillet, and add your okra. It does not matter one whit if the okra pieces are not completely covered with cornmeal.

Cook over medium heat for about 10 minutes, and then over medium-low for another 20 or 30.

"Okra takes a while," my mother said.

It should be so deep green it is almost black, and the meal should be crispy.

This is not the deep-fried, battered, still-raw okra you get in restaurants, she said.

"That ain't okra," she said.

Sweet Corn

WHAT YOU WILL NEED

3 to 3½ cups fresh sweet corn
1 teaspoon salt
¼ teaspoon sugar
¾ stick butter (at least)

HOW TO COOK IT

Shuck and remove the silk from your corn. How many ears you need will depend on the size; just try to end up with at least 3 cups. You will want leftovers of this; it is even good cold.

In a cast-iron skillet, combine your corn, salt, and sugar with about ½ cup water, and cook over medium-low heat for about 10 to 15 minutes, then add the butter and cook over low heat till the water has cooked out and the corn is stewing in the butter and its own sugars.

Time is relative. We like it a little crisp, and some people only cook it for about 20 minutes in all, for an even crisper taste. To be honest, "it's hard to mess up sweet corn."

She did not say, "Even you could do it," but I think she meant to.

Fried Green Tomatoes

WHAT YOU WILL NEED

1 cup lard or bacon grease
2 green tomatoes, as large as possible, just starting to
    turn
1 cup flour
1 teaspoon salt
½ teaspoon black pepper

HOW TO COOK IT

Heat your fat in a cast-iron skillet till it's good and hot, then lower the heat to medium.

Slice your tomatoes about ¼ inch thick. Mix your flour, salt, and pepper, and dust the tomatoes lightly with the dry flour, and cook until golden brown, then turn, and repeat.

A little of this goes a long way. For most people, two or three slices is enough.

Most people are used to battered, deep-fried green tomatoes cooked in cornmeal. This is obviously not that. Such a method, she believes, is fine for corn dogs at the fair.

If she is cooking for a large group, she will sometimes reduce the amount of fat, pile wheels of tomato in, and cook them slowly, stirring with a big spoon. This breaks up the tomatoes, and you end up with a kind of scramble of green tomatoes and crisped flour, which is pretty good, too.

The secret to any green tomato for frying is to pick one that has just, just started to turn and is showing the slightest bit of ripeness. These will be sweeter.

"It makes all the difference in the world," she said.

.   .   .

This is what she will cook.

I know there are few certainties in this world, but I know the old woman pretty well, even if I did spend much of my life away. The weeds, I believe, do not have a chance.

THE RECIPE THAT NEVER WAS

Quick Fried Apple Pies

The best cook in the world

WHAT YOU WILL NEED

2 cups apples

2 teaspoons sugar

1 teaspoon ground cinnamon

1 stick butter

1 pound biscuit dough (page 50 or store-bought)

1 teaspoon bacon grease

HOW TO COOK IT

Combine the apples, sugar, and cinnamon, and chill in the refrigerator, covered, for about 1 hour. In a large skillet, melt ½ stick of the butter and cook the apple mixture on medium heat for about 10 minutes. Let it cool.

Roll out the dough to a thickness of about ⅛ to ¼ inch, and—you can use a saucer for this—cut 4 circles of 6 or 8 inches in diameter. You may have enough filling for more. Brush the edges of the dough with a little butter. Spoon 2 tablespoons of the apple mixture into the middle of each circle, turn it over, and pinch the edges closed.

In a clean skillet, melt the bacon grease and remaining butter on medium heat, and—about 2 at a time—fry until golden brown on each side, adding more fat and butter as needed.

Serve warm, with a good cup of coffee.

"But I never made that," she said.

"I know damn good and well you did," I said.

My big brother Sam nodded.

"Well," she said, "I forgot."

"Well," I said, "I guess it's a good thing we did a book."

But how, I wondered, did she know how to make it, if she believed she never had?

Ghosts.

It had to be.

ACKNOWLEDGMENTS

I have many people to thank for helping me bring this book to its completion, so many I don't even know how to start. I guess I will just begin as I always have, by thanking my people, living and dead, who furnished me with the stories and memories that made it possible—not just this book, but my very life as a writer. Kin, and friends, and sometimes just chance encounters gave this book the flavor I hope it contains. There are, literally, hundreds of them; their lifetimes frame these stories, and color them.

I especially want to thank my aunt Juanita, aunt Jo, uncle John, sister-in-law Teresa, niece Meredith, hardheaded brother Sam, and other kin, for helping me gather the stories and photographs in this book, and for putting up with me as I fretted over it. I thank Kaylin Bowen, for her help and tolerance.

It is past time, too, to thank the readers who have been with me now for going on three decades, people who found something of worth in the stories of workingwomen and -men. It has been my great pleasure to write them down and share them. I am honored to do it.

I thank Amanda Urban for her guidance. I thank Jordan Pavlin for again taking the stories of my people and handling them with such great care. And I want to thank Maria Massey and all the others at Knopf for editing, designing, and creating books that I am honored to place on my shelves. I am always a little surprised, to look up and see them there.

But there is no book unless there is an idea. I want to thank

Dianne, who saw the value in a book such as this long ago, saw that a recipe is more than just a blueprint, but a kind of history.

And, of course, I have to thank the cook.

What joy you have brought to this life, one skillet at a time.

I'd cook you a meal if I only knew how.

With emotional generosity and effortlessly compelling storytelling, Rick Bragg continues his personal history of the Deep South. This time he's writing about his grandfather Charlie Bundrum, a man who died before Bragg was born but left an indelible imprint on the people who loved him. Drawing on their memories, Bragg reconstructs the life of an unlettered roofer who kept food on his family's table through the worst of the Great Depression. In telling Charlie's story, Bragg conjures up the backwoods hamlets of Georgia and Alabama in the years when the roads were still dirt and real men never cussed in front of ladies. A masterly family chronicle and a human portrait so vivid you can smell the cornbread and whiskey, *Ava's Man* is unforgettable.

Memoir

ALSO AVAILABLE

Somebody Told Me
The Prince of Frogtown

VINTAGE BOOKS
Available wherever books are sold.
www.vintagebooks.com